Contents

THIRD EDITION

Contemporary
SPAIN

Christopher J Ross
Bill Richardson
Begoña Sangrador-Vegas

HODDER
EDUCATION
PART OF HACHETTE LIVRE UK

First published in Great Britain in 1997.
Second edition published in 2002.
This third edition published in 2008
by Hodder Education,
a member of Hachette Livre UK.

www.hoddereducation.com

The advice and information in this book are believed to be true and accurate at
the date of going to press, but neither the authors nor the publisher can accept
any legal responsibility or liability for any errors or omissions.

Hachette Livre UK's policy is to use papers that are natural, renewable and
recyclable products and made from wood grown in sustainable forests.
The logging and manufacturing processes are expected to conform to the
environmental regulations of the country of origin.

British Library Cataloguing in Publication Data
A catalogue record for this book is available from the British Library

Library of Congress Cataloging-in-Publication Data
A catalog record for this book is available from the Library of Congress

ISBN 978 0 340 95874 2

Cover © Jorge Delgado / iStockphoto.com

1 2 3 4 5 6 7 8 9 10

Typeset in 10/12pt Goudy by Servis Filmsetting Ltd, Stockport, Cheshire.

Printed and bound in Malta.

What do you think about this book? Or any other Hodder Education
title? Please send your comments to feedback@hoddereducation.com

Preface

Every year more and more people are taking Spanish studies in higher education. Increasingly, too, those studies are focusing on contemporary Spanish society and the use of language within it. The two aspects are inseparable. An understanding of all but the most trivial of Spanish texts, both written and spoken, requires access to the body of knowledge about their own country and society which is common to all reasonably educated Spaniards. The aim of this book is to allow English-speaking students to access that same body of knowledge.

To illustrate the point, take the following (hypothetical) sentence from a UK newspaper: 'Labour's modernizers will this week tackle head-on two of the thorniest issues facing the party: selective education and electoral reform.' To understand it, the reader not only requires familiarity with English syntax and general vocabulary, but also needs to be aware of the meaning, and connotations, of the specific terms 'Labour's modernizers', 'selective education' and 'electoral reform', all of which form part of the cultural baggage of the educated UK-based English-speaker. This book's primary purpose is to equip English-speaking students of Spanish with the basis of the equivalent body of knowledge and understanding about Spain.

Even more than in general language, culturally defined terminology appears to give rise to problems of interference. Again, to take an example: the party which won Spain's 1996 election habitually figures in the English-language press as the 'Popular Party'. Use of this name, taken directly from the Spanish *Partido Popular*, removes an important element of meaning from the Spanish term and is significantly misleading – as well as faintly ludicrous. It makes no more sense than to say a Spanish text has been 'traduced' into English, merely because in appearance 'traduce' resembles the Spanish word *traducir* (to translate).

The book's second purpose is to help students to avoid some of the more glaring linguistic pitfalls of this type. Here a note of caution must be sounded. In some cases, English usage is too well established to be challenged. Even though 'Committees' would be much more appropriate, the trade union federation *Comisiones Obreras* is already widely known as 'Workers' Commissions'. Similarly, although 'coalition' is usually applied to a government, it is already widely used in the English-language names of

Spanish political parties such as *Coalición Popular*, which would be better rendered by 'People's Alliance'.

Another obvious problem in preparing the book was that of selection. I have attempted to cover those concepts and terms which seem to me to occur frequently in texts, together with sufficient background explanation to allow them to be understood. The task was complicated by the change of government which occurred during the final phase of writing. Inevitably there will be increasingly frequent reference to the party and individuals who now run Spain, and less to their predecessors. Nevertheless, the Socialists had been in power for so long and through a period of such rapid development that their names and actions will remain an essential point of reference for many years to come.

The book is arranged in a series of topic-based chapters, each of which attempts to introduce the main features of one facet of Spanish society and its institutions. It is intended for readers without specialist knowledge of any of the subjects concerned, and technical language is kept to a necessary minimum. Although not a reference book as such, the various sections and sub-sections are intended to be self-standing, so that readers can dip into a particular topic or aspects of it. There is frequent cross-referencing, indicated by section numbers in square brackets, to allow threads of interest to be followed across topic boundaries. Inevitably this approach makes for a degree of intrusiveness and repetition, but I have taken the view that it is desirable in the interests of easy usage.

The glossaries included after each chapter are in no sense intended to be comprehensive. They are meant to complement published dictionaries by picking out usages that I have found from experience to be difficult to locate, or potentially misleading, or both. The bracketed Spanish terms inserted in the main text are intended to give an indication of usage in context; there is no suggestion that they are the sole, or even the most usual, equivalent of the preceding English concept or phrase. Where fully assimilated English versions of Spanish terms exist, they are used in the text, e.g. Saragossa, Aragon. Where they do not, the original Spanish form is used, including any accents. This applies in particular to proper names, e.g. Felipe González.

Even more than the text as a whole, the listing of initials and acronyms is, of necessity, selective. I have attempted to include only those which are habitually used to refer to the organization or concept without further explanation, e.g. PSOE. Where sets of initials have effectively supplanted the full term, such as the radio station *Cadena COPE*, they are not included in the list.

A list of further reading is included at the end of the book. It is deliberately brief, including only items which seem to me reasonably accessible to the non-specialist reader. Particular mention should be made of John Hooper's *The New Spaniards*, an outstanding work of journalism that gives an extraordinarily vivid and sympathetic picture of contemporary Spain. There is, of course, no substitute for the quality Spanish press in keeping up with events in the country; a number of titles are now available on the internet. For more analytical material the best source is the *International Journal of Iberian Studies*, formerly the *Journal of the Association for Contemporary Iberian Studies*.

I owe a sincere debt of gratitude to various people who have helped in the production of this book. First and foremost among them are my wife and parents, for their unfailing support down the years. Second, my former teacher and colleague Diarmuid Bradley; that I could even think of undertaking such a project is due to his wisdom, inspiration and friendship. Last but very far from least, valued colleagues at Heriot-Watt University, especially Kent Sproule and Ann McFall for support and solidarity beyond the call of duty, and Graeme Lewis for his help in producing the maps. Needless to say, the errors and imbalances of the book have nothing to do with any of them, but are entirely my own responsibility.

Chris Ross
February 1997

Preface to second edition

Apart from the addition of two chapters, on the European tier of government and the individual regions, and updating of others, the main change with respect to the first edition is that the list of acronyms and abbreviations has been suppressed as a separate unit. This time I have taken the view that these are best incorporated in the (expanded) index, to enable interested readers to access all the information provided on a particular item from a single point.

I should like to thank those readers who kindly alerted me to errors in the first edition; their corrections have been gratefully taken up in the new one. On the other hand, I have not attempted to do as a number of comments suggested and extend the book's coverage to wider social developments. That would have exceeded both my competence and the space available. Happily, since the first edition's appearance a number of publications have come on the market which address such aspects specifically.

Chris Ross
March 2002

Preface to third edition

In this edition, we have updated the contents of the book, and have re-organized the chapters to give more space to certain topics which are now of crucial importance. We include of a chapter on 'social challenges' which addresses, among other topics, immigration and the situation of women, and another new chapter on the mass media. We also include a brief account of the events of 11 March 2004, now a seminal date in contemporary Spanish history, and have brought together in one chapter the various references to the army, the forces of law and order and the justice system. While the elimination of the old 'Interests and lobbies' chapter means that there is no separate section on the Catholic Church in Spain, references to the important role played by the Church are numerous throughout the book and each is contextualized within the topic being discussed.

We have extended the list of useful websites at the end of the 'Further reading' section. For a deeper understanding of the issues, however, the best sources are often still published books and articles; for this reason we also offer the reader who wishes to examine the topics in depth a longer reading list, one that includes advanced material as well as more accessible items.

We are extremely grateful to all those who took the time to read individual sections of the book and offer comments and suggestions. They include Pilar Alderete Díez, Mercedes Arévalo Catalán, Matías Bedmar Moreno, Mel Boland, Pedro-José Bueso Guillén, Óscar García García, Fiana Griffin, Ana María Lanau Larramona, Paula Lojo Sandino, Chris Monahan, Philip Ryan, Begoña Siles Ojeda, Karina Socorro Trujillo and Catherine Way. Tamsin Smith and Bianca Knights at Hodder Education were always extremely supportive and encouraging. We were given further invaluable assistance by Paula van Herk of the European Commission, by Niamh Walsh and Marie Reddan of NUIG Library, and by María Luisa Marteles Gutiérrez del Álamo and Miguel Ángel Miguel of the Spanish Embassy in Dublin.

Some of the technical aspects of keeping the text in good order were looked after by Karen Berry, Laura Daly, Robert Richardson, Deirdre Swain and Marina Wild.

Any errors or inadequacies that remain are, of course, the responsibility of the authors.

Bill Richardson
Begoña Sangrador-Vegas
June 2008

Contemporary Spain in context

With its population of around 45 million, Spain now ranks among the world's ten largest economies. Its area of 505,000 square kilometres, while relatively modest in global terms, is the second largest in the European Union, of which it is a fully-fledged and influential member. Beyond any doubt it belongs to the select club of industrialized Western democracies. Yet little over thirty years ago Spain was a relatively backward country, largely isolated from its European neighbours and ruled by a dictatorship. Even though it has since undergone immense and rapid changes, this radically distinct experience means that Spain – even more than other countries – cannot be understood without some knowledge of its history. This introductory chapter accordingly attempts to give an overview of that history, concentrating on the critical period from around 1800 which culminated in the lengthy dictatorship of General Franco. It then examines the process by which, after his death, Spain finally joined the mainstream of Western liberal democracy. Lastly it indicates the main features of the geopolitical context in which the country now finds itself, its principal ties with the outside world and their implications.

0.1 The nineteenth century and its aftermath

Spain's situation in 1975 was the product of a long process of decline (*decadencia*) that had been in train for over three centuries. The highpoint of its history had come in the century after the crucial year of 1492, which began with the completion of the country's seven-century-long 'Reconquest' from the Moors and ended with the arrival in the Americas of Spanish ships under the command of Columbus (*Colón*). During that time it emerged as the first genuinely global power, dominating Europe and controlling vast areas in the Americas. Thereafter, however, it steadily lost political influence while stagnating socially and economically.

The crucial phase came in the nineteenth century, when most of the Western world experienced the great advance into modernity, an advance made possible by the earlier intellectual revolution of the Enlightenment (*Ilustración*). But just as that movement made little impact on Spain, so the country was barely touched by the three phenomena which together brought about modernization – industrialization, liberalism and nationalism.

Where they appeared they tended to be mutually reinforcing, and their non-appearance in Spain was similarly interlinked. The failure to industrialize was both cause and consequence of the weakness of the middle class (*burguesía*), which proved incapable of replacing absolute monarchy (*absolutismo*) with a regime based on the rule of law and individual liberties. The lack of a dynamic middle class also deprived Spain of the key factor in forging a sense of common nationhood as occurred in other European countries. Furthermore, such industrialization as did take place served to accentuate the distinctiveness of two of the country's disparate regions, the Basque Country and Catalonia. In both it triggered off important political forces whose very essence was denial of Spanish nationhood.

The result was that, while for other Western countries economic advance went hand in hand with the acquisition of colonial empires, for Spain the loss of most of its American colonies was matched by domestic stagnation. The liberal movement frittered away what little strength it had in fighting three civil wars against the ultra-traditional Carlist movement (*carlismo*). For half a century from 1820 changes in government occurred typically as the result of a military coup (*pronunciamiento*), of which there were frequent examples. In 1868 one such rising made common cause with widespread popular discontent and turned into the 'Glorious Revolution' that expelled the hapless Queen Isabel II. There followed the period of deepening chaos known variously as the six revolutionary or democratic years (*sexenio revolucionario/democrático*), which culminated in the First Republic (1873–74).

The Republic came about not because most Spaniards had rejected monarchy as an institution, nor due to widespread support for the relatively progressive ideas it embodied, but merely since there was no real alternative at the time. Not surprisingly it proved to be a disaster; at one stage the government was faced by a number of so-called 'cantonalist' revolts that demanded extensive autonomy for individual provinces or districts. Spain, it seemed, was threatened with complete collapse.

At last a further coup restored the monarchy, in the person of Alfonso XII, and put in place a political arrangement known as the Restoration Settlement. Under this, the military was kept out of politics for half a century, but at a high cost. In a caricature of democracy the Liberal and Conservative parties conspired to produce alternation in government (*turno pacífico*). Elections were subject to widespread rigging (*fraude electoral*), of which the main agents were local party bosses (*caciques*).

In 1898 this system was shaken by a graphic demonstration of Spain's international decline. In several engagements lasting a total of only a few hours, the country saw its navy destroyed by a handful of US ships, and lost the remnants of its colonial empire: Cuba, Puerto Rico and the Philippines. This 'disaster' revealed to all with eyes to see, the extent of Spanish backwardness (*atraso*), and provoked much gloomy analysis of the country's condition. But, outside the field of literature, few results were produced by the ill-defined regenerationist movement (*regeneracionismo*).

Spain's non-involvement in the First World War underlined its negligible weight in world affairs. And, the obvious advantages notwithstanding, it actually served to aggravate the country's problems in one respect. For Spain, alone of the major Western countries, did not experience the surge of unifying national feeling which, for better or worse, the war evoked. Instead, it remained deeply split. A tiny, mainly well-off, more or less educated elite had little or nothing in common with the mass of rural poor or the small industrial working class.

Politically the country became ever more sharply divided into what were often referred to as the 'two Spains'. One comprised what we would now call the right, the forces of authority and tradition: the monarchy, the Church and the military, allied with landowners, small farmers and most of the urban middle class. On the left side of the divide was ranged an even more motley collection of industrial workers, landless peasants and urban intellectuals, influenced by ideas that ranged from anarchism through Marxist socialism to liberalism.

After the First World War, control over the country swung between these two mutually irreconcilable forces. First, in 1923, General Miguel Primo de Rivera staged a coup with the tacit blessing of King Alfonso XIII, and imposed a relatively mild form of dictatorship (*dictablanda*). When his support crumbled Primo abruptly abandoned

Spain in 1930, to be followed a year later by the King. For the second time in 60 years, Spain became a republic mainly because there was no obvious alternative.

During its five-year life the Second Republic itself underwent regular changes of government. Power was held first by the left, then by the right, during the so-called two black years (*bienio negro*). In February 1936 the combined forces of the left, in the guise of the Popular Front (*Frente Popular*), regained power. Five months later, on 18 July 1936, a military uprising against the elected government plunged the country into civil war. It was an unequal struggle.

The Republic, it is true, could count on considerable support from the worse off, and from the strategically vital industrial regions of Catalonia and the Basque Country. But, crucially, it received little backing from abroad. The main Western democracies, France and the UK, stood idly by; the Soviet Union, after initially providing much-needed logistic aid, abruptly withdrew its support in 1938. The uprising, meanwhile, received considerable supplies of both men and machines from the Fascist powers of Italy and Germany. Together with the support of most of the army – as well as significant sections of the people – this proved decisive, and in 1939 the Republican forces surrendered to the rebel Nationalists (*nacionales*).

0.2 Franco's dictatorship

By 1939 the victorious rebels' undisputed leader (*Caudillo*) was General Francisco Franco Bahamonde. His personal power was the first key feature of the regime he created. The second was its basis in the traditionalist ideas of the Spanish right, centred on Spain's glorious military past, the Catholic Church and the desirability of strong central authority. It was this traditionalism that distinguished the Franco regime from the fascist ones of Hitler and Mussolini. Nevertheless, its third main characteristic was an important fascist element, reflected in the idea of a distinctive Spanish 'race' and a strong strain of anti-semitism.

That derived from the Falange, the party founded by José Antonio Primo de Rivera, son of the country's ex-dictator, and modelled explicitly on Mussolini's Fascist party. Conveniently for Franco, the Falange's charismatic leader was killed at the outbreak of the Civil War by Republicans, who thus converted a potential rival into a martyr for the Francoist cause. While the war was still in progress Franco forcibly amalgamated the Falange with various other groups to form the National Movement (*Movimiento Nacional*).

As well as a powerful instrument of propaganda and social control, the Falange also provided Franco with an ideological basis for his regime, the notion of so-called organic democracy (*democracia orgánica*). Allegedly this was a purer form of the doctrine than the corrupt liberal democracy of the Western powers, and also more in tune with Spanish traditions. It rejected pluralist party politics and class-based trade unions as the creators of artificial divisions in society.

In line with these ideas the Franco regime outlawed all parties other than the Movement, and required all producers in a given industry, workers, managers and owners alike, to belong to a single trade union (*sindicato vertical*). Like other 'organs' of the Francoist state these were strictly government-controlled. Vigorous efforts were made to stamp out regional culture and identity in the Basque Country and Catalonia. In reality, organic democracy was a cover for an authoritarian and often brutally repressive regime, whose fascist connotations were evident in the name it adopted for its philosophy, National Syndicalism (*Nacionalsindicalismo*) – the parallel with National Socialism was unmistakable.

Franco's closeness to the fascist powers led to Spain's international isolation after their defeat. Most importantly the country was excluded from the American-funded Marshall Plan of economic aid which triggered recovery in the rest of Western Europe. The regime made a virtue of necessity, proclaiming its belief in economic autarky (*autarquía*), or self-sufficiency, and itself imposed restrictions on the movement of persons and goods across its frontiers.

In the 1950s isolation was somewhat relaxed. In 1953 a Concordat was signed with the Vatican; later the same year defence agreements were signed by which US military bases were established on Spanish soil. Yet Franco continued to block trade and travel, and even on occasion refused offers of outside economic assistance.

By the middle of the decade this course had proved economically disastrous. The country was near bankrupt and living standards remained perilously low; Spain was classified by the United Nations as a developing country until the 1960s. In these dire straits Franco brought into his government a group of technical experts, mainly lawyers and economists. Most were drawn from the conservative Catholic lay group Opus Dei and were unconnected with the Falange.

These experts (*tecnócratas*), of whom the best known were Laureano López Rodó and Alberto Ullastres, brought about a radical change in policy. Often identified with the 1959 Stabilization Plan (*Plan de Estabilización*), it in fact involved a range of measures adopted during that year and the following one. In essence they allowed foreign trade, tourists and investment into Spain, while allowing out those of its own people unable to find work at home. The result was the prolonged period of economic expansion, lasting up to 1974, which made the word *boom* part of the Spanish language and, allied with continued repression, served to dampen opposition to the regime.

The Franco regime itself also underwent an ideological change in its later stages. Even before the crisis of the 1950s discredited its economic doctrine of self-sufficiency, the defeat of fascism had made National Syndicalism an unhelpful concept with which to be associated. Latterly it was replaced as the regime's official ideology by so-called Catholic Nationalism (*Nacionalcatolicismo*). This lacked the overtly fascist overtones of the earlier concept, but also the more egalitarian and modernizing ideas associated with the Falange. Instead, the regime became identified ever more closely with the most conservative brand of Catholic thinking, which placed a dead hand over artistic innovation and free thought of virtually any kind.

Ironically, Catholic elements became one of the sources of discontent with the regime. The dissent of liberal lay Catholics, and some clergy, was fostered by the debates and decisions of the Second Vatican Council (*Concilio Vaticano II*) held between 1962 and 1965, while bishops and priests in the Basque Country and Catalonia became increasingly vociferous in their backing for regionalist feeling in the two regions. When the relatively liberal Cardinal Enrique y Tarancón took over as head of the Spanish Catholic Church in 1971, the bishops went so far as to issue a joint statement that implied disillusion with the Franco regime and regret for their failure to take a more even-handed approach to the Civil War conflict and its aftermath. Such attitudes were by no means universal in the Church, large parts of which remained deeply traditionalist in their social and political views. But they were sufficiently widespread to prevent it from providing concerted opposition to democracy.

Another focus of dissatisfaction was the business community, the more dynamic sections of which were increasingly frustrated by the European Community's refusal to countenance Spanish membership so long as the regime lasted [4.2.1], while more active resistance came from two sources.

The first of these was the industrial workforce. Organized with the help of illegal trade unions [5.5.1.1], strikes proved impossible to prevent and regularly escalated into street clashes with the police. Not infrequently the intervention of the army was necessary before they could be suppressed. The second source of active opposition was the regional nationalism which the regime had signally failed to stamp out. In Catalonia this centred on cultural issues and mainly involved the middle classes. In the Basque Country, however, it not only formed an alliance with the workers' movement and the lower clergy; it also developed an armed wing, ETA.

In fact ETA's main significance was as a catalyst which transformed Basque nationalism into a major political force [3.2.2.1]. Its actions never posed a serious threat to the regime while Franco lived. One, however, did have a significant effect on the prospects of its surviving him. In 1973 an ETA commando blew up the car carrying the first and only man to whom Franco had entrusted the office of prime minister, Admiral Luis Carrero Blanco, and a key element in plans to preserve authoritarian rule after his own death.

In one sense these depended on restoring the monarchy, an institution which commanded the loyalty of most conservative Spaniards, especially the army. Technically, the rightful claimant to the throne was Alfonso XIII's son, Juan de Borbón, about whose reliability Franco had long harboured well-founded doubts. The dictator had therefore persuaded Juan to entrust him with the upbringing of Juan's son, Prince Juan Carlos de Borbón, whom he groomed carefully to succeed him as head of state. The machinery of government, however, would remain in the hands of loyal Francoists, to be led by Carrero Blanco had he lived. Franco himself seems to have believed that these arrangements would ensure the survival of his regime; famously, he asserted that matters were 'all tied up' (*atado y bien atado*).

0.3 Transition to democracy

Even if Admiral Carrero Blanco had survived it is highly doubtful that this confidence would have been vindicated. Like many a dictator, Franco mistook acquiescence with his repressive regime for full-hearted support, which it had never enjoyed except among a small minority. Yet opposition remained muted by fear of another civil war, by the balm of rising material prosperity and because change appeared impossible while Franco lived. His death released the pressures that had built up during the later years of dictatorship, and which rendered virtually unthinkable a continuation of his regime (*continuismo*).

0.3.1 Pressures for change

In part, pressure for change derived from the economic progress the regime had itself stimulated. The contacts engendered by incoming tourism and temporary emigration in search of work had shown many ordinary Spaniards that, contrary to the regime's assertions, liberal democracy produced considerably higher living standards than the Francoist 'organic' variety [0.2]. To the liberal middle classes, for whom economic conditions were easier, democracy offered the attraction of greater intellectual and artistic freedom. To younger Spaniards in general it promised a more relaxed and enjoyable lifestyle.

Powerful external forces also favoured a move towards democracy. The US government had been greatly alarmed at the Portuguese revolution of 1974 and feared that an attempt to prolong dictatorship might result in Spain's turning Communist. More realistically, business interests in Western Europe were eyeing the Spanish market, to which access would only be possible if democracy were restored. Last but not least, democratic parties in Europe, especially those of the left, provided financial as well as moral support to those working actively for change within Spain.

These were divided, broadly speaking, into two camps. One was made up of individuals who, while working with or for the old regime, had come to accept that some form of meaningful democracy was necessary, even desirable, once Franco was dead. These liberalizers (*aperturistas*) were a disparate, unorganized group whose aims were in a sense negative; while they wished for change, they wished also to keep it within strict bounds.

The genuine opposition, considerably larger in numbers, covered an even wider spectrum of groups and opinions, ranging from revolutionary Maoists and Trotskyists to enlightened businessmen and liberal Catholics [0.2]. Its organized core lay in the umbrella organizations set up by the two historic parties of the Spanish left: the Democratic Council (*Junta Democrática*), headed by the Communist Party, and the Socialist-led Democratic Platform (*Plataforma Democrática*). Their aim was a complete break with the past (*ruptura*).

Exactly what that meant was unclear. Certainly it implied the establishment of a democratic regime in which those who had worked with the former regime should have no part to play. For sections of the opposition, however, it suggested rather more. Some Socialists and Communists, in particular, expected institutional reform to be accompanied by radical social and economic changes involving restrictions on the power of private capital. Such demands were anathema to other supporters of democratization, both inside and outside Spain.

After a lengthy illness Franco finally died on 20 November 1975 (*20-N*). Juan Carlos was immediately sworn in as King, and confirmed in office Carlos Arias Navarro, who had taken over as Prime Minister from Carrero Blanco [0.2]. Arias had the reputation of a timid liberalizer; in the event he proved to be more timid than liberal, taking only minimal steps towards democracy. His speeches consistently indicated an essentially authoritarian attitude that gave heart to reactionary opponents of democracy (*nostálgicos*).

Yet Arias was unwilling or unable to clamp down on pressure for change, as he was urged to do by the small group of diehard Francoists (*búnker*). Despite still being technically banned, opposition became ever more vocal and visible. In 1976 the Democratic Council and Democratic Platform came together in a Joint Platform (*Platajunta*). Even so, the opposition leaders' control over their followers was tenuous. On the streets, mass demonstrations frequently degenerated into clashes with the police. Widespread industrial unrest reflected workers' growing concern at rapidly rising prices, and at the same time served to worsen the economic situation. Events were getting dangerously out of hand.

0.3.2 Adolfo Suárez and political reform

At this crucial juncture, in July 1976, King Juan Carlos and his closest advisers took what proved to be a decisive step. Having encouraged Arias to resign as PM, they used the small room for manoeuvre left to them by Franco's complex arrangements to appoint in his place a high-ranking but relatively unknown Francoist bureaucrat, Adolfo Suárez. Their choice provoked consternation and fury from the opposition. In the event, however, it was to prove an inspired one. Effectively Suárez's appointment marks the true beginning of Spain's transition to democracy (*transición democrática*).

It was precisely Suárez's Francoist past that allowed him to move the situation forward. A former head of the regime's state broadcasting service [10.1] and secretary-general of the National Movement [0.2], he had immense knowledge of the operation of the old regime and many of its leading figures. That allowed him to achieve what, on the face of it, seemed impossible; to build a democratic state on Francoist laws and institutions.

The key to this process lay in the Parliament (*Cortes*), whose members (*procuradores*) had all been more or less directly appointed by the regime. Using a mixture of procedural manipulation and covert pressure on individuals, Suárez persuaded the existing Parliament effectively to vote itself out of existence. In 1976 it passed the Political Reform Act (*Ley de Reforma Política*), which provided for democratic elections to a new parliament. On 15 December 1976, in a referendum which was widely supported by most sections of the community – including the Catholic Church – the Act was overwhelmingly ratified in a national referendum.

Suárez had already ended the ban on political parties, provided they were formally approved by the government. Over the 1977 Easter holiday he took the decisive step of legalizing the Communists, thus allowing all significant elements of the opposition to contest the coming general election. It was held on 15 June 1977, and was won surprisingly but comfortably by Suárez's own party, the Democratic Centre Union (UCD) [2.2].

Yet the Prime Minister lacked an overall parliamentary majority, and so needed the opposition's support to undertake the further change clearly demanded by popular feeling. Moreover, the economic situation was deteriorating alarmingly. In the wake of the 1973 rise in oil prices, inflation was spiralling out of control [5.1.1]. Many workers were using their newfound freedom to strike for large wage rises, thus aggravating matters still further. Their actions increased rumblings from army leaders unhappy at the legalization of the Communists. For all these reasons Suárez was anxious to reach agreement with the left-wing opposition.

It was a desire shared by the Socialist and Communist leaders, Felipe González and Santiago Carrillo respectively, who had been taken aback by the results of the two recent polls. In the referendum their joint call for Spaniards to abstain had been almost completely ignored. Then, at the 1977 election, their parties had proved less popular than one led by a former Francoist. At the same time, they too were concerned that continued industrial unrest might provoke a coup and so rule out any further elections. And the Socialists especially were under pressure from their foreign allies and financial backers, the most important of whom were the German Social Democrats (SPD), to tone down their more extreme demands.

0.3.3 Compromise, disillusion, consolidation

These various pressures on the government and the main opposition leaders produced a willingness on both sides to make concessions in order to achieve agreement. The opposition had already done so in its decision to take part in the 1977 election, and so tacitly accept Suárez's gradualist approach. Now it was the Prime Minister's turn to back down. He abandoned his previous plan to base a new constitution on a report from government lawyers and accepted that it must be the task of the newly elected parliament.

How to draft the constitution was one of a set of agreements reached between government and opposition in 1977, known as the Moncloa Pacts (*Pactos de la Moncloa*). The other main thrust of the Pacts was economic. The opposition leaders committed themselves to ensuring that wage demands from their supporters did not push up inflation: the government promised to take measures against unemployment.

In the event, little or nothing was done to create jobs, so that the opposition – or at least its grassroots supporters – got few direct benefits from the Pacts. The government, on the other hand, gained considerably. The Pacts did much to restore the confidence of international investors in the Spanish economy, contributing crucially to its gradual improvement and to political stability. Furthermore, Suárez and his allies not only retained the largest say in formal, constitutional change, they also achieved their aim of averting broader socio-economic transformation.

In effect, the Moncloa Pacts marked the left's abandonment of the aim of breaking with the past [0.3.1]. Change, it was now clear, was to be restricted to political reform, and even that would proceed in agreement with important elements of the old regime. To cover the extent of these arguably unavoidable concessions, a new term was coined. The transition was now described as a negotiated break with the past (*ruptura pactada*) – which, given the original meaning of 'ruptura', was a contradiction in terms. The culmination of this process, the greatest success for the spirit of compromise (*consenso*) which characterized this period, was the approval of a democratic Constitution in late 1978. From the point of view of constitutional theory, that step marked the end of the transition.

Yet in another sense the process still had some way to run. Admittedly most Spaniards were unconcerned, even happy, that the notion of radical change in Spain's socio-economic structures had been quietly dropped. But they had expected democracy to make them materially better off – and many had yet to see any such benefits. Nor did the next few years bring any significant improvement in their situation, as the country's economic difficulties continued. In fact these were only partly due to the political upheaval of transition; understandably, however, many people could not or would not see it that way at the time. Their disillusion (*desencanto*) was obvious at the second post-Franco election, held in March 1979, when turnout fell sharply.

Over the next two years such feelings were amplified by a growing sense of political instability. First, despite winning its second election victory, the ruling UCD fell into increasing turmoil and, at New Year 1981, Suárez abruptly and mysteriously resigned [2.2]. Then the granting of devolution to the Basque Country and Catalonia sparked off widespread demands for regional autonomy [3.1.2]; these were seized upon by some on the right as proof that Spain was in danger of breaking up. And crucially, the Basque terrorist group ETA stepped up its murderous activities, of which the security forces were by far the principal target [3.2.2.1]. Their understandable, bitter resentment was ripe to be channelled by the military's most reactionary elements.

It was well known that these were considering a coup, to be justified by popular dissatisfaction with democracy and the country's alleged ungovernability. Indeed several times their plans were discovered and foiled when already well advanced. Eventually, though, on 23 February 1981 (*23-F*) civil guards under the command of Lieutenant-Colonel Antonio Tejero Molina stormed the Spanish Parliament during the investiture of Suárez's successor as PM, Leopoldo Calvo Sotelo. For 36 hours they held its members captive, along with journalists and parliament officials. Simultaneously various army units mutinied, led by their officers; in Valencia, General Milans del Bosch ordered tanks onto the streets.

Most sections of the army, however, remained loyal to the constitutional order. Together with the police they brought the revolt under control and released the captives. Although it was some time before all its leaders were identified, the attempted coup was effectively over in a day and a half. Briefly it seemed to confirm all the worst fears that Spanish democracy remained fatally unstable: in the event its effect was to dispel them. For the coup sparked off a massive popular and political reaction. No significant public figure spoke out in its support. Instead, political leaders ranging from the Communists to former Francoist ministers headed public demonstrations in support of the new regime. The largest, in Madrid, brought over a million people onto the streets. Spaniards might have been disillusioned with democracy, but they were virtually unanimous in preferring it to the alternative offered by the military extremists.

The next 18 months constituted a strange interlude. As his party steadily crumbled [3.2.2], Calvo Sotelo was prevented from taking decisive action to deal with the country's problems. Yet the opposition was reluctant to force him from office for fear of another coup attempt. Finally, however, his position became untenable and a third general election was called. Held on 28 October 1982 (*28-O*) it resulted in an overwhelming victory for the Socialist Party, whose leader, Felipe González, took over the reins of government in an atmosphere of complete normality. For the first time in Spanish history one freely elected government was replaced by another of a different political persuasion without any significant section of society seriously questioning the legitimacy of the change.

0.4 Spain in the contemporary world

As well as by its history, present-day Spain is conditioned by its relations with the outside world. In 1975, thanks to the nature of the Franco regime, these were extremely limited. Since then, however, they have expanded beyond recognition.

That was spectacularly symbolized in 1992. During the Quincentenary of the most famous date in Spanish history [0.1], the country hosted three major international events: the Olympic Games (*Juegos Olímpicos/JJOO*) were held in Barcelona and the Expo World Fair in Seville, while Madrid reigned as European City of Culture (*Capital Cultural Europea*). By far the most important of Spain's new links are precisely those with Europe, which are discussed separately in Chapter 4. But those with three other areas of the world also have considerable significance: with the USA, because of its role as dominant world power; with Latin America, for historical and cultural reasons; and with North Africa, because of its geographic proximity.

0.4.1 Spain and the USA

The removal of barriers to the outside world has inevitably meant Spain's growing exposure to the influence of the country that was long the undisputed leader of the Western world, and since the collapse of Communism has been the world's sole superpower. That is a thorny issue in the country, partly because, like France, Spain is the homeland of a great world language whose status is threatened by (American) English. But in the Spanish case other, historical, factors also play a role.

For one thing, the Spanish right contains a deep strand of anti-American feeling quite without parallel in Western Europe. The United States was instrumental in depriving Spain of its last significant colonies [0.1], having actively supported the earlier independence struggles of those on the Latin American mainland. The Franco regime swallowed the resultant resentment, to sign the 1953 Defence Agreements [0.2]. Yet for many Spaniards who shared its traditionalist ideals the sight of their country reduced to the status of a US client merely reinforced the sense of bitterness.

Such attitudes found an echo in the centre-right governments under Adolfo Suárez that steered the transition to democracy following Franco's death [0.3.2]. Suárez made much of the idea that Spain's international role should be that of a bridge between the first (Western) and third (developing) worlds. This position, which amounted to a form of non-alignment (*tercermundismo*), led him on occasion to oppose US policies, especially in Central America. Certainly it seemed to preclude Spanish participation in NATO (*Organización del Tratado del Atlántico Norte/OTAN*), the American-dominated pillar of the Western military alliance.

In this sense Suárez's departure from power was crucial, since virtually the only decisive action taken by his successor, Leopoldo Calvo Sotelo [0.3.3], was to take Spain into the alliance's political structure. This move, taken behind Parliament's back, evoked furious opposition from the left, even more anti-American than the right but for very different reasons: US sustenance of a regime which had backed Hitler and Mussolini, and the impact of the 1968 movement of student unrest which, as elsewhere in Europe, had a strongly anti-US tone. Indeed, a considerable number of those who came to occupy leading positions during and after the transition were involved in, or influenced by, the events of 1968.

Among these were the Prime Minister elected in 1982, Felipe González, and many of his Socialist cabinet colleagues. During the election campaign they had savagely attacked Calvo Sotelo's decision, and supported calls for the removal of US military bases. However, once in power González came up against the realities of international politics. Executing a dramatic change of tack he now called for Spain to remain in the alliance provided certain, rather spurious conditions were met. In March 1986 he fought and won a referendum held to confirm this new position [4.2.2].

Although the referendum brought anti-American feeling strongly to the surface, it subsided in the wake of that campaign. The issue of the bases was effectively resolved by a formula under which the facilities were handed over to Spanish control but remained available to the American military. During the first Gulf War in 1991 the revelation that US aircraft *en route* for the combat zone had indeed made use of the bases caused some revival of anti-American feeling. But at the same time Spanish naval units were themselves involved in the conflict, which on balance marked a further step in Spain's integration into the American-led structures of Western defence.

That process of integration appeared to deepen during the course of the invasion and subsequent occupation of Iraq in 2003. The conservative People's Party (PP) government – which had officially taken Spain into the military structure of NATO in 1996 – sent over a thousand Spanish troops to assist the US armed forces in that venture. The then Prime Minister, José María Aznar, seemed keen to identify with the American-led 'war on terror' in the aftermath of the 9-11 attacks in 2001, and lost no opportunity to associate with George W. Bush and Tony Blair in an apparent attempt to position Spain as a leading Western power.

The feeling across the country, however, was decidedly different, although the disapproval of the Spanish people had little impact on Aznar's policy in this respect. It was only when the PP lost the subsequent general election and the new Socialist government recalled Spanish troops from Iraq in 2004 [2.3.4] that foreign policy came more into line with popular feeling once again. One less positive result of that withdrawal, however, was a decided coolness in US-Spanish relations, at least at leadership level, from 2004 on.

As in other parts of the Western world, Spanish feelings about the USA tend to be a mixture of fascination with those dimensions of its popular culture which are accessible through a vast array of media resources – especially television – and a sceptical attitude towards the traditionally imperialist bent of its foreign relations. But the extent of the scepticism is limited, and, broadly speaking, Spaniards have the sense that their country's place in the world is firmly in the European and Western camp, allied inevitably, if at times reluctantly, to the USA. And today, while American cultural and political influence continues to evoke adverse reactions, these are on a scale much closer to that elsewhere in Europe than was the case 25 years ago.

0.4.2 Spain and Latin America

A major factor in Spain's complicated relationship with the USA is precisely its own close links with the superpower's own 'backyard', Latin America, which themselves have never been simple. While a shared language and significant elements of culture in common undoubtedly make for genuine feelings of solidarity on both sides, Spain's past role as the colonial power over much of the region has more ambiguous implications.

Some Spaniards at least still like to see their country in the role of motherland (*madre patria*) to its former subjects. But many in Latin America take a much more jaundiced view of the colonial experience, a feeling forcefully expressed at the time of the 1992 celebrations in Spain by members of Latin America's indigenous peoples (*indígenas*). Their protests had an impact in the sense that the concept of the Americas' 'discovery' was replaced by the less emotive one of a 'meeting' between their inhabitants and Europe's.

In comparison with the British version, of course, Spanish colonial domination ended relatively early. Nor was Spain's empire ever a commercial enterprise in the same sense as the UK's. Indeed, its ex-colonies have arguably had greater economic significance for the country since they obtained independence, as a destination for Spanish emigrants. Emigration was particularly marked from Spain's poorer regions; in some parts of the New World all Spaniards are referred to as Galicians. Many Spaniards have family ties in the Americas, and the wealthy returning emigrant (*indiano*) continues to feature strongly in popular consciousness.

Highest at the start of this century, emigration received a fresh boost when restrictions on leaving the country were relaxed after 1960 [0.2]. As well as allowing the Franco regime to export its unemployed, Latin America also provided one of its few sources of foreign support [6.1.1]. Most notably, the Argentinian populist dictator Juan Perón provided invaluable food aid during the early 1950s, when famine was a real possibility in Spain. Such support gave some basis to Franco's concept of a Spanish-speaking community (*Hispanidad*), inspired by his own reactionary ideas. But by the 1970s the era of dictatorships was coming to an end in Latin America as well. And, in any case, an impoverished Spain could not begin to compete for real influence in the region with its powerful 'northern neighbour'.

After Spain's return to democratic rule in the 1970s its leaders continued to place considerable importance on links with Latin America, while significantly reassessing their nature. Now Spain came to see itself more as a model for the process of transition from dictatorship to democracy, on which many of its former colonies were now themselves embarking. Support for institutional reform became an important focus of Spanish development aid (*ayuda para el desarrollo*), almost half of which goes to Latin America. Since it joined the European Community in 1986 [4.2.1], Spain has also portrayed itself as the defender of Latin American interests within the EC, arguing in favour of greater financial support and improved trading conditions for the sub-continent.

Successive Spanish governments were aware that this approach had decidedly paternalistic overtones, which they were anxious to play down. In order to foster a sense of more equal cooperation, they promoted a new, and more concrete version of the old Francoist concept of 'community'. Its basis is the Conferences of Iberian American States (*Conferencias Iberoamericanas*), the first of which was held in 1991 at Guadalajara, in Mexico; subsequently they have become regular events. The participants include not only Spain and its former colonies in South and Central America, but also Portugal and Brazil – hence the neologism 'Iberian America' (*Iberoamérica*) – although Spain, as much the larger of the European members, clearly regards itself as the driving force behind the project. Indeed, some of its rulers seem to have seen in the 'Iberian American community' the basis of a distinctive world role for Spain, independent of its European ties, rather as some in the UK still hanker after the notion of the 'English-speaking peoples'.

In practice, though, the new 'community' has developed minimal political weight, not least because of Spain's own increasing commitment to a common European foreign policy [4.2.2]. Moreover, Spain's pretensions to serve as Latin America's advocate on the European stage have turned out to be somewhat hollow. It has done nothing to alter the EU's seeming determination to keep out developing countries' products – its own trade with Latin America remains very limited – and little to loosen restrictions on immigration from the region (other than of suitably talented football players).

In terms of aid, too, Spain's position is less altruistic than appears at first sight. Since its overall aid budget remains very low by European standards, the absolute sums – as opposed to the share – channelled to Latin America by the Spanish International Cooperation Agency (*Agencia Española de Cooperación Internacional/AECI*) are not especially large. Moreover, a high percentage of aid is cultural rather than economic, while almost all the latter is tied, i.e. it must be spent on specific projects, often carried out by Spanish contractors. In 1999, Spain's credibility as a supporter of democratization also took a severe blow when the head of the AECI's Latin American operations was himself dismissed for corruption. For these reasons, Spanish government aid efforts are often criticized by the country's own non-governmental organizations (*organizaciones no gubernamentales/ONGs*), whose international activities are also highly concentrated in Latin America.

Spanish NGOs have also been critical of the attitude taken by successive governments to human rights in Latin America. Ever since the realignment of foreign policy along pro-American lines in the 1980s [0.4.1], this has tended to be relatively cautious. Indeed, Spain has often been markedly more hesitant than some of its new European partners in condemning continuing human rights abuses in the region, most of them committed by right-wing regimes with dubious democratic credentials.

Such caution was accentuated by a desire not to disrupt the Iberian America project by antagonizing the leaders of Spain's partners in it. One exception to this was the hard line which the conservative PP government took against the regime of Fidel Castro in Cuba in the period following their election in 1996; however, within two years, official condemnations of Castro had died away, and good relations were re-established, which grew even stronger during the period of the PSOE government after 2004.

Spain's refusal to speak out on human rights issues may have helped it maintain good relations with those who hold power in Latin America, but has not helped its standing among the region's population as a whole. Since the mid-1990s a new source of resentment has been added by an astonishing surge in Spanish investment in the region [5.2.1]. Again, there is a gap in perceptions here. For, while in Spain the investment flow tends to be seen as evidence of positive engagement, from Latin America it can look more like a new form of colonialism. Such feelings add an extra edge to industrial disputes in Spanish-owned firms, especially if they involve large-scale redundancies. Some major investors, such as *Telefónica* [5.4.1], have caused further resentment by trying to restrict competition from indigenous firms in their own interests, while the Spanish airline Iberia made itself particularly unpopular by its arbitrary behaviour in Latin American markets.

In more recent years, the arrival in power in Latin America of left-wing governments such as those in Bolivia, Brazil and Venezuela has led to further adjustments in the relationship between Spain and Latin America. These governments have been outspoken in their criticisms of Spain and in particular of the behaviour of the above-mentioned Spanish multinational firms (along with others) in Latin America. To date, however, they have continued to show an interest in maintaining strong diplomatic links with the country, and feel more comfortable with the Socialist government in Spain than they did with their predecessors, the People's Party.

The changing nature of the relationship came sharply into focus at the 2007 Iberian American summit in Chile when the Venezuelan President, Hugo Chávez, voiced trenchant criticism of the former Spanish Prime Minister, José María Aznar, accusing the latter of conspiring to remove him from power. The current Spanish PM, José Luis Rodríguez Zapatero, rebutted Chávez's attacks, and requested that he show due respect to Aznar. The spat ended with King Juan Carlos, who was also in attendance, asking the Venezuelan to stay quiet while Zapatero was speaking, and eventually walking off the platform when Chávez refused.

Incidents such as this one reflect the fact that there is a new maturity to the relations between Spain and her former colonies. The latter are keen to assert their position, which is one of increasing economic and diplomatic strength, and to be seen as equals to the former colonial power. And the fact is that, in the eyes of most Latin American governments, the principal foreign partner is – unsurprisingly – Washington, not Madrid. Meantime most Spaniards have come to see their links with Europe as much more significant than trans-Atlantic ones, albeit these retain considerable emotional force.

0.4.3 Spain and North Africa

The cultural and historical basis for Spain to see itself as a bridge between Europe and Latin America is well known. Rather less so are the similar grounds – to which can be added immediate geographical proximity – for its claim to play a similar role *vis-à-vis* North Africa in general, and Morocco in particular. It is true that the Moorish presence is now a very distant memory in Spain [0.1]. But it is only a little over thirty years since the country withdrew from its last colony on the southern shore of the straits of Gibraltar, and even today a sizeable Spanish-speaking community exists there. Moreover, it still retains as an integral part of its own territory the two enclaves of Ceuta and Melilla [11.18].

Given that historical background, it is hardly surprising that the 'bridge' analogy is just as problematic in this case as in that of Latin America. Perhaps for that reason, once Spain had returned to democracy after the death of General Franco, the country's new rulers attempted to subsume relations with North Africa in a broader context. The area was now to be seen as part of the Southern Mediterranean as a whole, whose political and economic development Spain was anxious to encourage. In fact there were some concrete grounds for a broader approach. Not only do a very large part of Spain's massive energy imports come from Algeria and Libya. Given its location, Spain's security is closely bound up with the stability of the Mediterranean as a whole.

Some attempts have been made to give substance to the new approach. In 1991 Madrid hosted the conference that gave rise to the Middle East peace process, having finally established diplomatic relations with Israel in the 1980s, and Spain has subsequently become one of the major donors of aid to the Palestinian territories. It also tried to interest its European Union partners in their southern neighbours, the highpoint of its efforts coming in 1995 when it promoted the first Euro-Mediterranean Conference, in Barcelona, during its presidency of the European Union [4.3.1]. It has also been a participant in the so-called '5+5 Dialogue' (*Diálogo 5+5*), a series of meetings that have been held since 1990 between five countries from the northern shore of the Mediterranean (Portugal, Spain, France, Italy and Malta) and the five countries from its southern shore that constitute the region called the Maghreb (*Magreb*): (Morocco, Algeria, Tunisia, Libya and Mauritania).

Despite this broadening of the agenda, it is still the case that most of the Spanish attention in this area is on Morocco. Prior to 1975 relations with Morocco were strained, even though the Franco regime – somewhat bizarrely, given its militant Catholicism and underlying racism [0.2] – made much of its positive links with the Arab world in general. In reality, though, these were based essentially on common hostility towards Israel, which for Morocco was less important than the continuing Spanish presence in Ceuta, Melilla and the much larger territory to Morocco's west, then known as the Spanish Sahara. In 1975, seizing on the power vacuum in Spain as Franco approached death, Morocco's King Hassan II organized the so-called green march (*marcha verde*), a mass civilian incursion into the colony, that effectively brought it under his control.

Subsequently relations between Spain and Morocco improved considerably, with the former aspiring to act as Morocco's advocate (*valedor*) inside the EU, representing its interests in the Union's internal debates. In 1991 the two countries signed a 'Treaty of Friendship, Good Neighbourliness and Cooperation' in the Moroccan capital Rabat. This was the model for a number of other such treaties which have since been agreed between Spain and various Noth African and Middle Eastern countries, including Algeria and Egypt. Since then high-level ministerial meetings have been held on a regular basis. Plans to build a rail tunnel under the Straits are well advanced.

In recent years, a number of issues and incidents have caused friction between the two from time to time. Most obviously, Spain's refusal to countenance withdrawal from Ceuta and Melilla is a constant irritant. When the two cities were given autonomous city status in 1994, confirming their place in Spain's new regionalized structure, relations were severely strained. This was exacerbated in November 2007 when the Spanish King and Queen paid an official visit to the cities, an act that provoked the government in Rabat to recall its ambassador from Spain until January of the following year. Meanwhile, in July 2002, Moroccan gendarmes entered Parsley Island, a tiny Spanish possession off the North African coast, just 250 metres from Morocco, and the manner of the 'reconquest' of the island by Spanish troops strained the relationship further. Another problematic issue is that of access to Morocco's considerable fishing grounds, which are of vital importance to Spain's hard-pressed fishing industry [5.3.1]. The fact that some Moroccan products, especially fruit and vegetables, compete directly with Spanish ones implies a conflict of interests over access to EU markets.

Possibly the most difficult issue for the two countries is illegal immigration. This has become increasingly significant as the numbers of Moroccans – and Africans generally – attempting to enter Spain by crossing the Straits of Gibraltar or sailing from the African coast to the Canary Islands have increased over the last ten years [6.1.1]. Given that Spain is a member of the Schengen Group [4.2.2], Spanish efforts to stem the entry of Africans by these routes in effect means that Spain is acting as the border guard for the EU, a position which seems to run counter to the country's supposed role of 'bridge' to its closest southern neighbour.

0.5 Glossary

20-N m	20 November 1975 (death of Franco)
23-F m	23 February 1981 (attempted coup)
28-O (m)	28 October 1982 (election of first Socialist government)
absolutismo (m)	absolute monarchy, rule
aperturista (mf)	liberalizer (at end of Franco era)
atraso (m)	backwardness
autarquía (f)	autarky, policy of economic self-sufficiency
ayuda para el desarrollo (f)	development aid
bienio negro (m)	'two black years' of right-wing government, 1934–36
búnker (m)	diehard Francoists
burguesía (f)	middle classes, bourgeoisie
cacique (m)	(corrupt) local party boss
Capital Cultural Europea (f)	European Capital of Culture
carlismo (m)	Carlist movement, ultra-traditionalist movement in nineteenth century
Caudillo (m)	'Leader', title assumed by Franco
Colón (m)	Columbus
Concilio Vaticano II (m)	Second Vatican Council
Conferencias Iberoamericanas (f)	Conferences of Iberian American States
consenso (m)	spirit of compromise (characteristic of transition period)
continuismo (m)	(support for) continuation of Franco regime after 1975
Cortes (fpl)	Spanish parliament
decadencia (f)	decline
democracia orgánica (f)	'organic democracy', Francoist term for regime philosophy
desencanto (m)	disillusion (with democracy, esp. *c.* 1978–81)
fraude electoral (m)	election-rigging, electoral fraud
Frente Popular (m)	Popular Front (left-wing alliance in 1936 election)
Hispanidad (f)	Spanish-speaking community (Francoist term)
Iberoamérica (f)	Iberian America, Spanish and Portuguese America
Ilustración (f)	The Enlightenment
indiano (m)	(rich) returning emigrant from Latin America

indígena (m)	indigenous inhabitant; Latin American indian
Juegos Olímpicos/JJOO (mpl)	Olympic Games
Ley de Reforma Política (f)	Political Reform Act
madre patria (f)	motherland, Spain seen from Latin America
Magreb (m)	the Maghreb
marcha verde (f)	mass intrusion of Moroccan civilians into former Spanish Sahara in 1975
Movimiento Nacional (m)	National Movement, single party of Franco regime
Nacionalcatolicismo (m)	'Catholic Nationalism', ideology of later Franco regime
nacionales (mpl)	Francoist forces (in civil war)
Nacionalsindicalismo (m)	'National Syndicalism', ideology of earlier Franco regime
nostálgico (m)	reactionary
Organización del Tratado del Atlántico Norte (OTAN) (f)	North Atlantic Treaty Organization
organización no gubernamental/ ONG (f)	non-governmental organization/NGO
Pactos de la Moncloa (m)	Moncloa Pacts
Plan de Estabilización (m)	Stabilization Plan (1959)
procurador (m)	member of Franco's (appointed) 'Parliament'
pronunciamiento (m)	(nineteenth-century) military revolt
regeneracionismo (m)	post-1898 regenerationist movement,
ruptura (democrática) (f)	clean break with the past (i.e. Franco regime)
ruptura pactada (f)	negotiated break with the past
sexenio revolucionario/ democrático (m)	six-year period of upheaval following 1868 Revolution
sindicato vertical (m)	Francoist government-controlled trade union
tecnócrata (mf)	technocrat; expert (adviser to Franco regime post-1960)
tercermundismo (m)	vision of Spain as bridge between first world and third (esp. Latin America); non-alignment
transición democrática (f)	transition to democracy
turno pacífico (m)	system of alternation in power based on electoral fraud
valedor (m)	advocate (e.g. of a country's or countries' interests inside the EU)

The Spanish state

The basis of a country's public life lies in the institutions and mechanisms by which it is governed, the state. The equivalent Spanish term (*estado*) is often used specifically to refer to Spain's own central government as opposed to the country's various regional governments. That distinction is followed here. The present chapter will examine the main central institutions – the monarchy, the Parliament, the political executive made up of the Prime Minister and his cabinet, and the administrative apparatus subordinate to it – leaving regional government to be studied in Chapter 3. Also dealt with in Chapter 1 is local government. Although clearly distinct from the central institutions, it shares with them one essential feature. Unlike the regions, which are the product of an open-ended process of development conditioned by the interplay of political forces over the last three decades, the structures of both central and local government derive from the new Constitution adopted in 1978.

1.1 The 1978 constitution

The Constitution's adoption marked a milestone in Spain's transition to democracy after General Franco's death in 1975, and the document itself was very much a product of that complex and delicate process [0.3]. The original intention of Adolfo Suárez, the Prime Minister who set change decisively in train, was that the basis of Spain's new democracy be drafted by government lawyers. But his hand was forced by the results of the 1977 election [0.3.2], which left him dependent on the goodwill of the opposition forces. And they were quite clear that the task must be undertaken more openly, by the democratic representatives of the Spanish people.

1.1.1 Constituent process

As a result, the newly elected Parliament became a constituent assembly (*cortes constituyentes*), that is, one charged with drawing up a new constitution. The Parliament, in turn, entrusted the bulk of the drafting process to a seven-man, cross-party committee whose members became known collectively as the 'fathers of the Constitution'. The draft they produced in January 1978 was then further debated and amended in both Houses of Parliament. On 31 October an agreed text emerged.

On 6 December 1978 (6-D) this text was submitted to a referendum; it received the support of 88 per cent of those who voted, representing 59 per cent of the total electorate. Only in the Basque Country was the result less clear. There, although just over three-quarters of the votes cast were favourable, the low turnout (49 per cent) meant that these represented only just over a third of the region's electorate. This fact, together with the circumstance that there had been no Basque representation on the drafting committee, was to provide an unfortunate excuse for some to question the legitimacy of the new constitutional order in the region [3.2.2.1].

Formally, the constituent process was not completed until some three weeks later, with the King's ratification of the agreed text and its official publication on 29 December. Nevertheless, the date most closely associated with the 1978 Constitution is that of its popular approval, now commemorated by a public holiday, Constitution Day.

1.1.2 Structure, principles, content

The Constitution is divided into 11 parts or 'titles'; the first is an Introductory Title (*Título Preliminar*), while the remaining ten are substantive and denoted by Roman numerals. The areas covered are mainly typical of previous Spanish Constitutions and other similar documents, the main original feature being the specification in Title VII of the principles on which the Spanish economy is to be run.

The titles are themselves subdivided into a total of 169 numbered articles, organized where appropriate into 'chapters' and 'sections'. The major concerns of those who framed the Constitution are apparent in the number of articles devoted to different topics. Well over half of them cover just three areas: basic rights and liberties (46 articles), the role of Parliament (31) and provisions for regional self-government (23).

In addition to the main text the Constitution includes a number of dispositions. The last, or Final Disposition, established the date when the Constitution would take effect. A single Revocatory Disposition (*disposición derogatoria*) revoked the Fundamental Laws of the Franco regime, a series of measures which had effectively acted as its constitution. Nine transitional dispositions (*disposiciones transitorias*) covered questions relating to the introduction of various of the Constitution's provisions.

Of the four additional dispositions, the last three clarify points relating to the age of legal majority (*mayoría de edad*), the special situation of the Canary Islands, and the court system. The first declares that the Constitution 'protects and respects the historic rights' of the Basque provinces and Navarre. This seemingly anodyne statement hinted at the complex issues bequeathed by history in those two regions [3.2.2, 11.15].

Returning to the text itself, the three fundamental principles of the Constitution are set out in Article 1.1. First, Spain is defined as a democracy. This principle is reflected not only in the central role accorded to a Parliament elected by regular popular vote [1.3], but also in provision for various forms of direct participation in the operation of the state (*participación ciudadana*). Such provision, however, is often cautious – for example, half a million signatures are required before a proposed law can be presented to Parliament by a so-called people's initiative (*iniciativa popular*).

Secondly, Article 1.1 defines Spain as a state under the rule of law (*estado de derecho*). On the one hand, this principle means that all actions of public authorities are subject to legislation, which in turn must conform to the principles set out in the Constitution itself. On the other, it is reflected in a lengthy catalogue of rights set out in subsequent articles. They include not only basic human freedoms but also other economic and social rights whose protection poses clear problems, most notably the 'right to work' (Article 35).

In such cases the text is regarded by experts as establishing an aspiration; it is seen not as a delimiting constitution, freezing the country's institutional development at a particular moment in time, but as an enabling one. Thus, even if the state cannot be forced to provide work, it is considered that the Constitution's provisions would prevent removal of public support for the unemployed. Equally, while discrimination of various types undoubtedly exists, by proscribing it the Constitution allows action to be taken against its overt practice by any social or economic body.

Similar considerations apply to the Constitution's third basic principle, one which has no direct English equivalent. The definition of Spain as a so-called social state (*estado social*) was inspired chiefly by the post-1945 (West) German socio-economic model, known in English as the social market economy. One aspect of Spain's adoption of this model is precisely the inclusion in the Constitution of social rights, such as that to work. The other is explicit constitutional authorization to state institutions of an active role in the country's economic affairs. Most famously, this role includes redistribution of income more fairly, not just between the country's regions [3.1.4], but also between its individual citizens. Here again, the Constitution has been observed more in the breach than the observance.

Nonetheless, the altruism of its basic principles is one reason why the Constitution has acquired an extraordinarily high status for Spaniards, especially those with access to power. The other is that its provisions are usually regarded as having resolved three fundamental conflicts that had split Spanish society for a century and more, relating to the roles of the monarchy [1.2], the regions [3.1.1] and the Catholic Church. In relation to the latter, the Constitution establishes equality of all religions and stipulates that none shall have official status, although it does implicitly acknowledge the Church as an objective feature (*hecho sociológico*) of Spanish society. But this approach was a reflection of the popular consensus that had already been reached on this issue as a result of various social and political factors. A similar consensus existed with regard to the monarchy, and any remnants of republicanism that existed were not so strong as to warrant significant opposition to the text. And, given that the regional question remains open even today, despite the progress that has been made [3.2.2], the perception that the Constitution had managed to resolve these three divisive issues is undoubtedly distorted.

That is not to say that the Constitution takes no credit for Spain's achievements since 1978. But it does suggest that its true importance lies less in any of its specific provisions than as a symbol of Spaniards' collective will to face the future rather than the past, and to place the highest priority on the concerns of the individual citizen. Precisely in that sense, however, it is worth noting that the text – like most documents of its type – has little or nothing to say on such increasingly crucial areas for the individual as the environment, the media and the activities of major corporations.

1.1.3 Interpretation

The complexity and imprecision of the Constitution's provisions mean that, even more than most legal texts, its meaning must often be officially interpreted. A mechanism for doing so is foreseen in the text itself, Title IX of which provides for creation of a Constitutional Court (*Tribunal Constitucional*). The details of the Court's membership and operation were laid down in legislation passed in 1979.

The 1979 Act establishes that the Court shall consist of 12 members, all of whom must be experienced and respected jurists. Of these, two are appointed by the government of the day, eight elected by Parliament (with at least a three-fifths majority), and two named by the governing body of the legal profession. Of the eight elected by Parliament, the Congress and the Senate elect four each. Under legislation introduced in 2007, aimed at enhancing the degree of parliamentary representation achieved by the regions, the latter four must be nominated for election by the regional parliaments. Like their nine-year term of office, the attempt to achieve balance in the membership of the Court was designed to ensure its independence of direct government influence. As in other areas, the efficacy of these legal safeguards has subsequently been called into question by political developments [1.4.1].

The Court, against whose decisions there is no appeal, is empowered to resolve two types of conflict over the Constitution's meaning. First, it adjudicates in disputes between the central government and the other bodies which enjoy legislative powers in Spain – the country's autonomous regions – over which of the two is competent to make law governing particular matters (*conflictos de competencias*). Because of their scope and, in many cases, the sensitive political issues involved, such disputes represent an important aspect of the Court's work, although they constitute only a small percentage of its cases.

The second way in which the Court interprets the Constitution is by deciding whether a particular act passed by the central or regional parliaments, or decree issued by the government, contravenes the Constitution. To this end the Court acts only on the initiative of certain authorized agencies. On the one hand, certain groups of politicians – the central government, regional authorities and groupings of at least 50 members of Parliament – may, within three months of a law's coming into effect, request the Court to rule on whether it complies with the Constitution (*recurso de constitucionalidad*). On the other, judges may question the constitutional status of a law applicable to any case with which they are concerned (*cuestión de inconstitucionalidad*). Although these types of appeals have been relatively rare in the history of the 1978 Constitution, there has been a notable increase in the number of *recursos de constitucionalidad* brought by the opposition People's Party since the Socialists assumed power in 2004. Indeed, in the period from March 2004 to August 2007, no fewer than 21 such appeals were put forward [2.3.4].

Since judges may act on behalf of litigants, this second procedure allows members of the public access to the Constitutional Court, albeit indirectly. Direct public access to the Court exists in that all Spaniards may make application to it for protection of certain of the rights and freedoms established by the Constitution, where these have allegedly been infringed by a public authority (*recurso de amparo*). The rights concerned are those contained in Articles 14 to 29, although application to the Court may be made only once all other forms of legal redress have failed. It is one of the positive signs of genuine public participation that, contrary to many predictions, this type of dispute has made up the vast majority of those which have come before the Constitutional Court, although it is also the case that just 4 per cent of these have been deemed worthy of detailed examination.

Private citizens, however, have no right to request the Court for a ruling on whether new legislation is or is not constitutional. To do that they must go through the only agency outside government and Parliament to which the Constitution gives such powers, Spain's Ombudsman (*Defensor del Pueblo*). More generally he – as yet there has been no Ombudswoman – is charged with monitoring the activities of all public authorities for possible contraventions of individuals' constitutional rights. In practice he acts in response to complaints; in doing so he has the right to priority assistance from those authorities whose alleged maladministration he chooses to investigate.

The Ombudsman is also required to present periodic reports of his activities to Parliament, by whom he is appointed. While most of the complaints he receives relate to the legal system [9.1.4], one of his most important roles has been in assisting immigrants threatened with expulsion, or subject to abuses by the authorities. However, the present incumbent, former Socialist minister Enrique Múgica, caused considerable controversy when he declined to challenge the restrictive new Aliens Act passed in 2001 [6.1.1].

1.1.4 Amendment

The rules governing amendments (*reformas*) to the Constitution are laid down in Title X. They may be introduced by the same agencies as ordinary legislation [1.3.3]. However, in a reflection of the overriding concern with stability felt by the Constitution's architects, the conditions attached to their passage are extremely strict. In most cases a two-thirds majority is required in both Houses of Parliament. In addition, a referendum must be held should a group comprising a tenth of the membership of either House demand it within 15 days of such parliamentary approval.

However, an even more exacting procedure is set out for any 'fundamental' amendment affecting the text as a whole or its most important provisions: those relating to the role of the monarch and individual rights and liberties, as well as the basic principles set out in the Introductory Title [1.1.2]. Such amendments must first be approved by a two-thirds majority in both Houses, which must then be dissolved immediately and a general election (*elecciones legislativas*) held. The newly elected Parliament must then confirm its predecessor's decision, again with a two-thirds majority in both Houses. Finally, a referendum must ratify Parliament's approval of the amendment.

Hardly surprising, then, that as yet only one attempt at change has been made, in response to obligations acquired by Spain as a member of the European Union. Given the overwhelming pro-European feelings of the country's political class [4.2.2], the success of that particular amendment (Article 13.2) which was passed in 1992 and which allows citizens of other EU member states to vote at local elections, is equally unsurprising – and far from indicative, given that there is an even greater barrier to amendment than technical rules.

That is the extraordinary veneration in which the Constitution is held by most of the Spanish political elite [1.1.2], who often seem to regard any proposals for amendment as a form of heresy. Even where the desirability of change in a major institution has long been generally acknowledged, as in the case of the Senate [1.3], the main parties have been inclined to shy away from the notion of change. The current Socialist Prime Minister, José Luis Rodríguez Zapatero, did propose a set of changes which would have a major impact on Spanish life if implemented, although the pace at which these proposals are being progressed has been – perhaps predictably – very slow.

The proposals would entail change in four constitutional areas: adjusting the composition of the Senate [1.3.1]; permitting first-born female offspring to ascend to the Spanish throne ahead of younger male siblings [1.2]; allowing the use of vernacular names in relevant autonomous communities, and achieving greater alignment between the Spanish Constitution and the terms of the Lisbon Treaty [4.1.2].

At least part of the reason why politicians have been reluctant to admit the need to amend the Constitution, however, is that they fear that reopening the debate on any fundamental constitutional matter would give nationalists, especially those in the Basque Country, the chance they have been waiting for, and bring the whole regional issue back to boiling point. The cynical might argue that such reticence is justified in that amendments will, in practice, rarely be needed because the Constitution's imprecision in many areas makes it highly flexible. But that ignores the text's silence on major issues for the twenty-first century [1.1.2], and the resultant need for positive amendment if it is to retain its relevance.

In practice, however, the main Spanish parties have shown that they are prepared to amend the Constitution by default if it suits them. Compulsory military service is enshrined in the text (Article 30), but was nonetheless suspended by new legislation in 2001 [9.2.2]. Arguably the same applies to those 'rights' supposedly conferred by the Constitution but which successive governments have ignored in practice [1.1.2]. Such behaviour is clearly at odds with their habitual rhetoric of respect for Spain's supposed fundamental charter (*Carta magna*).

1.2 The monarchy

The central constitutional role of the monarchy, or 'Crown' as it is called in the text, is apparent from its inclusion among those aspects whose amendment is subject to especially demanding procedures [1.1.4]. The relative ease with which this role was accepted by the traditionally republican left was seen at the time as a key aspect of the consensus achieved during the transition [0.3.2]. Moreover, both then and more recently there has been a tendency to play up the contribution of King Juan Carlos and his closest advisers to the transition's success, not merely in the period up to approval of the 1978 Constitution but also thereafter. It is therefore important to stress that the Constitution also specifies the essentially subordinate nature of the monarch's role – and that the course of events since 1978 has repeatedly borne this out.

Thus, despite being Spain's Head of State, the monarch exercises only negligible powers of initiative in that role. It is true that operation of the state at the highest level depends largely on his signature. It is the monarch that makes senior official appointments, including that of the Prime Minister; laws are issued and justice carried out in his name. However, these, like all his actions, are essentially formal in nature, and require the endorsement (*refrendo*) of another important constitutional figure – the government, its head, or Parliament – from which the actions in practice emanate. Similarly, the monarch's endorsement of their decisions, such as legislation or the appointment of ministers, is a purely formal act.

This is not to say that the monarchy lacks significance, but rather that its importance is not real but symbolic. On one level, the monarch's involvement in key aspects of public life represents the principle of national unity: that the state acts on behalf, and in the common interest, of the Spanish people as a whole. On another, certain specific actions serve to present a particular image of the country both to the outside world and to its own citizens.

It is generally agreed, for instance, that Juan Carlos's official visits abroad (*viajes oficiales*) have been a highly effective form of 'marketing' for Spain. Internally, the deliberately ostentatious exercise of his right to vote has reminded any Spaniards who harboured lingering doubts about democracy that the contemporary monarchy is a pillar of that form of government, not an alternative to it. Perhaps, too, maintenance of a relatively modest lifestyle and royal household (*casa real*) serves to underline the constitutional aspiration to greater equality.

There are two areas in which the monarch's influence might be seen as real. The first is his role in appointing a Prime Minister following a general election. Under normal circumstances the monarch has no discretion in this regard; he calls on the leader of the largest party to form a government and, once they have received the requisite parliamentary vote of confidence, swears them in. It has been argued that after a close election, where no party enjoyed a clear parliamentary majority, the monarch's role could acquire greater importance. However, there is no evidence that this was the case after either the 1993 or the 1996 general elections, neither of which produced a decisive result.

The second way in which the monarch is seen as possibly exercising real influence is through his role as Commander-in-Chief of the Armed Forces (*Mando Supremo de las Fuerzas Armadas*). Here again there is no question of the King's exercising planning or operational control; these functions lie clearly with the appropriate institutions (government and Parliament) and, like others, require only formal endorsement by the Head of State. Nevertheless, it does seem clear that Juan Carlos has been able to exercise a degree of moral authority over military – especially army – officers, thereby preventing their hostility to democracy from spilling over into active opposition, most famously on the night of the 1981 coup attempt [0.3.3].

Yet, in so far as such authority exists, it would appear to derive less from the provisions of the Constitution than from the particular traditions of the Spanish military, and from Juan Carlos's upbringing and experience. After all, there seems little reason why officers suspicious of the constitutional order should feel loyalty to the monarch because of the role he is assigned by that order. More generally, the undoubted esteem enjoyed by the monarchy in Spain today has essentially been earned in political practice rather than bestowed through constitutional theory. To a significant degree it is not so much enthusiasm for monarchy as an institution as respect for Juan Carlos's personal exercise of the monarch's role.

Juan Carlos assumed the throne under very delicate circumstances, not as the legitimate heir but as Franco's nominee [0.2]. Not until 1977, when the new King's father formally renounced his own rights, was the situation regularized. In terms of cementing his popular standing, however, the key event was probably his role in suppressing the 1981 coup [0.3.3]. Since then, he has shown consistent tact and no little political skill in establishing the monarchy as a bulwark of democracy rather than a threat to it.

At the same time, the fact that Juan Carlos and his consort Sofía perform many duties together, as the royal couple (*los reyes*), means that popular respect is not restricted to the King himself. It extends also in some degree to their children, who have been schooled in the same downbeat approach to monarchy. The two eldest are daughters, the Princesses (*Infantas*) Elena and Cristina. The youngest, Prince Felipe, has the title of Prince of Asturias. As the Constitution specifies the primacy of male offspring, he is also heir to the throne (*heredero*), and has been playing an increasingly prominent role in Spanish public life in recent years. His marriage in 2004 to Letizia Ortiz constituted something of a surprise for Spaniards since Ms Ortiz was a commoner and a divorcee, who had been known to the Spanish public as a TV journalist. Judging from the generally favourable – not to say fawning – coverage received by this couple in the Spanish press [10.2], it seems safe to assume that the royal family will continue to command high levels of popular respect in the future.

One possible change that may be introduced relates to the primacy of the rights of male descendants with regard to inheriting the throne. Already, the current Prime Minister has posited the notion of introducing gender equality to the relevant article (Art. 57) of the Constitution – a form of equality which is otherwise guaranteed to all citizens under Article 14 – although the political class have to date shown little enthusiasm for the proposal [1.1.4]. Given that both of the children born thus far to the Prince and Princess are female (Leonor, born in 2005, and Sofía, born in 2007), the issue of allowing a first-born daughter to take precedence over any younger male siblings may well need to be addressed in the not-too-distant future.

1.3 Parliament

Both the monarch and his heir – on coming of age – must swear an oath of loyalty. Its wording expresses the Crown's subordination to the law of the land and, above all, to the Spanish people as a whole. It is they who wield sovereignty under the 1978 Constitution, which ascribes the central role in the state to the body that makes law and represents the common will, Parliament. Indeed, the political form of the state is defined as not just a constitutional but also a 'parliamentary' monarchy (Article 1.3).

1.3.1 Election, structure and composition

The key role of Parliament (*Cortes*) in securing the fundamentally democratic nature of the state [1.1.2] derives from the fact that it is directly elected by the people. This takes place by means of a general election (*elecciones generales*), at which all Spaniards aged 18 and over may vote. The maximum period between elections is set by the Constitution at four years.

The Constitution also states that Parliament shall be organized in the form of two chambers (*Cámaras*), or Houses. The official title of the Lower House (*Cámara Baja*) is the Congress (*Congreso de los Diputados*); its members are deputies (*diputados*). The Upper House (*Cámara Alta*) is known as the Senate (*Senado*), its members being senators (*senadores*). In line with British usage, deputies are sometimes referred to in English as MPs, but strictly speaking the term 'members of parliament' (*parlamentarios*) applies to both Houses in the Spanish case.

As in the UK, the term 'Upper House' is misleading, since the Senate has little real power. Its impotence is reflected in the fact that there is no team of government ministers there, as there is in the British House of Lords. Effective parliamentary influence lies almost exclusively with the Lower House. In particular, Congress alone designates the Prime Minister, and hence indirectly the entire cabinet [1.4.3], and can effectively overrule the Senate if the two Houses disagree over proposed legislation [1.3.3].

According to the Constitution, Congress must have between 300 and 400 members; current legislation sets the total at 350. The constituencies (*circunscripciones*) that the deputies are elected to represent are Spain's 50 provinces; in addition, the North African enclaves of Ceuta and Melilla each elect one deputy.

The numbers of deputies returned by the various provinces are reviewed regularly. They are broadly proportional to the size of a province's electorate, subject to a constitutional minimum of two (currently, though, no province elects fewer than three deputies). This arrangement means that the smaller, rural provinces are significantly over-represented. The most populous province, Madrid, currently elects 35 deputies, roughly one for every 130,000 voters. That is over twelve times the figure for Soria, the province with the smallest electorate.

Rural over-representation is one reason why the results produced by the Spanish electoral system are less proportional than in any Western country except those which, like the UK, use majority systems in single-member constituencies. The other reasons are the relatively large number of constituencies, most of which return five or fewer deputies, and the requirement for a party to win at least 3 per cent of the votes to gain representation even in the larger provinces. Together these arrangements seriously disadvantage small parties, or at least those which operate throughout the country as opposed to within a particular province or region. As a result, the constitutional requirement that the electoral system for the Congress should 'respect the principle of proportionality' is met only partially, if at all.

However, criticism of the system has focused not on this point, but on the limited ability of voters to influence exactly who represents them, since they can choose only between lists of candidates presented by the competing parties. And, while the number of seats (*escaños*) allocated to a list depends on the number of votes it receives, the particular candidates elected are determined purely by their placing on the list, which is decided by the party. Over the years various proposals have been made to change this system of closed, blocked lists (*listas cerradas y bloqueadas*), by allowing voters either to adjust the order of candidates within a list or to choose candidates from several. But the present arrangement suits the major parties well, and they have had little difficulty in resisting the fairly mild pressure for change.

In any case, experience at elections for the Upper House, which are held concurrently with those to the Congress, suggests that the changes proposed would have little effect. At Senate elections voters may indeed cast their votes for candidates of several parties: in practice they opt overwhelmingly not to do so. In most constituencies, that is in the mainland provinces, voters cast three votes each for the Senate, and the four best-placed candidates are elected. Ceuta and Melilla elect two Senators each, while in the Canaries and Balearics the constituencies are individual islands or groups of islands, each of which returns a single Senator.

This system favours the rural provinces even more clearly than that used for the Congress. However, again debate about its reform has not centred on such bias. Instead it has been concerned mainly with the Senate's constitutionally defined role as a chamber of 'territorial representation'. At present that is achieved through the representatives of the various regional parliaments, which each designate one Senator, plus one more for each complete million of regional population. These indirectly elected Senators – currently there are 51 – are heavily outnumbered by their 208 directly elected colleagues. The question of whether, and how, to redress the balance forms part of wider debates on the Senate's general impotence and the developing relationship between central and regional government in Spain [3.1.6].

1.3.2 Organization and procedure

The internal organization of the two Houses is broadly similar. In each case overall responsibility for the running of day-to-day business and the maintenance of discipline lies with the Speaker of the House (*presidente/-a de la Cámara*), who is assisted in this task by a presiding committee (*mesa*), which he or she chairs. This committee establishes general rules of procedure for the House and the order of business for each day, that is, its agenda. Speaker and committee enjoy the support of legally trained parliamentary clerks (*letrados*).

The Speaker is elected by the House as a whole at the beginning of a new parliament (*legislatura*), i.e. after a general election, together with the remaining committee members. These are the four deputy Speakers (*vicepresidentes/-as*) and four secretaries. As a rule their election is in fact the product of consensus between the main parties, which agree on a share-out of the posts.

These arrangements are typical of those in contemporary Western legislatures. The second internal organ of each House of Parliament is, by contrast, a peculiarly Spanish institution. This is the Standing Council (*Diputación Permanente*), which traditionally acted as a watchdog over the powers of the House while it was not in session. With the increasing unlikelihood of coup attempts, this role seems happily now to be outdated. In practice the Council's main function is to ratify government regulations issued after a parliament has been dissolved.

The *Cortes* differs from the British Parliament in another, more significant way. Both formally and in practice individual elected representatives have even less influence than at Westminster, and political parties correspondingly more. This characteristic reflects a general constitutional recognition of the role of parties [2.1.1]. In terms of parliamentary procedure it is apparent in the formalized role accorded to the parliamentary parties, or groups (*grupos parlamentarios*), made up of all of the House's members belonging to a single political party. These are represented on the Standing Council in proportion to their size. More importantly, it is the groups which elect representatives to the spokespersons' committee (*junta de portavoces*).

This body is chaired by the Speaker, and acts as an interface between the House as a whole and the presiding committee. In particular it enables the latter to take into account the wishes of members in organizing the House's business. The workings of the chairpersons' committee again reflect the importance attached to the parliamentary groups, since the voting power wielded by representatives on it is proportional to the size of their groups.

For these and other reasons the conditions under which such groups may be formed are crucial. In the Congress a minimum of 15 deputies are required, or five if their party obtained at least 5 per cent of the votes cast throughout Spain at the previous general election. In order not to disadvantage regionally based parties, who have, in practice, no hope of satisfying either of these conditions, five members may also form a group provided the lists on which they were elected obtained at least 15 per cent of the votes cast in constituencies where they were presented. In addition, parties may band together to form groups if they so desire. In the Senate the minimum group size is ten, and cross-party groups may be formed by those Senators representing a particular autonomous region, whether directly or indirectly elected [1.3.1].

In both Houses those members who are not in a position to join a party group, or choose not to do so, automatically form part of the Mixed Group (*Grupo Mixto*). This group enjoys the same rights as others but naturally tends to lack the political cohesion to make full use of them. Nonetheless, both individual members of the Mixed Group, and the group as a whole, have on occasion played significant parts in parliamentary life.

In both Congress and Senate the full House (*pleno*) meets to exercise important symbolic functions, such as electing the leader of the largest Congress group as Prime Minister. Plenary sessions are also held regularly for substantive matters. However, most substantive debate takes place in committees of various types. Some standing committees (*comisiones permanentes*) may themselves pass laws. Also important are committees of investigation – known in the Senate as 'special committees' – set up to inquire into particular issues. Joint committees (*comisiones mixtas*) have members drawn from both Houses. In all cases representation on committees is in proportion to the size of parliamentary groups. A verbatim record of proceedings (*diario de sesiones*) is published for all committees, as well as for the Houses themselves.

1.3.3 Legislation

The Spanish Parliament's legislative work encompasses various different types of measure. Of these, only the most common has a direct British equivalent – the Act of Parliament (*ley ordinaria*). Spanish framework acts (*leyes marco*) and foundation acts (*leyes de base*) both set out objectives and principles to guide subsequent detailed legislation. Framework legislation relates to fields in which this latter is the responsibility of autonomous regions. Foundation acts lay down rather more specific guidelines for central government regulations (*decretos legislativos*).

Certain issues of outstanding importance are dealt with by means of 'entrenched legislation' (*leyes orgánicas*). These are laws which deal with crucial issues, specified in the Constitution, such as divorce, abortion, the status of autonomous regions and the ratification of international treaties. Parliamentary approval for these laws – and for their amendment – requires a majority of all members of the House, whereas approval for other types of legislation depends on a simple majority of those voting.

A further category of legislation consists of the 'royal decree-law' (*real decreto-ley*). Such decrees may be issued by the government to deal with urgent matters, excluding certain fundamental areas such as individuals' rights and liberties and the basic institutions of the state. In this case Parliament's role is restricted to debating the measure within 30 days of its issue and deciding whether to ratify or overturn its provisions.

With the exception of this last case, the procedure followed by the various forms of legislation in their passage through Parliament is similar. Legislation is usually initiated by the government, in which case it is often preceded by a White Paper (*Libro Blanco*) intended for public consultation. It then becomes a draft bill (*anteproyecto de ley*), which is subjected to preliminary scrutiny by the presiding committees of the two Houses. If accepted for debate this becomes a government bill (*proyecto de ley*).

Non-government bills (*proposiciones de ley*) may emanate from a number of sources, including a people's initiative [1.1.2], as well as the various regional parliaments or either House of Parliament. In the last case the initial proposal may come from a parliamentary group or an individual member with the support of 15 colleagues; this latter option provides the nearest equivalent to a British Private Member's Bill.

Non-government bills are subject to several handicaps relative to government ones. They are not permitted to refer to matters requiring entrenched legislation or to tax affairs. Nor can they ever be accorded priority or emergency status. Indeed, any government with an effective majority can prevent their ever being debated, since that depends on their first being accepted by a vote of the full Congress.

Once admitted for debate, bills of both types pass first to the Congress and then to the Senate. Most discussion takes place in the appropriate committee; it in turn generally appoints a working party (*ponencia*) which prepares a report (*dictamen*) for the full committee. The bill, incorporating any amendments made in committee, returns to the full House for further debate and possible amendment. In the Upper House the starting-point for this process is the bill as passed, and possibly amended, by the Congress. Senate approval for this text completes the bill's passage through Parliament.

Alternatively, the Senate may introduce amendments of its own or reject the measure in its entirety. In either case the bill is returned to the Congress, which may overturn Senate amendments merely by voting in favour of its original text. Even outright rejection by the Senate has little practical effect, since the Congress may approve its original proposal immediately with the support of a majority of its members; once two months have expired, a majority of those voting suffices. And even this minimal blocking power of the Upper House is reduced to a timespan of 20 days if either the government or the Congress itself declares the legislation concerned to be urgent.

Once a bill has successfully surmounted these various hurdles it is passed to the monarch for his endorsement [1.2]. Having thus become law, the measure – like other state documents – is published in the Official Gazette (*Boletín Oficial del Estado*).

1.3.4 Parliamentary control

Parliament's second main task is to exercise control over the government of the day, that is, to require it to account for its actions. In order to do so, both Houses have the right to demand from the executive any information they consider necessary and to require government members to appear before them. Indeed, parliamentary committees of investigation [1.3.2] may require the appearance of any witnesses they think fit. However, the most frequently used mechanisms are those which allow Parliament to demand a government response to two types of interrogation.

Questions on specific matters (*preguntas*) may be presented only by individual members of Parliament; they may require an oral reply from a government minister. Interrogative motions (*interpelaciones*) may also be presented by individual members. However, they may in addition be raised by parliamentary groups [1.3.2]; they relate to the general conduct of government and they may result in the presentation, and possible adoption, of a resolution by the House. In these latter respects they are similar to British opposition motions.

In addition to these, and the establishment of investigative committees, Parliament has two further devices by which to exert control over the government of the day. The first is the censure motion (*moción de reprobación*) condemning the actions of a particular government member. Such motions have purely moral force, as the Constitution establishes that Parliament can only require the resignation of the government as a whole, not of individual members.

This restriction also applies to the second device, the motion of no-confidence (*moción de censura*). In addition, and following the German model, such motions must be constructive in nature, that is they must not only condemn the Prime Minister in office but also propose the name of an alternative candidate. Moreover, to be approved they require a majority of all members of the Congress, not just of those deputies actually voting, which they must do in public. Given these restrictions, and the high level of discipline exercised by Spanish parties [2.1.2], the chances of such a motion succeeding are very low indeed.

In fact only two have been presented, neither successfully. In both cases (in 1980 and 1987) the focus of the debate fell on the alternative candidate presented in the motion rather than on the record of the incumbent and his government (to the opposition's advantage on the first occasion but the government's on the second). That was quite proper, given the constitutional provisions, but hardly suggests that the no-confidence motion serves as an effective means of control over the existing government. Indeed, as in most other Western countries, and whatever the Constitution may say about its supremacy, the extent to which the Spanish Parliament can exert such control in practice is extremely limited [1.4.1].

1.4 Government

Under the 1978 Constitution executive power lies with Spain's government, in the narrow sense – that is, the political head of the country's governmental body, made up of the Prime Minister and his cabinet of ministers. Conscious of their country's history, the Constitution's authors had two conflicting concerns about the executive's status. On the one hand, they wished to ensure the government's subordination to Parliament. On the other, they wished to avoid paralysing its power to act. In the event, they were much more successful in achieving the second of these aims than the first.

1.4.1 Pre-eminence of government

Effective domination of Parliament by the government of the day is a cause for growing concern in a number of Western democracies. In Spain, certain features of the state mean that the executive's domination is especially marked. To some extent this pre-eminence can be traced to constitutional and legal arrangements. Thus government bills enjoy a privileged position in the legislative process [1.3.3]. Similarly, stringent conditions attach to the presentation and passage of a parliamentary motion of no-confidence in the executive [1.3.4]. By contrast, a vote of confidence (*moción de confianza*) requested by the Prime Minister himself requires merely the support of a majority of deputies actually voting in order to pass.

However, the fundamental reasons for government pre-eminence have less to do with the Constitution itself than with subsequent developments unforeseen by those who drew it up. One is the arguably lax way in which the constitutional requirement for a proportional electoral system was interpreted [1.3.1]. This has produced not the minority or coalition governments envisaged by the Constitution's architects but a succession of single-party administrations. Moreover, the leading political parties have proved to be considerably more tightly disciplined than expected [2.1.2].

In conjunction, these factors have enabled the government to establish a high degree of influence over Parliament, and also to some extent over the judiciary [9.1.1]. This was especially so during the period 1982–93, when the Socialist Party enjoyed an overall majority. Then Parliament's legislative role effectively became a mere rubber stamp, as the government steamrollered measures through Parliament irrespective of opposition views [2.3.2].

During periods of overall majority, too, Parliament's theoretical powers to scrutinize the government's actions and call it to account for them are largely neutralized, since their exercise depends on the opposition's ability to muster a majority in at least one of the Houses. This applies, for example, to the establishment of committees of investigation, which can be blocked by the government majority. Similarly, censure motions against individual ministers are usually unsuccessful, and can sometimes reinforce the standing of their target rather than undermining it. During the 1980s, Prime Minister Felipe González made no secret of how little importance he attached to parliamentary control over him and his colleagues; at one stage he attended the Congress only twice in one year.

In the late 1980s the Parliament's manifest loss of power and prestige became a cause for concern about the health of Spanish democracy. In part as a result, the government showed decidedly greater attention at least to the formal aspects of its relations with the legislature. Again, however, this development owed more to political realities than to constitutional theory, in the sense that this period saw the emergence of a more coherent and effective opposition [2.4.2]. Only with the Socialists' loss of their overall majority after 1993 did real changes become apparent, and even then they were limited. One example was the opposition's success in forcing the establishment of a Senate special committee to investigate the government's alleged involvement in counter-terrorism during the 1980s [9.5.2].

However, the success was short-lived, since the committee's work was effectively stymied when the main Catalan regionalist party abruptly resumed its previous support for the government. Ironically, it was another about-face by the same grouping that effectively forced the Socialists from office [2.3.3]. But even then Parliament was not involved. Instead the Prime Minister, aware that he could no longer rely on getting legislation passed, simply exercised his right to dissolve the Houses, as he had done in both 1986 and 1989 in order to hold an election when it best suited him.

The result was another minority administration bolstered by Catalan support [2.4.3], and Parliament continued to have slightly more scope to exercise real control. Towards the end of this period, in 1999, the opposition actually succeeded in forcing important changes to a major piece of government legislation, a new Aliens Act (*Ley de Extranjería*), in parliamentary debate. But, as before, the key factor remained the political tactics of the government's Catalan ally rather than any change in the underlying conditions. At no stage did Parliament manage to channel obvious public concern about corruption and other executive abuses of power; indeed, it barely even attempted to do so.

Subsequently, under both the majority People's Party administration of 2000–2004 and that of the Socialists in power since 2004, government domination of parliament has been as marked as during the 1980s.

1.4.2 Prime Minister

Just as the Spanish executive occupies a pre-eminent position among the country's institutions, so it in turn tends to be dominated by its head, the Prime Minister (*presidente del gobierno*). Since the adoption of the 1978 Constitution, five men have held this post.

The first of these, Adolfo Suárez (1976–81), was effectively nominated by King Juan Carlos, and played a key role in the Spanish political scene under far from easy circumstances, cajoling the major political figures of the time towards an acceptance of democratic processes and compromise with each other on major issues. He never exercised full control over his leading colleagues, however, and they seem to have forced his eventual, abrupt resignation [2.2]. During the brief tenure of the second PM, Leopoldo Calvo Sotelo (1981–82), the political problems were so great and so numerous as to make him the servant rather than the master of events.

The full extent of prime ministerial ascendancy (*presidencialismo*) has been at its clearest, however, ever since the effective consolidation of a new political and party system in 1982 [2.1]. During the long premiership of Felipe González (1982–96) this was sometimes ascribed to his undoubted charisma and enormous personal popularity, which regularly exceeded that of his party [2.3.2]. His successor, José María Aznar (1996–2004), could not have been called charismatic even at the height of his powers during his second administration (from 2000), and when first elected his personal ratings in opinion polls lagged behind his party's. Yet not only was that position reversed with time; the extent of his authority over his government and party colleagues grew to be no less than González's had been, and may even have been greater. In fact, Aznar's period in office is often described as having been particularly authoritarian, especially in contrast with his successor, the current PM, José Luis Rodríguez Zapatero (2004–), who, while still enjoying the kind of dominance over parliament normally associated with the post, has been more conciliatory in the tactics he employs for dealing with government business.

As with executive dominance of the state, the reasons for the PM's influence, and its gradual accentuation, derive to a large extent from political factors. In particular, the highly centralized and disciplined nature of Spanish parties, especially when in power [2.1.2], is a key factor. As in other countries the increasingly personalized media coverage of politics in general, and elections in particular, also plays a role. However, the power of the Spanish PM is also due in part to certain provisions of the 1978 Constitution which were specifically designed to prevent his becoming a lame-duck figure, as so often had happened in the country's previous history.

Thus it is the Prime Minister personally who is given the support of a new Parliament in the form of a vote of investiture. Should a change of government occur as the result of a successful no-confidence motion, then the requirement for this to be constructive means that a candidate to the post must be named [1.3.4]. If a PM were to be removed by a failed vote of confidence or a successful motion of no-confidence, then the entire government would have to resign with him. Moreover, although the Constitution dictates that certain matters of major importance must be discussed by the government as a whole, it does not specify any method of decision-making – and it is the Prime Minister who is responsible for presenting the government's view to Parliament or otherwise acting on it.

Above all, certain decisions are effectively taken by the PM alone, subject only to the formal endorsement of the monarch [1.2]. In particular this applies to ministerial appointments [1.4.3]. It applies also to the decision to call a vote of confidence, or to dissolve Parliament and thus force an early general election (*elecciones anticipadas*). Both privileges give the PM an obvious means of control over recalcitrant colleagues and his own political party.

Finally, the PM's power is further bolstered by the support he receives from two institutions. One is the separate ministry encharged with managing his own and the cabinet's business [1.4.4]. The other is his group of political advisers (*gabinete del presidente*). Together with this entourage, the Prime Minister represents a sort of government within the government, often referred to obliquely by the name of his official residence, the Moncloa Palace.

1.4.3 Cabinet

Strictly speaking, the government consists of the cabinet (*consejo de ministros*), although there is a provision in the 1978 Constitution – never exercised – for members other than ministers to be included. Important parts of the government's work are carried out in cabinet committees (*comisiones delegadas del gobierno*), of which the Prime Minister and his Deputy are automatically members.

In effect, the Prime Minister makes cabinet appointments and dismisses ministers, although officially this is done by the monarch on his recommendation. Indeed, ministers are clearly subordinate to the PM, since their position is totally dependent on his [1.4.2]. On the other hand, they are relatively immune from parliamentary pressure, as they cannot be forced to resign by a censure motion [1.3.4].

Ministers are not necessarily members of Parliament, although they have the right to appear before both Houses, and the obligation to do so if required. Nor are they necessarily members of the party in power; successive governments have included non-party 'independents', although typically these have subsequently entered Parliament attached to a party list. Another difference from UK custom is the absence of a ministerial team in the Upper House, a reflection of the Senate's powerlessness [1.3.1].

Technically, a change of government is considered to have taken place in the event of a general election, the replacement of an incumbent Prime Minister, or a cabinet reshuffle (*remodelación/crisis de gobierno*). According to that definition there have been somewhat more than 30 different governments since Franco's death in 1975. Reshuffles were relatively frequent in the early years of the new democracy, and have been less so in recent years, particularly during the premiership of José María Aznar. The current PM, José Luis Rodríguez Zapatero, presided over four different governments during his first period in office (2004–2008).

Other than in the case of the Prime Minister, the Constitution makes no distinction between the members of the cabinet, although it does provide for the appointment of one or more Deputy Prime Ministers. The role of Deputy PM was given legal definition in 1983 in the Central Government Structure Act [1.5.2], where its functions were stated to consist essentially of assuming the PM's responsibility should he die, be indisposed through illness or leave the country. He or she is automatically a member of all cabinet committees. Felipe González's cabinets [2.3.2] had one – very powerful – Deputy PM – while his successor, Aznar, appointed two deputies, one with responsibility for the PM's office, the other in charge of a joint Economics and Finance Ministry [2.4.3]. This pattern has been retained since, with the only innovation occurring in 2004, when Rodríguez Zapatero appointed the first female Deputy PM, María Teresa Fernández de la Vega.

The Suárez governments of 1979–81 had between 22 and 24 members. This relatively large and unwieldy size reflected his need to balance factions and interests within his party at a time of major political change [2.2]. Under González cabinets were slightly smaller, with between 16 and 19 members. In his successful 1996 election campaign Aznar made much of his intention to cut alleged waste at all levels of government, and ostentatiously appointed a 15-member cabinet. But this was universally recognized to be a purely token gesture, and his fourth team, appointed in 2001, contained 17 members. The current government under Zapatero contains 17 members.

Up to recently, and in line with most Western countries, these cabinets were overwhelmingly male, especially during the transition period. Not until 1981 was a woman appointed to cabinet office, when Soledad Becerril became Arts minister. After González's election the following year there was a six-year period of all-male cabinets, broken by the appointment of Rosa Conde as Government Spokesperson with ministerial rank [1.4.4]. Only in 1990 was a woman again entrusted with a subject portfolio.

During the remainder of that period of the Socialists' time in power, cabinets included either two or three women, although their ministries were all relatively low-ranking ones. Aznar's first cabinet following his 1996 victory included four women, one of whom was given the relatively high-ranking Justice portfolio. But his fourth, appointed five years later, contained one fewer, again in middle- to lower-status portfolios. Admittedly, though, one of his female ex-ministers, Loyola de Palacio, had gone on to arguably higher things: the post of European Commissioner [4.3.2].

In the run-up to the 2004 elections, Zapatero promised to form a government with equal numbers of men and women (*gobierno paritario*), and he put this policy into practice on assuming office. His first three cabinets consisted of eight men and eight women, although his fourth team comprised nine men and seven women. On regaining power in 2008, however, he made the historical decision to appoint the first-ever cabinet comprising a majority of women. That cabinet consisted of nine women – one of them the first female Minister of Defence – and eight men. Several of the more senior ministries, including Economy, Justice, the Interior (Home Affairs) and Foreign Affairs, continue to be held by men, however.

Finally in this section mention should be made of the 'Council of State', a body roughly equivalent to the British Privy Council. Councillors of state (*consejeros*) are senior figures from local, regional and central government together with representatives of such bodies as professional associations and universities. They are either appointed by official decree – in practice by the cabinet itself – or are members ex-officio, i.e. by virtue of the post they hold (e.g. director of the Spanish Royal Academy, or attorney-general [9.1.2]). Their remit is to provide ministers with expert advice, in particular as to whether their proposed actions are compatible with the Constitution and other legislation.

1.4.4 Ministries

Within the cabinet, each minister – except the PM and, at times, his Deputy [1.4.3] – is charged with responsibility for a particular portfolio (*cartera*), or area of policy, and heads the corresponding ministry. There is constitutional provision for the appointment of ministers without portfolio but it has not been used since the 1970s. The Constitution also requires the government to obtain Parliament's approval before making changes to the number of ministers or the distribution of their responsibilities. This injunction, however, has been repeatedly ignored in the frequent restructuring of ministries since 1978.

Spanish ministries are frequently referred to merely by the name of their portfolio (e.g. *Agricultura* for the Agriculture Ministry). In addition, the Foreign Office (*Asuntos Exteriores/AAEE*) is sometimes known by the official residence of its minister, the Holy Cross Palace (*Palacio de Santa Cruz*). It has existed as a separate ministry throughout the constitutional era. By contrast there have not always been direct Spanish equivalents to the other two great departments of state in British terms: the Home Office and the Treasury.

In the case of the Home Office or Interior Ministry (*M. de Interior*) this was true only during Felipe González's last two governments in 1994–96, in which it was combined with the Justice Ministry [9.1.2]. Given the special nature of the Justice portfolio this amalgamation was highly controversial, especially coming at a time when senior Interior Ministry officials had themselves been indicted for involvement in covert anti-terrorist operations [9.5.2]. The motivation seems to have been political – a desire to give a high profile to the Justice Minister Juan Alberto Belloch, one of the few cabinet members untainted by corruption allegations [2.3.2].

Similar considerations played a role in an earlier amalgamation. Up to 1982 the portfolios of Economy (*Economía*) and Finance (*Hacienda*) had been kept separate, as is common practice in a number of Western countries but not in the UK, where the Chancellor of the Exchequer has responsibility for both. However, when Felipe González came to power that year he wished to deploy his party's leading financial expert, Miguel Boyer, to best effect. He accordingly merged the two, and made Boyer a 'super-minister' in charge of the new, joint ministry.

This arrangement was maintained when Boyer was replaced by Carlos Solchaga, and later Pedro Solbes. Under them the joint ministry routinely decided on and implemented economic policy without reference to either Parliament or the cabinet as a whole. In effect it became one of the very few competing power bases to that of Felipe González as PM. On replacing González in 1996, José María Aznar placed one of his chief lieutenants, Rodrigo Rato, in the role, but once his political hand and personal prestige was enhanced by re-election in 2000 Aznar once again separated the posts. More recently, when the Socialists regained power, joint responsibility for the two areas was re-established, again under the control of Solbes.

In other cases, changing political circumstances have given rise to alterations in the titles and responsibilities of individual ministries. Thus Suárez's first, pre-constitutional government included ministers for each of the armed services, posts which have not figured in any cabinet since 1977. Between 1979 and 1986 all cabinets included a Minister of Local and Regional Government (*Ministro de Administración Territorial*), responsible for the delicate process of devolving power to the regions. With the process complete, the title was changed to Minister of Public Administration (*Ministro para las Administraciones Públicas*).

More recently, the term 'environment' has come to figure in ministry titles [5.3.1]. Initially it was appended to the title of what had originally been the Ministry of Public Works (*Ministerio de Obras Públicas*/MOP) before adding first Town Planning (*Urbanismo*) and then Transport to its name. In 1996 Aznar finally set up a separate Environment Ministry (*Medio Ambiente*). The remaining functions were given to a new Development portfolio (*Fomento*), a title with distinctly Francoist overtones.

Especially worthy of note from a British perspective are two other ministerial portfolios, neither of which has a UK equivalent and both of which have come and gone from Spanish cabinets since 1975. The first, traditional in Spain, is the Prime Minister's Office (*Ministerio de la Presidencia*). The Office's official remit is for protocol and the premier's personal security, although it had always had an additional importance because of the direct access to the PM enjoyed by its Head (*Ministro de la Presidencia*). In the late 1980s, however, he became an increasingly influential political figure, with responsibility for the PM's schedule of appointments, the arrangement of cabinet business and, in the role of government secretary, the recording of its deliberations and decisions. Under Aznar the Office's status and importance were further enhanced when both successive Heads of the Office were given the rank of Deputy PM [1.4.3]. Within the current Socialist government, this arrangement is again in place.

The other Spanish cabinet post which appears rather odd to British eyes is that of Government Spokesperson (*Portavoz del Gobierno*). The portfolio was first given ministerial rank by González in 1985, initially in conjunction with that of Arts (*Cultura*), before acquiring its own ministry three years later. Between 1992 and 2000 its responsibilities were incorporated into the PM's Office, a reflection of the

Table 1.1 Cabinet composition, 2008: cabinet formed April 2008 (fifth Zapatero cabinet)

Cartera	Portfolio
*Presidencia	PM's Office
Economía y Hacienda	Economics and Finance
Interior	Interior (Home Affairs)
Asuntos Exteriores y Cooperación	Foreign Affairs and Cooperation
Justicia	Justice
*Defensa	Defence
*Fomento	Development
Trabajo e Inmigración	Employment and Immigration
*Igualdad	Equality
Industria, Comercio y Turismo	Industry, Trade and Tourism
*Ciencia e Innovación	Science and Innovation
Cultura	Culture
*Educación, Política Social y Deporte	Education, Social Policy and Sport
*Administraciones Públicas	Public Administration
*Vivienda	Housing
Sanidad y Consumo	Health and Consumer Affairs
*Medio Ambiente, Medio Rural y Marino	Environment, Rural and Marine Affairs

* = Portfolio held by a woman

latter's new political role. However, in 2000 Aznar again created a separate Spokesperson's Office (*Ministerio del Portavoz del Gobierno*) – rather ironically given that he had previously made a virtue of keeping cabinet size to a minimum. Under Zapatero, the position is held by the First Deputy PM, who is also head of the PM's office [1.4.3].

More recent changes, also introduced under Zapatero, include the creation of a separate ministry for Housing (*Ministerio de Vivienda*), an area which, under Aznar, had been included in Development, and the incorporation of responsibility for immigration issues in the Labour ministry, whose full name is now Ministry of Labour and Immigration (*Ministerio de Trabajo e Inmigración*). The cabinet appointed in April 2008 also included another innovation, the creation of a separate Ministry of Equality (*Ministerio de Igualdad*).

1.5 Administration

Clearly, running a modern country involves much more than the passage of laws or the operation of the cabinet. Below this top level of government there is necessarily a much larger apparatus, responsible for detailed implementation of policy and day-to-day administration. This is the task of Spain's public service (*función pública*) and its staff (*funcionariado*), a concept which extends well beyond that of the British civil service to include not only administrators in local government and quasi-governmental agencies but non-administrative public employees, such as teachers.

1.5.1 Franco's legacy

The first thing to note about this machinery is that, unlike the uppermost echelons of public life, its structure and personnel were relatively unaffected by the transition after Franco's death in 1975. To a large extent this was inevitable. After 1975 not only was there an overwhelming desire to avoid opening old wounds. Under Franco the state machinery had simply become too large and too complex to allow the sort of wholesale purge of public administration typical of previous regime changes in Spain; it would have brought the country to a standstill. Yet, while it may have been desirable for that reason alone, relative continuity within the public service has undoubtedly had serious implications for administration in contemporary Spain.

One was the extraordinarily complex arrangements which had grown up in a number of areas of government activity. Their most obvious symptom was the typically Spanish phenomenon of innumerable public counters (*ventanillas*), each with its narrowly defined area of business and idiosyncratic, often apparently arbitrary, opening hours. Another was the complex and outdated career structures of public servants (*funcionarios*), based on a series of corps which bore little relation to contemporary needs.

Moreover, the public service as a whole was imbued with attitudes typical of an authoritarian state, which were often inappropriate for dealing with citizens enjoying constitutionally guaranteed rights. Thus the lack of public scrutiny under the Franco regime encouraged practices such as the filling of jobs on the basis of contacts rather than merit (*enchufismo*) and influence-peddling (*tráfico de influencias*), that is, the allocation of lucrative public works contracts in return for money and favours. The succession of corruption scandals in the late 1980s was in part a reflection of how hard such habits die.

Most important of all, during the Franco era leading regime figures moved back and forward between the cabinet and the upper echelons of the administration. Furthermore, in both cases they were not merely permitted but obliged to join the governing party, and were equally subject to summary removal at Franco's behest. As a result a distinction which is basic to any democratic system, that between the government of the day and the permanent administration, was lost almost entirely. The situation today is, of course, very different, in that political posts are now subject to election. But some traces of it remain, in the system whereby senior administrators (*altos cargos*) are political appointees (*cargos políticos*), and often career politicians.

It should be stressed that this practice is not peculiar to Spain. On the contrary, in many democracies it is deliberately used to ensure an adequate link between two apparatuses that can otherwise become undesirably separated. Without it, many would argue, government policy which reflects the democratically expressed will of the people may simply be blocked by a reluctant civil service. But in Spain, not only does the system serve to conserve attitudes from the pre-democratic era. It further concentrates power in the hands of the cabinet and its head [1.4.1]. And it is also unusually widespread, extending to quangos [1.5.3], non-government agencies with constitutional status, such as the governing body of the judiciary [9.1.1], as well as administration at central, regional and even local level.

1.5.2 Civil service

The broad Spanish equivalent to what in the UK is known as the civil service – that is, the administrative apparatus of central government – is known as the central administration (*Administración General del Estado/AGE*). Other than at the highest levels it is staffed by career civil servants (*funcionarios de carrera*), appointed initially by competitive public examination (*oposición*). Subsequent promotion tends to be based on a points system, in which seniority plays a role but so also do other factors, such as in-service training.

The service's senior ranks, however, tend to be filled by political appointees [1.5.1] (and also to have potentially misleading titles for English-speakers). Their current structure was broadly laid down by the 1983 Central Government Structure Act (*Ley de Organización de la Administración Central del Estado/LOAE*), which brought together and consolidated a number of piecemeal changes introduced in the early 1980s. In particular, the LOAE introduced two new senior grades of administrator.

The higher of the two, containing the most senior non-cabinet posts, is that of Secretary of State (*secretario de estado*). It exists only in the larger ministries, and its role corresponds broadly to that of a British junior minister. That is, Secretaries of State may attend cabinet meetings but only to provide information, not to participate in discussion. That is a privilege denied to the other new grade, that of general secretary (*secretario general*), which also exists only in certain ministries. Holders of both types of post head sections of a ministry (*secretarías*), and have responsibility for a particular policy area or areas.

Intermediate between these two grades in seniority is another also filled by political appointees. Unlike the two grades created by the LOAE, however, that of Under-Secretary of State (*subsecretario de estado*) is a long-standing feature of the Spanish public service. While the post may carry responsibility for a policy area within a ministry, it has others which give it particular importance. One is the internal running of the ministry concerned, including personnel, financial and legal matters.

However, the crucial point is that it is in the interministerial Secretaries and Under-Secretaries' Committee (*Comisión General de Secretarios y Subsecretarios*) that two key types of decision are taken. The first is the allocation of budgets to the various ministries. The second is preparation of the cabinet agenda, which in practice means effectively predetermining its decisions on all but the most politically sensitive of issues. As a result, Under-Secretaries play a crucial role both in translating a ministry's projects into government action and in securing the financial means to implement them. In those ministries where the post has been abolished, the responsibilities have been assumed by a Secretary of State.

In addition to these political appointees at the head of the ministries' administrative structures (*organigramas*), all ministers, including the Prime Minister and his Deputy, have a private staff of political advisers (*gabinete*). As in the UK, these provide their masters with strategic and political advice on the work of the ministry as a whole, rather than on particular subject fields. Unlike the British case, they are technically civil servants, the office's Director having the grade of Secretary of State.

Below these various tiers of political appointees begins the administrative structure proper. Its highest grade is that of director-general (*director general*). Such posts have tended to grow in numbers and importance in recent years with the expansion of government activity in the 1980s. They carry responsibility for a directorate-general, a particular section or sub-section of the ministry's organization. By contrast, the grade of professional general secretary (*secretario general técnico*) has declined in importance, even though every ministry continues to have at least one such post. Its task is to provide advice and support across the whole range of a ministry's responsibilities, a function now largely usurped by the minister's political advisers.

As in other countries, the so-called central administration is by no means exclusively located in the capital city; virtually all ministries need local and provincial branch offices to deliver their services. This outlying administration (*administración periférica*) expanded enormously during the Franco era. On the one hand, government activity as a whole grew considerably; on the other, local government was placed under strict central control. The key institution of what had become a very large and highly centralized apparatus was the provincial civil authority (*Gobierno Civil*) – whose name derives from the existence of a parallel military structure, also based on the provinces [9.2.1].

With the transition to democracy, some of the outlying administration's responsibilities were handed over to democratic local authorities [1.6]; more were later transferred to the new autonomous regions as a result of devolution [3.1.3]. In 1983, the LOAE gave the civil authority overall responsibility for all remaining central government functions within its province. This arrangement was a constant cause of friction with regionalists, especially in the Basque Country and Catalonia, for whom it smacked of a continuing desire for centralization.

Meanwhile, the Constitution and subsequent devolution had given rise to a new arm of outlying administration in the shape of the central government representative (*delegado del gobierno*) in each region. His or her official role is to represent the state at official events in the region. Informally, he or she also acts as a channel of communication between central and regional governments, a function that is particularly significant in those regions where regionalist parties are strong, notably Catalonia and the Basque Country. Additionally, representatives were intended to coordinate the work of the various governors within their region.

This situation gave rise to obvious problems, and in the single-province regions the two posts were soon effectively combined. In 1997 the new conservative government went a step further. Under the Civil Service Organization and Operation Act (*Ley de Organización y Funcionamiento de la Administración General del Estado/LOFAGE*) the post of civil governor (*Gobernador Civil*) was abolished. Its functions were transferred to new assistant representatives located in each province where there was no representative proper (*sub-delegados*), and on each of the smaller Balearic and Canary islands (*directores insulares*).

This change was in line with the LOFAGE's main aims, which were to reduce the amount of administrative duplication and overlap [3.1.5] and to give Spaniards easier access to public authorities in general. From it has developed the idea of a local one-stop centre (*ventanilla única*) through which all individuals' administrative problems can be handled, irrespective of the authority – central, regional or local – which is responsible for the matter. The scheme depends on the government reaching agreements with individual authorities, and there progress has been patchy; so far just eight of the seventeen regions have come aboard. The LOFAGE also restricts certain civil service grades to career administrators – but by doing so, also implicitly institutionalizes the practice of political appointments.

1.5.3 Central government agencies

In addition to the civil service proper, Spain's central administration can also be regarded as including those bodies which are attached to ministries without forming part of their structure. What these quangos have in common is that appointments to their governing bodies are made by the Madrid government, and so are susceptible to political criteria. They are numerous and have widely varying natures and functions.

Thus the quangos include the Royal Academies of the arts and sciences, as well as the Cervantes Institute, charged with promoting the Spanish language world-wide. The Higher Council for Scientific Research (*Consejo Superior de Investigación Científica*/CSIC) is meant to encourage and oversee research activity, a task in which it has enjoyed strictly limited success [7.3.1.1.2]. Of particular importance are those operating in the spheres of business and economics. These include relatively new regulatory authorities, such as the National Stock Exchange Commission (*Comisión Nacional de Mercados de Valores*/CNMV) and the Competition Commission (*Tribunal de Defensa de la Competencia*/TDC) as well as longer-established bodies such as the Audit Commission (*Tribunal de Cuentas*).

Some quangos operate in fields where in other countries the initiative is taken not by the state but by civil society. Examples are the National Youth Bureau and National Women's Bureau [6.2]. Others control very considerable budgets, including the procurement agencies (*Juntas de Compras*) attached to various ministries. A number of quangos have been involved in the influence-peddling scandals of recent decades, including the national railway board, RENFE, and the agency responsible for producing the Official Gazette [1.3.3].

Of particular interest are the Constitutional Studies Centre (*Centro de Estudios Constitucionales*/CEC) and the Social Research Centre (*Centro de Investigaciones Sociológicas*/CIS). Both of these are attached directly to the Prime Minister's Office [1.4.4]. As a result, the very heart of government's political machinery enjoys privileged access to sensitive information which has been assembled with public money, in particular the results of regular opinion polls carried out by the CIS. This situation has given rise to justified concern.

1.6 Local government

In Spanish, local government is often referred to as 'local administration'. This usage reflects the conditions of the Franco regime, under which local government effectively became part of the central government's outlying administration [1.5.2]. Its role was to impose central decisions locally rather than to allow local responses to local issues, far less democratic ones. Further back in time, however, Spain enjoyed a tradition of relatively independent local government, a tradition re-established by the 1978 Constitution and confirmed by the holding of democratic local elections in 1979.

1.6.1 Municipalities

The Spanish local government unit with the longest tradition is also the smallest: the municipality (*municipio*). The country's municipalities vary widely in size and nature, from the largest cities, through medium-sized towns down to single villages or rural areas containing various hamlets. They are run by municipal councils (*ayuntamientos*). Councillors (*concejales*) are elected at four-yearly municipal elections (*elecciones municipales*) held on a single day for the whole of Spain, coinciding with those for most of the autonomous regions [3.1.3]. As in parliamentary polls, electors vote for a list of candidates [1.3.1].

The mayor (*alcalde*) is not a mere figurehead as in the UK, but the council's leader. He is formally elected by the councillors; in practice the post is almost always filled by the candidate on the list receiving most votes. In the largest authorities the mayor normally works closely with one or more deputy mayors (*tenientes de alcalde*), and with a team of senior councillors (*equipo de gobierno*). Within this, individual councillors have responsibility for the different departments (*áreas*) into which the council's administrative structure is divided. They are referred to by the name of the department concerned (e.g. *concejal de vivienda*) and correspond broadly to the committee chairpersons of UK local authorities.

Another feature of the larger authorities, with their extensive administrative structures, is the prevalence of political appointments to senior posts [1.5.2]. Apart from the very smallest councils almost all are now politicized, in the sense that councillors are elected from party lists. In the smaller ones only some, or none, of the institutions listed above are to be found. There the main weight falls on the mayor, and on the clerk to the municipality (*secretario municipal*).

The range of services which a municipality is required by law to provide is smaller the lower the population for which it is responsible. Many are very small indeed – of over 8000 in total, more than 60 per cent have fewer than 1000 inhabitants – and significant numbers lack the resources to provide even the most basic of services. One solution to this problem has been to amalgamate several councils into one. In such cases, villages deprived of their council usually retain an honorary mayor (*alcalde pedáneo*) for ceremonial purposes. Because of the difficulties posed by traditional loyalties, however, such rationalization of municipal boundaries (*concentración municipal*) has been relatively rare. As an alternative, in some areas councils have banded together in voluntary federations (*consorcios/mancomunidades*).

Structural problems are also apparent at the other end of the scale, in the largest population centres. There urban growth has meant that traditional municipal boundaries often make little administrative sense, cutting through what are now effectively single settlements. One means of addressing this problem is the creation of metropolitan area authorities with responsibilities across entire conurbations, such as that which exists in Barcelona, called the Metropolitan Association of Barcelona-Confederation of Municipalities (*Asociación Metropolitana de Barcelona-Mancomunidad de Municipios*).

The organization which represents all the country's local authorities is the Spanish Federation of Municipalities and Provinces (*Federación Española de Municipios y Provincias/FEMP*). Some ten more federations and associations of municipal authorities also exist; these bring together groups of municipal authorities within different regions of the country.

1.6.2 Provinces

Whereas Spain's municipalities date from the Middle Ages and even earlier, the country's 50 provinces were created only in the early nineteenth century. They also differ from the smaller units in that they were originally intended as a means of extending central government control down to local level. It is at provincial level that the last remnants of the central government's outlying administration continue to operate [1.5.2]. These factors inevitably lend a touch of anomaly to the position of the provinces in post-Franco Spain.

Their continuing existence is due to the fact that, after 1975, they were given a new role as the upper tier of a democratized system of local government. In part this was done by handing over to them some functions formerly exercised by the outlying administration. However, it was also a response to the problems posed by the small size of many municipalities [1.6.1]; in such areas responsibility for some service provision was taken over by the provinces.

The body which exercises these responsibilities is the provincial council (*diputación provincial*), made up of provincial councillors (*diputados*) and headed by a council chairperson. In most of Spain council members are elected indirectly, that is by the various municipal councils within the province concerned. The various islands of the Canaries and Balearics also have their own councils (*cabildos* and *consells* respectively), in the first case directly elected.

The other special case is that of the three Basque provinces (Alava, Guipúzcoa and Vizcaya), which, uniquely in Spain, are traditional units dating back to the Middle Ages. There the administrative authority (*diputación foral*) is controlled by a directly elected provincial council (*Juntas Generales*). The Basque Country, where the provinces also enjoy relatively strong powers, displays in extreme form a problem apparent throughout Spain: the proliferation of administrative tiers and the overlap of functions between them [3.1.5].

Given their ambiguous historical role and relatively minor functions, the provincial authorities are the most obvious candidate for elimination in any attempt to simplify the situation. Indeed, this has already effectively occurred in the six single-province regions (*comunidades uniprovinciales*), where the provincial councils have been absorbed by the respective regional governments. Elsewhere, especially in Catalonia, there has been pressure to replace the provinces by districts (*comarcas*) with greater relation to traditional sentiment and/or contemporary population patterns, as well as the needs of service delivery. Yet not everywhere are there obvious alternatives to the provinces. And, in any case, their abolition would not solve the underlying problems posed by the small municipalities – as well as inflaming Basque sensibilities.

1.7 Glossary

6-D (m)	6 December 1978 (date of referendum on 1978 Constitution)
administración general del estado (f)	central administration
administración periférica (f)	outlying administration (of central government)

alcalde (m)	mayor; leader of municipal council
alcalde pedáneo (m)	honorary mayor (of former municipality)
alto cargo (m)	senior public servant
anteproyecto de ley (m)	draft bill (for parliamentary scrutiny)
área (f)	department (of local authority)
Asuntos Exteriores/AAEE (m)	Foreign Office
ayuntamiento (m)	municipal council
Boletín Oficial del Estado (m)	Spanish Official Gazette
cabildo (m)	island council (Canaries)
Cámara (f)	chamber
Cámara Alta (f)	Upper House (of Parliament)
Cámara Baja (f)	Lower House (of Parliament)
cargo político/de confianza (m)	political appointee
Carta magna (f)	constitution
cartera (ministerial) (f)	(ministerial) portfolio; ministry
casa real (f)	royal household
circunscripción (f)	constituency
Centro de Estudios Constitucionales (CES) (m)	Constitutional Studies Centre
Centro de Investigaciones Sociológicas (CIS) (m)	Social Research Centre
comarca (f)	district
comisión delegada del gobierno (f)	cabinet committee
comisión especial (f)	special committee (of Senate)
comisión general de secretarios y subsecretarios (f)	secretaries and under-secretaries' committee
comisión mixta (f)	joint committee (of both Houses)
Comisión Nacional de mercados de Valores (f)	National Stock Exchange Commission
comisión permanente (f)	standing committee
comunidad uniprovincial (f)	autonomous region consisting of a single province
concejal (m)	municipal councillor
concejal de vivienda (m)	councillor with responsibility for housing
concentración municipal (f)	rationalization of municipal boundaries
conflictos de competencias (mpl)	central–regional government disputes over legislative competence
Congreso (de los Diputados) (m)	Congress; Lower House of Spanish Parliament
Consejero (m)	Councillor of State
consejo de ministros (m)	cabinet
Consejo Superior de Investigación Científica (CSIC) (m)	Higher Council for Scientific Research
consell (m)	island council (Balearics)
consorcio (m)	federation of adjoining municipalities to provide services
cortes constituyentes (fpl)	constituent assembly

Cortes Generales (las) (fpl)	Spanish Parliament
crisis de gobierno (f)	cabinet reshuffle
(cf. crisis en el seno del gobierno)	(government crisis)
decreto legislativo (m)	government regulation
Defensor del Pueblo (m)	Ombudsman
delegado del gobierno (m)	central government representative in an autonomous region
desarrollo (m)	detailed provision for a feature envisaged in the Constitution
Día de la Constitución (m)(6-D)	Constitution Day
diario de sesiones (m)	verbatim record of proceedings
dictamen (m)	report (from parliamentary committee)
diputación foral (f)	provincial administrative authority (Basque Country and Navarre only)
Diputación Permanente (f)	Standing Council (of the Spanish Parliament)
diputación provincial (f)	provincial council
diputado (m)	deputy/MP; provincial councillor
director general (m)	director-general (highest career public service grade)
director insular (m)	central government representative on a particular island; assistant to the representative for that region
disposición derogatoria (f)	revocatory disposition (to Constitution)
disposición transitoria (f)	transitional disposition (to Constitution)
elecciones anticipadas (fpl)	early election
elecciones legislativas (fpl)	general election
elecciones municipales (fpl)	local (municipal) elections
enchufismo (m)	practice of filling jobs on the basis of contacts
equipo de gobierno (m)	'cabinet' of leading councillors in local authority
escaño (m)	seat (in Parliament)
estado (m)	state; (Spanish) central government
estado de derecho (m)	state under the rule of law
estado social (m)	state whose economy is run on (German) social market lines
función pública (f)	public service
funcionariado (m)	public servants
funcionario (m)	public servant
funcionario de carrera (m)	career public servant
gabinete (m)	private office (staff)
Gobernador Civil (m)	provincial governor
Gobierno Civil (m)	provincial civil authority
gobierno paritario (m)	cabinet with equal numbers of men and women
Grupo mixto (m)	Mixed Group (of deputies/senators)
grupo parlamentario (m)	parliamentary group/party
hecho sociológico (m)	objective feature of Spanish society [recognition of Catholic Church in the Spanish Constitution]
heredero/-a (m/f)	heir (to the throne)

iniciativa popular (f)	people's initiative (procedure by which a proposed law can be presented to Parliament)
infanta (f)	princess
interpelación (f)	interrogative motion (requiring a government response to Parliament)
Juntas de Compras (fpl)	procurement agencies of government ministries
junta de portavoces (f)	(parliamentary) spokespersons' committee
Juntas Generales (fpl)	directly elected provincial council (Basque Country only)
legislatura (f)	legislature; Parliament (period between elections)
letrado (m)	legally trained parliamentary clerk
ley de base (f)	foundation act (basis for subsequent government regulations)
Ley de Extranjería (f)	Aliens Act
ley marco (f)	framework act (guidelines for regional legislation)
ley ordinaria (f)	Act of (Spanish) Parliament
ley orgánica (f)	organic act (entrenched legislation)
Libro Blanco (m)	White Paper (for public consultation)
listas cerradas y bloqueadas (fpl)	closed, blocked lists (electoral system)
mancomunidad (f)	federation of adjoining municipalities to provide services
Mando Supremo de las Fuerzas Armadas (m)	Commander-in-Chief of the Armed Forces
mayoría de edad (f)	age of legal majority
medio ambiente (m)	environment
ministro de la Presidencia (m)	Head of the Prime Minister's Office
moción de censura (f)	no-confidence motion (against PM)
moción de confianza (f)	vote of confidence
moción de reprobación (f)	censure motion (against an individual minister)
municipio (m)	municipality
oposición (f)	opposition (party); competitive public examination
organigrama (m)	structure (of an organization)
parlamentarios (mpl)	members of (Spanish) Parliament
participación ciudadana (f)	direct participation (by individuals, in machinery of government)
pleno (m)	plenary session; meeting of full House/municipal council
ponencia (f)	committee set up for a special purpose
pregunta (f)	question (to government minister, by individual MP)
presidencialismo (m)	presidential system; pre-eminence of PM in Spanish politics
presidente de la Cámara (m)	Speaker of the House
presidente del Congreso/Senado (m)	Speaker of Congress/Senate

presidente del gobierno (m)	Prime Minister
proposición de ley (f)	non-government bill
proyecto de ley (m)	government bill
real decreto-ley (m)	royal decree-law (urgent legislation)
recurso de amparo (m)	application for protection of constitutional rights and freedoms
recurso de constitucionalidad (m)	request for ruling on compliance of a law with the Constitution
reforma (constitucional) (f)	amendment (to the Constitution)
refrendo (m)	endorsement (of action of one state institution, by another)
remodelación (de gobierno) (f)	cabinet reshuffle
reyes (los) (mpl)	the King and Queen; the royal couple
secretaría (f)	section (of ministry)
secretario de estado (m)	Secretary of State (approx. equivalent to UK junior minister)
secretario general (m)	general secretary (ministry post, grade below Under-Secretary)
secretario general técnico (m)	professional general secretary (senior career public servant)
secretario municipal (m)	clerk to municipality
Senado (m)	Senate; Upper House of Spanish Parliament
senador (m)	senator
sub-delegado del gobierno (m)	assistant central government representative to a region, based in a particular province
subsecretaría (f)	section (of ministry) headed by Under-Secretary
subsecretario de estado (m)	Under-Secretary of State (Civil Service grade below Secretary of State)
teniente de alcalde (m)	deputy mayor
título (m)	title (primary divisions) of the Constitution
Título Preliminar (m)	Introductory Title
tráfico de influencias (m)	influence-peddling
Tribunal Constitucional (m)	Constitutional Court
Tribunal de Cuentas (m)	Audit Commission
Tribunal de Defensa de la Competencia (m)	Competition Commission
urbanismo (m)	town planning
ventanilla (f)	counter (in government office)
ventanilla única (f)	one-stop centre for government services
viaje oficial (m)	official visit
vicepresidente (m)	deputy (for full title see corresponding *presidente*)

2

Political parties

Throughout the Western world political parties are central to public life. They play a major part in setting the framework within which debate on issues takes place, at national level and often locally as well. In contemporary Spain they have acquired a particular significance, due to the nature of society and state institutions, and also to that of the parties themselves. This chapter begins by examining certain features of Spanish parties in general, features which to a degree distinguish them from their counterparts in other Western democracies. The remaining sections then consider the nature and development of the three parties to have governed Spain since Franco's death, in order of their coming to power, before looking briefly at some of the minor players on the political stage.

2.1 General features of Spanish parties

Political parties are crucial to modern notions of democracy. They are supposed to channel public opinion, in all its variety and even contradiction, into a manageable number of alternative visions of how to run the country, in the form of election manifestos (*programas electorales*). By the time Spain returned to democracy in the 1970s this bottom-up model already looked rather dubious as a description of reality because, even in countries where democracy was deeply-rooted, parties often appeared more like instruments to control public opinion than to express it. Since then, the doubts have increased. In Spain's case the situation was complicated further by tardy modernization and the Franco regime's ban on democratic politics, which together meant that in 1975 there were no parties with recent experience of such activity – and practically none with any experience at all. The result has been that the functions and behaviour of parties have tended to diverge even more than elsewhere from those described by political theory.

2.1.1 History, status and popular standing

The most obvious difference between Spanish parties and those in almost all other Western countries is their relative lack of historical tradition. The point is of contemporary importance. It is known that loyalty to a particular party, not just over the lifetime of a voter but over generations, often plays a significant part in determining voting habits. In Spain parties have had, as yet, little chance to build up a reservoir of loyalty. Indeed, in the period up to 1936 Spain remained so politically backward that there was little opportunity for the development of parties as they are normally understood [0.1].

On the one hand, those forces which favoured only gradual change or opposed it altogether – those we would today broadly term the right – controlled the country by means other than winning fair elections. As a result the parties they formed remained mere groups of notables, based in Madrid, with links to corrupt political bosses at local level (*caciques*). None developed a mass membership, and none re-emerged to play a significant role in politics after 1975. The only party permitted by

Franco, the government-run 'National Movement' [0.2], was dissolved the year after the dictator's death.

On the left the position was rather different. By the 1930s both the Socialists and the Communists were established political forces, with genuine party organizations and, in the former case, considerable electoral strength. Because of Spain's late and patchy economic development, however, these were restricted to some of those few regions where industry had developed (the Basque Country, Asturias and Madrid) and to the southern countryside. What is more, for almost 40 years both parties of the left were banned and vilified by the Franco regime. In so far as they operated at all, it was in exile or underground.

As a result, of all the myriad political parties which emerged after they were legalized in 1976 [0.3.2] – the media talked of an 'alphabet soup' (*sopa de siglas*) – none had in existence a normal structure of organization and membership. With the possible exception of the Basque PNV [3.2.2.2], none possessed a network of related associations through which to establish contact with society as a whole. And neither parties nor voters themselves had recent, or in most cases any, experience of democratic politics. Moreover, in the case of the Communists, who in 1976 were widely expected to emerge as a leading if not the largest political force, there were understandable doubts about their commitment to observe the rules of democracy.

For all these reasons, those who framed the 1978 Constitution were anxious to foster the growth of democratic parties. Their concern was expressed through recognition, in the Constitution's Introductory Title [1.1.2], of parties as a 'basic mechanism of political participation'. It was again demonstrated by the speed with which this special status was regulated in greater detail. Before the end of 1978, at a time when many major matters required urgent attention, a Political Parties Act was passed.

Under this law parties were given certain privileges, in particular the right to public funding once registered officially as such [2.1.3]. In return, they were required to satisfy certain conditions. In essence, parties' statutes, their own internal 'constitutions', had to conform to certain rules. Thus their stated aims must not be contrary to the Constitution itself, and their internal structure and operation must be democratic in nature.

The first provision had on occasion been applied to regionalist parties who aspired to break away from Spain, thus infringing the country's territorial unity stipulated in Article 2. It appeared to allow a refusal to register – effectively a ban on – fascist or other anti-democratic groups. The second was also mentioned as a possible ground for de-registering Basque parties linked to terrorism. In general, however, the conditions imposed by the 1978 Act had virtually no practical application.

This is not the case of a more recent law, the Political Parties Act of 2002 (*Ley de Partidos*). This facilitates the banning of parties that do not respect democratic freedoms, which advocate racism and xenophobia or which give political support to those who use violence. Under the terms of this Act, the radical Basque party Unity (*Batasuna*), formerly People's Unity (*Herri Batasuna*), was controversially banned by the Supreme Court in 2003 for refusing to condemn the actions of ETA; other radical Basque parties have also been banned under its provisions [3.2.2.1].

Developments have belied the widespread fear that Spanish parties would prove sickly creatures in need of careful nurture. One indication of their robust health is the turnout at general elections (*participación electoral*) or, to use the term usually adopted in Spain, the abstention rate (*tasa de abstención*) (see Table 2.1). After rising sharply in 1979 due to popular disillusion with the results of democracy [0.3.3], abstention fell to just 20 per cent in 1982 as a wave of popular enthusiasm swept the Socialists to power [2.3.1]. The turnout in elections since 1982 has not reached the 80 per cent level, but generally reaches levels that are as high as those in other developed countries, or higher. For instance, it rose to 78 per cent in 1996, when the Socialists were ousted by the People's Party (PP), and 76 per cent in 2004, when the reverse happened.

2.1.2 Leaders and members

A key factor in shaping public perceptions of parties has been the way in which they have operated. Central to that is the relationship between their upper echelons or leadership (*cúpula*) and rank-and-file membership (*bases*). In Spain, this has been crucially affected by the context in which parties rapidly developed after 1976. At that time the two country-wide parties which already had some form of organization, the Socialists and Communists, were used to the secrecy and discipline required by underground operation. On the right and in the centre, parties were initially little more than groups of public figures; such organization as they had was inherited, unofficially, from Franco's National Movement [0.2].

As a result, all the parties shared two features to a greater or lesser extent. One was the high degree of control exercised by the leadership, the other a low level of party membership (*afiliación*). In 1979, after the initial surge of enthusiasm for democracy, neither Socialists nor Communists could claim more than around 100,000 members (*militantes*), while no force on the centre-right had any significant membership at all. Overall, the percentage of the population belonging to parties was among the lowest in Europe; only the Socialists, in some of their industrial heartlands [2.3.1], and the Basque PNV [3.2.2.2], could claim a strong presence in society.

Quite apart from general concerns about the health of democracy, the lack of members posed a very practical problem for the new parties. As well as building up their own organizations, those that enjoyed success had somehow to fill elected posts, such as MPs and councillors, as well as numerous political appointments in national, regional and local government [1.5.1]. The solution adopted by the country's first ruling party was to absorb a considerable number of politicians and bureaucrats from the former regime [2.2]. However, when the parties of the left took over control of many local authorities after the 1979 municipal elections, they were faced with a major difficulty.

The Socialists were particularly affected; they won more votes and thus had more posts to fill, but had fewer members and activists than the Communists in many areas. Moreover, within four years the party gained control over central government and most of the new autonomous regions [2.3.2]. Its response was, in part, to expand its membership by incorporating individuals seen as potential ministers, local councillors and political appointees. But the reverse also applied; the enormous patronage wielded by the Socialists during the 1980s attracted new members for

Table 2.1 Results of principal parties in general elections, 1977–2008

		1977	1979	1982	1986	1989	1993	1996	2000	2004	2008
Turnout	%	79	68	80	71	70	76	78	69	76	74
Democratic Centre Union (UCD)	V	6310	6292	1429							
	P	34.8	35.5	6.2							
	S	167	168	11							
Social and Democratic Centre (CDS)	V			595	1863	1618	413				
	P			2.8	9.2	7.9	1.8				
	S			2	19	14	0				
Spanish Socialist Party (PSOE)	V	5371	5477	10,098	8887	8116	9150	9426	7829	11,026	11,064
	P	29.9	30.5	47.3	44.1	39.6	38.8	37.6	34.1	42.6	43.6
	S	110	121	202	184	175	159	141	125	164	169
People's Party (PP)[a]	V	1439	1068	5557	5245	5286	8201	9716	10,320	9,763	10,170
	P	8.4	6.1	25.9	26.1	25.8	34.8	38.8	44.5	37.7	40.1
	S	16	9	107	105	107	141	156	183	148	154
Spanish Communist Party (PCE)	V	1710	1940	845							
	P	9.3	10.8	3.9							
	S	20	23	4							
United Left (IU)	V				930	1859	2254	2640	1254	1,284	963
	P				4.7	9.1	9.6	10.5	5.5	5.0	3.8
	S				7	17	18	21	8	5	2
Convergence and Union (CiU)[b]	V	515	483	767	1012	1032	1166	1152	965	835	774
	P	2.8	2.7	3.6	5.0	5.0	4.9	4.6	4.2	3.2	3.1
	S	11	8	12	18	18	17	16	15	10	10
Basque Nationalist Party (PNV)	V	296	275	397	309	255	291	319	352	420	303
	P	1.7	1.6	1.8	1.5	1.2	1.2	1.3	1.5	1.6	1.2
	S	8	7	8	6	5	5	5	7	7	6
Esquerra Republicana de Catalunya (ERC)	V	144	123	138	84	84	189	167	194	652	296
	P	0.79	0.69	0.66	0.42	0.41	0.8	0.67	0.84	2.52	1.17
	S	1	1	1	0	0	1	1	1	8	3

Notes:
[a] Prior to 1989, variously People's Alliance (AP), Democratic Coalition (CD), People's Coalition (CP).
[b] Leading Catalan regionalist party.
V = votes (in thousands); P = per cent poll; S = seats.

Source: Interior Ministry

reasons which often had little to do with their beliefs or even with any interest in politics as such. Towards the end of the decade, as the People's Party captured control over many local and regional authorities [2.4.3], it was affected by a similar process.

As a result, membership of both the main parties has risen substantially, with the PP now claiming over 700,000 members and the Socialists somewhat fewer. In view of the Communists' disappearance as a major force [2.5.2], and given the decline in political activism visible in most Western countries, that brings Spain much more into line with its neighbours in terms of membership density. However, it remains unusual in the sense that party members consist, to a quite extraordinary degree, of political office-holders (cargos) of one sort or another. This phenomenon, in turn, has had two main consequences.

It means, first, that a very high proportion of party members have a strong personal, often financial interest in obtaining and holding on to public office. Not surprisingly, administrations formed by the main parties at all levels of government often appear more interested in holding on to power than in using it to implement their election manifestos. Even more seriously for parties' collective standing, the situation is a significant factor in corruption.

It also leads to another form of impropriety: opportunistic party-hopping (chaqueteo). During the transition period, when parties were still in the stage of formation, the practice of individuals moving between them was a frequent and even understandable one. Nevertheless it caused sufficient disquiet that its most visible form – MPs crossing the floor in Parliament (transfuguismo) – was made the subject of strict controls; if an MP leaves a party group he or she must now either resign or join the Mixed Group [1.3.2]. Switches of allegiance at lower levels are less easy to prevent. Their effect, in terms of public cynicism about politics and politicians, can be readily surmised.

Secondly, the make-up of the main parties has tended to strengthen the degree of control exercised by their leaderships. It is they that decide on the placing of individual candidates on the party lists presented to voters [1.3.1], and they who make political appointments to senior administrative posts [1.5.2]. Media-centred election campaigning, which became the norm relatively early in Spain precisely because of low party membership, further accentuates party leaders' dominant status. And, as elsewhere, it also tends to place a heavy emphasis on party unity; dissidents can expect scant rewards.

The electoral impact of national leaders is important even at lower levels, since local and most regional elections take place on a single day and the campaign for them is to a large extent a national affair [3.1.3]. Yet local and, especially, regional leaders also play a significant role and, perhaps more importantly, now control a considerable amount of patronage in their own right. Likened on occasion to Spain's pre-democratic party bosses [2.1.1], the more powerful of these city and regional leaders provide the only real counterweight to the leadership's power within the main parties.

2.1.3 Power and money

At the time the 1978 Constitution was being drawn up, there were genuine fears that Spain's fledgling parties would prove too weak to ensure the state's democratic nature. In so far as the strength of parties is concerned, they have proved wildly exaggerated. Not only do parties monopolize participation in politics, in the sense that only the candidates they present have any realistic chance of election to public office, the widespread system of political appointments means that their influence over the machinery of government goes far further than merely the elected sphere.

As a consequence, the most commonly voiced concern today about the health of Spanish democracy is that the country has become a party-run state (*partitocracia*). The description needs to be severely qualified, in two ways. First, within parties it is the leadership, not the membership as a whole, who exercise effective power [2.1.2] – and as elsewhere, leaders tend to pragmatism rather than ideology. Second, in the case of parties in power at national or lower levels, there is a considerable degree of contact and overlap between party leaderships and those who control the machinery of government (again the Basque PNV [3.2.2.2] is the exception to the rule). Arguably, rather than parties controlling the state, in such cases it is the executive that exercises a decisive influence over parties.

Ironically, one of the measures taken in the 1970s to strengthen parties has, in practice, served to increase their subordination. That measure is the state funding (*financiación*) introduced by the 1978 Political Parties Act [2.1.1]. As in other countries, reservations were expressed in Spain about the provision when it was introduced. However, given the country's highly unusual circumstances, there was no viable alternative; parties, in so far as they existed, lacked both funds and the means to generate them. Consequently the money they received from the state immediately became the main source of income for all parties of any significance, and remains so today.

During the 1980s there was growing public concern about the operation of party funding in general. In response, measures were introduced in 1987, under the Political Parties Finance Act (*Ley Orgánica sobre Financiación de los Partidos Políticos*), to regulate it in greater detail. Under these measures parties receive an annual sum from the state, based on their performance (votes and seats won) in the most recent election. In addition they receive special support for election campaigns on the same basis, including access to television time as well as finance. One effect of this arrangement is to intensify even further parties' concern with electoral success [2.1.2].

The 1987 legislation covers not only public funding but also income from other sources. Under this heading come, first, membership dues (*cuotas de afiliación*) and other income generated by the party itself. Given the low level of membership and activism this source is inevitably of only minor significance. The second means by which parties may raise money themselves is through bank loans (which clearly places a premium on good links with the banking sector). Finally, parties may receive private donations. These are subject to limits on their quantity and to stringent conditions on how they are made. While this strict control has decided advantages in terms of clarity – it would, for example, render illegal the vast majority of the private and company donations which have proved controversial in the UK – it also poses problems of its own. These arise because, perhaps inevitably, parties find the level of funding they receive, public and otherwise, to be inadequate in practice. As a result, many of the influence-peddling scandals of recent decades [1.5.1] have been concerned not with personal but with party enrichment.

The most notorious example was the Filesa affair (*caso Filesa*) of the 1980s, named after a company set up by the Socialist Party specifically to channel the proceeds of such activities into party coffers. In 1997, six party officials were convicted on related charges. To a greater or lesser degree, however, all the major country-wide and regional parties have financed themselves in this way, which represents yet another incentive, this time collective rather than individual, for parties to cling to office at all cost.

A revised Political Parties Funding Act (*Ley Orgánica sobre Financiación de los Partidos Políticos*) was passed in 2007, aimed at improving transparency and control in the area. Under this Act, state funding to political parties generally increases by some 20 per cent, not counting €4m which is allocated to the parties for increased security against terrorist threats, and €54m which the Ministry of the Interior contributes to the parties for their electoral expenses. Furthermore, with regard to the allocation of funding based on parties' share of the vote, the new law stipulates that all votes cast will be taken into account when allocating funding, rather than just those instances where parties received more than 3 per cent of the votes in the constituency, as had been the case previously. The law amends the provisions for private tax-free contributions, prohibiting anonymous donations as well as donations in excess of €100,000 per year, although this limit does not apply to donations of real estate (*bienes inmuebles*).

In short, Spanish political parties continue to be dependent on state contributions as their main source of funding. Most are heavily in debt, above all the Socialist PSOE, which currently has debts of €62m, while those of the People's Party amount to some €28m.

2.2 UCD and the 'centre'

To some contemporary observers, the brief history of the first political party to govern Spain after 1975 confirmed fears about the country's ability to sustain viable parties. While that view proved unfounded, the fact remains that the Democratic Centre Union (*Unión de Centro Democrático/UCD*) did not survive into the contemporary era of Spain's development [0.3.3].

UCD emerged by a process of clustering from the bewildering array of tiny parties that sprang up after Franco's death [2.1.1]. Its nucleus was the People's Party (*Partido Popular*), a grouping founded in 1976 by José María Areilza and unconnected with the party of the same name which later governed the country in the period 1996–2004. Areilza had occupied various senior official posts under the Franco regime but had latterly been prominent among those working for limited change from within it [0.3.1]. He was considerably better known at the time than the young man recently appointed Prime Minister by King Juan Carlos, Adolfo Suárez, and seen by some – not least himself – as a suitable successor.

In January 1977 Areilza's formation absorbed another similar group, changing its name to Democratic Centre. Thereafter it swallowed up or allied with a steady stream of smaller parties. In the spring came the decisive step when Suárez climbed aboard the bandwagon, imposing two conditions for his support. First, he became the grouping's leader, Areilza being summarily ditched. And many of his closest colleagues, like him former Francoist bureaucrats, also assumed leading positions within UCD, as the expanded electoral alliance was now re-christened.

UCD won the largest share of the votes in the general election (*elecciones generales legislativas*) held in 1977 [0.3.2], helped by Suárez's burgeoning personal standing as the PM in charge of government during the period of transition to democracy. In the wake of this success, Suárez was well placed to steer the process of democratization over the next few crucial years [0.3.2]. He showed a talent for deal-making, genuinely consulting with the chief opposition parties, and advocating and achieving consensus on a wide range of important issues, not least the wording of the 1978 Constitution [1.1.1].

With fundamental democratic institutions in place, fresh elections were held in March 1979, and, again, UCD achieved a victory. However, in reality, UCD was suffering from strong internal divisions, since it was in effect a conglomeration of different political groupings, each led by one or more powerful individuals (known as 'barons') who were jealous of their own status and, often, resentful of Suárez. In the UCD parliamentary party (*grupo parlamentario*) itself, divisions between supporters of different barons came together, explosively, with those between the party's four main ideological factions.

The first of these was closely linked to the Catholic Church. These Christian Democrats were conservative on social issues, but favoured the state intervention typical of the German model of a social market economy [1.1.2]. The liberal faction, by contrast, favoured a greater degree of social change, being less influenced by the Church if not mildly anticlerical. Economically they were concerned to remove the many restrictions imposed on business by the former regime, and were accordingly much less enthusiastic about the 'social' aspects of the German model. The Social Democrats, the third main grouping, were largely in agreement with the liberals on social issues but strongly opposed to them on economic ones. There they wanted to see not reduced state intervention but an expansion in welfare state provision and economic planning. The last of UCD's factions was a group of former Francoist bureaucrats, among them Suárez himself and Rodolfo Martín Villa. Not known as liberalizers before Franco's death [0.3.1], their concern seems to have been above all with avoiding insurrection by either the left or the military – with the process of transition rather than with its ends.

The splits in the party became increasingly obvious in late 1979 and into the early 1980s. One instance was the government's attempt to regulate divorce (*Ley del Divorcio*, 1981) which opened up splits between the Christian and Social Democrat factions which proved unbridgeable. As the party began to disintegrate, Suárez resigned abruptly in January 1981. Shortly after, the Spanish political system was rocked to its foundations by the coup attempt known as 23-F [0.3.3]. It was only the fear of further such attempts that held the opposition back from overthrowing what was now a weak UCD government. By summer 1982 it had lost a third of its deputies, forcing Calvo Sotelo to call an early election. In that election, the party suffered a catastrophic defeat and was reduced to a mere 11 seats in the Congress it had previously controlled. Within a year it had been dissolved.

By the time of the October 1982 election Suárez had left UCD and had set up a new party, the Social and Democratic Centre (*Centro Democrático y Social/CDS*). It fared badly that year but considerably better at the 1986 election. But at local elections held in 1988 CDS made the tactical mistake of joining with the People's Alliance to oust

Socialist administrations which lacked an overall majority. This step effectively undermined its claim to represent a pure centre (*centro-centro*), distinct from both left and right. Thereafter its electoral fortunes deteriorated rapidly; at the 1993 general election it failed to win a single seat. By then Suárez himself had admitted defeat and retired from active politics. Without its founder the party effectively withered away.

The demise of UCD and the CDS left Spain without an explicitly centrist party. Instead, the country has moved, in effect, to a two-party system (*bipartidismo*), in which both major contenders seek to occupy the centre ground from right and left respectively. Dissatisfaction with that situation occasionally leads to yearning for the less confrontational approach associated with UCD.

2.3 The Socialist Party

In its role as the governing party UCD was succeeded by the Spanish Socialist Party (*Partido Socialista Obrero Español/PSOE*). In power from 1982 to 1996, and again since 2004, the PSOE has undoubtedly exercised more influence over Spain's contemporary development than any other party. It is also by some way the country's oldest, having been founded in 1879. Prior to 1982 it had spent almost its entire history in opposition or underground, most recently during the Franco era.

2.3.1 From the underground to office

When Franco was in power the PSOE's leadership went into exile, and largely refrained from promoting underground opposition to the regime. Its attitude provoked growing resentment among members within Spain. In 1974 a group of these took control over the party at its 25th Conference (*Congreso*), held at Suresnes in southern France. A young lawyer, known by the codename of *Isidoro*, was elected leader. Together with his closest colleagues – most of them either from the Basque Country or, like himself, from Seville – he was to dominate the PSOE's development for the next two decades. His real name was Felipe González.

The strength of his grip on the party became quite clear in 1979. At that year's 28th Conference delegates rejected a proposal to drop the term 'Marxist' from the party's self-description, a step its leader considered vital if the party was to avoid scaring off potential voters. González promptly resigned. Before the year was out he had been overwhelmingly re-elected, and his proposal approved, at a special Conference hastily convened when it became clear that his opponents could offer no alternatives.

By 1979 the Socialists had already established themselves as Spain's second largest party, having clearly won the struggle with the more fancied Communists for left-wing votes (see Table 2.1). That same year they won control over most of Spain's important towns and cities at the first democratic local elections. In many councils their control depended on a mutual-support agreement with the Communists (*pacto municipal*). This agreement indicated the thrust of the PSOE's strategy at the time; to harness the support of all those who felt that under the then UCD government social and economic change had been too slow and too limited.

Already, in 1977, the PSOE had absorbed the smaller People's Socialist Party (*Partido Socialista Popular/PSP*), whose former leader Enrique Tierno Galván was a popular and successful Mayor of Madrid from 1979 to his death in 1986. When UCD's social democratic faction broke away in 1980 [2.2], it too was absorbed into the PSOE. The Socialists also received a steady flow of prominent defectors from the Communists, by now in seemingly permanent crisis [2.5.1]. Crucially, the PSOE also now attracted a large proportion of their support, particularly young, educated professionals previously influenced by the Communists' role in opposition to the Franco regime. Such voters proved highly susceptible to the PSOE campaign at the 1982 general election. Its slogan *Por el cambio* ('Vote for change') captured perfectly the image of non-ideological radicalism assiduously cultivated by González.

Along with the collapse of UCD [2.2], the attraction of former Communist voters was the key to the PSOE's sweeping 1982 victory; not until 2000, by when the electorate (*electorado*) was considerably larger, was its total of over 10 million votes exceeded at a Spanish election. Although just less than half of those cast, they were converted by the electoral system [1.3.1] into a handsome overall parliamentary majority. The election date, 28 October 1982 (*28-O*), marks a watershed in Spanish politics. Not only did it confirm that the transition was over [0.3.3]. It also ushered in a period of 14 years during which the PSOE dominated Spanish government and politics to an extraordinary degree.

2.3.2 Government under González

After winning the October 1982 general election, the PSOE went on to strengthen its position by its sweeping victory in the local elections held in 1983 and by increasing its strength in the regional elections held in the same year.

This enabled the party to provide the sort of strong, active government UCD had so patently been incapable of providing after 1979. During the 1980s, enormous and badly needed progress was made on a variety of fronts; taxation [5.2.3] and education [7.3.1] were reformed, industry was restructured [5.1.2], the welfare state overhauled [7.1.2, 7.2.1] and infrastructure, especially new roads, constructed on a vast scale. It introduced changes to government support for the Catholic Church, which meant that citizens could now opt to have a small percentage of their income tax designated as Church funding, although it also maintained the subsidization which had existed since Francoist times. In effect, the PSOE presided over Spain's belated socio-economic modernization, one of two words which increasingly dominated its discourse. The other was Europe, by which was meant specifically entry into the European Community, an objective achieved in 1986 [4.2.1].

The emphasis on modernization and EC entry brought a considerable change in the image and nature of the party which had traditionally claimed to defend the interests of manual workers. The policies pursued by its Economics and Finance Minister, Miguel Boyer – himself a leading banker – would eventually have the effect of strengthening the Spanish economy [5.1.2], but meant hardship in the short term as many workers lost their jobs. This led to a progressive estrangement between the PSOE and the Socialist trade union confederation, the UGT, which would reach crisis proportions in the 1988 general strike [5.5.1.2].

Perhaps the most striking example of a shift in policy, however, was the way the party went from opposing Spain's membership of NATO [4.2.2] while in opposition to urging voters to support that membership in the referendum called by the government on the issue in 1986. González managed to persuade first his party and then the country that membership of NATO was necessary in order to ensure that Spain could take its rightful place among its European neighbours.

Exploiting the advantage handed to him by the agreement on Spain's accession to the Community and his party's victory in the NATO referendum, González called a general election somewhat earlier than necessary, in June 1986, and won another overall majority. Three years later he again led the PSOE to victory, in an election called almost a year early to benefit from the economic boom that followed EC entry [5.1.2]. By then the PSOE's vote had been eroded to the extent that it won exactly half the Congress seats, thus technically losing its overall majority. Nevertheless, with the opposition split, this was a purely academic consideration.

González's Deputy Prime Minister during this period was Alfonso Guerra, another Andalusian Socialist, who also held the position of deputy secretary general of the party. Even more adept than González at appealing to working people, Guerra was also an expert tactician who orchestrated the PSOE's electoral victories. Between the two, they ran a highly centralized and efficient party machine which exercised a huge degree of control over all aspects of the administration of the country.

Given this situation, it is perhaps not surprising that the party leadership fell into practices that verged on the anti-democratic, showing scant regard for any opinions other than its own, and repeatedly steamrollering legislation through Parliament with only formal debate. With the power and influence it had over the country as a whole, however, it also appeared prone to corrupt practices, so that holding an official position in the PSOE, or at least being a member of the party, seemed to confer advantages on people at all levels, especially in terms of securing public contracts and even appointments in the public service.

One significant instance of this pattern of favouritism emerged in the early 1990s, when Alfonso Guerra's brother, Juan Guerra, was discovered to be occupying official premises in Seville, despite the fact that he held no government or even party post. Given that Juan Guerra was also able to amass a considerable fortune with suspicious ease at around the same time, the Guerra affair (*caso Guerra*) greatly damaged Alfonso's position. He eventually resigned as Deputy Prime Minister in 1991, although he continued in his role as deputy general secretary of the party.

The González–Guerra partnership foundered in the wake of the scandal, as Guerra increasingly aligned himself with those in his party who objected to the kind of neo-liberal economic policies being pursued by the government. Eventually the criticism from that sector of the party became so overt that González was forced to call a general election in early 1993. To the surprise of most observers, the PSOE won again; on this occasion, the election campaign had been managed by González himself, so that his own personal standing had been enhanced.

The government had been attacked during the election on the issue of corruption, as well as the downturn which the Spanish economy had experienced at the end of the 1980s and the beginning of the 1990s. But by 1993, the economy had started to recover, and, in relation to corruption, González went so far as to acknowledge the need for cleaner government and undertook to ensure that this would be the case in future. As part of the process, he invited some high-profile individuals from outside the party to stand for election on the PSOE's list. One of those star-signings (*fichajes*), who was duly elected, was the prominent prosecuting magistrate, Baltasar Garzón.

González promised that Garzón would have a free hand in dealing with corruption if the party were re-elected, but, as it turned out, the latter found his investigations blocked once they threatened senior party figures. This applied in particular to alleged government involvement in the 'dirty war' waged against ETA by the shadowy group known as the GAL [9.5.2]. In frustration, Garzón resigned and resumed his former career as a magistrate; his subsequent investigations brought the GAL affair into the very heart of the government, leading to the arrest and eventual conviction of former Interior Minister José Barrionuevo. There was speculation that the 'Mister X' with ultimate control over the GAL had been González himself, although this allegation was never substantiated.

Although they had won the 1993 election, the Socialists had not managed to secure an absolute majority and had to depend on the support of smaller parties, notably the Catalan nationalist party, Convergence and Union (*CiU*) [3.2.1.1]. The Catalan nationalists refused to enter a coalition, however, although they did agree a parliamentary pact (*pacto legislativo*) with the PSOE. This meant that CiU would give their support to legislation proposed by the government, but this did not stop it from also supporting the creation of committees of investigation whose work provided further evidence of financial and other irregularities by senior Socialists.

The government's political woes were made even worse by its determination that Spain be among the EU members to qualify for the first wave of Economic and Monetary Union [4.2.2]. The austerity measures it adopted to ensure this got off to an embarrassingly poor start and, once they began to take effect, hit hardest at the PSOE's own supporters [5.1.3]. Understandably, González's Catalan allies became increasingly alarmed at the implications of associating with an ever more unpopular government. In autumn 1995 they moved to distance themselves by refusing to support the following year's budget estimates.

As a result, González was forced to call an election for the following spring. Having previously stated that he would not stand for re-election as PM, he was eventually obliged to do so by a party conscious that he was still enormously popular with wide sections of the electorate. Even with the GAL allegations hanging over him, he once again proved a formidable campaigner. His efforts meant that the PSOE did not suffer the comprehensive defeat that was generally expected, but they could not prevent it from losing power at last [2.4.3].

2.3.3 Return to opposition

The PSOE's defeat at the polls in 1996 was a reflection of the fact that its support base had changed radically since its historic 1982 victory [2.3.1]. That had been won by extending its traditional base among manual workers – especially the industrial workforce – anxious to improve their material living conditions, to young, better-off urban dwellers who were attracted by the Socialists' image of social progressiveness. For both these groups the party's record in power had ultimately proved disappointing.

Material prosperity had risen, but workers, especially in older industries, had not been among the main beneficiaries. Since the legalization of abortion, under strict conditions, in 1985 the party had undertaken few major social reforms; while Spanish society had undoubtedly become much more relaxed, that was not primarily due to legislation and was in any case taken for granted by the new generation of voters who had no memory of the Franco era. Furthermore, the PSOE's progressive image was badly tarnished by controversial law-and-order legislation in the 1990s [9.5.2]. Corruption scandals [2.3.2], as well as its long hold on power, made it appear to many voters as the party of the establishment, an old party.

In fact these perceptions contained a considerable element of truth. In 1996 the PSOE relied disproportionately on the votes of two social groups. One consisted in the employees of a public sector vastly expanded under its rule, and possibly threatened by a right-wing government. The other was the elderly, who have come to form a very significant part of the Spanish electorate, and one which the PSOE had been careful to cultivate through allocation of state benefits [6.3.2]. The same applied, on a lesser scale, to the rural poor of the south [5.2.4.1]; it was no coincidence that the three southern regions of Extremadura, Castile-La Mancha and Andalusia were the only ones in which the PSOE topped the poll in 1996. But they also remain the most economically backward in the country, and the concentration of Socialist votes there underlined that the PSOE was now the voice of the least dynamic elements in Spanish society – in stark contrast to the 1980s, when it had been the party of modernization [2.3.2].

To be fair, some in the PSOE were aware of its plight and in the wake of its 1996 defeat they could be heard calling for complete overhaul of the party (*renovación total*). Their demand proved problematic, however. For one thing, it implied admission of past irregularities, financial and otherwise [2.3.2], on a scale far greater than the party's upper echelons were prepared to concede. It also implied González's replacement as leader – just when the 1996 results had confirmed him as the party's prime electoral asset, and when the only obvious successor had been ruled out by Javier Solana's appointment as NATO Secretary-General [0.4.1]. As González himself had pointed out before the election, and repeated thereafter, he was 'both a problem and a solution' for the party.

In the event he resolved the immediate dilemma by presenting his resignation, unannounced, at the party's 1997 Conference. But it became clear at once that his move was designed not to initiate but to thwart any wider change. With its proponents caught unaware, González's own choice of successor, Joaquín Almunia, was easily elected to replace him. Worthy but stolid, Almunia had been an ever-present in the Socialist cabinets of the early 1990s, and was clearly not about to undertake a serious critique of their performance. In any case, a mere change of personnel could not solve the PSOE's underlying problem: that for over a decade it had effectively been led from government [2.3.2], and had lost the capacity to lead itself.

Lacking González's position and charisma, Almunia could not hope to establish the authority of his former boss. Hoping instead to pacify discontent, he made one concession to demands for a new approach. To the concern of many in the old guard, he agreed that the party's prime ministerial candidate for the next election should be chosen by a one-member-one-vote election, on the lines of an American presidential primary (*elecciones primarias*). When it was held, in 1998, his colleagues' fears were borne out, with Almunia losing to the younger, more charismatic José Borrell.

Borrell was also a survivor of the González governments. Indeed, he had initially made his name as an efficient implementer of policies disliked by much of the party's rank and file. In opposition, however, he was the only leading Socialist to attack the new government on overtly left-wing grounds, a stance which enabled him to exploit the widespread but poorly articulated discontent among PSOE members.

His choice sparked an immediate 'Borrell effect'; the party's morale rose perceptibly, as did its opinion poll ratings. But his mildly radical views and open sympathy with regionalist ideas in his home region of Catalonia rendered him unacceptable to much of the party leadership. And, for all the party leader's patent willingness to make it work, 'cohabitation' with Almunia proved difficult. Then, in 1999, Borrell was distantly implicated in a minor scandal uncovered in one of his former ministries. Although the affair was trivial by recent Spanish standards he resigned immediately from his position as candidate, giving the distinct impression that he was relieved to be rid of a thankless task.

With a general election now looming the PSOE had no option but to fall back on Almunia to run for PM, a candidate who was not even the choice of his own party members. But that was the least of the Socialists' troubles. For one thing, as a political machine the PSOE had become caught in a vicious circle. Its former effectiveness had depended heavily on the party's strong grip on power [2.3.2], but that was now a distant memory. Even before 1996 it had lost control of most of local and regional government. With the accompanying powers of patronage and opportunities for graft [2.1.2, 2.1.3], the party had lost both funding and members, as well as the main means of maintaining discipline among those that remained. The results were increasingly apparent in an internal feud and, eventually, a singularly ineffective campaign when the election finally came, in March 2000.

Matters were not helped by the fact that the PSOE had failed utterly to develop a coherent programme or strategy with which to confront a government buoyed by economic success [2.4.3]. Its bankruptcy was laid bare shortly before the campaign got under way. For the best part of two decades the PSOE had treated anyone to its left with ill-disguised contempt, deriding the communist-led United Left (IU) as unrealistic and naïve; IU, for its part, had been relentless in its attacks on the Socialists, on occasion even tacitly allying with the PP against them [2.5.2]. Yet now the two parties agreed on a loose 'electoral pact', and a joint programme which lambasted the PP's record in power as irredeemably reactionary – conveniently forgetting that in many respects its policies were indistinguishable from those pursued by the PSOE up to 1996 [2.4.3].

The pact proved a disaster. In a complete reversal of events in 1993 and 1996, the PSOE fared much worse than predicted by opinion polls. IU may have lost proportionately more votes, but the PSOE's relegation to a distant second place was an equally traumatic result. Almunia, characteristically, assumed full responsibility for the defeat and resigned immediately as party leader. The election to replace him was held at a special conference a few months later. It was won by a virtually unknown forty-year-old, José Luis Rodríguez Zapatero, who narrowly defeated the leadership's favoured candidate, José Bono, the long-serving prime minister of Castile-La Mancha.

2.3.4 The Zapatero era

The new leader did not enjoy the support of any organized faction within the party. Instead, he succeeded in channelling widespread, if unfocused, grassroots discontent.

The confusion in the party was then underlined by the conferences subsequently held in the party's several regional sections, most of which were dominated by personalized struggles for power; in some regions, notably Madrid and Asturias, the followers of Alfonso Guerra [2.3.2] retained a strong hold. Moreover, especially in those regions where the Socialists still controlled the regional government, there was a growing tendency for local party leaders to act and speak on the basis of their own political needs, with little or no concern for nation-wide party policy. Rodríguez Zapatero, noted for his tolerance and conciliatory approach, initially found it hard to impose his authority and to define a clear policy line. Furthermore, he was perceived broadly as more left-leaning than his predecessor; as a personality, he was generally seen as lacking in charisma and leadership quality.

Nevertheless, early on in his tenure as leader, he concluded several cross-party agreements with the PP government on individual issues [2.4.3]. Then, late in 2001, he brought about a major policy change in his party in relation to the form of the state, viz., the decision to support Spain's conversion into a genuinely federal state, as long advocated by the PSOE's Catalan section [3.2.1.1]. The move was a radical break with the party's centralist traditions, not to mention the wishes of some of its most powerful regional 'barons'. Since then, little progress has been made in achieving this aim, perhaps reflecting the fact that doubts continue to be raised about the degree to which both party members and voters accept it.

Against all odds, and still under the leadership of Zapatero, the party won the general election held on 14 March 2004. Polls held just a few days before the election had predicted that the Socialists would lose. Thus, it is likely that the turning point in the electorate's voting intentions came in the aftermath of the appalling train bombings in Madrid three days earlier, in which 191 people had been killed [9.5.4], and was a reaction to what people perceived as the PP government's attempt to distort the true picture regarding the identity of the perpetrators of the bombings. The government's obstinate attempt to attribute blame for the atrocity to ETA rather than to Islamist terrorists seems to have encouraged voters to opt for the Socialist alternative [2.4.5]. In the event, the PSOE topped the poll, winning some 42.6 per cent of the vote and 164 seats, almost 5 per cent and 16 seats ahead of the PP.

On assuming office, the new Prime Minister declared that his legislature would be characterized by the adoption of a new approach to government (*nuevo talante*). This change was focused not just on the implementation of more liberal policies, but also on the stated objective of prioritizing openness, tolerance and dialogue, in contrast with what was generally perceived to have been Aznar's more authoritarian approach. Evidence of the new direction came in the form of a number of political decisions taken rapidly by the new government, including the revocation of the National Water plan [8.3.2] and the decision to annul the requirement, stipulated in the 2001 Education Act [7.3.1.2.2], that religion be a compulsory subject in state schools [2.4.4]. Along with these, laws were introduced to regularize the situation of the millions of immigrants in Spain (2005) [6.1.1], to help combat domestic violence (2004) [6.2], to update the situation with regard to both abortion and divorce [6.2], and to allow for same-sex marriage (2005) [6.3.1]. The government party was regularly supported during this period by IU [2.5] and ERC [3.2.1.1].

In the area of foreign policy, the key measure indicative of change was the immediate decision to recall the 1,300 Spanish troops serving in Iraq, as the PSOE had promised to do in the course of its election campaign. This measure signalled not only a diminution in Spanish government support for the foreign policies of the United States [0.4.1], but also a greater rapprochement with the EU. This in turn was reflected in Zapatero's support for the proposed new European Constitution, which was endorsed by referendum in Spain in February 2005, although it was later rejected by other EU countries [4.2.3].

Meanwhile, the PSOE's renewed electoral success was extended to other arenas. In the 2004 European elections it won 25 seats, one more than the PP (Table 4.3). At regional level the Socialists also fared well. Following their 2003 success in Catalonia [3.2.1.1], they made advances in both the Basque Country and Galicia [3.2.3.2] two years later. This electoral honeymoon appeared to be on the wane, however, when the PSOE was outvoted by the PP in the local elections held in 2007, even if it secured most council seats thanks to the peculiarities of the electoral system.

This reverse may well have reflected a certain sense that the Zapatero government was lacking in focus, a sense strengthened by the repeated cabinet reshuffles – three in all – between 2004 and 2008. During the second, in April 2006, the Minister of Defence, José Bono, stepped down from his position. Bono alleged personal reasons for his decision but was widely believed to have been at odds with the party leadership on key policy issues including its approach to the re-drafting of the Catalan Statute of Autonomy [3.2.1.3], its review of the status of religion in schools and its willingness to contemplate the emergence of alternative family structures, reflected in the law on same-sex marriages.

The apparent failure of the Basque peace process with the effective ending of ETA's ceasefire in December 2006 [3.2.2.4] was also a major setback for the ruling party, which was forced to re-define its policy in this area, and is aiming now to achieve a cross-party antiterrorist pact (*Pacto Antiterrorista*). The announced intention of the Basque *lehendakari*, Juan José Ibarretxe, to carry out a referendum on self-determination in the Basque Country [3.2.2.1] added more heat to the situation. And ETA's assassination of a former Socialist councillor in the Basque Country two days before the March 2008 general election was yet a further clear signal of the militant radicals' determination to defy central government and disrupt the political process.

That election was marked by the same kind of bitter hostility that had been evident throughout the period of the legislature since 2004. There were accusations and counter-accusations of deception and incompetence. The Church made clear its preference for the PP and, in the two leaders' debates that were televised in the run-up to the election, Rajoy made much of Zapatero's alleged inability to deal with the 'problem' of immigration [6.1]. Meanwhile, the latter scored points on the economy [5.1.3] and on his government's record on social issues [6.3], while managing to depict the PP as still being the inheritors of the Francoist legacy of repression and exploitation.

Most observers felt that Zapatero won the debates, and this was reflected in polls that showed the Socialists four points ahead of their rivals two days before the election. The result confirmed these predictions and the PSOE won 169 seats, which, although not an absolute majority, was five seats more than in 2004. Although this meant that the Socialists had 15 seats more than the PP, the latter also improved their position, their tally increasing from 148 to 154, with the result that Congress was now characterised by a greater degree of 'polarization' (*bipolarización*) than before. With the Communists down to a paltry two seats, Zapatero looked to the Catalan and Basque nationalists for support as he prepared for another four years of government.

2.4 The People's Party and its forerunners

The People's Party (*Partido Popular/PP*) first came to power at the general election of 1996, and remained in office for the next eight years; it is not to be confused with the short-lived party of the same name which formed the nucleus of UCD [2.2]. In direct contrast to the PSOE, the present-day PP is therefore an extremely young party, having adopted its current name only in 1989. Even its direct forerunner, People's Alliance (*Alianza Popular/AP*), was founded little more than 30 years ago. Yet in many respects the past has been just as important for the PP as for its main rival – in some even more so.

2.4.1 People's Alliance and People's Coalition

The reason why the past weighs so heavy on the PP is to be found in the origins of AP. This was set up in 1976 as an alliance of seven small right-wing groups, none of which was a party in any meaningful sense. Instead they were the personal followings of their respective leaders, parodied as the 'magnificent seven', all of whom had been prominent in the previous regime. Their leader was Manuel Fraga Iribarne who, though he counted as one of the regime's liberalizers [0.3.1], had served in several of the dictator's cabinets.

Nor were AP's links to the old regime merely a question of personnel. Fraga himself favoured a strictly controlled form of democracy. His party campaigned for the 1977 election on a platform of minimal change. Its crushing defeat showed clearly that this line was out of touch with popular feeling (see Table 2.1). Thereafter AP and its few deputies took part in the process of drawing up the 1978 Constitution, although doubts remained about its commitment to democracy. All its leading figures were wont to express reservations about the changes under way and a number of its MPs failed to vote for the Constitution. AP was particularly outspoken in its criticism of the constitutional arrangements for devolution [3.1.1], which it long remained committed to amend if elected.

For the 1979 election AP changed tack radically. It attempted to establish a more moderate image by allying with a number of groups and individuals unhappy with or excluded from UCD. This 'Democratic Coalition' performed even worse than AP had done in 1977. The setback prompted Fraga to abandon the idea of trying to compete with UCD as a centre-right option. Over the next few years he set about building a broad party of the right (*gran derecha*). His model was the British Conservative Party and his aim to make AP what the Tories then were – a natural party of government (*mayoría natural*).

Considerable efforts were made to improve AP's organization, and, indeed, to create a party structure for the first time in much of Spain, with limited success. In fact, the crucial factor in changing the party's fortunes was the disintegration of UCD

[2.2]. AP profited from this process, first by a steady stream of defections in Parliament, then by a large increase in its vote at the 1982 election, when for the first time its lists of candidates were not dominated by figures from the old regime. As a result it was transformed from a minor player in the political spectrum into the main country-wide opposition to the triumphant Socialists – indeed virtually the only one.

This in itself allowed AP to reap further benefits, such as the effective support of the Spanish Employers' Confederation, the CEOE [5.5.2]. AP also attracted into a new electoral alliance two splinter parties which had emerged from the wreckage of UCD, the Christian Democrat People's Democratic Party (*Partido Demócrata Popular/PDP*) and the Liberal Party (*Partido Liberal/PL*). Together with AP these made up the People's Coalition (*Coalición Popular/CP*).

The new recruits gave a modest boost to CP's appeal, but they also imported into it the problems that had destroyed UCD [2.2]. From the outset CP had within itself organized currents of opinion with differing political beliefs and mutually suspicious leaders. It proved unable to fix on a coherent line of opposition to a government whose unpopular economic policies were broadly in line with its own views. Most notoriously, in the 1986 NATO referendum [4.2.2] Fraga called on his supporters to abstain, even though he and his party were staunch supporters of Spanish membership, merely to avoid siding with the Socialist government.

Such inconsistency made it easy for the government to play down attacks from CP as opportunistic. At the same time, CP suffered from a lingering impression among large sections of the electorate that it would seek to return to the policies of the Franco regime, especially by restricting individual freedoms. These reservations were linked particularly to the person of Fraga. When CP failed to advance at the 1986 election, commentators spoke of an electoral ceiling (*techo electoral*). By this they meant a level of support (around 25 per cent of the electorate) through which no party led by Fraga could hope to break.

Almost immediately following the 1986 election the PDP withdrew from CP. Its leaders criticized CP's policies for being too right-wing, and declared that only a more moderate line offered hope of defeating the PSOE. When, in November, CP performed disastrously in a Basque regional election, Fraga resigned, publicly and emotionally, as AP leader. And in January 1987 CP effectively ceased to exist when the PL also abandoned it, leaving AP alone as well as leaderless.

2.4.2 From AP to PP

It was widely expected that Fraga would be succeeded as party leader by his experienced deputy, Miguel Herrero de Miñón. However, at a special party conference held in January 1987 Herrero's supporters were outmanoeuvred by those of a younger, relatively unknown challenger. Previously AP regional leader in Andalusia, Antonio Hernández Mancha was elected chairman, his choice clearly reflecting a desire among delegates for a fresh start.

This the new leader of the AP attempted to provide by changing the line of its attacks on the government. Whereas Fraga had concentrated on opposing liberal social policies, in areas such as abortion and education, Hernández Mancha focused on the impact of the Socialists' economic policies on less well-off voters [5.1.2]. For an essentially conservative party this was a radical departure which could only have been carried off by a strong, established leader, which Hernández Mancha was not. In addition, his populist line alienated the leadership of the business community.

Given these continuing travails, AP's poor results in the 1987 regional elections were predictable. They also added a further problem for the party; the advance of a number of regionally based parties of the right and centre-right [3.2.3]. In some areas – notably Aragon and Navarre – these even threatened to eclipse AP completely, and so undermine its credibility as a truly national party.

By 1989 Hernández Mancha's support had vanished and he did not even stand for re-election as leader. In desperation, it seemed, the party turned again to Fraga as its chairman. The impression of stagnation was reinforced at the 1989 election, when AP again failed to improve on its 1982 performance, despite the PSOE's deteriorating support. However, two significant changes had indeed taken place. AP no longer existed, having metamorphosed into the People's Party. And for the first time Fraga had not been his party's candidate for Prime Minister.

Both changes had been agreed, on Fraga's recommendation, at the foregoing party conference. Their first intention was to remove the 'ceiling' imposed by his own past [2.4.1]. But they also aimed to resolve the dilemma addressed by UCD and CP in different ways but with equal lack of success, the question of how to bring together the three main strands of the Spanish centre-right: conservatives drawn from the Francoist old guard, liberals and Christian Democrats [2.2, 2.4.1]. The change in party name was a clear sop to the latter, 'People's Party' being the designation adopted by Christian Democrats internationally; Fraga also agreed that the party's MEPs would join the Christian Democrat group in the European Parliament [4.3.1]. At the same time he brought Marcelino Oreja, an internationally known Christian Democrat and former UCD minister (see Table 4.2), into the party leadership.

These various moves were intended to give the newly-born PP the image of a modern, mainstream European party, linked to successful Christian Democratic parties in Germany and other EU countries. Yet in terms of economic policy, if anything the PP shifted away from Christian Democratic ideas towards more liberal ones, a move which enabled it to regain the support of the CEOE [2.4.1]. The resultant mix of social conservatism and economic liberalism brought the PP ideologically close to the British Tories, but in their contemporary, Thatcherite guise rather than the traditional brand Fraga had always admired.

The problem of Fraga's own person was solved by removing him with honour from the national political scene. In 1989 he headed the PP's slate at the Galician regional election; winning an overall majority he withdrew to govern his own home region, which he did until 2005. At his party's 1990 Conference – the first held under the initials PP – he was elected to the special post of founding chairman (*presidente fundador*). He was replaced as party leader by the man Fraga himself had chosen to be PP's candidate for Prime Minister the previous year, José María Aznar.

2.4.3 The PP under Aznar

Under Aznar the PP experienced a slow but steady recovery, with the party being presented as the only real option to the PSOE, especially given the collapse of CDS, its only real rival for centre-right votes in the country [2.2]. The Socialists' own increasing problems made them much more vulnerable than before [2.3.2], although Aznar's lack of popular esteem compared with that of Felipe González still made it difficult for the party to project itself as a genuine alternative government (*alternativa de poder*).

Although the PP failed to win the 1993 general election, despite the polls that had predicted it would, its results were by far the best achieved by the party or any of its predecessors. The failure was partly due to the PSOE's success in insinuating that the PP was still closely linked to the Franco regime, and, in response, Aznar stepped up his efforts to bring forward a new generation of leaders who, like himself, were not closely identified with that tarnished legacy. At the same time, he continued working to give the PP the strong, country-wide basis AP had never fully established.

The party also succeeded in marginalizing many of the regional centre-right parties which had emerged in the mid-1980s [2.4.2]. With the two largest, in Aragon and Navarre, it reached agreements to present joint lists for general elections. The result was that, by the mid-1990s, the PP was firmly established as a major political player in all the regions with the exception of the Basque Country and Catalonia, where most voters were still deeply suspicious of it.

These developments, along with the emergence of a new and more centralized management structure within the PP which allowed Aznar, as party chairman (*presidente*), to exercise a strong hold over other party leaders, eventually began to bear fruit. In 1994, the PP outpolled the PSOE in elections to the European Parliament, its first victory in a Spain-wide contest (Table 4.3). At the following year's regional and municipal elections it enjoyed further success, taking control of 12 out of 17 regions, and all the large cities except Corunna and those in the Basque Country and Catalonia. This triumph also had a knock-on effect in that it brought to public notice a whole series of the party's regional leaders who had previously been largely anonymous.

In the run-up to the 1996 general election – a time when the twentieth anniversary of Franco's death brought the transition into the spotlight – Aznar was at pains to identify his party with positive memories of UCD [2.2]. Its conference held in January of that year was dominated by the notion of the PP as a 'centre' party. Nevertheless, the PSOE was also able to exploit memories of the past in the subsequent campaign. On this occasion the focus of Socialist innuendo was the influence allegedly exercised over the PP by the Opus Dei organization, whose close involvement with the Franco regime is notorious.

The tactic succeeded to the extent that, while the PP did win the 1996 election, its victory was much narrower than predicted by the polls. Aznar had no overall majority, and for a while it looked as though he might fall at the final hurdle of securing enough parliamentary support from regional parties. However, after over two months of negotiations he succeeded in hammering out a deal with three of them; the tiny Canary Islands Alliance, the Basque PNV and, crucially, the Catalan CiU, which had previously maintained the Socialists in power [2.3.2].

The PP's policies during much of its first term sometimes evoked comparisons with the Francoist past, while at other times indicating an openness and moderation previously alien to the Spanish Right. Among the latter could be counted, first, what was initially a surprisingly good relationship with the trade unions – although the relationship was eventually to turn sour [2.4.4]. As well as improving the PP's image among floating voters at the time, this approach produced concrete benefits in terms of social security funding [7.1.2] and employment creation [5.2.4.2]. The PP also made no significant attempt to reverse social or legal reforms undertaken since 1978, declining, for example, to satisfy the Catholic hierarchy's demands for more favourable funding arrangements for the Church. It also scrapped its policy of advocating the return of the death penalty and its earlier proposal that convicted ETA terrorists be deprived of the right to remission of their sentences.

It also unequivocally accepted the new, devolved structure of government, something the old AP had always regarded with suspicion, and even introduced reforms aimed – in theory at least – at diminishing the role of central administration still further [1.5.2]. Aznar managed the tricky task of cooperating with his Catalan, Basque and Canary Islands nationalist allies surprisingly well, and made concessions to the Basques and Catalans on fiscal policy. The positive political impact of these various steps was evident at the regional elections held in the Basque Country in 1998 and in Catalonia a year later, in both of which the PP made significant advances (see Tables 3.2 and 3.1).

On the other hand, it took a very hard line against ETA, which was understandable, given that the party had itself become the main target of terrorism [3.2.2.3] and Aznar made no substantive response to the ETA ceasefire of 1998/99. This decision, while criticized by many at the time, was arguably vindicated by the subsequent resumption of violence. But Aznar also frequently insisted on treating the PNV as if it were directly allied with terrorism, an allegation that, for all the PNV's ambivalence about violence, was patently absurd. The PP's hope that this confrontational attitude would pay electoral dividends was dashed at the 2001 regional election, the results of which greatly strengthened the PNV. Much more importantly, its attitude was likely to hinder attempts to heal the wounds in Basque society, not help them.

More generally, the PP government tended to display signs of a reactionary Spanish nationalism for which notions of the country's diversity were anathema. The crassest example came in 1997 when the then Education Minister Esperanza Aguirre unsuccessfully attempted to impose a standard history curriculum throughout the country. Its strong emphasis on Spain's supposed historical unity was both contrary to most academic opinion, and unhappily reminiscent of Francoist ideas. A similarly combative approach, but of a very different nature, was apparent in the government's health policy, which displayed a dogmatic preference for the private sector over the public [7.2.2]. This reflected the PP's conversion to a neoliberal view of economics that was also apparent in the enthusiasm for deregulation and privatization displayed by the Economics and Finance Minister Rodrigo Rato.

2.4.4 Aznar ascendant

The payoff for Aznar and his party came on 12 March 2000 (*12-M*). Against all expectations, the PP was not only re-elected but secured a comfortable overall majority in both Houses of Parliament. By consolidating its gains in the Basque Country and Catalonia it also established itself, at last, as a truly national party. The triumph, quite unprecedented for a Spanish conservative, owed not a little to the steady growth in Aznar's personal standing, once such a handicap for the party

[2.4.3]. And it, in turn, strengthened his position still further, confirming him as the PP's unchallengeable leader.

Moderation of the PP's image may have been one factor behind its spectacular victory in the 2000 general election. But more important were the Socialist opposition's utter disarray [2.3.3] and, above all, the country's good economic performance. The reasons for that can be debated. Some would give the credit to the PP's slightly more liberal approach; others would argue that the groundwork was laid by the previous government, whose policies the PP largely took over unchanged.

Whatever the reasons, the results were undeniable. Not only did Spain comfortably meet the strict criteria for entry into Economic and Monetary Union [4.2.2]. The benefits were felt in the form of rapid growth and falling unemployment. Aznar's repeated assertion that 'Spain's doing well' (*España va bien*) was derided by his opponents, but it struck a chord with much of the electorate.

The cabinet he subsequently appointed reflected Aznar's greatly enhanced personal position. The most prominent minister, Rodrigo Rato, saw his power-base curtailed with the separation of the finance and economics portfolios [1.4.3]. Moreover, unlike that of four years earlier the government was now dominated by figures who had made their careers inside the PP itself, under Aznar. The most important of these was Mariano Rajoy, initially in charge of the Prime Minister's Office [1.4.4], but moved to Interior in 2001.

The margin of his 2000 victory also freed Aznar from his dependence on outside parliamentary support, a circumstance that some expected to see reflected in more distinctively right-wing policies. In the field of immigration these expectations were borne out in a tougher new Aliens Act, introduced in 2001 [6.1.1]. Generally, though, the policy mixture was much as before. A broadly neoliberal economic policy was tempered by a willingness to reach negotiated agreements with the unions, for example on pension reform, although relationships between government and unions were strained again when new employment regulations introduced in 2001 allowed for easier dismissal of workers and new types of short-term contracts. These reforms provoked the unions into calling a general strike in 2002 [5.2.4.2]. The desire for consensus, however, extended also to the Socialist opposition, with whom the government entered agreements (*pactos de Estado*) on the approach to ETA terrorism [3.2.2.4] and reform of the legal system [9.1.4].

Less consensus was evident in relation to some other issues. These included two controversial laws in the area of education, the University Regulation Act (*Ley de Ordenación Universitaria/LOU*) [7.3.1.1.3] and the Education Quality Act (*Ley Orgánica de Calidad de la Enseñanza/LOCE*), the latter stipulating, *inter alia*, that religion would be a compulsory subject in second-level schools [7.3.1.2.2]. Despite student protests, public criticism and the opposition of the PSOE, these measures became law in 2001, with the PP government relying on support from the Canary Islands Alliance.

Aznar's second term also saw the continuation of another trend. Having made much of its predecessors' alleged abuse of power while in office, the PP's record in that regard was not noticeably better than the PSOE's. Thus in a number of cases state enterprises privatized by it finished up in the hands of individuals and interests closely linked to the party, the most notorious example being the appointment of Aznar's schoolfriend Juan Villalonga to head the telecommunications giant Telefónica [5.4.1]. In turn, Telefónica was heavily involved in blatant attempts to control private television news reporting [10.4]. Given that manipulation of state television continued more or less unabated [10.1], coverage of the 2000 election was just as heavily weighted as ever in favour of the government of the day.

Corruption scandals also continued to emerge, albeit not with the frequency of the early 1990s [2.3.2]. One of the most serious involved Josep Piqué, a Catalan businessman first brought into government as Government Spokesperson and subsequently appointed Foreign Minister. Another, centred on Gescartera, a Madrid financial services firm, was especially significant because it indirectly implicated Rato, who had been widely seen as Aznar's heir apparent (*delfín*). When it came to it, Aznar in fact gave his support to Mariano Rajoy, who was made second-in-command in the party and candidate for the PM position in September 2003. Meanwhile, Rato's career took a different path as he was appointed Director General of the International Monetary Fund in June 2004, a position he stayed in until he resigned from it in 2007.

By then a number of other developments had damaged the government's standing and gradually eroded Aznar's own position, including the increasingly confrontational approach that Aznar was taking towards Basque and Catalan nationalists [3.1.6], and the apparent tendency within the party leadership towards reactionary Spanish nationalism. Some were relatively minor, such as the PM's decision to erect a giant Spanish flag in the centre of Madrid in 2001 or the high-handed way in which Spanish troops moved to re-possess Parsley Island after Moroccan gendarmes had landed on it [0.4.3].

Other issues were more serious. The government was heavily criticized for its clumsy management of the environmental disaster caused by the sinking of an oil tanker off the Galician coast in 2002 [8.1.2]. Its support for the American invasion of Iraq in March 2003, when hundreds of Spanish troops were sent into the region, met with massive opposition from Spaniards generally [0.4.1]. Finally, the loss of 62 Spanish servicemen when a military aircraft crashed in Turkey while returning from Afghanistan led to another public relations disaster. On that occasion, the Ministry of Defence was accused of hiring an antiquated aeroplane and of mishandling the collection of DNA evidence from the victims' bodies, leading to some thirty families unknowingly burying other people's relatives.

Although these were clearly setbacks for the PP, they were mitigated somewhat in the minds of the electorate by the obvious strength of the Spanish economy, which was booming at this time [5.1.3]. This probably helped to buoy up their electoral situation. In the 2003 regional elections, the party held onto power in eight out of thirteen regions; its most notable loss, in Aragon, was attributable mainly to the controversial plan to divert part of the Ebro's flow to other regions [3.2.3.2]. In Catalonia the party added two extra seats to its tally, although, with the overall results enabling the formation of a broad left-wing coalition, they lost their previous indirect influence over the region's government [3.2.1.1]. At the local elections also held in 2003, the PP failed to obtain most votes country-wide for the first time since

1993, but it held onto power on Madrid City Council, which it has dominated since 1991, as well as in 29 other major towns and cities.

2.4.5 In opposition again

In the run-up to the 2004 general election, then, there was no serious expectation that the PP would be defeated, given its economic successes and the relative disarray of the PSOE [2.3.3]. But the reaction of the government to the 11-M massacre [9.5.4] was such that public opinion swung against it in spectacular fashion. Given the magnitude of what had happened, and the international impact that it had, Spaniards generally expected that the election would be postponed. The response of the government, however, was first to announce that the planned election would proceed. Then it openly – and repeatedly – blamed ETA for the atrocity, despite the apparent paucity of evidence, and even though, uncharacteristically for ETA, there was no warning given and the victims were mainly commuters on their way to work. While the Interior Minister immediately declared that ETA members were the prime suspects, the Foreign Minister instructed Spanish embassies abroad to brief the media along those lines.

Spaniards generally were suspicious of the government's behaviour. Many believed that its attempt to link ETA to the attacks was a convenient way of aligning events with the zero-tolerance policy it had adopted towards ETA and the strong antipathy it had shown towards Basque nationalism. The government's actions gave many people the impression that it was attempting to capitalize on the massacre for the sake of electoral gain. On the eve of the election, demonstrations took place outside the headquarters of the PP in Madrid and in other cities, and popular sentiment was clearly swinging against the government. Voting patterns in the election reflected the public's sceptical view of their government's pronouncements, and by the time the polls closed it was clear that the PP would lose power. In the event, the turnout was some 7 per cent higher than in 2000 and the PSOE had won 164 seats to the PP's 148.

In the wake of this election defeat, Aznar's preferred candidate, Mariano Rajoy, became leader of the party, while the man who had functioned as Interior Minister under Aznar, Ángel Acebes, took his place as second-in-command. In opposition, Rajoy's strategy was hardline and confrontational, and his criticisms of the PM and the government were expressed in strong and, at times, intemperate language. The party's behaviour appeared to reflect a feeling among its members that it had been cheated out of government, and it consistently opposed the view that the 11-M massacre was the work of al-Qaeda, even in spite of court rulings that supported that interpretation [9.5.4].

The party has also been consistently critical of the PSOE's approach to the Basque problem [3.2.2.1], condemning that party for agreeing to negotiate with ETA and depicting Zapatero as naïve and foolish. Party leaders claim that the breakdown in the Basque peace process vindicates their scepticism, and advocate a hardline, law-and-order approach to the issue.

Although the party did not oppose the 2004 Domestic Violence Act [6.2] or the law on gender equality passed by the Cortes in March 2007 [6.2], its statements on government proposals have generally been characterized by their right-wing tenor. For example, it joined the Catholic Church in vociferously condemning the government's 2005 plan to introduce same-sex marriage and to grant homosexuals and lesbians the right to adopt children [6.3.1]. Indeed, over the course of the PSOE legislative period, the PP has appeared happy to be seen as increasingly aligned with the Church's views. For its part, in the run-up to the March 2008 election, the hierarchy encouraged the electorate not to vote for any political party that would be prepared to negotiate with terrorists, thereby implicitly giving its support to the PP.

Its record in opposition has been leaving an electoral mark. In 2005, regional elections took place in both the Basque Country and Galicia. In the former, the PP lost the second place it had won four years earlier to the Socialists, a result widely interpreted as an expression of support for the government's strategy of resolving the Basque conflict by negotiation [3.2.2.1]. The outcome in Galicia constituted an even greater setback, since the PP's losses there were sufficient to see it removed from power for the first time in 16 years [11.12]. Local election results in May 2007, however, were generally more positive for the party, which regained its position at the top of the country-wide poll. In Catalonia, though, the party's vote slipped by 20 per cent as Acebes, in his role as party manager, relegated those candidates identified with the more progressive figure of Josep Piqué, president of the Catalan PP, down the party's lists.

This clash was symptomatic of the divisions among senior party figures that have surfaced in recent years. The most prominent has been the rift between Esperanza Aguirre and Alberto Ruiz-Gallardón, the main contenders to succeed Rajoy as leader. It came to a head in the competition between the two for the position of PP leader in Madrid. Aguirre, a former government minister and currently First Minister of the Madrid region [11.13], is seen as a conservative. The more liberal Gallardón, Aguirre's predecessor as First Minister and mayor of the city of Madrid since 2003, is viewed with suspicion within the party and was criticized for his decision to conduct a gay marriage in 2006 [6.3.1]. His offer to put his name forward as second on the party's general election list for the Madrid region for the March 2008 election was refused by the party leader. In fact, Rajoy omitted him completely from the PP's list and made Manuel Pizarro, former head of the energy company Endesa [5.2.1], the second listed candidate. In the wake of this, Gallardón promptly announced he was considering retiring from politics.

The 2008 election constituted another defeat for the PP, despite the fact that the party increased its number of seats in Congress from 148 to 154. Still 15 behind the PSOE [2.3.4], it had failed to prepare the ground appropriately by building bridges with potential coalition partners, as it had failed to dispel the lingering doubts among the electorate with regard to its behaviour at the time of the 11-M massacre [9.5.4]. With a haste which may have indicated a note of desperation, Rajoy declared his intention to continue as party leader immediately after the result was announced, and secured his party executive's support for that stance. In the wake of the election, however, numerous PP members expressed their doubts about the policy direction the party had been pursuing.

2.5 United Left

Spain's third largest political force – in terms of members and votes, although not parliamentary seats – is United Left (*Izquierda Unida/IU*). IU is in fact an alliance involving both parties and individual members. By far its largest component, however, is the Spanish Communist Party (*Partido Comunista de España/PCE*). Indeed, it is fair to say that until recently IU was a mere vehicle for the PCE, its existence a reflection of the latter's failure to make a significant impact on Spanish politics in its own right.

2.5.1 IU's origins

That failure contrasts with expectations at the time of Franco's death. Both the PCE and outside observers believed that the party would emerge as a major political force – that was why its legalization by the Suárez government before the 1977 election was such a delicate moment in the transition [0.3.2]. The PCE had been the only force to undertake significant opposition activity throughout Spain and had close links to the Workers' Commissions, the strongest trade union federation [5.5.1.1]. Many younger educated Spaniards outside its traditional working-class base had been attracted by its activism.

However, these advantages proved illusory, for a variety of reasons. The emergence of so-called Euro-communism in the 1970s caused turmoil in Western Communist parties. At the very time of Spain's transition to democracy the PCE was hit by deep internal divisions. Furthermore, it had been portrayed for 40 years by regime propaganda as the incarnation of evil and chiefly to blame for the Civil War; even many on the left had bitter memories of its behaviour then. Alone of the major party leaders, the PCE's Santiago Carrillo was old enough to have participated in that conflict.

The desire felt by most Spaniards to bury the memory of the Civil War was a lesson read by many into the results of the 1977 election (see Table 2.1). Both then and in 1979 the PCE performed poorly. In 1982 it suffered a further catastrophic defeat; many former supporters, especially those who had seen the PCE essentially as a means of opposing Franco, now opted to cast a tactical vote (*voto útil*) for the Socialists in order to ensure a government of the left. After this debacle Carrillo resigned and was replaced as general secretary by the much younger Gerardo Iglesias, who continued in the post until 1989. But he proved unable to turn the party's fortunes around, at a time when the euphoria of the PSOE's arrival in power rendered a left-wing opposition seemingly superfluous. The party was racked by internal dissent, and suffered several splits [2.6].

The 1986 NATO referendum offered a fresh opportunity to the PCE, since it was the only major party to oppose the government outright, and was strongly represented on the Citizens' Platform (*Plataforma Ciudadana*) which coordinated the 'no' campaign. Although this campaign was ultimately unsuccessful [2.3.2], it did attract considerably more support than the PCE had proved able to do at elections. The party's leadership attempted to capitalize on this, by forming a broad grouping of those involved in the Platform to fight the general election held three months later.

The new alliance was christened United Left (*Izquierda Unida/IU*), and succeeded in marginally improving on the Communists' vote four years before. Later in 1986 IU was given a more formal structure. Originally seven parties formed part of it, but, other than the PCE, only one proved of any lasting importance: the Socialist Action Party (*Partido de Acción Socialista/Pasoc*), made up of PSOE dissidents.

During the late 1980s the collapse of Communist regimes in Eastern Europe made it difficult for IU to make electoral headway, given its domination by the PCE. On the other hand, it received a fresh impulse from the same direction in the shape of a new, more dynamic leader. This was Julio Anguita, the Mayor of Cordoba from 1979 to 1986, and known as the 'Red Caliph' because of his success in turning the city into a Communist electoral bastion. Elected PCE general secretary in 1988, the following year he took over as IU's 'general coordinator', or effective leader.

Along with the unpopularity of the government, Anguita's high standing among voters helped IU to double its share of the vote at the 1989 election. Given the Socialist government's abandonment of left-wing policies [2.3.2], this result was actually not particularly impressive. But with the government in ever deeper political trouble [2.3.2], IU's hopes were high in the early 1990s.

2.5.2 Isolation, division, decline

In fact, though, IU's breakthrough never came. Its disappointing showing at the 1993 election, when it made only an insignificant advance, was ascribed at the time to the heart attack suffered during the campaign by its leader, Julio Anguita [2.5.1]. However, Anguita's return to the helm after a rapid recovery revealed that his leadership was more problem than solution, owing to his extreme intransigence in three respects.

First, Anguita refused to allow dissolution of the PCE into IU, a step that would have allowed the latter to become a party in its own right with a simpler organizational structure. It would also have got rid of the Communist name, at a time when it was even less helpful than ever. Second, he was extremely critical of the direction of European integration [4.1.2], and the government's determination to keep Spain at the forefront of the process [4.2.2]. While his criticisms may well have been justified, they – and their harsh tone – were simply not in tune with public sentiment.

Finally, Anguita pursued an unrelentingly hard line against the PSOE, refusing absolutely to cooperate with the Socialists unless they radically changed their economic policies. He was especially loud in condemning the various corruption scandals which affected the Socialists in the 1990s [2.3.2]. In Andalusia IU went so far as to join with the conservative PP in forcing the Socialist regional government to resign. The move gave substance to damaging accusations from the PSOE, who claimed that IU was involved in a 'pincer movement' on the party, an unholy alliance of left and right that favoured only the latter.

Inside IU too many were unhappy with Anguita's strategy and aloof style. The main focus of dissent was a faction known as the Democratic New Left Party (*Partido Democrático de Nueva Izquierda/PDNI*), whose main leaders were Cristina Almeida, a combative and popular Madrid lawyer, and Diego López Garrido. These modernizers (*renovadores*) wished to see IU take a more flexible attitude to possible alliances with the PSOE, and to place more stress on new issues, such as feminist and environmentalist ones.

Ranged against the modernizers were those loyal to the Anguita leadership (*oficialistas*). Most of these belonged to the PCE, the only group within IU with a well-established organization. Moreover, like other Communist parties it was used to operating in a highly centralized manner. IU's own structure, by contrast, was weak and ill-defined, which not only presented problems at election times but also made it more difficult for the modernizers to bring about change.

Anguita might have won the internal battle but he had lost the external war, as became crystal clear at the 1996 general election. Despite securing the support of environmentalists in some areas [2.6], IU failed almost entirely to profit from the Socialists' defeat. In theory, the election results brought IU tantalizingly close to power, as they made a coalition government with the PSOE possible. But in practice the deep antagonism which had built up between the two parties – admittedly by no means all Anguita's fault [2.3.3] – ruled that option out. And to rub salt in the wound, at the Andalusian regional election held on the same day the PSOE was re-elected with an increased majority, while IU actually lost ground.

In 1997 IU's already parlous situation was worsened still further when Anguita made a futile attempt to assert his authority. Relations with IU's sections in several regions were severely disrupted, and its semi-independent Catalan organization, Initiative for Catalonia (*Iniciativa per Catalunya/IC*), was prompted to break away entirely. Anguita also expelled the PDNI, whose leadership subsequently opted to link up with the PSOE. Meanwhile the Communists who provided his sole remaining prop were further weakened by the progressive breakdown of their relationship with the trade union federation Workers' Commissions [5.5.1.2].

Finally, in 1999, Anguita stood down as PCE leader, to be replaced by his former deputy Francisco Frutos. In an astonishing reversal of his strategy, Frutos opted to fight the 2000 general election in a loose alliance with the PSOE [2.3.3]. The move cost IU much of its remaining credibility and half of its support; thanks to the vagaries of the electoral system [1.3.1] IU even lost its place as third largest parliamentary party, being overtaken by the Catalan CiU in terms of seats.

Later the same year IU held a special conference to elect a new 'coordinator'. In a very close vote Frutos was defeated by Gaspar Llamazares, a virtual political unknown, who thus became IU's first non-Communist leader. That change in itself removed a major handicap for IU, and Llamazares has enjoyed some success in rebuilding bridges to IC, the Workers' Commissions and some sections of PDNI. He has also attempted to strengthen IU's links with leftist regionalist parties, especially in Galicia, Aragon and Catalonia. In the Basque Country, in 2001, IU (there called *Ezker Batua-Berdeak*) joined mainstream, centre-right nationalists in a coalition government, which has continued in power since then.

In recent years, IU has opted to focus more strongly than hitherto on ecological concerns, cultivating an 'ecosocialist' image while maintaining a strong commitment to federalism and republicanism. Despite ongoing dissension in the party, Llamazares has managed to continue as leader, although his position has looked increasingly tenuous. Election results have not been favourable. Given that it operates on a Spain-wide basis, any small decline in its share of the vote means a significant loss of seats. With its vote slipping by half a percentage point in the 2004 general election (from 5.5 to 5 per cent), IU won just five seats in parliament (down from eight). This pattern was further accentuated in 2008, when its share of the vote slipped again, to 3.8 per cent, and it ended up with a mere two seats, one held by Llamazares himself, the other by the party's Catalan wing, ICV [3.2.1.1].

IU has lent its support to most of the policy positions adopted by the PSOE since 2004, although it did oppose the proposed European Constitution. When this was ratified by a large majority (77 per cent) in the 2005 referendum [4.2.3], it only served to confirm IU's distant third place in the Spanish party ranking.

2.6 Minor parties

The last thirty years have seen an extraordinary flowering of small parties in Spain. However, almost without exception, these operate at regional level [3.2.3]. Since the demise of the centrist CDS [2.2], no Spain-wide party other than the PSOE, PP and IU has come even close to being represented in Parliament.

The absence of a substantial environmentalist party even comparable to the UK Greens reflects the fact that – at least until recently – there has been a general lack of awareness about environmental issues in Spain [8.3.2]. As well as being weak the country's Greens have also been divided, with no less than five different groups contesting elections in the 1980s. Ecologist groups in some regions have stood jointly with United Left, an ally which has done little to help their cause [2.5.2]. Only in Catalonia, where Greens have taken part in a more wide-reaching realignment of the left [11.10], is their situation slightly more hopeful. At the 2008 general election various ecologist groupings again stood, the largest of them obtaining just 0.16 per cent of the votes.

That was still more than any party of the extreme right or left could manage, both of which have been perpetually divided into numerous tiny groupings (*grupúsculos*), many ephemeral. This has been particularly true on the left. Immediately following the legalization of parties in 1976 an enormous number of small revolutionary groups professing Trotskyist, Maoist and other revolutionary ideas sprang up. In total these received some 3 per cent of the votes cast at the 1979 general election. Subsequently they have all sunk into insignificance or disappeared altogether.

In the early years after Franco's death the far right enjoyed a modicum of success under the leadership of Blas Piñar, a devoted follower of Franco. In 1979 his National Union (*Unión Nacional/UN*) won one seat in Congress. Subsequently he was associated with the groupings New Force (*Fuerza Nueva*) and National Front (*Frente Nacional/FN*), the latter modelled on Jean Marie Le Pen's party of the same name in France. However, neither achieved any significant support and by the late 1980s they appeared to have effectively withdrawn from electoral politics, occasionally re-emerging under a variety of names, but to no serious effect in terms of share of the vote.

Two smaller parties which made a slight impact in the 1980s and 1990s were both maverick formations serving essentially as vehicles for the egos and interests of their leaders – who were also similar in being shady right-wing business figures. José María Ruiz Mateos had originally achieved a degree of dubious fame in 1983 for his involvement in a scandal that led to the expropriation of his Rumasa group of companies. The Grouping (*Agrupación*) he set up in 1989 won two seats at that year's European election, but that was its only success and Ruiz Mateos himself subsequently faded from the political scene altogether.

Jesús Gil y Gil's Independent Liberal Group (*Grupo Independiente Liberal/GIL*) never won seats in parliament or in Europe, although it enjoyed a fair degree of success in local elections, mainly in the late 1990s. Gil (who died in 2004) was the controversial mayor of Marbella for 11 years (1991–2002), a position he held with an absolute majority. He was also the charismatic president of the football club Atlético de Madrid from 1987 to 2003, with a reputation for high living and fiscal laxity. In 1999 he was imprisoned for misappropriation of public funds, after he had been convicted of diverting more than a quarter of a million euros from the accounts of the Town Council of Marbella into Atlético's accounts. This was just one of the scandals in which he was implicated; in total, he was involved in more than 80 cases, and was imprisoned three times.

The party's stronghold was in southern Andalusia, principally in parts of the provinces of Cádiz and Málaga. Its members dominated Marbella from 1991 to 2006, and many of them were implicated in the corruption scandals that emerged towards the end of that period. The scandals centred on both the misappropriation of funds and the wholesale flouting of planning regulations in an affair known as the Malaya Operation (*Operación Malaya*) which led to several councillors being accused of criminal activity and subsequently jailed [8.2.3]. One of the more notable figures involved was Julián Muñoz, who had succeeded Gil y Gil as mayor of Marbella and who, at the time of writing, is completing a jail sentence. The party has now disappeared and most of the politicians previously associated with it have joined the PP.

In the run-up to the general election of 2008, a new and very different kind of party emerged called Union, Progress and Democracy (*Unión, Progreso y Democracia*/UPyD). This was created by a group which had been set up in the Basque Country in 1999 to denounce ETA's terrorism, to express support for the victims of its violence and to oppose any notion of negotiation with it. UPyD's leaders include prominent figures such as the philosopher Fernando Savater and an ex-MEP and former leading PSOE figure, Rosa Díez, who managed to break through and get elected to parliament in 2008. The party claims to reject the traditional left-right view of politics and professes a new concept of Spanish citizenship based on a sceptical attitude towards regional nationalisms and the defence of democratic freedoms.

2.7 Glossary

28-O (m)	28 October 1982 (first PSOE general election victory)
afiliación (f)	membership
agrupación local (f)	local (party) branch
alternativa de poder (f)	alternative government
bases (fpl)	rank and file members
bienes inmuebles (mpl)	real estate (property donated to political parties)
bipartidismo (m)	two-party system
bipolarización (f)	polarization of Congress (between PSOE and PP)
cacique (m)	(corrupt) local party boss
cargo (m)	post, office; office-holder
caso (m)	affair, scandal
centro-centro (m)	pure (political) centre
chaqueteo (m)	party-hopping

coalición electoral (f)	electoral alliance
Comisión Ejecutiva (f)	National Executive (of party)
conflicto de humanidades (m)	dispute over proposed new history syllabus in 1997/98
Congreso Federal (m)	National Conference (of party)
cuota de afiliación (f)	membership fee
cúpula (f)	upper echelons (of party)
delfín (m)	heir apparent (to political post)
elecciones generales/legislativas (fpl)	general election
elecciones primarias (fpl)	primary election (to select party's candidate for PM)
electorado (m)	electorate, voters
felipismo (m)	personalized leadership style of Felipe González
fichaje (m)	signing; prominent personality incorporated onto party's slate of candidates
financiación (f)	funding
gobierno de coalición (m)	coalition government
gran derecha (f)	broad party of the right
grupo parlamentario (m)	parliamentary party
grupúsculo (m)	microparty
guerrista (m)	supporter of Alfonso Guerra in PSOE internal disputes
independiente (m)	non-party member brought onto party slate or appointed to political office
mayoría natural (f)	natural party of government
militante (mf)	(party) member, activist
Nuevas Generaciones (fpl)	New Generation (PP youth wing)
nuevo talante (m)	new approach to government (post-2004)
oficialista (mf)	supporter of party leadership in internal dispute (especially of J. Anguita within IU)
pacto antiterrorista (m)	antiterrorist pact
pacto de Estado (m)	formal agreement between government and opposition on major issues
pacto municipal (m)	mutual support pact in local government
participación electoral (f)	(election) turnout
partitocracia (f)	state dominated by parties
presidente (m)	chairman
presidente fundador (m)	founding chairman (of PP), honorary title given to Manuel Fraga
programa electoral (m)	election manifesto
renovación total (f)	complete overhaul (of a party, or other organization)
renovador (m)	modernizer (in PSOE or IU)
sopa de siglas (f)	'alphabet soup', myriad small parties which appeared after legalization in 1976

tasa de abstención (f)	abstention rate
techo electoral (m)	electoral ceiling, level of support that a party is unable to break through
transfuguismo (m)	practice of crossing the parliamentary floor, i.e. switching parties
unión nacional (f)	national union
voto útil (m)	tactical vote/voting

Regionalization and regionalism

Spain is a famously diverse land, partly because of topography and climate. Yet diversity is also the result of the country's belated and partial economic development which, in the late nineteenth century, led to political regionalism, in the form of demands for self-rule in the Basque Country and Catalonia. These soon became an important issue in Spanish politics, and Franco's brutal attempt to resolve it only increased its salience. This chapter begins by examining the very different response of the democratic regime installed after his death, and how the process of devolution that was put in place developed over time. It then looks at how this process interacted with feelings of regional identity in the various autonomous regions that emerged.

First, however, a point of terminology: throughout, the term 'region' is used in a purely geographical sense, to mean a part of Spain. It is in no sense contrasted with 'nation', which is understood to be a political and social concept. 'Regionalism' is used to describe political activity based on the notion that the people of a particular area have shared interests and a right to some form of self-rule. It includes some movements or parties that consider the inhabitants of their particular region to form a nation, and are therefore often termed – and term themselves – 'nationalist'.

3.1 Devolving power to the regions

Arguably the most sweeping of all the changes which Spain underwent following Franco's death was the rapid devolution of power to the country's regions. Within eight years the dictatorship's highly centralized power structures had been replaced by the regionalized form of state known as the *Estado de las Autonomías*. The change is widely regarded, inside and outside Spain, as perhaps the major achievement of the 1978 Constitution. That is a misleading view, however – and not only because it is by no means clear that devolution has been an unequivocal success. Quite simply, the Constitution's architects did not set out to establish a new form of state but to solve a specific political problem. And the form which emerged was as much a reflection of political manoeuvring as of the framework laid down by the Constitution.

3.1.1 Regions in the Constitution

It is no exaggeration to say that the single most important challenge facing the Constitution's framers was the pressure for self-rule in Catalonia and the Basque Country. A major issue in its own right, this pressure was also closely linked to the danger of military insurrection, since the army was highly sensitive about Spanish national unity and because the security forces were bearing the brunt of terrorism in the Basque Country [3.2.2.1]. The purpose of the Constitution's provisions for the regions was accordingly to strike a delicate balance between satisfying Basque and Catalan demands, on the one hand, and keeping the army pacified, on the other.

These provisions were contained in the lengthy Title VIII, and it is little wonder that they gave anything but a precise blueprint for nation-wide devolution. In fact they did none of the things that would normally be expected from such a blueprint. They did not define clearly the powers to be wielded by regional authorities; they did not specify how these were to be funded; they did not even establish a set of regional boundaries.

What the Constitution did do was to stipulate that regions might accede to a degree of limited self-rule if they chose to do so. Any province or group of provinces which could demonstrate the existence of popular demand for devolution would have the right to become an autonomous region (*Comunidad Autónoma*/CA). The mechanism for achieving such status was defined as a Statute of Autonomy. A region's Statute would serve as a sort of mini-constitution, establishing institutions of regional government (*gobierno autonómico*) and defining the policy fields in which they could exercise powers, either legislative or executive.

Title VIII also defined upper and lower limits to the extent of such powers. Article 148 listed subject areas in which powers would be assumed by any region becoming autonomous, while Article 149 defined those in which powers were to be reserved to the central government. Since the lists were far from exhaustive, this arrangement left open the possibility of regions acquiring powers in areas appearing on neither. There was also provision for central government to devolve its own powers to particular regions by decree.

Within this framework, two different procedures were established by which a region could become autonomous. The simpler, specified in Article 143, required only the approval of a sufficient proportion of the region's municipalities. However, regions going down this track would accede only to the powers set out in Article 148. Before taking on any others – up to the limit set by Article 149 – it would have to wait for five years. Moreover, it would then have to get parliamentary approval for amending its Statute of Autonomy, a potentially difficult process since Statutes have entrenched status [1.3.3]. Because of this time lapse, the procedure established in Article 143 is known, rather confusingly, as the slow route (*vía lenta*) to autonomy.

If a region wished to follow the fast route (*vía rápida*) to more extensive powers it was required to satisfy much more complex and demanding conditions. Set out in Article 151, these included holding a referendum, in which the proposed Statute must be approved not just in the region as a whole but also in each of its provinces. However, in three cases this requirement was waived by the Constitution's second Transitional Disposition [1.1.2].

That was devoted to regions which had previously 'approved by referendum a draft Statute of Autonomy', giving them the status of 'historic nationalities' – an invented term which avoided the use of either nation or region. Along with Galicia, this formula conveniently singled out Catalonia and the Basque Country. The particular complexity of the latter case was reflected in a further Transitional Disposition, the fourth, which explicitly allowed for Navarre's eventual incorporation into a Basque autonomous region.

3.1.2 Rolling out devolution

Thus, in constitutional terms, devolution could perfectly well have affected only the 'historic nationalities' [3.1.1], plus perhaps a few more regions with clear historical claims to be considered distinctive. Indeed, that may well have been the intention of those who framed the Constitution. If so their plans went dramatically awry; within five years devolution had extended to the whole of Spain.

Ironically, the reasons why the process went so far so fast were to a large extent of their own making. For, by singling out some regions for privileged treatment they laid the basis for feelings of resentment and discrimination elsewhere. And, by placing such complex obstacles in the way of other regions who wished to catch up, they not only aggravated such feelings but also ensured that resolving any resultant disputes would be a messy and conflictual process.

The political reality that devolution was essentially meant to pacify Basque and Catalan pressure was emphasized by the fact that it was under way even before the Constitution itself was approved. In the three 'historic nationalities', bodies were set up to prepare for forthcoming autonomy (*órganos preautonómicos*) – specifically, to negotiate with the central government over the details of their Statutes [3.1.1]. By the autumn of 1979 drafts including wide-ranging powers had been agreed in the crucial Basque and Catalan cases and, on 25 October of that year, both received overwhelming popular approval in their respective regions. In Galicia the process took rather longer, reflecting the lack of political and popular pressure there [11.12], but by the end of 1980 it too had achieved autonomy, albeit with significantly fewer powers.

By then, however, the focus of attention had moved elsewhere, to Andalusia. Politicians in Spain's largest region were acutely concerned that their region's grave economic backwardness [11.1] would be aggravated still further if it were left behind politically as well. They therefore took the initiative in drawing up proposals for an Andalusian Statute that went well beyond the basic level of autonomy specified in Article 143 of the Constitution. Having been agreed with representatives of the central authorities, on 28 February 1980 these were submitted to a referendum and obtained a clear majority in the region as a whole.

However, a narrow 'no' vote in one province (Almería) prevented the Statute from coming into force [3.1.1]. Whatever the Constitution might say, this result was politically intolerable. Recognizing as much, the government defied explicit constitutional restrictions and allowed a second referendum on a slightly revised text. Held on 20 October 1981, it resulted in a favourable majority in all eight Andalusian provinces.

These convoluted and highly publicized developments were largely responsible for triggering off so-called devolution fever (*fiebre autonómica*) in the rest of Spain. Even in regions where there was little sense of a distinct identity, and where self-rule had never previously been an issue, demands grew loud for a measure of autonomy – for coffee all round (*café para todos*) in the phrase of the day. They were viewed with alarm by the centrist government and the main opposition party, the Socialists. Especially after the 1981 attempted coup [0.3.3], both were concerned that the army might use Spain's alleged disintegration as an excuse for further interventions. In the summer of 1981 they therefore reached a pact on the regions (*pacto autonómico*) intended to keep devolution within bounds.

Specifically they agreed that they would block any attempts by other regions to follow Andalusia down the fast route to autonomy [3.1.1]. They also agreed on a

Devolution Standardization Act (*Ley Orgánica de Armonización del Proceso Autonómico/LOAPA*), bulldozed through Parliament with their joint support. The LOAPA laid down that, in the numerous policy areas where both the Madrid government and the regions enjoyed legislative powers, central laws would always take precedence. It also asserted Madrid's right to pass 'coordinating' laws to constrain regional legislation, even in fields where regions' Statutes had given them exclusive legislative powers.

The main effect of the LOAPA was, once again, far removed from what had been intended. In Catalonia and, especially, the Basque Country, it was widely seen as an attempt to snatch back much of what had only just been granted. Regionalists mounted ferocious campaigns against the Act that undoubtedly greatly strengthened them politically. They also challenged its provisions in the Constitutional Court [1.1.3]. To the government's considerable embarrassment, the Court found almost entirely in their favour and in 1983 all the LOAPA's key provisions were struck from the statute book.

The other main point of the 1981 pact proved largely irrelevant. No more regions made any real attempt to follow the fast route. On the other hand, devolution itself proved unstoppable; the question was no longer whether it would extend to the whole of Spain but how the country would be divided up. The main issues in that regard arose in and around the two Castiles, Old and New, and were resolved by giving autonomous status to the Castilian provinces of Madrid, Cantabria and the Rioja, while denying it to the historically separate region of Leon (*León*).

Overall, these decisions served to increase markedly the disparities between the new autonomous regions in terms of population and resources, and in doing so stored up certain problems for the future [3.1.6]. But in the short term they enabled much more speedy and complete devolution than had seemed likely in 1978. By the end of 1983 only the two North African enclaves of Ceuta and Melilla had still to have their status regulated; not until 1994 did they finally become 'autonomous cities' [11.18]. The remainder of the country – mainland Spain (*España peninsular*) and the two island groups (*archipiélagos*) of the Balearics and Canaries – had been divided into autonomous regions, 17 in total.

3.1.3 Regional institutions and powers

The maps which soon appeared showing Spain neatly divided into regions gave the impression that these constituted a homogeneous tier of government. Another Spanish neologism, *autonómico*, was coined to refer to it, once again to avoid hurting Basque and Catalan sensibilities. The impression of homogeneity was misleading, but it was reinforced by the remarkable similarity in the institutional structures of the new regions.

In effect, all of them adopted the model prescribed by the Constitution for those following the fast route to autonomy [3.1.1], itself largely a copy of that applying at national level. Thus, each of the regions has a High Court of Justice [9.1.3]. A regional First Minister (*presidente*) leads the regional government, the official designation of which often reflects historical or linguistic factors (see Chapter 11). It is made up of regional ministers (*consejeros*), who head the various departments (*consejerías*) into which the regional administration is divided.

Every region also has a single-chamber parliament elected for a four-year term, using electoral systems which, with minor differences, are copies of that used for general elections [1.3.1]. In the Balearics and Canaries each island elects its own regional MPs, while in Murcia special regional electoral divisions have been created. Otherwise the provinces serve as constituencies, the more rural ones being generally over-represented as for general elections. This effect is especially marked in the Basque autonomous community, whose three provinces are equally represented in the regional parliament (*parlamento autonómico*) despite their widely differing populations [11.5].

Another area of difference is in the timing of elections. The four regions which achieved more extensive autonomy following a regional referendum (Andalusia, the Basque Country, Catalonia and Galicia) [3.1.2] have their own electoral calendars, both because their initial polls were held on individual dates and because in all four the government has exercised its right to call an early election. In the remaining 13 regions, those which followed the slow route to autonomy [3.1.1], elections are held on a single day, coinciding with the nation-wide municipal elections. These polling days have acquired importance as indicators of the national political situation.

However, by far the most significant differences among the regions at the end of the initial devolution process lay in the extent of their powers (*competencias*) or, more precisely, of the fields in which they could legislate independently. In the case of the four fast-route regions these were wide, and in many fields virtually untrammelled once the central government's right to impose 'coordinating' legislation had been limited by the Constitutional Court [3.1.2]. The precise extent of these regions' autonomy varied according to provisions of their Statutes. All had education powers, for instance, whereas only the Basques, the Catalans and the Navarrese had the capacity to operate their own police forces [9.3.2].

The remaining regions' powers were limited to the fields specified in the Constitution's Article 148 [3.1.1], which excluded all major economic functions as well as education and policing. In other fields these regions had powers to legislate only if authorized to do so by the Spanish Parliament, and then only within the guidelines of framework laws passed by it [1.3.3]. Otherwise they were restricted to carrying out administrative tasks delegated by the central government.

Special arrangements were made for three regions where, for various reasons, there was significant pressure for extended powers [3.2.3]. In the cases of the Canary Islands and Valencia, the government made use of the constitutional provision to devolve legislative responsibility by decree in a number of fields excluded from the minimum list [3.1.1]. In Navarre, however, this solution was rejected by regional representatives. Instead they insisted that autonomy be treated as a reaffirmation of the historical rights (*fueros*) which Navarre, alone of all the new regions, had retained through even the Franco era [11.15]. In practice, though, the effect was identical, placing Navarre too among a group of seven regions all with slightly different powers in excess of the minimal level enjoyed by the remaining ten.

3.1.4 Funding

Crucial to any system of decentralized government are the arrangements for funding (*financiación*) of the various sub-state units. In the Spanish case this, too, is an area of differences between the various regions. Here, though, the reasons were less political than historical, and the outcome was that the Basque Country – along with Navarre – was placed on a separate footing from all the other regions, this time including Catalonia.

These 15 regions were covered by a common funding scheme (*régimen común*), the basis of which was set out in 1980 in the Autonomous Regions' Funding Act (*Ley Orgánica de Financiación de las Comunidades Autónomas*/LOFCA). Under this measure they received a block grant, dependent on the cost of carrying out the responsibilities transferred to them. They were also allowed to retain the revenues from certain relatively unimportant taxes, and from other sources such as fines, once authorized to do so by the central government. Within this common scheme certain regions had a lighter taxation regime because of their geographical distinctiveness. Thus, special arrangements applied to the Canary Islands [11.6] and to Ceuta and Melilla [11.18], where certain products, such as wine and tobacco, were allowed to be sold free of VAT.

In practice, this system meant that much depended on political negotiations. Officially they took place in a body established by the LOFCA, the Joint Fiscal Policy Council (*Consejo de Política Fiscal y Financiera de las Comunidades Autónomas*). This Council was made up of the central government Ministers of Finance and Public Administration, and the various regional finance ministers (*consejeros de hacienda*). Unofficially, deals were inevitably struck behind the scenes, between and within parties.

That gave a double advantage to the regions with the greatest autonomy – and therefore the largest block grants – which were almost by definition those with most political clout. Moreover, in a number of cases, specifically that of Catalonia, they were also already among the wealthiest. The system thus threatened to widen the already considerable economic disparities between regions [5.3.5].

This effect acquired particular significance once the Socialist Party (PSOE) came to dominate Spanish politics in the mid-1980s [2.3.2], since it relied heavily on support from the country's three poorest regions (Andalusia, Castile-La Mancha and Extremadura). In 1985 the PSOE introduced various reforms designed to reduce the system's imbalances. The most important was to activate an instrument provided for in the Constitution but previously unutilized: the Inter-regional Compensation Fund (*Fondo de Compensación Interterritorial*/FCI). Drawn from central resources, the FCI is distributed on the basis of regions' needs and so provides a mechanism, albeit relatively limited, for redressing the disparities between them.

Two regions, the Basque Country and Navarre, were not covered by these arrangements. Instead, they had their own funding system (*régimen foral*) which, like other special features of their autonomy, derived from their historical rights (*fueros*) [11.5]. Under it most taxes, in particular income and corporation tax, in the two regions were collected by the provincial authorities. These then paid a certain sum – a reverse block grant (*cupo* in the Basque case, or *aportación* for Navarre) – to the central government in respect of the services it provided. Along with the precise range of taxes covered, the amount of the reverse grant was laid down in a special financial agreement (*concierto económico* or *convenio económico*).

This system placed the two regions in a much stronger position than those covered by the common scheme. First, they negotiated directly with the central government and did not have to face up to the competing demands of other regions. Secondly, their tax collecting role meant that any delay in reaching a decision prejudiced not them but the central government, so that any pressure to reach a rapid agreement fell on Madrid. Given that the two regions are also among the country's more prosperous, their special treatment added weight to the argument that devolution aggravated regional differences.

During the 1990s, concern grew in Madrid around the question of regional funding, given in particular the differences between the two regions governed by special arrangements – the Basque Country and Navarre – and the remainder. In the view of central government, the regions were having their cake and eating it. On the one hand, they now enjoyed a high profile as providers of public infrastructure and services. On the other, under the block grant arrangements that applied to most of them, they reaped none of the opprobrium attached to collecting the corresponding taxes.

Nor was it merely a question of political profile. By the 1990s regional spending accounted for a major part of the total public budget, and failure to control it might threaten Spain's efforts to meet the criteria for European Monetary Union [4.2.2]. As a result the central authorities were increasingly anxious to introduce a measure of shared fiscal responsibility (*corresponsabilidad fiscal*), that is, to link regional budgets more directly to taxes.

At the same time, Catalan premier Jordi Pujol had been eyeing with increasing interest the alternative arrangements operated by the Basques and Navarrese. Aware that he could not realistically expect to achieve a situation where the Catalans too could collect most taxes in their region and negotiate their contribution to the state with the Madrid government, in 1992 Pujol began to push the idea of a mixed scheme. Under this, tax raising would remain a central government responsibility, but regions would have an automatic right to 15 per cent of income tax receipts within their territory. Implementation of this proposal was Pujol's main demand in return for supporting the minority Socialist government elected in 1993.

It was vociferously attacked by the opposition People's Party as a threat to Spain's essential unity. Yet, since Pujol's assumption that the system would greatly favour the richer regions – in particular Catalonia – was widely shared, the subsequent debate brought divisions not just along party lines but also along those of economic geography. The most vociferous opposition came from the Socialist Juan Carlos Rodríguez Ibarra, premier of Extremadura, but he was backed by the heads of government of other poor regions, irrespective of party allegiance. Conversely, their counterparts in better-off parts of Spain tended to support Pujol, as did the PSOE's own Catalan section.

When the scheme was finally introduced on a trial basis in 1994 it accordingly contained various provisions to cushion the effects on the poorer regions. Even so, three of them – conservative-run Castile-Leon and Galicia, along with Extremadura – refused to join it and remained covered by the old block grant arrangements. Galicia's refusal was particularly interesting. Evidently Galician First Minister Manuel Fraga's awareness of his region's economic weakness remained stronger than his enthusiasm for wider autonomy [3.2.3.2].

His party's narrow victory in the 1996 general election left it even more dependent than its Socialist predecessor on Pujol's party, Convergence and Union (*Convergencia i Unió/CiU*) [2.4.3]. To secure CiU's support the PP was forced to abandon its resistance to fiscal decentralization; indeed it made a further concession, increasing the proportion of income tax revenue retained by regions to 30 per cent. In 2001, agreement was reached on further changes, which also enjoyed the backing of Catalan and other regionalists. They were based on bringing regions' revenue more into line with the taxes actually collected there. Thus, as well as increasing to 33 per cent the proportion of income tax receipts they retained, the new system also allotted regions 35 per cent of VAT receipts from their territory and 40 per cent of those from certain other taxes, in particular that on hydrocarbons (mainly petrol). In addition, the powers they had been given in 1996 to set the rates of certain taxes (*capacidad normativa*) within strict limits were extended.

At the end of 2001 these changes were put in jeopardy. The government insisted that they be linked to its plans for a general levelling off of autonomy [3.1.6], and in particular that they would only apply to regions which accepted responsibility for health care. Yet eventually all agreed to this transfer, thus clearing the way for the new system. This new approach only applied to the fifteen regions covered by the common funding scheme. Navarre and, most importantly, the Basque Country continued to have their own separate arrangements, with all the potential for grievance that implies [3.1.4]. In 1996/97 the Basque government exploited the PP's need for its parliamentary support to renegotiate its agreement with the government on favourable terms.

The debate about regional funding has been ongoing, and was re-kindled with some vigour in the context of the drafting of the latest Statute of Autonomy for Catalonia [3.2.1.3]. Thus, in 2006, the PSOE government put forward new proposals for regional funding, which take effect from 2008. Under these terms, each region will have its own independent 'regional revenue service' (*agencia tributaria consorciada*) associated with it. This body will collect any taxes for which the region would normally be responsible, and will share responsibility with central government for the collection of any other taxes. In this system, each region is set to retain 50 per cent of income tax and VAT receipts and 58 per cent of special taxes (*impuestos especiales*). Furthermore, the amount of the investment by the state in each region will be proportionate to the contribution which the region makes to the national GDP.

The new arrangements also introduced the so-called 'ranking principle' (*principio de ordinalidad*). Based on this, the funding which regions receive from, for example, the Inter-Regional Compensation Fund cannot be such as to alter the rank order of per capita income, thus ensuring that the status quo is maintained in terms of regions' relative wealth. In response to this agreement, the opposition PP has advocated reforming the LOFCA, since it claims that the ranking principle goes against principles of equality and solidarity.

3.1.5 Ongoing regionalist issues

Barely had the initial devolution round been completed in 1983 than pressure began for autonomy to be extended, both from the Basque Country [3.2.2.2] and from some of the regions which had fared least well so far [3.2.3.2]. Understandably, the central authorities and Spanish politicians generally were reluctant to touch the much-lauded edifice so recently created. But they were also becoming aware that the *Estado de las Autonomías* had brought problems as well as solutions for them and the country as a whole. At the start of the 1990s they therefore embarked on a new round of changes.

The transfer of powers from central to regional governments (*transferencias*) was carried out in a context where most of the latter did not have to raise the taxes to pay their new employees [3.1.4]. The result was that they often showed a distinct lack of restraint in expanding their wage bills, allowing their own bureaucracy to continuously grow to huge proportions as they took on an increasing range of responsibilities, while central government itself showed little tendency to shrink correspondingly. The autonomous governments also displayed an inclination towards their own form of centralization, taking on functions already carried out by the municipalities and provinces [1.6]. The resultant overlap and duplication were aggravated still further in 1986 when Spain joined the EU, thereby adding yet another tier of administration. For all these reasons devolution pushed government spending sharply upwards. Undesirable in itself, this became especially problematic after 1992, as the government strove to fulfil the stringent criteria for European Monetary Union [4.2.2].

Another important issue for central government was the sheer complexity of a system involving eight distinct grades of autonomy – the minimal level in the ten slow route regions, and one each for the remaining seven [3.1.3]. As a result the latter, particularly the richer among them, were sometimes able to offer higher levels of service in particular fields. That not only increased resentment elsewhere. Coming in such key areas of state activity as health it raised questions about Spain's fundamental unity.

Moreover, in many areas responsibility was shared between the regional and central tiers, leading to severe problems of coordination. The government attempted to resolve them by setting up joint sectoral working groups (*conferencias sectoriales*), each dealing with a single subject area and bringing together representatives of all the regions and of the central government. Nevertheless, the costs in terms of administrators' time remained high. Similar problems resulted from the existence of two separate funding schemes, themselves including various exceptions and involving regular lengthy negotiations [3.1.4].

These difficulties highlighted another problem of the regionalized system. It lacked a formalized structure through which regions could have an input into the workings of the state – or, after 1986, into those of the EU. Of course, that may have suited Madrid well enough in one sense. But it also meant that there were no clearly defined mechanisms for resolving conflicts between the central government and the regions, or between different regions. And, as such conflicts showed no sign of vanishing, that implied not just administrative costs but also persistent political turmoil.

By the end of the 1980s the governing Socialist Party was seriously concerned about the administrative and other costs of devolution. It accordingly resolved to try and remove some of the inconsistencies of the existing system. To be politically feasible such a move would have to involve an increase in regional powers, and not just because of the pressure for this in Aragon and elsewhere [3.2.3.2]. Any move in the other direction would inevitably antagonize Basque and Catalan regionalists, and thus undermine devolution's original purpose [3.1.1].

In order to proceed with its plans, the government would have to amend some or all of the various regional Statutes of Autonomy [3.1.1]. That implied a hurdle, part constitutional, part political. For Statutes have the status of entrenched legislation [1.3.3], and so require to be approved by an overall parliamentary majority. And that, as well as political prudence given the delicate nature of the issue, meant that the PSOE would need the support of the conservative People's Party.

Happily for the government the PP, having shed much of its earlier suspicions about devolution [2.4.2], was anxious to counter the electoral threat of the right-wing groupings that had emerged in several regions under regionalist banners [3.2.3.1]. It was accordingly disposed to reach agreement, and in 1992 a second pact on the regions (*pacto autonómico*) was signed. Like the first [3.1.3], it involved only the two largest Spanish parties and excluded all the regional ones, even those from Catalonia and the Basque Country.

In the pact, the PSOE and PP agreed to hand over more powers to the ten regions which had received only minimum autonomy in the first round (all of which they governed, either alone or in coalition). This was achieved partly by the government's delegating powers as allowed by the Constitution [3.1.1], and partly by amendment of the relevant Statutes of Autonomy, which took place in 1994. The powers that were thus transferred to regional control concerned issues related to education (by far the most important), social services and a number of other areas. Deliberately excluded was the health service, responsibility for which most regions were reluctant to assume because of the complexity and cost.

The 1992 pact also covered steps to counterbalance this further loss of central government control. As well as extending the role of the various joint working groups, it hoped to set a definitive ceiling (*techo*) on devolved powers. But the hope proved illusory. Before the changes agreed by the main Spanish parties had even been implemented, regionalists in the 'historic nationalities' [3.1.1] began demanding further changes to restore the differential between their regions and the rest. During 1993 and early 1994 their governments issued a series of demands for powers in the grey areas which the Constitution did not explicitly reserve to the central government [3.1.1]. Although the Basques and Catalans were particularly vociferous, their claims acquired extra weight from the unexpected backing of Galician premier Manuel Fraga [3.2.3.2].

Moreover, with the Socialist government having lost its overall majority in 1993, the Basques and Catalans were in a strong position to force concessions. The price of their parliamentary support was apparent in Felipe González's investiture speech, where he spoke of giving new momentum to the process of devolution (*impulso autonómico*). His government began efforts to agree exactly which areas of responsibility could, under the Constitution, be devolved to regional control (*competencias transferibles*). In parallel, discussions were opened on the handover of specific powers, even in the previously taboo area of social security administration.

In the event little progress was made on this front over the next four years, during which the Basque and Catalan governments focused more on funding issues [3.1.4].

However, once the PP came to power in 1996, again with Basque and Catalan support [2.4.3], progress resumed. The next year the PP reached a third pact with the PSOE on transfer of a further tranche of powers, including control over active measures to fight unemployment, and the ten slow route Statutes were amended for a second time.

While the Basque and Catalan governments were happy enough to see their own powers extended, they were also worried by the further erosion of their privileged position. Relations deteriorated, especially with the Basques, who took the lead in asserting the 'sovereignty' of the 'historic nationalities' [3.2.2.3]. They also stepped up their demands for powers over social security benefits (*políticas pasivas de la Seguridad Social*), the uniform level of which is generally seen as one of the fundamental features of a modern state.

Not surprisingly, this twofold challenge to Spain's basic unity was utterly rejected by the PP government. Yet it remained anxious to resolve the devolution issue once and for all. Once re-elected with an overall majority [2.4.4] it therefore introduced plans to standardize the level of autonomy throughout the country. As a sop to the 'nationalities' the plan included a further extension of their competences.

But the main aspect was devolution of powers over health, the one remaining major area of difference between the fast and slow route regions [3.1.1]. Several of these latter, including conservative-controlled Cantabria and the Rioja, were unhappy about taking on the very high costs involved, especially as they felt the central government was deliberately underestimating the amounts concerned [7.2.2]. Eventually, however, the government used financial pressure to force them to concede, and in 2001 health finally joined the list of subjects for which all regions were responsible.

3.1.6 Towards federalism?

The reforms that have taken place over the last two decades have done much to reshape the *Estado de las Autonomías*, but did not resolve several fundamental problems. For one thing, the distribution of functions between regions and centre remained ill-defined, so that problems of overlap and duplication persisted. One proposal for dealing with these came from a rather surprising source: the veteran conservative politician Manuel Fraga.

Once installed as regional premier of Galicia [3.2.3.2], Fraga suggested the creation of a single administrative structure (*administración única*) along German lines. This would mean the regions carrying out all administrative tasks within their territories, irrespective of whether the tasks related to central or regional legislation. To some extent this idea was taken up in government by Fraga's party, the PP [1.5.2]. However, quite apart from the difficulty of implementing such a solution in practice, it was concerned only with administering the existing situation, not with redefining it. Nor did it provide any means of resolving disputes between the central and regional governments and among the latter, another current lack [3.1.1].

As part of its efforts to introduce greater standardization in 2001 [3.1.5], the PP government proposed legislation to regulate centre–region and inter-regional relations (*cooperación autonómica*), under which, for example, the various joint sectoral working groups [3.1.5] would be given an enhanced role.

Another issue which arose in relation to the powers of regions *vis-à-vis* central government was the question of regional representation at the level of the European Union. This is considered important because regions are affected by many EU decisions, and not least because of the regions' role in allocation and distribution of resources provided by the EU's Structural Funds [4.1.1]. The government had already attempted to meet regional demands by setting up a special joint working group on EU-related affairs (*Conferencia para los Asuntos Relacionados con la Comunidad Europea/CARCE*), and had also been forced to allow the regions to maintain official representative offices in Brussels [4.3.3]. By 2001 the debate had come to focus on the question of regional representation in Spain's delegations to the heart of Union decision-making, the Council of Ministers [4.1.3]. Although Prime Minister José María Aznar rejected this idea, it was implemented by his successor after the change of government in 2004 [4.3.3].

Aznar had also set his face firmly against any meaningful reform of the Upper House of Spain's Parliament, the Senate, defined by the Constitution as a 'chamber of territorial [by implication, regional] representation'. In theory it should provide an arena in which centre–region and inter-regional disputes can be settled [3.1.5]. In practice, however, the Senate's current method of election renders this impossible, since only a fifth of its members are regional representatives [1.3.1]. Changing this model is therefore regarded by most experts as an essential step towards improving the operation of Spain's system of government.

In 1993 a first attempt was made at reform, when the Socialist government reached agreement with the PP and CiU on setting up within the Senate a General Committee on the Regions (*Comisión General de las CC AA*). In addition, an annual debate was to be held in the House as a whole, devoted to the situation and further development of the *Estado de las Autonomías*, to be attended by the Spanish prime minister and his regional counterparts. A motion was even adopted that the Senate be converted into a genuinely regional chamber, possibly along the line of the German *Bundesrat*. The Basque PNV [3.2.2.2] bitterly opposed the proposed changes, since these would have been a step towards putting the Basque Country on the same footing as any other region, and their representative boycotted the annual debates. In the event only two of these ever took place, and overall the changes had no discernible effects.

The essential problem lay in the reluctance of both major parties to consider any amendment to the Constitution (*reforma constitucional*), for fear that such a move would open the door to other, more drastic changes. Particularly after winning an overall majority in 2000 the PP remained unbending on this point, and its plans of the following year contained only the most bland of proposals with regard to the Senate: provision for the Upper House to consider bills with regional implications, and for regional First Ministers to attend the Senate without voting powers. The timidity of his party's proposals was attacked by Manuel Fraga, one of the Constitution's architects [1.1.1], who publicly rejected the idea that amending it was unthinkable.

The main attacks, though, came from the PSOE, which had shifted its stance considerably. Having previously accepted the idea of federalism, it now posited the possibility of amending those parts of the Constitution relating specifically to the

Senate, to allow half of its members to be elected on a regional franchise. In addition the sectoral working groups, far from being strengthened, would be abolished; instead, central and regional governments would be given a statutory duty to cooperate, as in Germany, and the Senate would become the first port of call for regional matters. There would also be a further – supposedly final – extension of regional powers, designed to clarify the division between central and regional responsibilities once and for all.

The PSOE's proposals – which it has not pursued with any great urgency while in power subsequently – undoubtedly had a certain coherence lacking in the system that had been in place, but they also glossed over a number of questions. For one thing, genuine federalism would pose obvious practical problems. The problems faced by the smaller regions in taking on the same responsibilities as the larger and more powerful ones have already been apparent in the case of health. Indeed, the PSOE's Catalan section, the PSC [3.2.1.1], which largely determined the party's new line, talks openly of 'asymmetric' federalism – essentially a contradiction in terms. For no less than pure Catalan regionalists, not to mention their Basque counterparts, the PSC is not prepared to accept that all Spain's regions are equal.

As long as that idea receives strong support in two such important regions, the tensions and inequalities so apparent within the current regionalized system will almost certainly continue whatever name it is given. For some, especially on the Right, that is a major drawback, and even a danger. However, it is also possible to take a less gloomy view – and not merely because the *Estado de las Autonomías*, with all its faults, has on balance worked fairly well. Most observers would agree that even by the standards of other contemporary democracies, power within the Spanish state is concentrated [1.4.1] and political debate constrained. Against that background, the diversity and conflict generated by the country's territorial structure can be seen as welcome if not downright necessary.

3.2 Regionalist movements

The uneven outcome of the initial round of devolution, and the fact that it was to a large extent the result of overt political pressure, meant that it could only be the first stage in a continuing process. On the one hand, it posed considerable administrative problems. On the other, far from neutralizing regionalism as a political force, it gave rise to new regionalist pressures. Admittedly the immediate aim of containing the situation in the Basque Country and Catalonia was achieved. But in both areas demands for greater self-rule continued, and in some ways even became more radical. And at the same time, parties claiming to represent distinctive local interests sprang up in virtually every one of the newly created autonomous regions, in some cases gaining sufficient strength to become a force not just in regional but in Spanish politics.

(NB. This section concentrates on developments of significance at the Spanish level. For further information on those internal to a particular region, readers should refer to the appropriate section(s) of Chapter 11.)

3.2.1 Catalonia

Of the two regionalist movements to which devolution was in large measure a response, historically much the stronger was that in Catalonia. On the other hand,

Catalan regionalism (*catalanismo*) was also noted for its moderation and flexibility. The result was that, after the dictator's death, devolution of powers to the region took place in an atmosphere of consensus. Subsequently, however, the very fact of autonomy, combined with political developments across Spain as a whole, has led to significant changes in the nature of regionalism and in its relationship with the central authorities.

3.2.1.1 Catalan regionalism and the emergence of CiU

The notion that Catalonia's distinctive character should be reflected in some form of self-government has long been shared by much of the region's industrial elite and the broad mass of its population. Yet generally regionalists have wanted no more than extensive self-government within Spain, and were disposed to reach agreements with the Spanish authorities on this and other issues (*pactisme*). They were thus satisfied by the establishment of a devolved regional government (*Generalitat*) under the Second Republic [0.1].

That was subsequently abolished by Franco, as part of his efforts to stamp out regionalism [0.2]. While these backfired spectacularly and only succeeded in greatly reinforcing it, they did not alter its rational and peaceable nature. For regionalist opposition to his rule centred on cultural issues, and on building a broad consensus on the need for wide-ranging self-government once democracy was restored, both inside Catalonia and with opposition forces throughout Spain. These efforts were so successful that Catalan regionalism and its demands were closely integrated into the transition process of the late 1970s.

Thus the people who drafted the 1978 Constitution [1.1.1] included a regionalist, while Catalonia produced a massive 'yes' vote in the referendum on the final text. And the original Catalan Statute of Autonomy of 1979 was relatively easily agreed between the region's representatives and the central government, before it too was overwhelmingly approved by popular vote [3.1.1]. This was hardly surprising since, with the exception of the right-wing People's Alliance [2.4.1], whose presence in Catalonia was minimal, all significant political forces in the region backed devolution.

Support was particularly strong among the two main left-wing parties, both of which themselves enjoyed a considerable degree of autonomy from their Spanish counterparts. Indeed the Catalan Communist Party (*Partit Socialista Unificat de Catalunya/PSUC*) was formally independent of the Spanish PCE [2.5.1], although in practice the two cooperated closely. The PSUC had been a major force in the 1930s and ran a strong third in Catalonia at the first elections after Franco's death. From 1982, however, its fortunes declined dramatically. Eventually it split over the decision to dissolve itself into Initiative for Catalonia (IC), the autonomous Catalan wing of United Left [2.5.2]. When this group in turn merged with the Catalan Green Party (*Els Verds*) to form Green Initiative for Catalonia (*Iniciativa per Catalunya Verds/ICV*), its capacity to make a political impact improved. One ICV candidate succeeded in getting elected to the European Parliament in 2004, and since the 2003 regional election (*elecciones autonómicas*), the party has governed as one element of a three-party coalition in Catalonia. ICV also returned one deputy to the Congress after the 2008 general election.

The fortunes of the Catalan Socialist Party (*Partit dels Socialistes de Catalunya*/PSC) have been consistently good. The party has topped the poll in Catalonia at every general election since 1975; indeed, in the 2008 election, it was largely responsible for the increase in the overall Socialist majority in the Madrid parliament [2.3.4], with its tally of seats rising from 21 to 25. It also has a strong presence in local government, especially in the regional capital Barcelona.

The PSC's leading figure since the transition to democracy has been Pasqual Maragall. He was mayor of Barcelona from 1982 to 1997, later serving as President of the *Generalitat* between 2003 and 2006. Technically the PSC, which was set up as recently as 1978, is the Catalan regional section of the Spanish Socialist Party (PSOE). However, it was created largely outside the PSOE, which had virtually no roots in Catalonia before the Franco era. It also continues to enjoy a uniquely wide degree of autonomy within the PSOE, whose leadership it has frequently defied. In particular, the PSC has consistently advocated Spain's conversion into a fully-fledged federation.

In that respect the PSC's position, like that of the PSUC, is indistinguishable from that of traditional regionalists. Prior to the Franco era the largest such force was Catalan Republican Left (*Esquerra Republicana de Catalunya*/ERC), which dominated the region's politics during the 1930s. Both then and since 1975 ERC has occasionally voiced demands for outright independence, but has generally returned to backing devolution eventually. Over the last decade the party has experienced a resurgence, with its membership doubling during the period 2002–07 to about 10,000. ERC has been in government in the region since 2003 in a three-party left-wing coalition, the so-called 'Tripartite' (*Tripartito*/Catalan: *Tripartit*), with the PSC and ICV-EUiA. The party did well in the 2004 general election, winning eight seats in parliament, but both the dominance of the PSC in the region as well as persistent internal divisions in the party have since weakened its position, with the result that its share of the vote dropped dramatically in the most recent general election in 2008, when it won just three seats.

In the inaugural general election of 1977 the newly formed Convergence and Union (*Convergència i Unió*/CiU) emerged as the strongest regional political force in Catalonia. Even CiU came only fourth in the region, however, behind the parties that operated across Spain as a whole, these being the PSC, PSUC and the local section of the centrist UCD [2.2], a performance it repeated in 1979. It was therefore a major surprise when CiU, which fully backed devolution as the best option for Catalonia, topped the poll at the first regional election held in 1980. Although it fell well short of an overall majority, the degree of consensus prevailing in the region meant that it was able to form a government alone. Over the next few years, too, it could usually rely on broad cross-party support for its legislation, which was concerned mainly with organizing the new regional institutions and with promoting the regional economy.

Although Convergence and Union has been regularly outpolled at general elections by the PSC [3.2.1.1], it has won most seats at every single regional election since 1980, and from 1984 to 1995 held an overall majority in the regional parliament. From 1980 to 2003 it ran the regional government (*Generalitat*) alone, being ousted in 2003 by the Tripartite coalition.

The party began as an alliance of two separate parties. One, the Catalan Democratic Union (*Unió Democràtica de Catalunya/UDC*), was a Christian Democrat formation set up in the 1930s. The other partner was Catalan Democratic Convergence (*Convergència Democràtica de Catalunya/CDC*), a party set up only in 1976. CDC, which was and is much the more important component of CiU, originally defined itself as centrist, even centre-left, in socio-economic terms. Its founder, and the man who was to dominate both CiU and the Catalan political scene for almost three decades, was Jordi Pujol.

3.2.1.2 Pujolism

Pujol had been a leading figure in opposition to Franco, and his prestige was a major factor in CiU's initial success. He was to occupy the post of regional First Minister (*president de la Generalitat*) for no less than 23 years, from 1980 to 2003. His and his party's dominance of the new Catalan institutions had a profound effect on CiU as an organization. Like other governing parties in Spain it was able to exploit its powers of patronage and, on occasion, the opportunities for illicit financing [2.1.3] to consolidate its position. Like them, too, it tended to become highly centralized [2.1.2]. The party also strengthened its links with business, especially the powerful banking sector, and was even involved in setting up a new bank, *Banca Catalana*. Indeed, while never fully abandoning the rhetoric of social solidarity among Catalans, it has become increasingly aligned with business interests.

Above all, CiU's success allowed it to project itself as the champion of regional interests, especially *vis-à-vis* Madrid. In the 1980s the regional government repeatedly clashed with the central authorities over aspects of the devolution process, such as the speed at which powers were transferred or attempts by Madrid to constrain their use [3.1.2]. Catalonia accounted for more cases of this nature referred to the Constitutional Court than any other region at this time, even the Basque Country [3.2.2.2]. At the same time, CiU took to attacking Spanish parties operating in Catalonia, especially its main rival, the PSC, as mere 'subsidiaries' of their Madrid headquarters with no real loyalty to the region. This gross distortion of the PSC's position in particular [3.2.1.1] was a clear attempt to claim the sole right to speak for Catalonia as a whole, something quite new in Catalan regionalism.

Also foreign to traditional regionalism was the sense of hostility towards things Spanish. It went hand in hand with Pujol's tendency to hint at a desire for more than mere autonomy, most notoriously following the Baltic states' achievement of independence. The CiU leader was extremely active in promoting Catalan interests internationally, especially once Spain joined the European Community in 1986 [4.2.1], within which the region was economically well-placed to go it alone if necessary [5.3.5]. Linked to these implications that Catalonia was more a part of Europe than of Spain was a growing tendency to assert Catalonia's status as a nation and not a mere region.

For over two decades Pujol was CiU's major electoral asset and its unchallengeable leader. Not for nothing did CiU's new, more assertive brand of regionalism become known as Pujolism (*pujolisme*). But, rather like the *felipismo* associated with long-serving Spanish premier Felipe González [2.3.2], Pujolism was less a philosophy than a political style. In Pujol's case that meant a hard-headed concern to squeeze the maximum benefits for Catalonia from the Spanish state, often with little apparent regard for the effects on the rest of the country.

In 1993, the Socialist government in Madrid turned to CiU for support, but, rather than entering a formal coalition with the PSOE, Pujol only agreed to provide parliamentary support. The result was that, over the next seven years, Pujol was in a position to exert enormous pressure on successive Madrid administrations, while keeping to a minimum the constraints on his own freedom of manoeuvre. Thus he made sure that the Socialists never strayed from the tough economic line required to join European Monetary Union [4.1.3], a strategy strongly favoured by his own business backers but painful for many Socialist voters [5.1.3]. Yet he pursued policies at odds with those of the central government in several policy areas, notably health [7.2.2], a sort of de facto extension of Catalonia's already wide autonomy.

Meanwhile, however, the formal basis of the region's privileged position was coming under threat. For the second round of devolution, begun in the early 1990s [3.1.5], undermined the special status enjoyed by it along with the other 'historic nationalities' [3.1.1]. Pujol responded by demanding for Catalonia the exceptional funding arrangements enjoyed by the Basque Country and Navarre, which had proved to give those regions significant practical advantages [3.1.4]. There was no real ground for this claim, which was essentially a negotiating device and in the end Pujol settled for lesser changes [3.1.4] that were nonetheless seen as highly beneficial for his region. Despite this success, late in 1995 he abandoned his hitherto ally on the thinnest of excuses [2.3.2] and called an early regional election on even more spurious grounds. This allowed him to exploit the weakness of CiU's main rival, the Socialist PSC [3.2.1.1], before the conservative People's Party, a growing force in Catalonia, could profit from its inevitable general election victory.

When the PP duly won the Spanish poll held early the following year Pujol was able to exploit its lack of an overall majority to re-assume his powerbroker position with a different ally [2.4.3]. Part of the price was a further major concession on the question of regional finance [3.1.4]. The whole episode reinforced the popular impression of Pujol as the most powerful politician, not just in Catalonia but in Spain. But, during the PP's first term in office, cracks soon began to appear in his power edifice. For one thing, the financial settlement he imposed on the new government further aggravated the growing ill-feeling that his aggressive style of regionalism had already aroused in the rest of Spain. Secondly, within Catalonia itself, there was hostile reaction among the region's Spanish speakers to the steps which CiU had taken to downgrade the status of (Castilian) Spanish vis-à-vis Catalan. These feelings of resentment were particularly acute among middle-class, centre-right Spanish-speaking voters, for whom CiU competed directly with the Catalan section of PP. The latter party made significant gains at the 1995 regional election, although any risk that they might overtake CiU was mitigated for the moment by the PP's need for Pujol's support in Madrid.

Before long the new Prime Minister, José María Aznar, purged his party's Catalan leadership and imposed a new, much more moderate one. Moreover, he made clear that the PP now accepted autonomy as a fact, renouncing the Right's earlier pledge to revoke or at least curtail it. But, at the same time, he was also keen to tidy up the devolution process by standardizing the level of autonomy exercised by regions. And that ran directly counter to the thrust of Pujolism.

Pujol's response was not long delayed. Soon he began placing renewed emphasis on ensuring that Catalonia would have its own voice in the European Union. He reacted suspiciously to the attempt at administrative reform contained in the measure known as the LOFAGE [1.5.2]. He explicitly rejected any idea of converting Spain into a federation – precisely the solution traditionally advanced by Catalan regionalists! In 1998 he even put his name to a joint declaration with Basque and Galician regionalists [3.2.2.3] proclaiming the 'sovereignty' of the three 'historic nationalities' [3.1.1].

Subsequently, though, Pujol distanced himself somewhat from a type of rhetoric more usually associated with Basque nationalism in general, and ETA in particular [3.2.2.1]. He also went along with steps – admittedly minimal – to move the Spanish Senate in the direction of a federal upper house [3.1.6]. His radicalism had definite limits, it seemed, so long as he retained his strong influence in Madrid. That, however, came to an abrupt end with the PP's unexpectedly decisive victory at the 2000 general election [2.4.4].

Indeed, due to the results of the Catalan poll held the previous year the relationship between Pujol's CiU and the PP was now reversed. Admittedly the PP had itself lost ground in 1999, but it was also now Pujol's essential ally in a regional parliament where, for the first time, CiU faced a strong and coherent opposition. Indeed it was only able to form a government at all thanks to the electoral system's bias towards more rural areas [3.1.4]: in terms of votes it had been outpolled by a broad left-wing slate put together by the PSC.

Thereafter the sense of realignment in Catalan politics was heightened when the small regionalist party ERC [3.2.1.1] agreed that its representative in the Senate would join with those from the PSC in a new grouping to be known as Catalan Unity (*Entesa Catalá*). In the early 1980s ERC had sided with CiU on most issues. Its change of line now challenged the notion, central to Pujolism, that politics is essentially a struggle between Spaniards and Catalans. As if recognizing that an era had come to an end, in 2001 Pujol stepped down as regional First Minister, and, in 2003, as CiU leader, to be succeeded as party president by Artur Mas. Under the arrangements for Pujol's succession, CiU was turned into a party in its own right, its Secretary General being named as Josep Antoni Durán i Lleida, head of UDC, a man who previously had frequently displayed unhappiness at CiU's moves away from traditional regionalism.

3.2.1.3 Catalonia after Pujol

The outcome of the regional election of 2003 left neither CiU nor the PSC with enough votes to be able to form a government, but, after some negotiation, a coalition was formed consisting of the PSC, the ERC and ICV-EUiA. Known as the 'Tripartite' [3.2.1.1], it was led by the PSC's Pasqual Maragall, with Josep Lluís Carod-Rovira (ERC) as Deputy First Minister.

The first political crisis for the Tripartite government was brought about by Carod-Rovira when in January 2004 he held a secret meeting with ETA [3.2.2.1] in France. Maragall himself only discovered what had happened when news of the meeting broke in the national press. The issue intensified a month and a half later

Table 3.1 General and regional election results in Catalonia, 1977–2008

| | | General elections | | | | | | | | | |
		1977	1979	1982	1986	1989	1993	1996	2000	2004	2008
Convergence and Union (CiU)	P	17	16	22	32	33	32	30	29	21	21
Catalan Republican Left (ERC)	P	5	4	4	3	3	5	4	6	16	8
Catalan Socialists (PSC)[a]	P	28	29	45	41	36	35	39	34	40	45
Initiative for Catalonia (IC)[b]	P	18	17	5	4	7	7	8	4	6	5
People's Party (PP)[c]	P	26	23	16	16	15	18	18	23	16	16

when ETA declared a ceasefire exclusively for Catalonia. Despite claiming that he had not negotiated this ceasefire, Carod-Rovira resigned as Deputy First Minister. He was replaced in this role by another ERC man, Josep Bargalló, although Carod-Rovira ran as leader of the ERC in the 2004 general election, when ERC obtained a spectacularly favourable result (see Table 2.1). On being elected, however, he yielded his seat in the Spanish Congress to another ERC candidate.

Further embarrassment was caused to the Catalan government by Carod-Rovira's ungracious behaviour during an incident in May 2005 when he and Maragall travelled to Jerusalem to take part in a tribute to the assassinated Israeli ex-PM Yitzak Rabin. Due to some miscommunication between the parties involved, a mistake in protocol occurred when a Spanish national flag and not a Catalan one was displayed at the ceremony, although the tribute was being offered by a Catalan delegation. Carod-Rovira's reaction in appearing to take deep offence at the error was widely viewed as lacking in proportion and common sense.

On 30 September 2005 the Catalan Parliament approved the draft of a new Statute of Autonomy, which entailed several enhancements to the level of autonomy being granted to the region. At that stage, the draft Statute even included references to Catalonia as a 'nation', as well as provisions for financing the region that were similar to those that obtained in the Basque Country and Navarre. The latter would have meant that the regional authorities themselves would have collected all taxes due in Catalonia and would have arranged for payment of a proportion of these to Madrid.

When this draft was debated in the Spanish parliament, however, amendments were introduced which had the effect of removing these elements from the Statute. At that point, ERC – a party that had supported the draft Statute in the regional parliament – now expressed opposition to it, and urged the electorate to vote against it in the referendum which took place in Catalonia in June 2006. Ironically, that party then found itself joining the opposition People's Party in rejecting the text, albeit for diametrically opposed reasons, since the latter argued that too much power was being devolved. In the event, Catalan voters approved the new text by a large

Regional elections								
	1980	1984	1988	1992	1995	1999	2003	2006
P	28	47	46	46	41	38	31	32
S	43	72	69	70	60	56	46	48
P	9	4	4	8	10	12	16	14
S	14	5	6	11	13	12	23	21
P	22	30	30	28	25	38	31	27
S	33	41	42	40	34	52	42	37
P	19	6	8	7	10	3	7	10
S	25	6	9	7	11	3	9	12
P	13	8	9	7	15	10	12	11
S	18	11	9	7	17	12	15	14

Notes:
[a] In 1999 headed joint candidature including IC and Citizens for Change (CPC) [11.10].
[b] Prior to 1986, Catalan Communist Party (PSUC). Since 1996 allied with Catalan Greens (EV). In 1999 stood separately in Barcelona province only. Since 2003 allied also with Esquerra Unida i Alternativa (EUiA).
[c] Prior to 1989, People's Alliance (AP) plus other Spanish centre-right parties (UCD, CDS).
P = per cent poll; S = seats.

majority. Just under 50 per cent of the electorate participated in the referendum, however, a fact that reflects the controversial nature of the proposals contained within it and the strength of opposition to it.

The Statute which was eventually approved includes the stipulation that the regional government will collect 50 per cent of all VAT receipts and income taxes in Catalonia, that it will have responsibility for deciding on quotas for immigrants and for issuing permits to them and that the High Court of Catalonia will become the highest tier of the judicial system in the region. A further significant advance was the articulation in the Statute of the principle of 'bilaterality' (*bilateralidad*), which meant an explicit acceptance of the fact that any legal measures negotiated between the region and Madrid would entail the granting of rights and the imposition of obligations simultaneously on *both* parties.

Since the Statute was approved, the PP has continued to challenge its legality and has brought several aspects of its provisions to the Constitutional Court, despite the fact that some of these are similar in nature to provisions included in the revised Autonomy Statutes of Andalusia, Valencia, Aragon and the Balearic Islands – which the PP has not opposed.

The ERC's rejection of the Statute left the First Minister, Pasqual Maragall, with no option but to remove all ERC members of his government from office. This he did in May 2006, replacing them with members of his own party, a move which effectively brought the Tripartite coalition to an end. Maragall then called an early regional election for 1 November, where the PSC lost five seats but again ended up entering into a coalition with the same partners. Meanwhile, Maragall stepped down in late 2006 and was replaced as leader of the PSC and as First Minister by José Montilla, with the same ERC man, Carod-Rovira, in position as Deputy. Serious differences emerged however, between the PSC and ERC on the question of the level of autonomy or sovereignty that Catalonia ought to have, with the ERC calling for a referendum on 'self-determination' for Catalonia by 2014. When combined with the sharp drop in support for both the ERC and ICV [3.2.2.1] at the 2008 general election, the prospects for a continuation of the Tripartite coalition look bleak at the time of writing.

3.2.2 The Basque Country

Apart from the fact that it also emerged in Spain in the late nineteenth century, Basque regionalism has virtually nothing in common with its Catalan counterpart. By 1900 the Basque language (*euskera*) had disappeared from most of the region without giving rise to any significant literature; Spanish was the native language of most Basques, including early regionalists. The movement they created was long politically weak, with limited popular support and very little from the region's economic elite. Yet when Spain returned to democracy after the death of Franco 'the Basque problem' had become probably the country's most important. It has remained so ever since.

3.2.2.1 The ETA factor

The intractability of the 'Basque problem' is mainly due to the activities of the armed group known as ETA. The initials stand for *Euskadi ta Askatasuna*, or 'Basque Homeland and Liberty' in the Basque language. ETA was set up in 1959, to resist Franco's attempts to stamp out Basque culture and national consciousness, and was initially linked to the traditional vehicle of Basque regionalism, the PNV [3.2.2.2]. However, from the outset ETA differed from the PNV in three crucial respects: it espoused revolutionary left-wing ideas; it demanded nothing less than outright independence for the Basque Country; and it was prepared to use violence, to which it first turned in 1968.

ETA's active resistance to the dictatorship, at considerable cost to its own activists (*militantes*), brought it widespread popular sympathy by no means confined to the Basque Country. In particular, its assassination of Franco's designated successor [0.2] enjoyed much unspoken approval. Moreover, its success in establishing links with the region's well-established workers' movement gave regionalism there the broad base it had previously lacked. It is no exaggeration to say that the wide-ranging provisions of the Basque Statute of Autonomy, and the massive 'yes' vote it received at the referendum held in 1979 [3.1.1], were largely attributable to ETA's activities.

Equally, it was the group's reaction to devolution that effectively scuppered hopes of a quick solution to the 'Basque problem'. For ETA maintained that, despite the return of democracy and the granting of autonomy, essentially nothing had changed. In its eyes, the Basque Country continued to be occupied by a foreign power – the 'Spanish state', as ETA always refers to Spain – just as repressive as the Franco regime. And, instead of desisting from violence, it actually stepped up its 'armed struggle', the death toll from which rose to a peak in 1980 and declined only slowly thereafter.

The range of its victims also widened. Initially these had been confined almost entirely to the security forces. Then, during the transition period, representatives of Madrid-based political parties, as well as businessmen, became regular targets. Once the Basque Autonomous Community (*Comunidad Autónoma Vasca*/CAV) was set up, its employees, particularly officers of the regional police force or *Ertzaintza*, came into the firing-line. So too did those ETA activists who took advantage of the government's arrangements for early release [9.4]. Members of the public also died as ETA turned increasingly to random bombings.

As a result of these developments public sympathy for ETA's activities fell sharply, even in the Basque Country, where it was increasingly concentrated among the region's large pool of disaffected and disoriented young people. At the same time, however, the continued use against ETA of methods inappropriate in a democracy, such as arbitrary arrest, torture or harassment, were almost equally offensive to many people in its home region as terrorism itself. Above all, the 'dirty war' of the mid-1980s [9.5.2] was always believed by many in the Basque Country, by no means all of them extremists, to be government-orchestrated. For these reasons ETA continued to enjoy both a small but steady stream of recruits and a lingering basis of sympathy in Basque society.

At various times such sympathy was expressed in support for two political organizations. The older was Basque Left (*Euskadiko Ezkerra*/EE), created in 1977 under the auspices of ETA's then 'politico-military' branch, ETA-pm. It soon rejected violence, and in 1981 persuaded the *poli-milis* to do so too. Thereafter EE aspired to act as a bridge between nationalists and their opponents. And, although it had rejected the 1978 Constitution for failing to recognize Basques' right to self-determination, EE enthusiastically backed devolution and opposed any suggestion that it be widened in the short term. Indeed, it became an outspoken opponent of ETA, and was instrumental in the drawing up and approval of the 1988 Ajuria Enea Pact (*Pacto de Ajuria Enea*), a cross-party agreement designed to isolate the organization and its supporters.

By then, sympathy for ETA and its aims was expressed exclusively through another grouping. People's Unity (*Herri Batasuna*/HB), later renamed Unity (*Batasuna*) was set up in 1978 by ETA-m, the 'military' branch that was to persist with the 'armed struggle', and which since 1981 has been the sole ETA. Throughout, HB has acted as its political wing (*brazo político*), subservient to its wishes, with the purpose of justifying violence and generating conditions propitious to its continuation. Thus HB's supposed programme is set out in the so-called 'KAS alternative', which demands that the Spanish government should negotiate independence for the Basque Country – to include Navarre – directly with ETA. The point of these extreme demands, and others made periodically by HB, is precisely that no Spanish government could ever concede them.

In the 1978 constitutional referendum HB campaigned for a 'no' vote. Subsequently it asserted that the ambiguous outcome in the Basque Country [1.1.1] means that 'Basques rejected the Constitution'. It denounced devolution, not just as an inadequate response to Basque aspirations but as the product of an illegitimate regime. For long it boycotted both the Spanish and regional parliaments, refusing to take up the seats to which it was entitled.

It also ran numerous campaigns centred on the alleged denial of Basques' right to self-determination (*autodeterminación*), and the situation of imprisoned ETA activists, particularly the government's policy of holding them far from their homes (*dispersión de presos*). But in classic populist style HB exploited other issues as they arose. Examples were the proposals for a nuclear power station at Lemoniz and a motorway through the Leizarán valley, which were abandoned and amended respectively as a result of campaigns orchestrated by HB.

From its formation HB succeeded in attracting 15 per cent and more of the vote at elections in the Basque Country; it became particularly strong at local government level, where it has always taken up its seats. Unlike most regionalist parties it performed no better in regional than Spanish elections. And that was wholly logical, for from the mid-1980s at the latest its support had little to do with political issues; instead it was based largely on support for, and identification with, ETA's violence.

When HB's leaders were imprisoned in 1997 for distributing a video featuring ETA members, the organization re-named itself Alliance for the Basque People (*Euskal Herritarok/EH*). This name in turn was abandoned in 2001, and the name 'Unity' (*Batasuna*) was adopted, apparently in response to the fact that both EH and HB were under threat of being declared illegal organizations by the Spanish government, in the wake of the 9-11 terrorist attacks in the USA. Batasuna itself, however, declared its intention as being simply to bring together members of HB and some militants from another pro-independence sub-group from the French Basque Country, thereby creating a political party which would operate at the 'national' level, in the sense of covering all the territory which radical Basque nationalists (Basque: *abertzales*) would lay claim to, in both Spain and France. As this new grouping emerged, new splits occurred, as two further groups, Aralar and Basque Nationalist Action (*Acción Nacionalista Vasca/ANV*), broke away, the former due to its disapproval of ETA violence, the latter because its members wished to maintain their status as an autonomous political party.

3.2.2.2 The PNV; from crisis to renewal

Notwithstanding the electoral success of HB [3.2.2.1], Basque regionalism's largest political force was and is the Basque Nationalist Party (*Partido Nacionalista Vasco/PNV*). The PNV is one of Spain's oldest parties, having been founded in 1895 by Sabino Arana. Prior to the Franco era it was effectively regionalism's sole vehicle, and tended to regard its supporters as the only true Basques. The PNV's demands lacked a clear cultural basis, due to the early decline of the Basque language, and it failed to attract the backing of the region's industrial elite. But in much of the countryside its supporters formed a substantial and tight-knit 'nationalist community' focused on the PNV's local clubs (*batzokis*), giving the party a popular base unrivalled in Spain [2.1.1].

It was these deep roots in Basque society that enabled the PNV to survive the Franco era, although it took no great part in popular opposition to the regime. Thereafter, despite the intervention of ETA's political wing, HB [3.2.2.1], it emerged as the region's largest political force. As a result it had the largest representation in the body set up to prepare the ground for devolution there [3.1.1], and in effect negotiated directly with the central government the terms of Basque autonomy.

Above all because the PNV insisted that this should reflect traditional Basque rights (*fueros*) [1.1.1] this proved a tortuous process, during which the party was able to pose as the Basques' champion against the central government.

Once the PNV won the inaugural regional election held in February 1980 and formed the regional government it cultivated this role further. Repeatedly the PNV administration engaged in disputes with Madrid over the implementation of devolution in practice, many of which ended up in the Constitutional Court; the most serious was that over legislation designed to place limits on the devolution process [3.1.3]. Not only that, it also began to criticize as inadequate the extensive autonomy overwhelmingly approved at the 1979 referendum [3.1.1] – an arrangement it had itself negotiated.

This adversarial attitude gave spurious credibility to ETA's contention that Basques were locked in a continuing conflict with the 'Spanish state'. Even more dangerously, the PNV echoed HB's claims that the Constitution – which it had played no part in drafting and subsequently refused to endorse – had no validity in the Basque Country [3.2.2.1]. Moreover while never condoning violence, the party habitually linked it to the government's refusal to consider even greater self-government, thus appearing to justify it. And the PNV's contacts with both ETA and HB, whose parliamentary boycott alone allowed it to govern alone, were an open secret.

The PNV's ambivalence greatly aggravated the already high level of tension in the region. But, initially at least, it proved highly successful for the party. At the 1984 regional election it increased its vote still further, having extended its hold on local government the year before. Subsequently, though, signs of a backlash began to emerge. One cause was that, like parties elsewhere in Spain in similarly dominant positions, the PNV had indulged in various practices verging on corruption [2.1.3]. More importantly its links – real and perceived – with ETA were becoming a liability, especially once its own members and supporters in the regional institutions came under terrorist attack [3.2.2.1].

The PNV was also hit by disputes between its party apparatus and its representatives in the regional government, two groups which in the PNV – unlike other parties in Spain [2.1.2] – are kept strictly separate. The latter, who tended to favour a more flexible approach, were led by the regional First Minister (*lehendakari*) Carlos Garaikoetxea. In late 1984 he was forced to resign by hardline party boss Xabier Arzalluz, increasingly seen as a 'sovereignist' (*soberanista*), that is, as an advocate of independence. Two years later Garaikoetxea left the PNV and formed a new party, Basque Solidarity (*Eusko Alkartasuna/EA*). The split forced the PNV to call an early election, at which it suffered severe losses.

The election results added a hopelessly fragmented political system to the Basque Country's woes, which as well as violence included a grave economic crisis and severe social disruption. The negotiations to form a new government were long and tortuous. Eventually, however, the PNV agreed to form a coalition with the Socialists, previously its bitterest opponent [3.2.2.3]. The decision had profound effects. It effectively forced the PNV to distance itself from ETA/HB by joining the Ajuria Enea Pact [3.2.2.1]. Indeed, largely owing to his close identification with the agreement the new regional First Minister José Antonio Ardanza, originally a rather grey figure, became the region's most popular politician.

The coalition also made the PNV tone down its rhetoric, especially its demands for independence. Pressure came also from the Basque business community, to which the PNV had now become much closer, and which was keenly aware that entry to the EC had if anything increased the region's need for economic ties to Spain [5.3.5]. Happily for the party the vogue for a 'Europe of the Regions', given substance in 1991 by the EU's creation of a Committee of the Regions [4.1.3], allowed it to argue that inside the Union devolution was indistinguishable from independence.

Finally, the PNV began to show interest in using the powers devolution had provided [3.1.4]. During its first years in power it had introduced virtually no legislation other than to regulate the regional institutions themselves. Towards the end of the 1980s, however, it became much more active, especially on the economic front. In 1992 a new party programme talked of replacing 'nationalism of the heart' by a more pragmatic 'welfare nationalism', to be implemented by the regional authorities. In 1993 the PNV even showed an unaccustomed concern for Spanish politics when it agreed to help prop up a minority government in Madrid [2.3.2].

In parallel with these various changes in the PNV's attitudes went a strong recovery from the electoral disaster of 1986. By the mid-1990s, although unable to dispense with coalition partners, it was again clearly in command of the regional government. Of the other regionalist parties, its bitter critic EE had disappeared as a separate force [3.2.2.3] and EA was reduced to the status of permanent junior coalition partner. In this situation, the PNV's hardliners scented the opportunity of a 'nationalist front' with the other Basque force, ETA/HB.

3.2.2.3 The sovereignty issue

In the early 1990s, the more moderate course taken by the PNV [3.2.2.2] was one reason to believe that the 'Basque problem' might finally be on the verge of solution. The feeling was strengthened by a number of successful security force operations against ETA. One, carried out at Bidart, in the French Basque Country, in 1992 led to the arrest of its then leadership and the capture of much useful information on its activities. There were also signs of movement in ETA's political wing HB [3.2.2.1], which from 1990 attended not only the Basque but also the Spanish Parliament. Some leading figures even questioned HB's complete subjugation to ETA, and were expelled from its ranks as a result.

Meanwhile major changes were taking place in the region's second party, the Socialists, which had traditionally enjoyed strong support among the region's industrial workers. Many of these were either incomers or their descendants, and understandably suspicious of the PNV. In the early 1980s the PSOE had aggravated their fears by portraying devolution as a threat to a supposed immigrant 'community'. But thereafter a younger generation of Basque Socialists actively enthusiastic about autonomy took control of the party's regional section, the Basque Socialist Party (*Partido Socialista de Euskadi/PSE*). In 1993 the PSE absorbed the majority faction of Basque Left (EE) [3.2.2.1] and became known as the PSE-EE.

At the same time the conservative People's Party (PP) dropped its opposition to devolution in general and Basque autonomy in particular. The change was helped by the nature of the language issue in the region. Given that so many Basques, even nationalists, cannot speak Basque, there was no question of the aggressive 'normalization' undertaken in Catalonia [3.2.1.2] – and thus less to worry the PP's centralists.

Unfortunately, however, the 1990s also brought virtual proof that the 'dirty war' of the previous decade had been organized by the Madrid government [9.5.2], as well as revelations of continuing security force malpractice. Regionalists in general were resentful and, once again, ETA was given fresh life. In 1995 it launched a new campaign of killings. This time the victims were mainly individually chosen, and included several local representatives of the PP. Public revulsion was widespread; in 1997 the particularly callous killing of Miguel Ángel Blanco, a young councillor in Ermua, sparked off massive demonstrations inside and outside the region.

Another factor in generating renewed tensions was the central government's moves to standardize the level of autonomy across the country [3.1.5]. These were anathema to the PNV, which boycotted the minimal attempts made to reform the Senate along federal lines [3.1.6]. Relations with Madrid temporarily improved with the election of a minority PP government in 1996 which badly needed support [2.4.3]; the PNV used the opportunity to negotiate a favourable renewal of the Basque Country's special financial arrangements [3.1.4]. But with the PP determined to press ahead with standardization – and understandably bitter about its assassinated Basque colleagues – relations between the two parties soon deteriorated again.

It was against that background that the PNV proclaimed the doctrine that the three 'historic nationalities' [3.1.1] enjoy sovereignty (*soberanismo*). By that it meant that they have the right to decide their own futures, without reference to the rest of Spain. In 1998 this idea formed the basis of the 'Barcelona Declaration' issued jointly by the PNV, the Catalan CiU [3.2.2.1] and the Galician BNG [3.2.3.2]. But the joint approach was disingenuous at best. For, whereas there is no dispute as to the boundaries of Catalonia or Galicia, the PNV and other Basque regionalists claim as their 'sovereign' homeland not just the present autonomous region but also Navarre and the French Basque Country (the 'seven historic territories'). And only in the Basque case has the claim been backed up by violence.

There is no doubt that the PNV's moves followed contacts with ETA, under severe pressure at the time. Its renewed violence had cost the group any residual popular sympathy; at the 1996 general election HB's vote fell significantly for the first time ever. In 1997 the party's mouthpiece, the newspaper *Egin* [10.2], was raided by the police and closed down (a replacement, *Gara*, soon appeared), and its entire leadership jailed for inciting terrorism. The leaders were released two years later on the basis of a Supreme Court decision.

HB's new leadership, headed by Arnaldo Otegi, was disposed to seek new options. First, it founded a new front organization to be known as Alliance for the Basque People (*Euskal Herritarrok/EH*). Then, in September 1998, EH signed a joint declaration with the PNV and various smaller associations. Named after the Navarrese town where it was signed, the Pact of Lizarra (Spanish: *Estella*) asserted the 'sovereignty' of the Basque Country defined as the seven territories. Four days later ETA declared a ceasefire (*tregua*).

3.2.2.4 New millennium, same problem

The PNV's decision to join the Pact of Lizarra brought down the regional government, which the Socialists abandoned in protest. The outcome of the resultant election reflected the enormous optimism unleashed by the ceasefire [3.2.2.3], particularly among left-wing nationalists opposed to violence. Under the EH banner HB's vote rose to a new high, while the PNV held its own. It immediately formed a new coalition with its offshoot EA [3.2.2.2] under a new regional First Minister with a more hardline reputation, Juan José Ibarretxe. Crucially its majority depended on the agreed parliamentary support from EH/HB.

This tacit alliance was furiously denounced by the Spanish parties. The PP, which had overtaken the Socialists to become the PNV's main challenger in the region, took a particularly tough line. It made little attempt to open talks on a permanent end to violence, citing ETA's demand that they should also address political issues. In early 2000 ETA began killing again, with critical journalists now joining local Spanish politicians among its chief targets. At the same time HB withdrew its backing for the regional government, and refused to present candidates at the 2000 general election.

That poll brought the Basque PP further gains. Seeing their intransigent strategy vindicated, the conservatives stepped up their attacks on the PNV, accusing it more or less directly of backing terrorism and claiming that it no longer had a mandate to run the region. In December 2000 the PP attracted Socialist backing for its hard line, when the two parties signed an anti-terrorism pact which, among other things, debarred any agreements with the PNV so long as it held to the notion of sovereignty [3.2.2.3]. The two main Spanish parties now formed a 'constitutionalist' front, with the PSOE making clear that it would back a conservative-led Basque government should the PP win the regional election scheduled for May 2001.

The campaign for this poll reached depths of bitterness not seen since the 1980s, whipped up by fervid denunciations of the PNV in the Madrid-based media. In the event the PP, although it again increased its support, fell well short of victory. To ETA and its allies Basque voters delivered a more decisive defeat – EH's vote was 50 per cent down on 1998. The big winner was the PNV, whose support rose strongly. Yet its euphoria was tempered by the fact that the total backing for regionalist parties had reached an all-time low. The result thus had salutary lessons for all, and brought welcome moves back towards sanity.

Thus the 'constitutionalists' toned down their anti-PNV rhetoric, and accepted without question the party's right to form a new coalition with EA. It was subsequently joined in a very junior role by the Basque section of United Left, so that – at least symbolically – it now straddled the Basque–Spanish divide.

But relations between Madrid and the government of the Basque Country were put under strain by the announcement of a plan, devised by the *lehendakari* and known, after him, as the 'Ibarretxe Plan'. This was aimed at reforming the Basque Statute of Autonomy so as to stipulate that the Basque Country would become a territory 'associated to Spain' but with a right to self-determination. This proposal was conceived as a 'third way', as opposed to the 'constitutionalist' approach of the PP and PSE-EE, and the outright independence advocated by Batasuna and ETA. In practice, the *Plan Ibarretxe* was so close to a call for independence that the 'constitutionalist' parties were outraged by it from the very beginning. It was duly approved in the Basque Parliament, however, on 30 December 2004, with the support of the PNV, EA and the Basque version of United Left (*Ezker Batua Berdeak/EBB*). Rather surprisingly, given that the Plan stops short of a demand for independence, it was also supported by three of the seven representatives of SA (*Sozialista Abertzaleak*), the name under which Batasuna had re-emerged after it had been outlawed for its alleged support of ETA [2.1.1].

What was no surprise, of course, was its subsequent rejection in the Cortes in February 2005, when the Plan was defeated by 313 votes to 29. Despite this overwhelming parliamentary opposition, Ibarretxe continued to assert the Basque government's right to proceed with the Plan, and his intention to hold a referendum on it in the Basque Country in October 2008. Both the current PM, José Luis Rodríguez Zapatero, and José María Aznar before him, have indicated their clear disapproval of the *lehendakari*'s conduct and their view that such a referendum would be illegal and unconstitutional. Indeed, in November 2003, the Madrid government had pre-emptively passed a law explicitly threatening with imprisonment those who advocated the holding of elections or referenda not previously authorized by the Spanish parliament. This measure – viewed by the PSOE as draconian – was annulled by Zapatero's government in 2005.

In line with the banning of Batasuna under the terms of the 2002 Political Parties Act [2.1.1], further pressure was placed on ETA sympathizers by the country's legal system. Judicial procedures were undertaken against organizations and media outlets broadly supportive of the group's aims. This fight against the so-called 'ETA fellow-travellers' (*entorno de ETA*) led to the controversial closing down of another Basque-language newspaper, *Euskaldunon Egunkaria*, as had happened in 1997 with *Egin* [3.2.2.3], on suspicion of its having provided financial support to ETA [10.2].

Towards the end of the PP's second term of government, relations with Basque nationalists, even the moderate PNV, were badly strained, with the PP government taking a strongly 'law-and-order' approach to the Basque problem. In the wake of the arrival in 2004 of a new government team led by the more conciliatory Zapatero, however, the 2005 Basque election was a less bitter affair than the 2001 poll. The PNV and PP lost four seats each, while the Communist Party of the Basque Lands (*Euskal Herrialdeetako Alderdi Komunista/EHAK*), the new party representing Batasuna, gained two seats and the PSE-EE five. Aralar, the new splinter group which had broken away from Batasuna and is opposed to ETA violence [3.2.2.1], ran for the first time and won one seat.

The interpretation of these results is complicated. On the one hand, the PNV's losses could be viewed as signalling voters' rejection of the Ibarretxe Plan, which would explain the increase in votes for the Socialists, but not the losses suffered by the PP, who were also opposed to the Plan. On the other hand, the increase in seats for the more radical parties, EHAK and Aralar, could reflect an increase in the number of voters committed to independence. In effect what this meant was that the balance of power between nationalists and constitutionalists in the Basque Parliament remained pretty much the same as it had been.

ETA's activities have declined significantly in the last few years and their violent actions are down to a historical minimum. The group has been under constant

Table 3.2 General and regional election results in the Basque country, 1977–2008

		General elections									
		1977	1979	1982	1986	1989	1993	1996	2000	2004	2008
Basque Nationalist Party (PNV)[a]	P	29	28	32	28	23	24	25	30	34	27
Basque Left (EE)	P	6	8	8	9	9					
People's Unity (HB)[b]	P		15	15	18	17	15	12			
Basque Solidarity (EA)[c]	P					11	10	8	8	7	4.5
Alavese Unity (UA)	P										
Basque Socialists (PSE-EE)[d]	P	28	19	29	26	21	24	23	23	27	38
Basque United Left (IU-EB)[e]	P	5	5	2	1	3	6	9	5	8	4.5
People's Party (PP)[f]	P	20	20	13	16	13	15	18	28	19	19
Aralar	P									3	3

pressure, with numerous successful police operations, in France as well as in Spain. Many of its erstwhile leadership are either under arrest or in jail and the organization is led by a younger generation, veterans of the street violence (*kale borroka*) orchestrated by Batasuna's youth wing. With the 'dirty war' [9.5.2] finally fading from public memory, and with its actions producing ever greater revulsion among Spaniards generally, support for the organization declined precipitately. In February 2004, ETA declared a ceasefire applicable only in Catalonia [3.2.1.3], while the devastating 11-M Islamist bomb attacks the following month [9.5.4] so horrified the Spanish people that revulsion against terrorism intensified to a new level, further eroding support for ETA.

In June 2005, the organization announced that it would no longer target politicians, and, in March 2006, a 'permanent ceasefire' was declared. Three months later the government announced the beginning of peace talks (*proceso de paz*). Hopes of fruitful negotiations leading to peace were higher than ever. The PP voiced strong opposition to the talks, insisting that the government should not talk to terrorists, even though that party, when in government, had negotiated with ETA during a previous ceasefire. Opposition also came from a group calling itself the Association of Victims of Terrorism (*Asociación Víctimas del Terrorismo/AVT*) [9.5.4], who accused the PSOE of surrendering to terrorists.

However, on 30 December 2006, ETA planted a bomb in a van in the parking area of Terminal 4 in Barajas Airport in Madrid. They gave the usual telephone warning, but the bomb killed two Ecuadorian citizens who were sleeping in their cars. Rather cynically, ETA declared that the ceasefire was still in place, but the political gridlock caused by this incident was insurmountable and the ceasefire was called off in June

| | \multicolumn{8}{c}{Regional elections} |
	1980	1984	1986	1990	1994	1998	2001	2005
P	38	42	24	29	30	28	43	39
S	25	32	17	22	22	21	33	29
P	10	8	11	8				
S	6	6	9	6				
P	17	15	18	18	16	18	10	13
S	11	11	13	13	11	14	7	9
P			16	11	10	9		
S			13	9	8	6		
P				1	3	1		
S				3	5	2		
P	14	23	22	20	17	18	18	23
S	9	19	19	16	12	14	13	18
P	19	4	1	1	10	6	6	5
S	1	0	0	0	6	2	3	3
P	13	9	8	9	14	20	23	17
S	8	7	4	6	11	16	19	15
P								2
S								1

Notes:
[a] In 2001 headed joint candidature with EA.
[b] Did not stand in 2000. In 1998 and 2001 stood under the initials EH [3.2.2.3]. In 2001, name changed to Unity [3.2.2.4]. In 2005, name changed to EHAK.
[c] In 2001, 2004 and 2005 stood jointly with PNV.
[d] Prior to 1993, PSE-PSOE.
[e] Prior to 1986, Basque Communists (EPK).
[f] Prior to 1989, People's Alliance (AP) plus other Spanish centre-right parties (UCD, CDS).
P = per cent poll; S = seats.

2007. Two days later, Arnaldo Otegi, the leader of Batasuna, was convicted of supporting terrorism and given a 15-month jail sentence. In the months that followed, ETA continued to plant bombs and issue threats. These attacks did not have fatal consequences until, in December 2007, ETA members shot dead two Spanish civil guards operating in southern France, followed, in March 2008, by the assassination of a former Socialist councillor in Guipúzcoa. At the time of writing, the prospects of re-starting the peace process seem to be diminishing steadily.

Meanwhile, tensions emerged again within the PNV in 2007 when the more moderate Josu Jon Imaz, who had taken over the leadership of the party from the sovereignist Xabier Arzalluz three years earlier, resigned due to disagreements with the more hardline Ibarretxe. Batasuna in turn has continued to suffer from the attentions of the examining magistrate Baltasar Garzón [9.1.4] who arrested twenty of the party's leaders in October 2007 when they were in the process of holding a meeting and thereby allegedly breaking the ban debarring them from political activity. Garzón was also instrumental in securing a ban on ANV and EHAK [9.1.4] in February 2008, which precluded them from fielding candidates in the March 2008 general election.

3.2.3 Other regionalist movements

When Spain returned to democracy, only in the Basque Country and Catalonia were Spaniards' undoubted feelings of association with a particular area expressed politically to any significant degree. At the time conservatives feared that the prospect of devolution would unleash their latent force, causing the country to fragment into numerous small units (*cantonalismo*) [0.1]. Their concerns proved utterly unjustified. But the following decades did see the appearance, virtually across Spain, of new regionalist movements (*regionalismos*) whose emergence was indeed closely linked to the devolution process.

3.2.3.1 Andalusia, Valencia, Navarre and the Canaries

The process began in historic regions with a distinct sense of identity. Yet such feelings were not in themselves enough; witness the distinctly muted reaction to the disappearance of Leon, one of Spain's most venerable units [11.9]. What Leon lacked was any distinct political tradition, something present in all the regions where new movements first appeared. These also had another factor in common. They were triggered off by the advantage given to the three 'historic nationalities' under the Constitution's complex provisions for devolution [3.1.1], and their subsequent fortunes were often heavily conditioned by developments outside the region concerned.

The point is well illustrated by the region where devolution ceased to be a constitutional issue and became a political one: Andalusia [3.1.2]. Beyond doubt it can lay claim to a distinctive character (*hecho diferencial*). It also has a tradition, albeit a weak one, of regionalist activity, and during the campaign to obtain more extensive autonomy for the region a regionalist party emerged, the Andalusian Socialist Party (*Partido Socialista de Andalucía/PSA*, later re-named *Partido Andalucista/PA*). Yet the very success of the campaign meant that by 1981 Andalusia had achieved its aims in that respect.

Thereafter, as a poor region, its interests tended to lie in holding the devolution process as a whole in check, while attempting to extract the maximum of central government support. For much of the last twenty-five years, that role has been effectively monopolized by the PSOE's local section, which controlled the regional government on its own from its creation until 2000, in coalition with PA from 2000 to 2008, and again on its own from 2008 onwards. It also exercises huge clout within its own party, heavily dependent on Andalusian votes as it now is [2.3.4].

Thus the PA is no longer represented in its regional parliament [11.1], a situation it shares with its Valencian counterpart, Valencian Union (*Unió Valenciana/UV*). Yet during the 1980s UV enjoyed considerable support and influence. For a while it even became an essential coalition partner in the government of a region which also had a low-key regionalist tradition of its own, and which had to wait longer than Andalusia to have its autonomy upgraded to the point where it was deemed to be a 'nationality'. The region's status was a particularly thorny issue in Valencia, where some conservatives purported to believe that it was threatened with incorporation into a Greater Catalonia (*Països Catalans*). This idea, essentially a cover for reactionary Spanish nationalism, underlay UV's rise, which also coincided with a time of chronic weakness for the mainstream Spanish Right [2.4.1]. With the success of the PP in the 1990s – and in the complete absence of any signs of Catalan expansionism – UV's support evaporated.

To some extent a similar phenomenon was observable in Navarre, which, despite having special funding arrangements [3.1.4] and despite being one of only three regions with their own police forces, was also briefly in danger of being left behind in the first devolution round. There, too, there were fears of possible annexation by one of the 'historic nationalities', in its case the Basque Country, while the Spanish Right's weakness left conservative voters feeling unprotected. And in Navarre, too, the result was the emergence of a new party, the Navarrese People's Union (*Unión del Pueblo Navarro/UPN*), which also entered the regional government.

There the similarities end, however, for UPN not only became Navarre's largest party, it remains so today. It also continues to provide the regional First Minister and has forced the PP to give it a free run in regional elections, in return for its support at general ones. The reasons for its continuing strength lie both outside and inside the region. Unlike their Catalan counterparts, Basque regionalists – some of them violent – explicitly claim Navarre as part of their homeland, so that the threat of incorporation cannot be dismissed.

Thus, moderate Basque nationalists have been consistently out-voted in Navarre by their more radical counterparts. The PNV [3.2.2.2] has never managed to hold more than three seats in the regional parliament, and when EA split from that party in 1986 [3.2.2.4], the new formation secured all its seats. Herri Batasuna/Batasuna has also been represented there since that parliament's inception in 1979, holding between five and nine seats. Since 2004, moderate and radical Basque nationalists have worked together within the Coalition for Navarre (*Nafarroa Bai/NaBai*), now constituted by Aralar, EA and PNV [3.2.2.4]. NaBai came close to entering the regional government in coalition with the PSOE after the 2007 regional election [11.15].

The final region to receive special treatment in the first devolution round was the Canary Islands [3.1.2]. The Canaries had produced a number of small regionalist groups in the 1970s. However, not until 1986 did these come together to form a single coherent force, Canary Islands Alliance (*Coalición Canaria/CC*). Its creation was prompted by Spain's accession to the EU, which potentially placed the Canaries as a whole in a position of dangerous isolation.

Subsequently CC established itself as the Islands' strongest political force, at least until the regional elections of 2007, when the PSOE won the highest number of seats in the region. To prevent the Socialists from forming a government, the PP entered a coalition with CC, as well as the latter's ally, the Canarian Nationalist Party (*Partido Nacionalista Canario/PNC*), with whom they had a pre-election pact.

A new draft Statute of Autonomy for the Canary Islands was approved by the regional government in September 2006 and, at the time of writing, is awaiting approval from Madrid.

3.2.3.2 Aragon, Galicia, other regions

By the end of the 1980s regionalist parties had been formed in virtually every region, and were represented in the parliaments of most. Their emergence was one reason for the start of a second devolution round in the 1990s [3.1.5], the course of which has in turn conditioned their own development along with other factors, both regional and national.

One reason why autonomy actually stimulated regionalism was that the new regions provided a fresh, and powerful, focus of identity and action. At the most basic level, every region now had its own flag, ubiquitously and prominently displayed. Interest groups of all types began to organize on a regional basis. Regional politics, above all regional election campaigns, tended to suggest that a region's people had common interests, perhaps even a common character, implicitly distinct from those of other parts of Spain. Typically this was expressed in terms of some disadvantage allegedly suffered by a region. And, crucially, the uneven result of the first devolution round [3.1.2] meant that most regions had cause to feel a sense of discrimination specifically in terms of autonomy.

Such feelings surfaced most dramatically in Aragon. This region, which has an undoubted sense of identity, had remained quiescent during the first devolution round, perhaps because its only distinctive political tradition, anarchism, provided no basis for action in Spain's new democracy. However, its relegation to the group of slow route regions [3.1.1] provoked a dramatic upsurge of popular opinion which included the formation of the Aragonese Regionalist Party (*Partido Aragonés/PAR*). Like Valencia's UV and Navarre's UPN a basically conservative grouping, the PAR profited from the weakness of the Spanish Right [2.4.1], heading the regional government for a number of years before the rise of the PP in the 1990s. In contrast to UV, it remained an important player in regional politics; since 2003, the PAR has participated in a coalition government in Aragon along with the strongest political force in the region, the PSOE.

Perhaps the most successful new regionalist party of recent decades, however, was the Galician National Alliance (*Bloque Nacionalista Galego/BNG*). As an avowedly leftist formation the BNG has only loose connections with traditional Galician regionalism, which was mostly conservative and generally weak. Culturally distinctive but socially and economically backward, Galicia long remained the fief of corrupt party bosses controlled by their Madrid masters [2.1.1]. Its privileged treatment in the constitutional provisions for devolution bore no relation to demands from the region itself, but was a by-product of the overriding need to satisfy Basque and Catalan feeling [3.1.1]. In the 1981 referendum on its Statute of Autonomy a mere 30 per cent of the electorate bothered to vote.

Nonetheless, the Statute was approved and Galicia acceded to the extensive autonomy to which it was entitled as a 'historic nationality' (*nacionalidad histórica*) [3.1.1]. The fact that in the 1990s successive central governments seemed intent on undermining this special status may have been one reason for the belated emergence of Galician regionalism. Certainly the BNG enthusiastically joined a Basque initiative to protest against these developments [3.2.2.3]. But probably rather more important was another, very different factor; the attempts by the region's own government to revive and foster Galician culture.

Ironically these were the work of Manuel Fraga [2.4.1], who in 1989 returned to lead the PP in his native region and subsequently won four successive regional election victories, each time with an overall majority. In the course of his subsequent career in regional politics, this former arch-centralist displayed an unexpected enthusiasm for Galician distinctiveness and for the idea of devolution in general [3.1.6]. At times, he even showed open sympathy with the aspirations of Catalan regionalists and pursued a policy of language 'normalization' along roughly Catalan lines, provoking some of the same tensions [3.2.1.2].

In the 2005 regional elections, the PP again won the highest number of seats of any single party in Galicia. This came as a surprise to many observers since there was widespread dissatisfaction with how the PP governments in Galicia and Madrid had handled the *Prestige* disaster in 2002 [8.1.2]. Nonetheless, it was the Galician Socialists (*Partido Socialista de Galicia/PSdeG*) who formed the regional government in the wake of those elections, in coalition with the BNG.

Many regional sections of the main country-wide parties now typically seek to portray themselves as defenders of local interests; in a sense, all parties are regionalists now. That may be one reason why the growth of specifically regionalist groupings seems to have slowed down recently, and in some cases been reversed.

Another is the fact that some such parties have been essentially vehicles for the personal ambitions of individual local politicians; such is the case of URAS in Asturias and, to some extent, the Basque Country's EA [3.2.2.2], as well as the now defunct Galician Alliance (*Coalición Galega/CG*) and Cantabrian UPCA. In addition, insofar as devolution has become more standardized, some of the grounds for regional grievance have been removed – at least outside the 'historic nationalities'. But in several regions and for various reasons new regionalist parties appear so well established as to remain part of the political scene for the foreseeable future.

3.3 Glossary

Acción Nacionalista Vasca (f)	Basque Nationalist Action
abertzale (mf)	(militant) supporter of Basque regionalism; Basque nationalist
administración única (f)	(system of) single administrative structure
Agencia Tributaria Consorciada (f)	regional revenue service
Ajuria Enea	residence of Basque PM
aportación (f)	reverse block grant (paid by Navarre to central government)
Asociación Víctimas del Terrorismo (f)	Association of Victims of Terrorism
autodeterminación (f)	self-determination
autonomía (f)	autonomy; autonomous region
autonómico (adj)	relating to the regionalized Spanish state, or to the regions themselves
batzoki (m)	PNV local branch premises
brazo político (m)	political wing
cantonalismo (m)	cantonalism, demands for local self-rule
capacidad normativa (f)	power to legislate (especially to set tax rates)
catalanismo (m)	Catalan regionalism
competencias (fpl)	powers, responsibilities (of government)
competencias transferibles (fpl)	areas of responsibility susceptible to being handed over to the regions under the 1978 Constitution

Comunidad Autónoma (f)	autonomous region
concierto económico (m)	financial agreement (between Basque Provinces and central government)
conferencias sectoriales (fpl)	joint sectoral working groups
consejería (f)	regional ministry
consejero (m)	regional minister
consejeros de hacienda (mpl)	finance ministers (of the regions)
constitucionalista (m)	(in Basque Country) opponent of *soberanismo*
convenio económico (m)	financial agreement (between Navarre and central government)
cooperación autonómica (f)	centre–region and inter-regional cooperation
corresponsabilidad fiscal (f)	shared fiscal responsibility
cupo (m)	reverse block grant (paid by Basque Provinces to central government)
dispersión de presos (f)	policy of holding ETA prisoners in jails which are a long distance from their homes
elecciones autonómicas (fpl)	regional election(s)
entorno de ETA (m)	ETA fellow-travellers (groups associated with ETA and allegedly providing it with financial support)
Ertzaintza (f)	Basque police force
España peninsular (f)	mainland Spain
Estado de las Autonomías (m)	present regionalized form of Spanish state
Estatuto de Autonomía (m)	Statute of Autonomy
Euskadi (m)	Basque homeland; Basque Country
euskera (m)	Basque language
fiebre autonómica (f)	'devolution fever', outbreak of demands for devolution in 1980–82
financiación autonómica (f)	regional funding
Fondo de Compensación Interterritorial (m)	Inter-regional Compensation Fund
fueros (mpl)	historic rights (esp. of Basque Provinces and Navarre)
Generalitat (f)	Catalan regional government/Valencian regional government
hecho diferencial (m)	distinctive character (of an autonomous region)
gobierno autonómico (m)	regional government
Junta (f)	name of government of various regions, esp. Andalusia
kale borroka	street violence (in the Basque Country)
lehendakari (m)	Basque First Minister
militantes (mpl)	activists
nacionalidad histórica (f)	'historic nationality', region granted autonomy under Second Republic
órganos preautonómicos (mpl)	bodies set up specifically to prepare for devolution
pactisme (Cat.) (m)	(Catalan) traditional readiness to reach negotiated agreements
pacto autonómico (m)	pact on the regions (1981; 1992)
Pacto de Ajuria Enea (m)	Ajuria Enea Pact
Països Catalans (Cat.) (mpl)	Greater Catalonia (incl. Valencia and Balearics)
parlamento autonómico (m)	regional parliament
políticas pasivas de la SS (fpl)	social security benefits
presidente autonómico (m)	regional First Minister
principio de ordinalidad (m)	(regional) ranking principle

proceso autonómico (m)	(process of) devolution
proceso de paz (m)	peace process
pujolisme (Cat.)/*pujolismo (m)*	contemporary Catalan regionalism, associated with Jordi Pujol
reforma constitucional (f)	constitutional amendment
régimen común (m)	funding scheme applicable to most regions
régimen foral (m)	traditional system (esp. of funding) applicable to Basque Provinces and Navarre
regionalismo (m)	regionalism; regionalist movement
soberanismo (m)	doctrine that a region (especially the Basque Country) has the untrammelled right to decide its own future
soberanista (mf)	(especially Basque) politician committed to *soberanismo*
techo (m)	ceiling, upper limit (on devolved powers)
transferencias (fpl)	handover of powers to regional governments
tregua (f)	ceasefire
Tripartito/Tripartit (m)	three-party coalition government in Catalonia
vía lenta (f)	slow route (to autonomy)
vía rápida (f)	fast route (to autonomy)

The European tier of government

Until recently government in Spain, as in other developed Western countries, was essentially a domestic matter. Today, however, decision-making within considerable areas of government activity falls within the remit of the European Union (*Unión Europea/UE*), so that policies formulated at European level translate into national legislation in the various member states, including Spain. In tandem with that process, structures exist to permit Spanish citizens to participate, either directly or indirectly, in EU decisions that affect them. This situation is the result of the process known as European integration (*integración europea*). Like the UK, Spain initially stood on the sidelines. But subsequently it became an enthusiastic participant, with the result that the emerging European tier of governance is of particular importance there. This chapter will examine Spain's involvement in the continuing process of integration, and the principal mechanisms which currently bind it into the EU's supranational structure. First, however, it will give a brief overview of integration and the EU's machinery, for those unfamiliar with one or the other.

4.1 European integration and the EU

The idea that Europe forms a natural unit and should be governed as such is an old one, and down the centuries various attempts were made to realize it by conquest. However, the first moves towards bringing the peoples of the continent together on a peaceful, democratic basis were taken in the aftermath of the Second World War. They were motivated by the need for economic reconstruction, by the desire to prevent further conflicts and by the perceived threat from the Soviet Union, and they set in train a process that became known as European integration. By the beginning of the 21st century its main product, the European Union, had not only assumed a wide range of legislative and administrative competences over much of the continent, but had also expanded its borders as far as the former Soviet Union.

4.1.1 The beginnings of integration

The first postwar moves towards integration involved a number of organizations in various fields. In 1948 the Organization for European Economic Cooperation (OEEC) (*Organización para la Cooperación Económica Europea/OCEE*) – later to become the Organization for Economic Cooperation and Development, or OECD (*Organización para la Cooperación y el Desarrollo Económico/OCDE*) – was founded to administer the American aid provided under the Marshall Plan. The following year saw the formation of the Council of Europe (*Consejo de Europa*), which was concerned mainly with fostering educational and cultural contacts on a voluntary basis. And in 1954 the Western European Union (*Unión Europea Occidental/UEO*) was set up to coordinate European defence policy, although in practice it was strictly subordinated to NATO – dominated, then as now, by the USA.

The origins of integration as it was later to develop lay in a fourth organization. In 1952, a group of OEEC members (France, West Germany, Belgium, the

Netherlands, Luxembourg and Italy) formed the European Coal and Steel Community (ECSC) (*Comunidad Europea del Carbón y del Acero/CECA*). Crucially 'the six', as they became known, ceded powers of decision over their own affairs to the ECSC institutions. In 1957, they set up two more organizations on a similar basis: the European Atomic Energy Community, or Euratom, and the European Economic Community (*Comunidad Económica Europea/CEE*). The latter was to form the nucleus of subsequent integration.

The Treaty of Rome which established the EEC included a statement of its members' intention to proceed towards 'ever closer union', implicitly political in nature. But, as the name implied, the EEC (or 'Common Market' as it was generally known) was essentially economic and had two main aspects. First, it was a common market (*mercado común*). In other words, its members established a free trade area (*zona de libre comercio*) by abolishing all internal tariff barriers (*barreras arancelarias*) to trade in goods, and also agreed to impose a common external tariff (*arancel aduanero común*) on imports from outside, or 'third countries'. Secondly, the six established a Common Agricultural Policy (*Política Agrícola Común/PAC*) designed to ensure stability of food supplies and farm incomes by a system of supports and guaranteed prices. These measures were an immediate success, providing a massive boost to trade and prosperity among the member states (*estados miembros*).

In 1973 the United Kingdom was admitted to the EEC, along with Denmark and Ireland (while voters in Norway at that time rejected the proposed terms of accession in a referendum). This first enlargement (*ampliación*) was followed by two more in the next decade, Greece being admitted in 1981 and Spain, together with Portugal, five years later [4.2.1]. Together these moves represented a major step towards one of the main aims of integration, the creation of a genuinely pan-European entity.

Meanwhile steps were also taken towards the other, known as deepening (*profundización*); that is, extending the scope and intensity of cooperation between the Community's members. Crucially, the system of institutions set up to manage the ECSC, Euratom and the EEC were merged in 1967, resulting in a single Commission and a single Council [4.1.3]. The late 1970s saw the creation of a European Monetary System, as part of which most – but not all – members of the EEC agreed to peg their currencies' values against each other by means of an Exchange Rate Mechanism (*mecanismo de cambios*).

The enlargements of 1973, 1981 and 1986 had brought some less wealthy countries into the Community, and this prompted the EEC to extend its arrangements to help poorer regions through various Structural Funds (*Fondos Estructurales*). These changes were enshrined in the 1986 Single European Act, or SEA (*Acta Única Europea/AUE*), which also saw a change of title from EEC to EC, or European Community (*Comunidad Europea/CE*). This change of name reflected the gradual inclusion of social and environmental policies within the Community's remit, as well as the development of common foreign policy. The SEA's main purpose, however, was to streamline the Community's decision-making procedures, in particular by limiting member states' ability to block proposals to which they objected [4.1.3].

This, in turn, was intended to enable a massive programme of legislation to complete the Community's single, or internal market (*mercado interior*) by removing a multitude of non-tariff barriers (*barreras no tarifarias*) to trade, and to enable the free movement between the members of persons and services as well as goods. The target date for this programme was set at 1992, and on 1 January 1993 the single market was declared complete, although a number of measures were still to be finalized. In their original, trading terms the aims of economic integration had now been achieved, at least on paper.

4.1.2 The development of the EU

By then, however, the member states had signalled their intention of going further. In February 1992 they had signed the Treaty on European Union, or TEU (*Tratado de la Unión Europea/TUE*), at Maastricht in the Netherlands. A complex and unwieldy document, it marked a major development in the EU's move from economic to political integration. To signal this decisive step it formally instituted a further change of name from 'European Community' to 'European Union'.

The TEU established two new fields, or 'pillars', of Union activity in the political sphere. These were concerned with developing a Common Foreign and Security Policy (*Política Exterior y de Seguridad Común/PESC*) and cooperation in justice and home affairs (*Justicia y Asuntos de Interior*), and were to function intergovernmentally, that is, by separate agreement of the member states rather than through the Union's decision-making structures and institutions. The Treaty also included a Social Chapter (*Acuerdo Social*) establishing certain minimum standards of social provision and economic justice.

But the key aspect of the Maastricht agreement was once again economic: its plans for Economic and Monetary Union, or EMU (*Unión Económica y Monetaria/UEM*). Under these a single currency (*moneda única*) was to be adopted in 1999, with national currencies disappearing three years later. Originally termed the *ecu*, by the time it appeared on the streets of the eleven member states where it was adopted on 1 January 2002 it had been renamed as the euro. Currently, the euro is the currency of 15 EU member states, known collectively as the Euro area or Eurozone (*zona euro*).

Also under the Maastricht agreement, a European Central Bank (*Banco Central Europeo/BCE*) was created to manage the new currency's exchange rate, and monetary policy in general. In order to qualify for EMU, member states would have to meet five convergence criteria relating to their economic performance. These greatly restricted their autonomy to set their own budgets (Table 4.1).

This selective approach tacitly recognized the existence of a two-speed Europe (*Europa de dos velocidades*), in which not all Union members would proceed towards integration at the same pace. It reflected both the concerns of some, especially the UK, at the gradual loss of their own sovereignty involved in integration, and the frustration of those anxious to push ahead. Such divergences had already led to the 1985 Schengen Agreement, under which some countries had agreed on the gradual abolition of controls at their common borders. Both the new pillars introduced at Maastricht also effectively involved a two-speed approach, while the opt-out clause (*cláusula de exclusión*) negotiated by the UK from the Social Chapter represented a further example. Yet another was the decision later in 1992 to create a Eurocorps (*Euroejército*) made up of military contingents from several countries.

The 1990s also brought a revival of activity on the second dimension of integration.

Table 4.1 The Maastricht convergence criteria

Indicator	Condition
1 Exchange rate	Currency must remain within narrow band of European Monetary System for two years prior to adoption of single currency.
2 Inflation rate	Inflation must be no more than 1.5 per cent higher than average of three member states with lowest rates.
3 Interest rates	Long-term rates must be no more than 2 per cent higher than average of three member states with lowest inflation rates.
4 Public debt	Total debt must be less than 60 per cent of country's GDP.
5 Public sector deficit	Annual deficit must be less than 3 per cent of country's GDP.

Accession negotiations were begun with Austria, Finland, Norway and Sweden; in 1995 all joined the Union bar Norway, which for a second time voted to remain outside [4.1.1]. This fourth enlargement brought the number of EU members to 15.

Despite the fact that good progress was being made on monetary union, integration in general hit a number of problems in the 1990s. Completion of the single market failed to provide the expected economic boost. The inadequacies of the Common Foreign and Security Policy were repeatedly shown up in the weakness of European responses to crises in ex-Yugoslavia and elsewhere. Germany, still struggling to cope with the immense task of incorporating its formerly Communist eastern part, was increasingly unhappy at providing the lion's share of the Union budget, and pressed for a reform of its finances. And there was increasing evidence that many of its citizens regarded the EU with indifference at best, a situation known in Union jargon as a 'democratic deficit'.

The 1997 Treaty of Amsterdam attempted to address this issue by tinkering with the Union's institutional structure. More concretely, the then members of the Eurozone agreed on a Stability and Growth Pact (*Pacto para la Estabilidad y el Crecimiento*), which committed them to maintain the budgetary discipline imposed by the Maastricht criteria once the single currency was introduced. The new Treaty also effectively institutionalized two-speed Europe by providing for subgroups of members to engage in enhanced cooperation (*cooperación reforzada*) under certain conditions.

None of these steps did much to relieve the Union's problems, however, and 1999 brought further setbacks. First, there was the embarrassing spectacle of the entire European Commission – in a sense, the central European institution – being forced to resign [4.1.3]. And then, after the euphoria surrounding its launch at the start of the year, the euro slumped in value against both the dollar and the pound, the main European currency to have remained outside EMU.

Yet, despite these travails, the Union continued to press ahead with its most ambitious project yet. This was a further enlargement, designed to incorporate up to twelve Central and Eastern European countries (*países de Europa central y oriental/pecos*), most of them from the ex-Communist bloc. By the Treaty of Nice signed in February 2001, the EU states reconfirmed their determination to press ahead with this project. The Treaty was implemented in 2003, and, in May 2004, the following ten countries joined: Cyprus, Czech Republic, Estonia, Hungary, Latvia, Lithuania, Malta, Poland, Slovakia and Slovenia. A subsequent enlargement, in January 2007, brought Bulgaria and Romania into the Union. The majority of the new member states are considerably poorer than those who joined earlier, and their accession has placed enormous strains on the Union's finances, notably the Common Agricultural Policy and the Structural Funds. Their arrival has also had implications for the Union's institutional arrangements [4.1.3].

Partly motivated by the need to streamline the EU machinery, and partly out of an underlying commitment to achieving greater unity across the Union, efforts were made in the wake of the 2004 enlargement to draft a new treaty which would apply to all the countries of the Union. This 'European Constitution' (*Constitución Europea*) made explicit the proposed new arrangements for the Union's institutions, and in that sense it contained several elements of a constitutional nature, although much of the document was aimed simply at collating and formalizing existing EU agreements. The first attempt to do this failed when voters in two of the original member states, France and Holland, rejected the text in referenda in 2005. After the controversial term 'constitution' had been abandoned, a new, shorter document, similar in content to the original, though somewhat less ambitious was agreed by the EU heads of state and government in Lisbon in October 2007. This document, known as the Lisbon Treaty, was due to be ratified by all member states and implemented in 2009. The process suffered a serious setback, however, in June 2008, when the Lisbon Treaty was rejected by the electorate in Ireland, a member state where any treaty that affects the state's constitution must by law be voted on in a referendum, and thus the only country that held a vote on the Treaty. At the time of writing, negotiations are taking place to try to find ways of moving forward with the process.

4.1.3 The EU machinery

At the apex of the EU's institutional machinery stands the European Council (*Consejo Europeo*). It is composed of the various member states' heads of government, and by heads of state with executive powers (including, for example, the presidents of Finland and France). It meets between two and four times a year. The Council's role is to give direction to EU policy formulation. It also sets out the broad headings for the discussions that are held amongst government ministers responsible for particular subject areas when difficulties arise in their decision-making processes. These latter meetings, which take place on a regular basis between the summit meetings (*cumbres*) of heads of state and government, were known until recently as the 'Council of Ministers' (*Consejo de Ministros*) but are now called the Council of the European Union (*Consejo de la Unión Europea*).

At any one time all the various Council meetings are chaired by the representatives of a particular member state. This function is known as the Presidency (*Presidencia*) and rotates on a six-monthly basis. During its term, the country holding the Presidency is also responsible for representing the Council of Ministers *vis-à-vis* other EU institutions, and the Union as a whole *vis-à-vis* the outside world. A Presidency acquires particular significance if it coincides with the preparation or holding of a so-called Intergovernmental Conference (*Conferencia Intergubernamental/CIG*), the process of consulting all member governments before carrying out a change to the EU's fundamental treaties.

Until recently, most Council decisions, including all those on the new pillars introduced by the Maastricht Treaty, had to be taken unanimously, effectively giving each state a veto. However, as a result of the same treaty, and of the Single Act

[4.1.1], a majority of the issues to be decided are now put to a ballot, using a system of 'qualified majority voting'. This means that each member has a certain number of votes; of the 345 in total, 255 constitute the qualified majority (*mayoría cualificada*) needed for a proposal to be approved. The allocation of votes is weighted towards the smaller states; currently the Union's 'big four' (France, Germany, Italy and the UK) have 29 votes, and tiny Malta three.

Under the terms of the Lisbon Treaty, a new 'double majority' voting system will be implemented in 2014. That system requires that decisions should have the support of 55 per cent of member states' votes, which must also represent 65 per cent of the Union's population, thus ensuring majority support in terms of both member states and proportion of the EU population. The provisions of that Treaty will also usher in a new version of the Council, which will become an independent institution, headed by a President elected by qualified majority for a term of two and a half years.

Currently, although the Council is a powerful entity within the EU machinery, by its nature its position cannot be compared to that of the cabinet in a single state. Apart from anything else, it lacks the requisite administrative support. The bulk of the Union bureaucracy – which, contrary to popular myth, is not all that large in total – works for the European Commission (*Comisión Europea*). The Commission is the most distinctive Union institution and in many ways its driving force: in effect, no decision can be taken by the Council and Parliament except on the basis of a proposal from the Commission. It combines some of the traditional features of an (elected) cabinet with those of a permanent civil service, being responsible both for the Union's day-to-day operation and for initiating new legislation or projects.

The Commission is headed by a President, appointed by the European Council for a five-year term. In consultation with national governments he – as yet there has been no female president – selects the 27 Commissioners (*Comisarios*) who make up his governmental team. He also assigns them responsibility for particular policy areas and chooses two to act as his deputies, or vice-presidents. In its broader sense the Commission also includes a considerable underlying administrative apparatus, divided up into 37 Directorates-General (*Direcciones Generales*) and Services (*Servicios*). Currently, each member-state nominates one Commissioner, although, under the terms of the Lisbon Treaty, from 2014 onwards only two out of every three member states would nominate Commissioners, with states taking turns in rotation. The President of the Commission would then be elected (not appointed as now) by a simple majority of MEPs, following a proposal from the European Council and taking into account the results of the European parliamentary elections.

At least up to the present, the European Parliament (*Parlamento Europeo*) has been markedly less powerful than either the Council or the Commission, although its ability to influence decisions was increased by the Single Act and the Maastricht Treaty [4.1.2], and its powers are further enhanced by the Lisbon Treaty. In 1999 it caused something of a sensation by pressurizing the Commission to resign en bloc after its investigations suggested that several Commissioners had engaged in corrupt practices. Originally its members, or MEPs (*eurodiputados*), were appointed by national governments, but since 1979 they have been directly elected at EU-wide polls held every five years, for which each country is free to choose its own electoral system.

With the accession of Bulgaria and Romania, the total number of MEPs stands at 785, although this number is due to be capped at 751 at the next elections. As in the case of the weighted voting used in the Council, although less dramatically, the allocation of seats currently favours the smaller members, ranging from 99 for Germany to 78 for France, Italy and the UK, to 54 for Spain, 13 for Ireland and down to five for Malta.

The Parliament's sessions are chaired by a speaker, or president (elected for 2.5 years) or by one of the vice-presidents. Together these make up its bureau, or presiding council. The vast majority of members opt to join one of the Parliament's official 'groups', usually known by their French initials (Table 4.4), around which the Parliament's work revolves. In particular, representation on the Committees (*Comisiones*), where most substantive work is done, is allocated to the groups on the basis of their relative strength, while the influential committee chairpersons (*presidentes*) are appointed on a similar basis.

In addition to these three, the EU has a number of other institutions and bodies of which four can be singled out here.

- The Court of Justice (*Tribunal Europeo de Justicia/TEJ*) is the final arbiter on disputes arising from the Treaties or legislation based on them, having ultimate authority over the various national judicial systems for the matters concerned.
- The Court of Auditors (*Tribunal Europeo de Cuentas/TEC*) is responsible for control of Union expenditure.
- The Economic and Social Committee (*Comité Económico y Social/CES*) is an advisory body bringing together representatives of European civil society – in practice, chiefly those of the social partners (*agentes sociales*), in other words employers and trade unions.
- The Committee of the Regions (*Comité de las Regiones*) also has advisory status; set up by the Maastricht Treaty, it is made up of representatives of regional and local authorities.

In all of these, as in the three main institutions, each EU country is guaranteed a certain degree of representation; one member on each of the Courts and a number roughly proportional to population on the other two bodies.

The system of guaranteed representation is a tacit admission that the politicians and administrators who staff the Union's institutions are in an ambiguous situation. While their responsibilities are, in theory, to their electors or to the Union as a whole, in practice they are almost certain to retain a degree of allegiance to their respective countries. Similarly the Union Presidency offers an excellent chance for the holder to promote its own agenda as well as serving common interests. This ambiguity is part and parcel of a larger one. For, while the Union is ostensibly a framework for the members to cooperate, it is also an arena in which they attempt to advance their individual, and sometimes competing interests.

Those interests are often best served by member states succeeding in filling as many influential EU posts as possible with their own nationals or by entering into alliances with other member states, particularly the larger ones. It also usually helps for a country to display strong commitment to integration, although the opposite strategy – of expressing Euroscepticism – especially when combined with an intransigent attitude, can sometimes be effective in gaining concessions from other members, as was the case of the UK in the 1980s under PM Margaret Thatcher.

4.2 Spain and integration

Marginalization from the rest of Europe was Spain's experience for much of its modern history. Moreover, Spaniards seemed to have internalized their isolation, showing a tendency – like that of the British – to refer to 'Europe' as an alien place. The 'disaster' of 1898 [0.1] prompted some reaction against such attitudes; most famously the philosopher Ortega y Gasset became one of the first proponents of a federal Europe, which he saw as the remedy for Spain's many problems. By a sad irony, though, when his vision finally started to take real form Spain found itself more marginalized than ever. Yet events were soon to change the situation radically, creating both a tremendous enthusiasm within Spain for the idea of Europe (*europeísmo*) and the conditions for its fulfilment.

(NB. Throughout this section reference is made to the general description of the integration process in sections 4.1.1 and 4.1.2.)

4.2.1 From pariah to partner

When the integration process began Spain was ruled by the Franco dictatorship, whose support for the Fascist powers during the Second World War had made it an international outcast [0.2]. In return, the regime purported to regard its democratic neighbours as corrupt and unjust, so that there was no question of Spain's forming part of the various international organizations formed between 1948 and 1957. However, shortly thereafter the regime was forced into a radical change of economic course, which in 1962 led it to apply to join the European Economic Community.

The application was a disaster for Franco. Not only was it rejected outright, but it provoked the EEC into making his regime's pariah status explicit. Spanish membership, it stated, was out of the question so long as the country remained a dictatorship, although in 1970 it did agree to sign an Association Agreement with Spain.

By this time, Europe had already acquired very positive connotations for Spaniards, especially among the many who had experienced at first- or second-hand the higher living standards and greater political freedom enjoyed by their northern neighbours. Among those who already wished for a return to democracy, the EEC's stance reinforced that appeal. It also helped swing key parts of the business community, who were keen to join the Community for economic reasons, firmly behind the process of democratization after Franco's death. Indeed generally, the idea of becoming more like the rest of Europe (*europeización*) became closely linked to the transition process, and so profited further from its success [0.3].

Not surprisingly, then, popular and political opinion was massively behind the renewed application submitted, to what was now the EC, by the first democratically elected government of Adolfo Suárez, in 1977. In principle the Community's existing members, too, were well-disposed to it; that same year they welcomed Spain into the Council of Europe. As well as a sense of guilt that Spain had been abandoned to its Francoist fate after 1945, there was also a clear feeling that a Europe without Spain (and Portugal) would always be incomplete. In the case of the EC, economic considerations also played a crucial role. By now the initial boost to growth in its founder members had begun to slacken, and the nine – above all Germany, the Community's economic powerhouse – saw in the large and relatively unexploited Spanish market the potential for renewed momentum.

In practice, though, economics also rendered the subsequent negotiations long and tortuous. One major problem was that of integrating Spain's fishing fleet, considerably larger than those of existing members, into the EC's arrangements. Even more serious were France's concerns about its agricultural sector; much Spanish farm produce, especially fruit and vegetables, was in direct competition with French, and once inside the EC's common market would be able to undercut it considerably. Moreover, from 1979 both Suárez and his successor were assailed by massive political problems at home [0.3.3]. As a result, they had little energy left over for European matters, and less credibility.

The arrival in power of the Socialists under Felipe González in 1982 marked a turning point. Not only did the new government enjoy a clear mandate. Unlike most of their predecessors, Spain's new rulers had impeccable democratic credentials, and enjoyed contacts with politicians in the EC countries built up during the twilight of Francoism and the transition. The two men who now took charge of the negotiations, Foreign Minister Fernando Morán [4.3.2] and Manuel Marín (see Table 4.2), were both cases in point. Indeed Marín, who was responsible for the details of the talks, was already a senior figure in the Party of European Socialists [4.3.1]. Together they drove the talks on with new vigour and tenacity and, despite several crises caused by French misgivings, Spain's Treaty of Accession (*Tratado de Adhesión*) was finally signed in mid-1985.

When it came into force on 1 January 1986, the country became a full EC member state, with all the attendant rights in terms of representation in its institutions [4.1.3]. However, Spain was forced to wait for some of the economic gains it expected from joining the common market. While her duties on imports from her new partners were to be removed at once, their tariffs on some Spanish agricultural products would be phased out only gradually, over a seven-year transitional period (*período transitorio*). Spain obtained no reciprocal concessions for its vulnerable dairy sector [5.3.1], while the treaty terms arguably failed to provide adequate protection for its fishing industry. In addition, in order to prepare for the inevitable shock to its economy, the country was already engaged in a painful process of industrial restructuring [5.1.2]. All in all, accession did not come cheap.

On the other hand, Spain succeeded in ensuring that the forthcoming Single European Act would include a major increase in the EC's Structural Funds, from which it would be by far the greatest beneficiary [5.1.2]. Even here there was a price to be paid, in that the country effectively surrendered the ability to set its own priorities for regional assistance. Yet very few doubts indeed were expressed about the terms that had been negotiated, and they were swamped in the general euphoria surrounding what was widely seen as the end of Spain's isolation. Significantly, the option of holding a referendum on the terms of entry, taken up in several other prospective members before and since, was never seriously considered. It would have been a pointless exercise, as no one, euphoric or not, was in any doubt as to the outcome.

Table 4.2 Spain's European Commissioners

Manuel Marín	1986–99	PSOE	Former Secretary of State for EC Relations Senior official in Party of European Socialists Key figure in negotiations for Spanish accession [4.2.1]
Abel Matutes	1986–94	AP/PP	Leading businessman and politician in the Balearic Islands MEP (1994–96) Foreign Minister (1996–2000)
Marcelino Oreja	1994–99	PP	Foreign Minister (1976–80) Secretary-General of Council of Europe [4.1.1] (1984–89) Key figure in foundation of PP [3.4.2] MEP 1989–94
Ignacia de Loyola de Palacio	1999–2004	PP	Senior figure in the PP Minister of Agriculture (1996–99)
Pedro Solbes	1999–2004	PSOE	Former Secretary of State for EC Relations Minister for Agriculture, Fisheries and Food (1991–93) Finance Minister (1993–96) Second Deputy PM (2004–) Finance Minister (2004–)
Joaquín Almunia	2004–	PSOE	Minister for Employment and Social Affairs (1982–86) Minister for Public Administration (1986–91) Former Secretary General of the PSOE (1997–2000)

4.2.2 In the vanguard

The situation regarding Spain's membership of another international organization could not have been more different. Spain had become a member of NATO in 1982, almost certainly in defiance of public opinion. The decision had been bitterly contested by the Socialists in opposition, and they came to power pledged to reverse it. However, it soon became clear to Prime Minister Felipe González at least that his EC counterparts were deeply unhappy at the prospect of having a new and important partner which was not integrated into the Western world's common defence system. Although never explicit, staying in NATO became a sort of unspoken condition for EC accession.

González had no doubt where his priorities lay, and seems to have persuaded EC leaders to accept his ability to impose them on Spanish voters. Their trust proved well-placed. González first convinced his party to drop its demand for immediate withdrawal and concede that, on this point, the Spanish people should decide. Then he managed to hold off the promised referendum until March 1986, when he was basking in the glory of recent EC accession [4.2.1]. And finally, in a highly personal campaign, he managed to reverse the opinion poll findings and obtain what was eventually a clear majority in favour of remaining in NATO's political – although not its defence – structure. In a postscript to these dramatic events, Spain was admitted to the Western European Union in 1988.

At the time, the NATO referendum was bitterly divisive. Opposition to membership reflected anti-American feeling spread right across society [0.4.1], but the organizers of the 'no' campaign were mainly on the political left. They provided the seed of a new party, United Left (IU), which over the next few years became increasingly hostile towards European integration in general, and the EC in particular. This might have been expected to strike a chord with several groups of voters: the victims of restructuring in the early 1980s [5.1.2]; those who failed to benefit from the post-accession boom; and the many who were badly hit in the subsequent slump [5.1.3]. Yet IU was dismally unsuccessful [2.5.2]. Its performance was in line with the surveys which consistently showed Spaniards to be very positively disposed towards the EU, more so than almost all their fellow Europeans.

Several reasons can be suggested for their enthusiasm. On balance, Europe had brought some benefits to most Spaniards, and very substantial ones to some. The role of the Structural Funds in a range of major infrastructure projects was highly visible. In some regions, including the Basque Country, Europe provided a means of side-stepping the conflicts caused by regionalism [3.2.2.2]. And the fact that many Spaniards had, under Francoism, been deeply alienated by the Spanish state meant that surrendering some of that state's sovereignty caused few of the fears felt elsewhere, especially in Britain. But the key factor was probably the absence of any equivalent to the UK's large – and well-resourced – eurosceptic lobby. Apart from IU, the political class was united in its europhilia (*europeísmo*), and the same was true of the vast majority of other key opinion formers in business and the media.

As a result, once inside the EC Spain showed practically none of the suspicion towards further integration that surfaced in other member states. The government signed the Single European Act without hesitation. Then, in 1989 it took the peseta into the Exchange Rate Mechanism of the European Monetary System, despite the fact that, for one of the Community's less developed economies, that was likely to prove problematic – as indeed it later did [5.2.2]. Nor did Spain show any of the reservations about the Maastricht Treaty displayed by some of its partners, adopting the Social Chapter and participating actively in the first moves to develop a Common Foreign and Security Policy. In 1992 it was one of the founder members of the Eurocorps, and three years later it signed the Schengen Agreement.

Above all, the González government immediately pledged Spain to join Economic and Monetary Union. The decision to try and meet the convergence criteria set for prospective EMU members was brave, even foolhardy. It was bound to bring significant economic hardship for Spain in the short term and, in any case, seemed likely to end in embarrassing failure. The government's Convergence Plan did indeed prove painful for many [5.1.3], at a time when González was under massive political pressure at home [2.3.4]. Yet EMU was one area in which the opposition steered clear of political point-scoring. And when the conservatives finally came to power in 1996 they maintained intact the commitment to joining EMU. In the event, the criteria were achieved with some comfort and Spain had made good its aspiration to be in the vanguard of integration.

This strong commitment to integration undoubtedly helped Spain to become, surprisingly quickly, an important player in internal Union politics. And if some suggested that its excellent record on incorporating EU legislation into its own national code was not necessarily accompanied by the requisite enforcement – for instance on environmental matters [8.3.1] – that only underlined how well it had learnt the rules of internal Union politics [4.1.3].

In addition, Prime Minister González was careful to fill the EU posts to which Spain was entitled with close and trusted colleagues, who had a good knowledge of the EU's complex workings [4.3.1]. And he also cultivated close relations with other major EU leaders, especially his German counterpart Helmut Kohl. As a result, although Spain acquired a reputation for defending its interests as tenaciously as the French, or even more so, it attracted none of the opprobrium reserved for Margaret Thatcher's Britain [4.1.3].

On one occasion, González did act in a manner distinctly reminiscent of Thatcher. It came at the 1992 Edinburgh Summit and concerned the Cohesion Fund (*Fondo de Cohesión*) which had been agreed at Maastricht earlier in the year. This was designed to alleviate the problems that joining Economic and Monetary Union would place on the Union's weaker economies and – as with the Structural Funds [4.1.1] – its main beneficiary by far would be Spain. At Edinburgh the majority of members wanted to drop the Fund because of its high costs. González threatened to block further progress on EMU and brought the Summit to the point of breakdown, until they finally relented.

Significantly, his obduracy seemed to have little effect on Spain's standing, or his own; thereafter he continued to be quoted as a possible Commission President [4.1.3]. His appointment, had it come about, would have been merely the last in a string of influential Union posts which Spain's partners awarded it during its first decade of membership [4.3.2]. All in all, life in Europe was turning out to be something of an extended honeymoon.

4.2.3 A maturing relationship with Europe

González's successor, José María Aznar, never actually questioned Spain's commitment to integration as such, and indeed oversaw his country's completion of the difficult journey to EMU [4.2.2]. However, while still in opposition and keen to attack the Socialists on every front, he had tended to seize on any minor concessions made to Spain's partners – inevitable in any working partnership – as proof that González was failing adequately to stand up for Spanish interests. To avoid charges of back-pedalling once elected, he found himself forced to maintain the rhetoric of 'national interests'.

Partly as a result, his premiership was also marked by poor personal relations with a number of EU leaders, especially his German counterpart Gerhard Schröder, and a growing tendency for Spain to be seen by its fellow members as a ruthless and even unreasonable negotiator. Of course, this cannot all be put down to Aznar, who also showed himself in domestic politics to be a good learner of political skills. Other factors were also at work, one being the differences between his and González's party bases.

The relative youth and peculiar origins of Aznar's People's Party [2.4.1] meant that it had nothing like the extensive connections with counterparts in other countries enjoyed by the Socialists; indeed only since 1989 has it been integrated in one of the main EU party groupings [4.3.1]. Additionally, while the Socialists' move to the right under González [2.3.3] placed them in the ideological mainstream of the continental EU, especially France and Germany, the PP remained somewhat of an ideological outsider. For, in its move away from authoritarian conservatism, it tended towards the sort of market-based ideology associated with Margaret Thatcher. It is no coincidence that in several internal EU battles Aznar found himself allied with the UK, still – despite Thatcher's departure – very much the EU's odd-man-out.

The crucial point, though, is that integration had lost some of its attraction for Spain. For one thing, the Union's Common Foreign and Security Policy, apart from its overall weakness, proved to be of little relevance for the country's two main foreign policy concerns outside the EU itself, Latin America [0.4.2] and North Africa [0.4.3]. CFSP focused almost exclusively on the Eastern Mediterranean and especially Eastern Europe, partly for security reasons but above all because of enlargement. Not surprisingly, Spain's enthusiasm for it slackened.

Enlargement to the East in 2004 and 2007 shifted the EU's economic centre of gravity, and brought in new members whose interests are mostly different from those of the Mediterranean countries in general, and Spain in particular. Such considerations lay behind the unease displayed by the González administration about the 1995 enlargement. But the countries admitted then were too small to greatly affect the EU's economic geography, and all were richer than the Union average so that their accession actually reduced common budgetary costs for the existing members.

With the latest enlargements, the Iberian Peninsula has, in a sense, become a peripheral area, remote from the Union's economic core. All but two of the twelve newest member states are non-Mediterranean in character and some, notably Poland, are large enough to wield significant influence in their own right. Most important of all, given their relative poverty the admission of these countries has entailed an end to the Structural and Cohesion Funds [4.2.2] in their original form, and a significant reduction in the massive financial support Spain has received under them.

Aznar had no real option but to resist such developments. Although he was shrewd enough not to question the principle of enlargement, in practice his battle to preserve Spain's generous receipts from the Funds for as long as possible was one of the main reasons why financially viable arrangements for an enlarged Union proved so hard to devise. Nor was he helped in presenting his case by Spain's economic success since joining the Union [5.1.3] and its determination to be at the forefront of integration [4.2.2], both of which sat ill with pleading poverty.

The result was that, in the run-up to the 2004 enlargement, Spain exasperated most of her fellow EU members, a situation Aznar himself occasionally aggravated. In particular, a threat to veto Germany's proposal for a transitional period on free movement of workers from the East – a delicate political issue in Germany but of no immediate concern to Spain – backfired badly. True, Aznar succeeded in preserving Spain's funding virtually intact up to 2006. But there were some indications that relations with its partners and the Union authorities themselves suffered [4.3.2].

Renewed marginalization in Europe, in terms not just of economic geography but also of ability to influence the EU's overall direction, was indeed a far from attractive prospect. It became less of a threat, however, once Zapatero took over as PM from Aznar in March 2004. With his European credentials intact, and with a more conciliatory approach to negotiation, Zapatero managed to improve relations with the Union and with Spain's fellow member-states. And the more positive attitude of its leader may have bolstered the country's sense of commitment to Europe: in a referendum held on 20 February 2005, Spaniards voted by a large majority to support the proposed new 'European Constitution'. This enabled Spain to become the first country to ratify the document when the Congress in Madrid endorsed it in April of that year. The proposed text was later abandoned after French and Dutch voters rejected it, to be replaced by a less ambitious version, the Lisbon Treaty [4.1.2].

At the time when the distribution of EU funds for 2007–13 was being negotiated, Spain had few if any grounds for claiming financial aid, given that per capita income in the country already exceeded 90 per cent of the EU average. Nevertheless, it was still agreed that Spain would continue to receive Cohesion Funds for that period, although the total would be less than a third of the amount received in 2000–06. Only those regions with a per capita income of less than 75 per cent of the EU average (Galicia, Extremadura, Castile-La Mancha and Andalusia) will receive the same level of Structural Funds as previously. Other regions, such as Madrid, stand to have their funding reduced by as much as 41 per cent. Special financial help was also made available for the Canary Islands and Ceuta and Melilla.

Of particular concern to the latter is the entry of illegal immigrants into Spain, especially of people from sub-Saharan Africa [6.1.1]. Given its position on the frontier of the EU, Spain requested special assistance with this problem. The most significant form this has taken has been the creation in 2004 of a new EU body, the European Agency for the Management of Operational Cooperation at the External Borders (*Agencia Europea para la gestión de la cooperación operativa en las fronteras exteriores*), or Frontex. This agency supports member states in controlling the Union's external borders and gives operational assistance with such surveillance. It has helped to reduce the numbers of immigrants entering through Spain. In line with this, Spain has been advocating the development of an EU-wide common immigration policy.

4.3 Spain in the EU machinery

As a result of its involvement in the integration process, Spain has handed over to the EU responsibility for wide areas of its own affairs, above all in the economic field. In return, it has acquired access to the Union's decision-making machinery in three ways. One is through the representation in the EU's various institutions to which it is entitled under the Union's various defining treaties and the terms of its accession. The second is through Spanish politicians and public servants appointed to senior EU posts. And third, a range of public bodies exists in Brussels and within Spain itself to act as links between the country and the Union machinery.

(NB. Throughout this section reference is made to the general description of the EU machinery in 4.1.3.)

4.3.1 Spain's assured representation

Spain's representation in the most senior of EU institutions is identical to that of its fellows: through the Prime Minister in the European Council and the responsible government ministers in the Council of Ministers. In the enlarged Union, Spain now has 27 votes for the purposes of qualified majority voting in the Councils, giving it a status which is close to that of the 'big four' (France, Germany, Italy and the UK) who have 29 each, and equal to that of newcomer Poland. Next in voting strength comes Romania with 14 votes, while the lowest number of votes is held by Malta, with just three.

Spain has so far taken on the role of Union President three times, its terms falling in the first half of 1989, the second of 1995 and the first of 2002. On the first two occasions the customary end-of-term summit was held in Madrid; in 2002 the venue was Seville. As a relatively new and less developed member, in 1989 Spain was content merely to show that it could meet its obligations in an efficient manner, an aim generally agreed to have been achieved. By 1995 it was rather more ambitious, but the efforts of the then Socialist government to promote Spanish interests were hampered by its domestic political troubles [2.3.4].

During its second presidency Spain organized the first Euro-Mediterranean Conference in Barcelona, an initiative that has been slow to produce any concrete effects [0.4.3], while in the Madrid summit held that year the euro was christened. In 2002, the conservative People's Party administration was in an awkward position, since its main concern was to block, or at least slow down, progress on expansion to the East, the EU's major project [4.2.3]. Not surprisingly, it took a rather low-key approach to its responsibilities.

One important success achieved by Spain under the terms of its accession was the right to nominate two Commissioners, a privilege previously enjoyed only by the 'big four'. Like them, however, it lost this right after enlargement under the terms agreed at Nice, and now nominates just one. Up to the point (in 2004) when this change occurred, in nominating its Commissioners Spain followed the same practice as the UK, putting forward one from each of the two largest political parties irrespective of which was in power. This arrangement enabled Spain to avoid the political horse-trading nomination causes in some countries and send a succession of well qualified Commissioners (Table 4.2). Since 2004, the single Commissioner appointed by the Socialist government has been the Socialist Joaquín Almunia.

On accession Spain was allocated 60 seats in the European Parliament, raised to 64 in 1994; under the terms of the Nice Treaty, this fell to 54. Its first MEPs were appointed by the King pending a special election in 1987, since when Spain has taken part in the five-yearly Europe-wide elections for the Parliament (see Table 4.3). For these, like several other Union members, Spain uses a single, country-wide constituency (*circunscripción única*), for which the parties present lists as in domestic elections [1.3.1].

Theoretically, this arrangement should make it easier for smaller, country-wide parties to obtain seats. However, only in 1989 was such an effect apparent, and then purely because the mainstream right was then so weak [2.4.1]. The system makes it harder for regionalist parties to gain representation than in general elections [1.3.1], so, in order to counteract this effect and ensure some level of representation, a number of such parties have joined together in alliances (*coaliciones*) with their fellows in other regions or with broadly like-minded parties to fight European elections. The only electoral success obtained by the Spanish Greens at this level, for instance, was achieved in 2004 when they secured two seats within an alliance formed between them and two other small parties, one a left-wing Catalan party.

Table 4.3 Results for the principal parties in European elections, 1987–2004

[P = % of vote; S = seats]

		1987	1989	1994	1999	2004
Social and Democratic	P	10.2	7.1	1	1.2	0.1
Centre (CDS)	S	7	5	0	0	0
Spanish Socialist Party (PSOE)	P	39	39.6	30.8	35.3	43.4
	S	28	27	22	24	25
People's Party (PP)[a]	P	24.6	21.4	40.1	39.7	41.2
	S	17	15	28	27	24
United Left (IU)[b]	P	5.3	6.1	13.4	5.8	4.1
	S	3	4	9	4	2
Convergence and Union (CiU)[c]	P	4.4	4.2	4.7	4.4	
	S	3	2	3	3	
Herri Batasuna[d]	P	1.9	1.7	1	1.4	
	S	1	1	0	1	
Agrupación Ruiz Mateos	P		3.8	0.4		
[2.6]	S		2	0		
Europe of the Nations Alliance[e]	P	1.7	1.5	1.3		2.4
	S	1	1	0		1
Nationalist Alliance (CN)[f]	P		1.9	2.8	2.9	
	S		1	2	2	
Andalusian Regionalist Party	P		1.9	0.8		
	S		1	0		
Nations' Left	P		1.8			
	S		1			
European Alliance (CE)[g]	P				3.2	1.3
	S				2	0
Galician National Alliance	P				1.6	
(BNG)	S				1	
GALEUSCA[h]	P					5.1
	S					2

Notes:
[a] AP in 1987.
[b] In coalition with Esquerra Unida i Alternativa in 1999. In coalition with Iniciativa per Catalunya Verds and Esquerra Unida i Alternativa in 2004.
[c] Leading Catalan regionalist party.
[d] Basque radical party. EH in 1999. Banned since 2003.
[e] Included Basque Solidarity (EA), Catalan Republican Left (ERC) and Galician Nationalist Party (PNG) in 1987. In coalition with National Alliance (CN) in 1999. In 2004 included EA, ERC, Aragonese Regionalist Committee (CHA), Andalusian Socialist Party (PSA), Asturian Nationalist Party (AA), Cantabrian Nationalist Party (CNC) and Citizens' Initiative of The Rioja (ICLR).
[f] Included Basque Nationalist Party (PNV), Canary Islands Alliance (CC), Valencian Union (UV), Aragonese Regionalist Party (PAR), Galician Alliance (CG) and Majorcan Union (UM) in 1989 and 1994. In 1999 some of these parties formed a different alliance (see g).
[g] Included Canary Islands Alliance (CC), Aragonese Regionalist Party (PAR), Andalusian Regionalist Party (PA), Valencian Union (UV) in 1999 and 2004.
[h] Included Galician National Alliance (BNG), Basque Nationalist Party (PNV) and Convergence and Union (CiU).

Source: Interior Ministry

Public interest is also strictly limited. As elsewhere in the EU, turnout is consistently lower than in domestic elections, even when these are held on the same day, as was done with some local and regional polls in 1987 and 1999. The lowest turnout to date has been for the most recent European elections in 2004. On the other hand, Spanish parties seem to place a relatively high value on European representation. The candidates they present, or at least those with realistic chances of election, tend to carry some political weight; there are few of the mavericks or marginal figures common among British MEPs. Four former or future Spanish Foreign Ministers have served as MEPs: Fernando Morán [4.2.1] and Carlos Westendorp [4.3.2] in the Socialist ranks and Marcelino Oreja and Abel Matutes – both also Commissioners in their time – on the right. Among current Spanish MEPs, Jaime Mayor Oreja (PP) and Josep Borrell (PSOE) are former government ministers.

Almost all the Spanish parties represented in the Parliament have opted to join one or other of its trans-national groups (see Table 4.4). Three points are worthy of additional note here. First, before People's Unity (*Herri Batasuna*), now Unity (*Batasuna*), ETA's political wing, was banned from taking part in elections, their participation in European elections secured them one MEP, who was cold-shouldered by all other Spanish parties because of that party's attitude to violence. Its single MEP therefore sat among the non-attached members (*no inscritos*). Second, members of regionalist electoral alliances may sit in different groups once elected.

Finally, the position of the conservative People's Party (PP) is of interest. From 1987 to 1989 its forerunner, People's Alliance [2.4.1], formed part of a minor right-wing group whose only other significant component was the British Conservatives. However, as part of the operation that led to the creation of the PP, its MEPs joined the European People's Party, the Christian Democrat umbrella organization, even though hardly any were previously known for such views. Their admission to the EPP prompted the Basque Nationalist Party, a long-standing member of the organization, to resign in protest.

In addition, Spain has assured representation on various other EU institutions and bodies. It nominates one judge and one advocate general (*abogado general*) to the Court of Justice and one representative to the Court of Auditors, while the governor of its central bank, the Bank of Spain, sits on the Governing Council (*Consejo de Gobierno*) of the European Central Bank. It also has 24 representatives on the Economic and Social Committee.

Spain also appoints 21 members to the Committee of the Regions (*Comité de las Regiones*). Here again the practice of nominating relative political heavyweights contrasts sharply with the UK's. Spain's seats are occupied by the First Ministers of the country's 17 regions, and the mayors of Madrid, Barcelona and two other major cities. Catalans have been particularly assiduous in using the Committee to lobby for their region's interests; former Barcelona mayor Pasqual Maragall [3.2.1.3] has served as its Vice-President, and former regional First Minister Jordi Pujol [3.2.1.2] was one of its most active members.

4.3.2 Spaniards in appointed posts

As well as its assured representation in Union institutions, a member state can also hope to improve its situation in EU internal politics by having its nationals

Table 4.4 Party groups in the European Parliament (2004)

Group[a]	Spanish name	Spanish representatives
European People's Party (Christian Democrats) and European Democrats (PPE-DE)[b]	Partido Popular Europeo (Demócrata-Cristianos) y Demócratas Europeos	People's Party (PP)
Socialist Group in the European Parliament (PSE)[c]	Grupo Socialista en el Parlamento Europeo	Spanish Socialist Party (PSOE)
Alliance of Liberals and Democrats for Europe (ALDE)[d]	Alianza de los Demócratas y Liberales por Europa	Convergence and Union (CiU) Basque Nationalist Party (PNV)
Union for Europe of the Nations (UEN)[e]	Unión por la Europa de las Naciones	None
Greens / European Free Alliance (Verts/ALE)[f]	Verdes / Alianza Libre Europea	Confederación de Los Verdes Iniciativa per Catalunya Verds Basque Solidarity (EA)
Confederal Group of the European United Left – Nordic Green Left (GUE-NGL)[g]	Grupo Confederal de la Izquierda Unitaria Europea – Izquierda Verde Nórdica	United Left (IU)
Independence / Democracy (ID)[h]	Independencia / Democracia	None
Identity, Tradition and Sovereignty (ITS)[i]	Identidad, Tradición y Soberanía	None

Notes:
[a] In most cases the French initials/abbreviation are generally used.
[b] Christian democrats, conservative, centre-right.
[c] Social democrats, democratic socialists.
[d] Assorted independents.
[e] National conservatives.
[f] Ecologist / Stateless nations.
[g] Socialists, communists.
[h] Eurosceptics.
[i] Far-right.

appointed to a wide range of posts that are not reserved for any particular country. In a sense this applies to its nominees on the European Commission since, unlike their number, their responsibilities are not fixed. Instead, Commissioners are appointed to portfolios by the Commission President, and it is clearly in a member state's interests for these to be as broad and as influential as possible.

In this respect Spain's policy of nominating Commissioners with good knowledge of Union matters paid dividends immediately, when Manuel Marín [4.2.1] was appointed a Commission Vice-President, a considerable coup for a new member. Marín went on to become one of the longest-serving Commissioners ever, retaining his position for thirteen years. During that time he held a number of important portfolios and became an influential figure in internal EU politics. Latterly, however, he rather fell from grace, being the subject of allegations about irregularities in the administration of development aid under his authority in the 1999 affair that led to the resignation of the entire Commission [4.1.3].

Although none has been as prominent as Marín, Spain's other Commissioners (see Table 4.2) have also tended to be given fairly significant portfolios, which could be seen as either a recognition of their calibre, or a pay-off for Spain's commitment to integration, or both. Between 1994 and 1999 Marcelino Oreja, a highly experienced international administrator, had a broad portfolio including responsibility for the crucial telecommunications sector. Loyola de Palacio succeeded Marín as a Vice-President in 1999 while also controlling a weighty portfolio that included transport and energy until 2004. During that same period Pedro Solbes had responsibility for the key area of Economic and Monetary Affairs, which is also the area now controlled by the current Spanish Commissioner, Joaquín Almunia. In the top rank of the Commission administration, three directors-general (out of 35) are from Spain.

Spaniards have also tended to hold more than their fair share of important posts in the European Parliament. Three have served as the chamber's president: Enrique Barón Crespo (1989–92), José-María Gil-Robles Gil-Delgado (1997–99) and Josep Borrell (2004–07). Currently, a Spanish Socialist MEP, Miguel Ángel Martínez Martínez, is Vice-President of the Parliament, while Spain also provides the chairs of two of its 23 standing committees. Finally, Barón Crespo chaired the Parliament's second-largest political group, the Party of European Socialists, from 1999 to 2004.

The expansion of Union activity following the Treaty of Maastricht created a new range of appointed posts within the ambit of the European Council, a number of which went to Spaniards. One who emerged as an archetypal Union figure was Carlos Westendorp who, like several of Spain's representatives and appointees, was responsible for European policy in the Foreign Ministry before becoming Foreign Minister. Among other jobs, Westendorp headed the group which prepared the ground for the 1996 Intergovernmental Conference and was thereafter the Union's High Representative to Bosnia, before going on to chair the Parliament's Industry Committee. Another senior Spanish appointee was Miguel Ángel Moratinos, who acted as the EU's envoy to the Middle East peace process during the period 1996–2003.

But the highest-ranking Spanish appointment within the Union came in 1999, when the European Council decided to name a High Representative (*Alto Representante*) for the Union's Common Foreign and Security Policy [4.1.2]. This position, which incorporates that of Secretary-General of the Council of Ministers, is arguably the second most influential post within the entire Union structure. The man chosen to fill the role of *Míster PESC*, as it is often called, was Javier Solana, Spanish Foreign Minister from 1992 to 1995. Solana unquestionably had impressive credentials for the job, having been a cabinet minister for thirteen years in total and Secretary-General of NATO from 1995 to 1999. In this position, he has performed so impressively that his tenure has been renewed for the period 2004–09. Shortly after his initial appointment he was also named as Secretary-General of the Western European Union [4.1.1], further increasing his already substantial influence.

As High Representative, Solana has mediated in conflict situations in the Middle East, Latin America and the former Yugoslavia, while also dealing with the tensions that arose between the UK and some other EU member states (notably France) over the former's involvement in the US-led invasion of Iraq. In 2002, he defied the USA by calling – albeit unsuccessfully – for that country to treat as prisoners of war the suspected terrorists being held in the Guantánamo Bay detention camp.

The Council post held by Solana merged with the role of Vice-President of the Commission responsible for External Relations, to become that of High Representative for the Common Foreign and Security Policy (*Alto Representante para la PESC*), which Solana holds as well as being Secretary-General of the Council of the European Union (*Secretario General del Consejo de la UE*). Solana's appointment to these key positions would have been unthinkable without Spain's ostentatious commitment to the CFSP under the Socialist governments in which he served [4.2.2] – a further dividend from the government's strategy of establishing Spain as a 'good European'.

4.3.3 Communication with the EU

The Union's role in internal Spanish affairs, and the need to defend Spanish interests within its structures, have led to the creation of various mechanisms designed to facilitate communication between the EU, national and regional levels of government. The first of these is Spain's 'permanent representation' in Brussels. Intended to assist the country's representatives in the Council of Ministers [4.3.1], it is headed by an ambassador and composed of senior diplomats and civil servants seconded from ministries in Madrid. It also represents Spain on the two so-called Coreper committees (*Comités de Representantes Permanentes*) in which Council business is prepared.

Regular contact with the Brussels representation is maintained by a special division within the Ministry of Foreign Affairs, which is responsible for all EU matters and is headed by a Secretary of State [1.5.2]. Its task is to coordinate the stances taken by all those ministers and civil servants who, in one forum and another, represent Spanish interests within the EU. It is assisted in this task by the Interministerial Working Group on Community Affairs (*Conferencia Interministerial para Asuntos Comunitarios/CIAC*), on which all the ministries are represented. Any disputes that cannot be settled there are referred to the cabinet committee on economic affairs.

In addition, other ministries which have to deal with Brussels on a regular basis – the great majority – have set up special units to do so, usually under a Director-General [1.5.2]. That in the Ministry of Economics is especially important, as it coordinates all initiatives connected with the Structural Funds [4.1.1]. It also administers the receipts from the European Regional Development Fund (*Fondo Europeo de Desarrollo Regional/FEDER*), which deals mainly with infrastructure projects.

The Ministry of the Environment, Rural and Marine Affairs is responsible for agricultural matters, so that it administers the guarantee section of the European

Agricultural Guidance and Guarantee Fund (*Fondo Europeo de Orientación y Garantía Agrícolas/FEOGA*). This supports prices under the arrangements of the Common Agricultural Policy [4.1.1]. The guidance section, which constitutes the second structural fund, is managed by the National Land Reform and Agricultural Development Agency (*Instituto Nacional de Reforma y Desarrollo Agrario/IRYDA*).

The third structural fund, the enormous European Social Fund (*Fondo Social Europeo/FSE*), aimed at promoting employment and improving living standards in the Union, is administered by the Ministry of Labour and Immigration. The Ministry of Education, Social Policy and Sport is responsible for administering the Lifelong Learning Programme (*Programa 'Ámbito del Aprendizaje Permanente'*), the newly created designation which includes a number of sub-programmes, chief among them being Comenius (for schools); Erasmus (for higher education); Leonardo da Vinci (for vocational training) and Gruntvig (for adult education).

The Spanish Parliament, too, has made arrangements for coordination by creating a Joint Committee of both its Houses [1.3.4] to deal with EU affairs. First, this Committee deals directly with the European Parliament, having the right to comment on any EP proposals. Secondly, it seeks to exercise parliamentary control over the Spanish government's policy towards the Union. Finally, it cooperates with the national parliaments of the other member states on matters of mutual concern.

Links with the EU are also of prime importance for Spain's autonomous regions. On the one hand, they are now responsible for a major part of the country's system of governance and administration, making the need for coordination almost as great as at national level. Not surprisingly, all seventeen now have a department for EU affairs; most have a special unit to administer Structural Funds money; and nearly all of them have set up offices in Brussels whose job is to lobby the Union institutions concerned. For years the demand by the regions for direct representation at meetings of the Council of Ministers was resisted by Madrid. In 2004, however, under PM Zapatero, an agreement was reached whereby the regions could send one representative to each of four Councils of Ministers as well as having the power to appoint two civil servants to Spain's Permanent Representation.

The status of Spain's regional languages in the EU has also been an issue. The Spanish government proposed in 2005 that the co-official languages of Galicia, Catalonia and the Basque Country should become official working languages of the Union. Although this request was rejected, many EU documents are translated into Basque, Catalan/Valencian and Galician. In 2006 it was agreed that citizens would be allowed to address the European Parliament and to direct complaints to the European Ombudsman in those languages.

In addition to these arrangements made by Spanish authorities, the EU has established a number of bodies in Spain, as in other member states. These are intended to allow Spanish society and business access to the Union and its institutions, the largest being the offices of the European Commission and Parliament in Madrid. European Documentation Centres (*Centros de Documentación Europea/CDE*) are scattered throughout the country, while several of the main cities host European Business Information Centres (*Centros de Información Empresarial*), commonly known as *Euroventanillas*. There is also a more extensive Business Cooperation Network (*BC Net*) intended to provide support for small and medium enterprises. The locations of all these types of office vary widely: a few have their own premises; some are located in regional government offices, universities or business associations [5.5.2]; others – especially among the last group – are hosted by private firms.

Finally, three EU specialist agencies are located in Spain. The office concerned with health and safety at work in Europe (*Agencia Europea para la Seguridad y la Salud en el Trabajo*) is located in Bilbao. The EU's Satellite Centre (*Centro de Satélites de la Unión Europea*), which works on exploiting information made available from observations of the Earth from space, is at Torrejón de Ardoz, near Madrid, while one of the largest of all the EU agencies is the Internal Market Harmonization Office (*Oficina de Armonización del Mercado Interior/OAMI*), located in Alicante.

Spain is exceptional in terms of the number of bodies of this type located in the country. While Belgium stands out as the single EU country to have five of them, the only other countries with three are France and Greece. That can certainly be seen as another fruit of the Spanish government's determination to establish the country as an important player in Union affairs. Whether it, or indeed the various European offices, do much to reduce the democratic deficit [4.1.2], by making Spaniards feel more involved in the Union, is less clear.

4.4 Glossary

abogado general (m)	advocate general
Acta Única Europea/AUE (f)	Single European Act
Acuerdo Social (m)	Social Charter (of the Maastricht Treaty)
adhesión (f)	accession (to the EU)
agentes sociales (mpl)	social partners
alto representante (m)	high representative
ampliación (f)	enlargement (of the EU)
arancel aduanero común (m)	common external tariff
asuntos de Interior (mpl)	home affairs
Banco Central Europeo (m)	European Central Bank
barreras arancelarias (fpl)	tariff barriers
barreras no tarifarias (fpl)	non-tariff barriers
Centros de documentación europea (mpl)	European documentation centres
Centros de información empresarial (mpl)	European business information centres
circunscripción única (f)	single, country-wide constituency (for European elections)
cláusula de exclusión (f)	opt-out
Comisario (m)	(European) Commissioner
Comisión Europea (f)	European Commission
conferencia intergubernamental (f)	intergovernmental conference
Consejo de Gobierno (m)	Governing Council (of European Central Bank)
Consejo de Ministros (m)	Council of Ministers
Consejo Europeo (m)	European Council
Constitución Europea (f)	European Constitution

cooperación reforzada (f)	enhanced cooperation
cumbre (m)	summit
Dirección General (f)	Directorate General (within the Commission)
estados miembros (mpl)	(EU) member states
eurodiputado (m)	MEP
Euroejército (m)	Eurocorps
Europa de dos velocidades (f)	two-speed Europe
europeísmo (m)	enthusiasm for (the idea of) the EU, europhilia
europeización (f)	process of (Spain's) becoming more like the rest of Europe
fondos estructurales (mpl)	structural funds
Fondo Social Europeo (m)	European Social Fund
integración (f)	entry (into the EU)
integración europea (f)	European integration
mayoría cualificada (f)	qualified majority
mecanismo de cambios (m)	Exchange Rate Mechanism
mercado común (m)	common market
mercado interior (m)	internal market
moneda única (f)	single currency
no inscrito (m)	MEP who is not a member of any of the European Parliament's groups
pecos (mpl)	Central and Eastern European countries
período transitorio (m)	transitional period
Política Agrícola Común (f)	Common Agricultural Policy
presidencia (f)	presidency
presidente (de una comisión) (m)	(committee) chair
profundización (f)	deepening (of the EU)
Tratado de Lisboa	Lisbon Treaty
Unión Europea (f)	European Union
Unión Europea Occidental (f)	Western European Union
zona de libre comercio (f)	free trade area
zona euro (f)	Eurozone, Euroland

5

The Spanish economy

For all the enormous political transformation Spain has undergone since Franco died, perhaps the greatest changes to affect the country in recent decades have been economic. In the 1950s it was still regarded by the United Nations as part of the developing world: now it has the planet's ninth largest GDP and its firms have turned it into the sixth biggest net investor abroad in the world. The first section of this chapter traces the course of economic change since 1975, highlighting two major themes. The second then considers four areas of imbalance in the economy that have clouded Spain's success story, and to some extent still do so. The third section describes briefly the major sectors of economic activity in Spain, and its distribution between regions. This is followed by a section which looks at the main features of Spanish companies, and, in the final section, there is an outline of two of the key economic lobby groups in Spain, viz., trade unions and employers' organizations.

5.1 *Apertura, ajuste* and *boom*

In 1975 the Spanish economy remained largely isolated from the outside world. By far the most important factor in its development since then has been a gradual process of exposure to international and especially to European markets (*apertura*). That process has been fundamental in promoting the country's development; almost universally it is seen as positive. Yet, especially coming at a time of unprecedented economic change in the world as a whole, it gave Spain enormous problems. The country was repeatedly obliged by economic circumstances to undertake policy changes (*ajustes*), usually painful ones, before it eventually recovered and experienced strong and consistent economic growth in the early part of this century.

5.1.1 Prelude: boom and bust

In today's rapidly globalizing world it is hard to comprehend just how cut off the Spanish economy was in 1975. Even if the Franco regime had long since abandoned its pretensions to self-sufficiency [0.2], the country's trade and investment flows remained very low. Indeed, it was only this isolation that had enabled Spain's belated but rapid economic modernization under the dictatorship. But even before Franco died the limitations of this approach were being cruelly exposed.

Spain's economic boom of the 1960s and early 1970s was based largely on heavy industries such as mining, shipbuilding, metalworking of various sorts, and basic chemicals. The firms involved were severely lacking in modern equipment. Instead they relied on relatively primitive technology and an abundant supply of poorly paid labour. Many, whether or not state-owned, received substantial government subsidies (*subvenciones*). Virtually none were in a position to compete with their better-equipped counterparts in other countries.

Consequently, Spanish industrial exports were minimal, while the country's manufacturing firms relied heavily on the protection of their own domestic market (*mercado nacional*) from foreign imports. Most obviously Spain imposed unusually high tariffs on many incoming goods. It also operated an elaborate system of quotas (*contingentes*) on particular products, as well as other forms of non-tariff barriers (*barreras no tarifarias*). By these various means the availability and prices of imported goods were regulated in such a way as to prevent them forcing Spanish ones off the market.

Yet, ironically, restrictions on foreign trade could not prevent Spain from falling prey to the development which brought growth in Western Europe as a whole to an abrupt end. Lacking significant energy reserves of its own, Spain had become even more highly dependent than other Western countries on cheap oil imports, above all from the Middle East. It was thus especially hard hit when, in 1973, OPEC (*Organización de los Países Exportadores del Petróleo/OPEP*) imposed a massive rise in oil prices. The effects on the economy were devastating. Unemployment started to rise, the balance of payments suffered severely, and inflation rose sharply – even though the government ill-advisedly kept energy costs artificially low by subsidizing them.

The impact was magnified further by the political situation following Franco's death. For almost a decade the attention of Spain's leaders was focused almost exclusively on the problems of building a democratic state. Economic issues were pushed into the background. Meantime many workers were understandably concerned for their living standards in the face of rising prices, and vigorously demanded wage rises to match. Even after trade union leaders agreed to moderate their claims in the 1977 Moncloa Pacts [0.3.3], wage rises continued to fuel price inflation for some years.

Consequently, during the early 1980s Spain's inflation rate (*tasa de inflación*) ran consistently well above the average for the European Community. The difference was of particular significance because, after 1975, all the major political parties were convinced that the country must join the EC. Doing so would, by definition, involve free trade with other member states. Unless inflation were brought down to EC levels, the country's products would be unable to compete in the Common Market.

5.1.2 Into Europe

When the Socialists came to power in 1982 intent on joining the EC [4.2.1], inflation was accordingly a major priority for them. The government's response was to promote a series of agreements with employers and unions, all of which set national benchmarks for wage increases designed to bring inflation down. The resultant wage moderation (*moderación salarial*) played a big part in bringing inflation under control. But it was also the first of a number of painful 'adjustments' for many.

The new government's second priority was to overhaul the antiquated industries bequeathed by the Franco regime [5.1.1], to give them a chance of competing inside the EC. Some attempts had already been made to tackle this task, but they were sporadic and ineffectual. As a result the Socialists had little option but to undertake a massive programme of industrial restructuring (*reconversión industrial*), the second key element of 'adjustment'.

The programme involved changing the structure of Spanish manufacturing industry at two levels. First, the intention was to shift its basis from out-dated industries to those with good future prospects. Secondly, within individual industries or branches, the government aimed to create firms of a scale large enough to compete with their European competitors. Restructuring thus implied a managed run-down of older industries which were in decline not just in Spain but throughout the developed world.

A prime example was shipbuilding. During the 1960s, Spain had become the industry's world leader, essentially because its shipyards paid lower wages than those elsewhere in the West. By the 1980s, however, it had been undercut in wage terms by new competitors, above all the newly-industrialized countries of South-east Asia. Similar considerations applied to a range of older industries, including iron and steel manufacture and the chemical industry. In all of them there was a need to eliminate loss-making firms (*empresas deficitarias*). Previously these had been kept alive by state financial support, much of which was now phased out to prepare for conditions within the EC.

For many companies the result was closure. The healthier ones were concentrated into potentially viable units through mergers (*fusiones*) and takeovers (*absorciones*). The survivors of this process were subject to tough measures designed to rationalize them, that is, put them on a sound financial footing (*saneamiento*). In essence that meant a stringent reduction in costs, typically through radical downsizing (*ajustes de plantilla*) – in plain English, job cuts.

Many workers were required to take early retirement (*jubilación anticipada*). Their younger colleagues were offered, at least in theory, retraining in new skills (*reciclaje*) as preparation for redeployment in the second stage of restructuring – re-industrialization, or the establishment of new industries. This policy, however, proved less easy to implement than the first. For many, 'adjustment' turned out to mean long-term unemployment (*paro de larga duración*).

In terms of their overall objective the policies pursued by the Socialists proved remarkably successful. Not only did Spain's economy survive entry to the EC, it actually flourished. Between 1985 and 1989 GDP grew at an annual rate only marginally short of 5 per cent, the highest in the Community and, indeed, among the major developed countries. This 'second economic miracle', as it became known, was partly due to internal factors. Restructuring had put parts of the country's economy on a much sounder footing. Political stability seemed assured and the country had a government with the will to act and the parliamentary majority to allow it to do so [2.3.2]. However, the main cause was precisely Spain's entry into Europe.

As an EC member, Spain was in a position to benefit from the expansion enjoyed in the late 1980s by the Community, and by the Western world as a whole. Foreign investment, the great majority now from its new partners, flowed into the country [5.2.1]. And, as one of the poorer members, Spain was also a major recipient of grants from the Community's Structural Funds [4.1.1] designed to reduce imbalances between different parts of the EC (*desequilibrios territoriales*). Such support was fundamental to the sharp increase in public spending, especially on education and infrastructure, which in turn was one of the principal driving forces behind rapid growth.

5.1.3 Recession and recovery

Throughout Western Europe the brief boom of the late 1980s was followed by the deepest recession (*crisis*) for 60 years. Spain was particularly hard hit. By the middle of the 1990s the ratio of its per capita GDP to the EU average had fallen back to around three-quarters, barely different from the level in 1975. There were various reasons for this setback.

One was the rise in government spending at the end of the previous decade [5.1.2]; although badly needed, it was simply too fast for the country's economy to bear, particularly in regard to social welfare. Another was the partial nature of restructuring [5.1.2]. A third cause was the fact that growth had been concentrated heavily in the services sector, and financed to a dangerous degree by short-term foreign capital which could be – and was – withdrawn when the international economic climate changed.

As a member of the EC club, Spain was no longer cushioned from such unpleasant developments. Moreover, their impact was aggravated by the Spanish government's slowness to react. By 1989 it was already clear that the economy had reached the stage of overheating (*calentamiento*). Yet the government failed for some time to take the steps necessary to produce a gradual cooling-down (*enfriamiento*). Instead, partly because of the impending prestige events of 1992 [0.4], it continued to spend heavily well into the 1990s. The results were very severe indeed. Inflation rose again and in 1993 economic growth went into reverse, that is, the economy contracted.

Because Spain had waited too long to adjust to the changing economic climate, the necessary deflationary measures were all the more severe when they finally came. By then wage moderation by agreement had been ruled out by the split between government and unions [5.5.1.2]. Instead, the emphasis fell on public spending cuts (*ajustes presupuestarios*). Infrastructure projects came to an abrupt halt, and in 1992 the government introduced a package of measures slashing entitlements to unemployment and other forms of benefit. Issued initially by a surprise decree, they became infamous under the name of *decretazo*.

These austerity measures eventually proved successful in getting recovery under way, albeit rather more slowly than elsewhere in the EU, as it now was. In the meantime, however, the government had committed itself to meeting the conditions set in 1991 for Economic and Monetary Union (EMU) (see Table 4.1). It was clear that meeting these convergence criteria would be a hard task for Spain, even with the help of the Cohesion Fund (*Fondo de Cohesión*) set up at her insistence [4.2.2]. To meet the challenge, Economics Minister Pedro Solbes drew up a Convergence Plan (*Plan de Convergencia*) which brought further restrictions on government spending and monetary policy (*política monetaria*).

Over the next few years convergence placed considerable strains on even the healthiest European economies. In Spain the situation was aggravated by the further opening up brought about by the Single European Act in 1993 [4.1.1]. Within a year the government had been forced to alter radically the forecasts on which its Convergence Plan was based. Nevertheless, it persisted with its restrictive policies. By the time it was defeated at the polls in 1996 Spain had been set firmly on the road to convergence, which was pursued with equal determination by the new conservative government. In 1997 these efforts were crowned with success when Spain was officially given the go-ahead for EMU [4.2.2].

By then, too, the country's economic fortunes were once more rising sharply, and continued to do so over the years that followed, with Spain once again outstripping most other Western nations in terms of growth. As a result it began to close the gap between it and the rest of the EU once more; in 2000 its per capita GDP stood at just 83 per cent of the Union average and by 2005 it had reached 98.5 per cent. Admission to EMU was not a fundamental cause of these developments, but it did act as a psychological boost to public and business morale.

One clear sign of this was that, for the first time, Spain's economy was opening up in a much more active sense. In the 1990s a growing number of Spanish firms began to penetrate foreign markets and to invest abroad [5.2.1], above all in Latin America. This trend continued in the following decade, when many Spanish firms invested in the new Eastern European member states of the EU [4.1.2]. Although this active participation in globalization is usually seen as positive, the massive losses suffered by Spanish companies when the Argentinian economy imploded in 2001/02 was a reminder of the possible dangers associated with it.

Growth in Spain's GDP was consistently good over the five years to 2008, averaging around 3.3 per cent (with a low of 2.7 per cent in 2002, and peaking at 3.9 per cent in 2006). This growth has been well ahead of both the Eurozone average and the average for OECD countries. In tandem with this, perhaps the most spectacular aspect of the recent success of the Spanish economy has been a dramatic drop in unemployment, which has gone from 13 per cent in 2001 to just 8.5 per cent at the beginning of 2008.

While this economic buoyancy represents a tangible improvement in the financial well-being of most Spaniards, there are negative aspects to it. Inflation, for instance, has increased significantly, and in 2007 stood at 3.5 per cent, with house prices having risen some 180 per cent over the previous ten years. The country's heavy dependence on the construction sector (18 per cent of the country's total economic activity in 2007) could yet prove perilous, given trends in that sector in early 2008 that indicate that it is slowing down. Meanwhile, improvements in productivity levels in Spanish industry have been sluggish: of the thirty richest countries in the world, Spain had the second lowest growth in productivity after Mexico between 1996 and 2006. In particular, Research and Development is chronically underfunded, with investment in R & D and Innovation (*investigación, desarrollo e innovación/I+D+i*) running at just over 1 per cent, around half the European average in that area.

5.2 Imbalances

Spain's impressive progress over the last twenty-five years was far from a smooth process; in fact it was more like a roller-coaster ride. By the same token, the advances achieved were by no means uniform across all aspects of its economy. At various times, four areas of imbalance have caused particular concern. One is that aspect most obviously affected by the process of integration into the world economy – the balance of payments. Two more – the value of money and the state of public finances – relate directly to the criteria laid down for entry into Economic and Monetary Union. The fourth is unemployment, which did not figure in the convergence criteria, but which was gravely affected by the efforts made to meet them.

5.2.1 Balance of payments

Spain's balance of payments deficit (*déficit exterior*) has been a problem for the country since the 1950s. Under the Franco regime, however, the country's foreign trade (*comercio exterior*) was so limited that in absolute terms the deficit was very small. The mild liberalization measures undertaken by the regime in 1959/60 [0.2] considerably increased the trade gap (*déficit comercial*) although money sent home to their families by emigrant workers abroad and revenue from tourism had the effect of moving the balance of payments into surplus (*excedente*) by the early 1970s.

From 1986, however, the situation was again reversed by the dismantling of customs barriers (*barreras aduaneras*) on EC entry [4.2.1]. As a result the Spanish market was invaded by goods from other EC countries, above all France and Germany. Indeed, the influx was actively encouraged by the government, which was conscious that, in order to build up new industries, Spain must import capital goods (*bienes de equipo*). Although Spanish exports also rose, it was at nothing like the same rate. The result was that the trade deficit increased fourfold between 1985 and 1989.

The opening up of trade in services in 1993 which resulted from the Single European Act [4.1.1] was another severe blow for the country's balance. Spain's own service sector was small and inefficient, and the country offered a tempting new market for European firms. Nor was it any longer feasible to cover the deficit by non-trade earnings.

Later in the 1990s, an upturn in tourist numbers and receipts [5.3.4] helped improve the balance. More important for the long term, however, was the fact that, for the first time in the country's history, recovery from recession was export-driven; in other words, firms' export earnings were the first means by which new demand was injected into the economy. In addition, the composition of exports started to shift away from traditional agricultural products to higher-value manufactured goods. Another factor was Spain's growing attractiveness to Foreign Direct Investment or FDI (*Inversión Extranjera Directa/IED*), which rose rapidly in the decade after 1986.

Thanks to these various effects, by 1997 Spain's current account was actually back in the black; the following year it recorded the highest surplus ever. Ironically, by then, inward investment had not only slowed but been overtaken by the investment of Spanish firms abroad which rose by a factor of ten between 1995 and 1999. The great majority of the large outflow was destined for Latin America. There, for instance, companies such as the country's two biggest banks, BSCH (Banco de Santander) and BBVA [5.3.3] became major investors, along with the privatized state monopolies Telefónica (telecommunications), Repsol-YPF (hydrocarbons) and Endesa (energy).

Although Spanish investment in Latin America dipped in 2002, as the economies of several key countries in the region went into recession, the pace of that investment has generally been steady since. This is despite other setbacks such as the nationalizations carried out by populist leaders such as Hugo Chávez in Venezuela and Evo Morales in Bolivia. The main focus of that investment has been in Mexico, Chile and Brazil, but many other countries have been targeted, with the result that many of the biggest banking, telecommunications and energy concerns in the region are owned by some of the Spanish transnational companies or TNCs (*empresas transnacionales*) mentioned above.

While Latin America has continued to be an important destination for FDI from Spain, the bulk of that investment since the turn of the century has been directed towards European Union countries. A considerable proportion of that has gone to the new member states of Eastern Europe, but other countries have felt the effects too. In fact, the single European country where Spanish FDI has had the greatest impact has been the UK. Some of the more spectacular British catches landed by Spanish firms have included Ferrovial's acquisition of BAA, the company that controls several major airports, including Heathrow; Telefónica's acquisition of the mobile phone company O2, and Iberdrola's purchase of ScottishPower.

The renewed balance of payments deficit recorded in 2000 was more the result of a worsening in the terms of trade for Spain, notably rising oil prices. The country's dependence on foreign energy is one reason why, despite the real progress made, its balance of payments remains vulnerable. And, with the coming of EMU [4.2.2], it can no longer use devaluation of its currency to boost exports, as happened in the 1990s. The most recent figures continue this negative trend, showing a deficit of 9 per cent of GDP, the highest in the developed world with the exception of the USA. This is caused mainly by high levels of borrowing, growing inflation (which is running well ahead of the EU average) and the deficit in the country's balance of trade, as Spanish imports heavily outweigh its exports. This deficit stood at more than €92 billion in 2006, for example, an increase of some 19 per cent over the figure for 2005.

5.2.2 Monetary aspects

Spain's former currency, the peseta, was traditionally weak. That is, it tended to lose value against other currencies, which made imports expensive. Thus, when the government was keen to facilitate the import of capital goods in the late 1980s [5.2.1], its exchange-rate policy (*política cambiaria*) was aimed at maintaining a strong peseta. In an attempt to underpin its value, in 1989 the then Finance Minister, Carlos Solchaga, took the peseta into the European Monetary System [4.1.1], effectively pegging it against the other main European currencies at a relatively high level.

As the country's economy deteriorated over the next few years [5.1.3], the peseta came under increasing pressure. This the government resisted, determined to meet the criteria for EMU (see Table 4.1). Even when the pressure became irresistible, the Spanish government was reluctant to acknowledge the extent of the peseta's overvaluation. The result was that on 13 May 1993 Spain was forced to devalue by a full 13 per cent, far more than allowed by the criteria. The date became known as Black Thursday (*jueves negro*).

This setback was a humiliation for the government but by no means disastrous for the economy; in fact it helped the balance of payments by improving export performance. In any case, only a few months later the EMS itself effectively collapsed. When a new, more flexible system was cobbled together in late 1993 the Spanish government re-joined, even though it seemed likely that the peseta was still too high for comfort.

This time, however, the gamble paid off. Rapid economic recovery, along with a weakening of the German mark, enabled the Spanish currency to maintain its value until, with the onset of EMU in 1999, it found shelter beneath the protective umbrella of the new European Central Bank [4.1.2]. Three years later, at the start of 2002, the peseta was replaced by the euro, at a rate of 1 euro to 166.386 pesetas.

Spanish participation in EMU was only possible because of a dramatic reduction in inflation. Conversely, one reason why successive governments were so keen to join first the EMS and then EMU was that the discipline they imposed was seen as a means of maintaining the peseta's internal value, its purchasing power (*poder adquisitivo*), by slowing down the rise in prices. For, although inflation had been brought down from the dramatic levels of the late 1970s [5.1.1], it remained significantly above the EU average into the 1990s.

Cutting it further was the main aim of the austerity measures adopted from 1991 on [5.1.3]. They had the desired effect, and by 1998 the rate was at a record low of 1.4 per cent, one of the best figures in the EU. This situation could not be maintained, however, and strong growth has pushed inflation back up to around 3–4 per cent in the first years of the new century. Even so, this represents a considerable improvement on past performance.

Keeping the peseta high and inflation low long required Spanish interest rates to be held well above the EU average. Not only did that infringe a third convergence criterion (see Table 4.1). It also held back the investment needed to ensure recovery after the recession of the early 1990s [5.1.3]. However, as inflation fell and confidence grew that Spain would indeed qualify for EMU, it proved possible to ease monetary policy as well. In 1998 base rates fell to their lowest ever level of 3 per cent. And the advent of EMU the following year meant that, in this respect too, the differentials between Spain and the other euro countries were effectively removed.

5.2.3 Public finances

The annual public sector deficit (*déficit público*) has been very high in Spain over the period since the transition to democracy. There are several reasons for this. One is the high cost of building a modern welfare state [7.1.1]; another is the state's involvement in a number of unprofitable economic activities [5.4.1]. While some of the latter were sold off as part of industrial restructuring in the 1980s [5.1.2], that process added new burdens on the public purse in the shape of redundancy payments, early pensions and unemployment benefit [5.2.4]. Moreover, even after the massive expenditure of the 1980s, Spain continued to need costly investment in infrastructure and technology, much of which had to come from the state. A further pressure on state spending was high interest rates [5.2.2], which pushed up the interest payments on government bonds or debt (*deuda del estado*).

Yet, despite all these pressures on expenditure, the deficit's main cause lay on the income side, in the tax system of the Francoist era. Not only was the overall tax burden (*presión fiscal*) then extraordinarily low by the standards of the developed world. It was also very oddly distributed. Direct taxes (*fiscalidad directa*) were levied almost exclusively on those whose wages were easily monitored, which, in practice, meant employees (*trabajadores por cuenta ajena*) who figured on the payroll of a large firm. Little attempt was made even to establish the tax liability of workers in the small firms which dominate the country's economy [5.4.2], or of the self-employed (*autónomos*). More than half of all tax revenues came from indirect taxation (*fiscalidad indirecta*), the rates of which were higher on basic than luxury items.

In the late 1970s and 1980s this system was reformed and efforts were made to increase revenue, so that, by 1989, the rates of both personal income tax (*impuesto sobre la renta de las personas físicas/IRPF*) and corporation tax (*impuesto de sociedades*) had increased substantially. In addition, Spain's entry into the EC brought the introduction of value added tax (*impuesto sobre el valor añadido/IVA*). Even so, the system had become much more progressive, in the sense that more tax income now came from direct taxes, the rates of which rise with income levels. As a result, growing prosperity in the late 1980s and again a decade later brought proportionately more into the government's coffers (*arcas del estado*).

There was, however, considerable public resentment of these activities on the part of the tax authorities (*hacienda*) among many Spaniards who were not used to the role of taxpayer (*contribuyente*). This resentment was reflected in the growth of a large informal economy (*economía sumergida*). By that is meant all those economic activities carried on outside the state's knowledge and so omitted from official statistics; in Spain's case studies have suggested that this may account for as much as 20 per cent of GDP. Industries believed to be particularly affected are construction and footwear. The effect of the reforms was to bring about a reduction of the deficit to the 3 per cent required for EMU entry [4.2.2] in 1997; in fact, by the turn of the century, it was down to around 1 per cent.

Since then, the improvements that have taken place in the economy have led to a situation where the government is in a position to register a surplus in its accounts for the first time in three decades. In 2005, mainly on the strength of higher taxation revenues, the government accounts (*cuentas de las Administraciones Públicas*) recorded a surplus of 1.1 per cent of GDP, which increased in the following year to 1.8 per cent. These figures mean that Spain is well within the budgetary criteria laid down within the EU's Stability and Growth Pact [4.1.2]. The latter allows for a maximum deficit of 3 per cent, while also permitting a maximum public debt of 60 per cent of GDP. In Spain the debt was just 39.8 per cent in 2006, which left the country in a more favourable position than most other EMU members, including key states such as Germany, France and Italy, all of whom were running public debts in excess of 60 per cent.

The Socialist government elected in 2004 used this surplus to finance a series of social measures which, among other things, helped to present it in a good light as it approached the March 2008 general election [7.1.2]. Only time will tell whether the surplus would have been better spent in reducing the country's national debt (*endeudamiento público*), as some critics maintained.

5.2.4 Labour market

For a long time stubbornly out of line with the rest of the developed world, Spain's unemployment rate (*tasa de desempleo*) has only recently dropped to around the level of the EU average. Attempts at resolving the problem have focused mainly on making the country's job market (*mercado laboral*) work more efficiently, and in recent years this strategy has finally begun to show some positive effects. Thus, while the unemployment rate in 1994 was around one in five of the labour force, today the level has dropped to about 8.5 per cent; furthermore, since the Eurozone was set up in 2002, some two fifths of all new jobs created within it have been created in Spain.

5.2.4.1 Unemployment

For lengthy periods in the 1980s and 1990s, over three million Spaniards were officially recorded as out of work by the government-run National Employment Agency (*Instituto Nacional de Empleo*/INEM). Using the rather higher figures of the Official Labour-force Survey (*Encuesta de Población Activa*/EPA), unemployment peaked in 1994 at 24 per cent, thereafter declining slowly, until the turn of the century when it dropped more dramatically. It should be noted, however, that the unemployment figures given here are almost certainly inflated due to the existence of a large informal economy [5.2.3].

Joblessness was a major issue as far back as 1982, when a Socialist government arrived in power promising to create 800,000 jobs. The fact that unemployment not only persisted but rose steeply during its term of office was often quoted to show that this pledge had been broken. Such accusations betrayed a misunderstanding of the causes of unemployment. In fact, over the next decade the number of people in work rose by well over a million. The problem was that the labour force (*población activa*) – the number of Spaniards working or seeking work – grew even more.

There were several reasons for this. By the 1980s, few Spaniards were working outside the country, and the high birth rates of the Franco era had worked through into the numbers of working age. Most important of all, relatively more adults were now seeking jobs than before. Since 1970 Spain's participation rate, or economic activity rate (*tasa de actividad*), has increased steadily. The rise would have been even greater had not many men made redundant in older industries ceased to seek work. By contrast, the female participation rate – previously very low indeed – rose dramatically. The trend is set to continue, since the Spanish participation rate is still below the EU average, substantially so in the case of women.

In the late 1980s and during the 1990s there was also a severe mismatch between the skills of the unemployed and the jobs becoming available. Thus most job losses (*destrucción de empleo*) were in traditional heavy industries or agriculture, whereas most new employment had been created in light industries and, above all, in the service sector. Successive governments attempted to counteract this problem by improving training provision in general [7.3.2.3], and by providing specific retraining (*reciclaje*) for those thrown out of work. The impact of these and other 'active' employment policies was limited.

The direction of 'passive' policies, that is those designed to cushion the effects of unemployment, has been varied. On the one hand, pressure on public finances [5.2.3] has several times brought cutbacks in the level and coverage of unemployment benefit. On the other, general welfare provision has been greatly expanded since 1980. That is usually seen as a major reason why Spaniards have shown little inclination in recent decades to move in search of work (*falta de movilidad laboral*); internal migration, previously high, has almost dried up. And, since new jobs were mainly outside the areas worst hit by unemployment [5.3.5], this posed another barrier to reducing it.

Since the turn of the century, however, Spanish unemployment figures have been improving significantly. Changes in employment law [5.2.4.2] have been one factor in this improvement, mainly because they have introduced greater flexibility into the system. Along with this, there has been a marked improvement in the general economic climate, both globally and within Europe. These conditions have helped create many new employment opportunities, especially in the services sector. Meanwhile, the influx of immigrants [6.1.2], most of whom are keen to take up these opportunities, has also meant that a greater proportion of the population is now at work. One final factor, and not a negligible one, is the possibility that the data on which employment figures are based may now be of better quality than they were heretofore. The result has been that numbers recorded as being out of work have fallen from 13 per cent in 2001 to 10.4 per cent in 2004 and 8.5 per cent by the beginning of 2008.

Notwithstanding the good news overall, it is still the case that there are worrying disparities in the figures. Unemployment continues to be high among young people (*paro juvenil*), for example, the rate in 2006 being almost 29 per cent for 16–19-year-olds and just under 15 per cent for 20–24-year-olds. Regional disparities are also quite striking, with the rate in Navarre, at 4.4 per cent, comparing favourably with the EU average of 8.2 per cent, whereas the Andalusian rate, for instance, remains stubbornly high at 12.5 per cent.

5.2.4.2 Revising employment legislation

According to most economists, at the root of the Spanish labour market's problems have been various forms of inflexibility, or rigidity (*rigideces*); that is, features which constrain the market's ability to meet rapidly changing economic conditions. In large measure they resulted from the complex system of employment regulation instituted by the Franco regime.

One aspect was the standard minimum wage (*salario mínimo interprofesional/SMI*) introduced in 1963 and set annually by the government after consultation with unions and employers' organizations. In fact, employers have shown little concern over the SMI, as its effect on wage levels is negligible. Even in theory only 5 per cent of the workforce are affected by it: in practice, high unemployment has meant that workers have been willing to collude with employers in working for lower rates in the informal economy [5.2.3]. Altogether more important in holding back job creation were employers' social security contributions (*cuotas empresariales*). Appreciably higher than in other EU countries, they have often been referred to as a jobs tax (*impuesto sobre el empleo*).

However, the principal causes of labour market rigidity derived from the legal conditions on employing workers, which were updated in the 1980 Workers' Charter (*Estatuto de los Trabajadores*) [5.5.1.1]. The Charter made collective agreements (*convenios colectivos*) between unions and employer representatives binding, thus restricting individual firms' ability to respond to their circumstances. It also consolidated the existing strict regulations on terms and conditions of service, and on the nature of employees' contracts, almost all of which were automatically permanent (*contratos de duración indefinida*), all of which made it difficult and costly for employers to reduce the size of their workforce.

During the 1980s this situation increasingly worried not only employers but also the government. In 1984 the latter introduced a first set of reforms, including legalization of fixed-term contracts (*contratos temporales*) which encouraged employers to take on new workers in the knowledge that they were not saddled with the related costs indefinitely.

In 1994, a broader set of changes was introduced. Under these, employers were permitted to issue part-time contracts (*contratos a tiempo parcial*), thus regularizing a situation already common in the informal economy. More significantly in terms of employment policy, two new contract types – work placements (*contratos en prácticas*) and apprenticeships (*contratos de aprendizaje*) – were introduced, allowing for greater flexibility in terms of wages and conditions. These reforms also relaxed the obligations on employers to respect national or sectoral agreements and eased the restrictions applying to dismissals (*despidos*).

While not worthless, these new reforms proved inadequate either to bring down unemployment or to satisfy employers. They also had the unforeseen effect of greatly reducing job security; in 1996, only 4 per cent of new contracts were permanent. As a result, the conservative government elected in 1996 was able to persuade unions and employers to reach an agreement the following year as the basis for a further round of changes.

These 1997 reforms restricted the use of temporary contracts (*contratos temporales*) while introducing a new type of permanent one to which much less onerous conditions on severance pay (*indemnización*) applied. These new contracts were available only to certain groups of employees – basically, younger and older workers, the long-term unemployed and the disabled. In addition, employers' social service contributions were reduced. Combined with the general economic upswing [5.1.3], these measures finally brought some concrete success. In 1998, 450,000 new jobs were created, 80 per cent of them permanent. And by 2001 unemployment had fallen to 13 per cent [5.2.4.1], still well above the EU average but a major improvement nonetheless.

Further reforms were instituted in 2001, in the form of an entrenched law [1.3.3], given that negotiations between employers and trade unions lasting some eight months had failed to yield an agreement. In response to the employers' expressed wish, more flexibility was allowed in relation to part-time contracts, while severance pay was reduced from 45 days per year worked to 33. On the other hand, the aspirations of the unions were reflected in an eight-day severance pay arrangement for fixed-term contracts, and a new subsidy for unemployed women who wished to return to the workplace after having children.

What was to prove by far the most controversial measure, however, came in 2002. This was a set of revisions to the legislation relating to unemployment (*reforma de la protección por desempleo*). The law took the form of a government decree stipulating new obligations on the unemployed and cutting their benefits. It included conditions such as the requirement that unemployed people would have to accept any position deemed suitable up to 30 kilometres (or a two-hour journey) from their home. Further, after a year's unemployment, they would be obliged to accept any job which they were considered capable of doing, along with having to attend obligatory training courses.

The reaction of the trade unions (CCOO and UGT [5.5.1.1]) was to call a general strike for 20 June 2002 (*20-J*), the fifth general strike in the new democracy, and the first under a PP government. Estimates of the numbers who took strike action on the day varied enormously. Demonstrations held in Madrid and Barcelona attracted half a million participants, according to the unions, or just 20,000, according to the government – whose dubious version of events was also supported by state TV [10.4]. As for the decree, it was eventually declared unconstitutional by the Constitutional Court, and annulled.

The most recent reform in this area was a 2006 agreement between government, employers and unions. This made it more attractive for employers to set up permanent contracts by offering a reduction of €800 in social security contributions if they converted fixed-term contracts into permanent ones before the end of 2006. It also made it obligatory, however, for employers to offer a permanent contract to any employee who had occupied the same post on the basis of two or more fixed-term contracts in a row amounting to two or more years of employment within a 30-month period. In spite of these changes, however, about 30 per cent of all workers in Spain are on temporary contracts, the highest proportion of any country in the EU.

5.3 Sectoral and geographical structure

The continuing existence of imbalances, including unemployment, is a reminder that Spain's recent economic history has not been an unbridled success story. And, in terms of the rate of advance, progress has been very uneven, with periods of rapid growth followed by stagnation or even recession. But in other respects change has been enormous and irreversible, especially when one looks beyond the features of the economy as a whole to its constituent parts: the different sectors of economic activity and the country's various regions.

5.3.1 Primary sector

Spain's primary sector has been shrinking for decades. In 1960 it accounted for over 20 per cent of GDP; by the 1990s the figure had fallen to around 6 per cent, and in 2006 it stood at just 3.9 per cent. As in other countries it is made up of various subsectors. Of these both forestry (*sector forestal*) and the mining industry (*sector minero*), although of significance in particular local areas and especially in environmental terms, play purely minor roles in the economy as a whole.

Spain's fishing industry (*sector pesquero*) is by far the largest in the EU, although for obvious reasons its significance is restricted to certain areas. It also faces a number of problems. Inshore fishing (*pesca costera*) has declined due to severe overfishing (*sobreexplotación*). More generally, EU conservation measures have forced reductions in the size of the fleet, especially in the main centres of Galicia and the Basque Country. Fishermen from these regions have led the way in seeking new fishing grounds (*caladeros*) on the high seas. Their often aggressive methods have led to confrontations with the authorities of several countries, including Ireland, Morocco and Canada. The development of aquaculture (*acuicultura*), mainly in the form of fish-farming and the cultivation of seaweed, has been an important related development in recent years, with Spain currently providing over a quarter of the entire aquacultural production in the EU.

The great bulk of the primary sector is made up of agriculture (*sector agropecuario*). In proportional terms it still accounts for considerably more employment in Spain than in the EU as a whole. Indeed, the country contributed 11 per cent of total EU agricultural production in 2006, making Spain the fourth largest agricultural producer of the 27 countries, after France, Italy and Germany.

Nevertheless, since 1960 Spain has experienced a massive drift of population from the land (*éxodo rural*), with just 4.5 per cent of the population employed in agriculture in 2007 (although, given the casual nature of much of the employment, this percentage varies considerably from one month to the next). This process began under Franco when the sector was accorded a low priority by the regime. The results of its neglect were clearly apparent in 1975, when Spanish agriculture was extremely backward and unproductive.

One pressing issue was the structure of agricultural landholding (*estructura agraria*), which in the south was linked to the question of ownership. In much of Spain farmers, whether owners or tenants, have traditionally enjoyed reasonable security of tenure. In wide areas of Andalusia and Extremadura, however, the countryside was dominated by large estates (*latifundios*). The bulk of the rural population consisted of day-labourers (*jornaleros*), employed at low wages and on extremely poor conditions. During the Second Republic their parlous situation had inspired attempts at land reform (*reforma agraria*), that is changes in the structure of land ownership. But little was achieved in terms of breaking up the estates, while under the Franco regime virtually all were returned to their former owners.

The question of land ownership overlapped with another, that of the size and nature of farm units (*explotaciones*), for the large southern estates were often notoriously ill-managed. In other parts of the country, on the other hand, many holdings were uneconomically small. To make matters worse, tiny smallholdings (*minifundios*) were often split up into plots (*parcelas*), sometimes widely separated. The first attempt at combating these interconnected problems was made during the transition, when a Landholdings Rationalization Service (*Servicio de Concentración Parcelaria*) was established to encourage the creation of larger, unified holdings through the exchange and sale of plots between smallholders. Government grants were provided to help the process along.

When the Socialists came to power in 1982 attention was extended to the question of the big estates, and the Service absorbed into a new Land Reform Agency (*Instituto de Reforma Agraria*). Working in conjunction with regional governments, and spurred on by the protests of the Landworkers Union [5.5.1.1], the Agency has enjoyed some success in transferring previously unused land to new owners, although the pressure to do so was to some extent relaxed by the extension of unemployment support to landworkers [5.2.4.1].

Instead, the focus of attention has shifted to the more general issue of agriculture's efficiency. In that sense the small scale of most farms continues to be a problem, because it makes the use of modern machinery difficult for both technical and financial reasons. Only recently have tractors been widely introduced into some areas; Galicia is especially notorious in this regard. Small farm size also militates against the establishment of effective distribution and marketing networks. One response to this problem has been to set up cooperatives.

Small farmers are also disproportionately affected by lack of knowledge about new techniques and alternative crops. As a result, attempts to increase productivity by these means have often created fresh problems. By and large they have involved bringing more land under irrigation (*riego*), a practice which is not only often harmful to the environment but also of doubtful utility in the longer term [8.2.2].

Provision of information on crops and techniques, and incentives to apply it, is one purpose of the EU's Common Agricultural Policy [4.1.1], from which Spanish farmers have benefited since 1986. Unfortunately for them, however, the bulk of its resources are devoted to the system of guaranteed farm prices, while under the CAP most resources are still focused on farmers in the original, more northerly EC member states.

The impact of EU membership on Spanish agriculture varies dramatically between different types of farming. Especially hard hit has been the dairy industry (*sector lácteo*). Concentrated on small, hilly farms in the northern coastal regions, it is poorly placed to compete with the much larger and more easily worked holdings common elsewhere in Europe.

Cereal farming, traditionally the backbone of the Castilian economy, has been another victim. On the other hand, new opportunities have opened up for some farmers, especially in the south and east where the climate is truly Mediterranean. There intensive techniques, using greenhouses (*invernaderos*) and extensive irrigation, have allowed profitable specialization in fruit and vegetables (*productos hortifrutícolas*). The southerly location gives a particular advantage in early season products (*primicias*).

Recent EU agreements on economic issues, including agriculture, will have further negative implications for Spanish agriculture. In the context of further enlargements of the Union, financial aid to this sector will be reduced during the period 2007–2013 [4.2.3]. This will entail a significant reduction in the area of land under cultivation, with the aim of cutting overall agricultural production and fostering more ecological approaches to agricultural activity. Despite this, however, Spain's most competitive products such as citrus fruits and other Mediterranean produce will remain relatively unaffected, given that, for the most part, the newcomers to the Union are not Mediterranean countries.

5.3.2 Industry

In contrast to the situation in other advanced countries, industry (*sector secundario*) was only briefly the largest and most important sector of the Spanish economy. Dwarfed by the primary sector until the 1960s, it was overtaken by services when the economy finally modernized thereafter. Its share of GDP and employment has changed little since the 1970s.

By 2006 the share of GDP accounted for by industrial activity was just under 30 per cent, and the sector employed approximately 17 per cent of the active population. Currently Spain ranks fifth in the EU in terms of turnover attributable to the industrial sector, with the country's industrial output accounting for nearly 8 per cent of total turnover for the sector in Europe, well behind the UK's 12 per cent or France's 14 per cent.

Most industrial activity is concentrated in northern Spain and the region around Valencia. In 2005, the regions with the largest industrial turnover were Catalonia (with 25 per cent of the total); Madrid (11 per cent); Valencia (10 per cent); Andalusia (10 per cent) and the Basque Country (9 per cent). The regions with the lowest industrial turnover were Cantabria, La Rioja, Extremadura and the Balearic Islands (which between them register just 2 per cent of the total).

The main feature of industrial development over the last forty years has been restructuring [5.1.2], a process that remains unfinished. Spanish industry still displays many of the same problems as before, albeit to a lesser degree. It lacks adequate technology and know-how. It suffers from fragmentation into a large number of small, often very small firms (*atomización*); some of the larger indigenous ones remain within a public sector of dubious efficiency [5.4.1].

These conditions are probably both cause and consequence of what has been described as a lack of entrepreneurial spirit (*mentalidad empresarial*) in Spanish society (especially if we exclude the Basques and Catalans). Although the situation has changed significantly in the last decade, and the large number of people who now run their own businesses means that a recent study could put Spain in fourth place in the entrepreneurial league table in Europe, the traditional dearth of entrepreneurs has been ascribed to a number of factors. These include an alleged Castilian disdain for manual work and the negligible influence of Protestantism, although, coming nearer to the present, enterprise was stifled by the Franco regime's policies of state intervention and protectionism [0.2]. Observers point also to the slow speed at which vocational training adapted to changing economic circumstances [7.3.2.3].

The food and drink industry (*sector alimenticio*) – actually one of Spain's most buoyant – provides a good illustration of the sort of problems associated with a lack of entrepreneurship. Domestic firms (*empresas nacionales*) within it were often slow to grasp the opportunities offered by the country's wealth of produce, much of it high quality and well adapted to consumer tastes in the developed world. Yet rather than being processed in Spain, olives have traditionally been exported to Italy. Typically Spanish meat products, such as cured ham, have not always been marketed adequately. The establishment of a promotional initiative in 1995 was, significantly, driven by public authorities, in this case the Andalusian regional government, and the existence of other supports and campaigns has also ensured that there is now more inclination for Spaniards to create their own businesses, most often in the services sector, but also in food processing and the like.

Given that traditional lack of private initiative and investment, Spanish firms have tended to rely on the state, or on foreign capital. In the nineteenth century foreign firms virtually monopolized the only two industrial activities of any significance outside the Basque and Catalan regions – railways and mining. Indeed, the protectionist policies pursued by successive governments up to and including the Franco regime were in large part a reaction to this situation.

With the opening up of Spain's economy after Franco's death, and especially after EC entry in 1986 [5.1.2], penetration of foreign capital greatly increased. Such investment has brought Spain many benefits, generating industrial development where none existed and preserving firms and industries that would otherwise have disappeared. On the other hand, it has involved loss of control over decisions in many of the country's largest firms.

These various aspects can all be seen in Spain's automobile industry (*sector automovilístico*). The country is the third largest manufacturer of vehicles in Europe and the seventh in the world, and this sector accounts for 22 per cent of all Spanish exports. The only major Spanish car producer, SEAT (*Sociedad Española de*

Automóviles de Turismo), was founded in 1950 and long produced models under licence from the Italian manufacturer Fiat. Gravely affected by the post-1973 recession [5.1.1], SEAT was bailed out by a 1982 cooperation agreement with the German Volkswagen company, which now has a controlling share. Similarly, the production of Pegaso trucks, begun by the state-owned firm ENASA (*Empresa Nacional de Autocamiones SA*), is now in Italian hands.

All other vehicle production in Spain is the result of inward investment. The longest established foreign manufacturer is the French FASA-Renault, which began production in 1951. Subsequently it has been joined by its compatriot Peugeot-Citroën, and by leading firms from the USA (Ford, General Motors) and Japan (Toyota, Suzuki). Many dependent component manufacturers (*industria auxiliar*) are also wholly or partly foreign-owned.

In conjunction these various operations are a major source of employment. However, it is a source which is highly vulnerable to changing business conditions. When economic times are hard the first to be hit are often subsidiaries based outside the home country of the parent company (*casa matriz*). The results can be traumatic. Thus in 1993 Suzuki announced its intention to close the Santana jeep factory on which the town of Linares in Jaén was almost entirely dependent.

Their importance as job providers gives multinationals enormous bargaining power *vis-à-vis* public authorities. Also in 1993, Volkswagen invested heavily in a new hi-tech SEAT plant at Martorell in Catalonia. Yet almost immediately VW announced its intention to pull out of the existing factory in the Barcelona Enterprise Area (*Zona Franca*) to which it had been lured by tax breaks and other incentives. The plans were only altered after further financial concessions from regional and national governments desperate to preserve jobs.

5.3.3 Financial sector

Lack of investment in Spanish industry is closely linked to another aspect of the country's late modernization: the relative underdevelopment of mechanisms for the supply of business finance. Spain's stock exchanges (*bolsas*) were, until recently, minuscule operations by international standards. Even though trading on them has increased substantially in recent years, Spanish companies remain heavily dependent on credit to finance their operations.

Here too, the state stepped in during the Franco era, when state agencies were set up to provide businesses with loans. They included an Overseas Trade Bank (*Banco Exterior de España*), as well as a number of institutions designed to channel credit to specific industries. In 1971 these were brought together as the Official Credit Agency (*Instituto de Crédito Oficial/ICO*). Nevertheless, the principal source of credit remained the banking system.

Traditionally this was divided into two parts. The first – slightly the smaller – consisted of the savings banks (*cajas de ahorros*). Locally based and managed, they served a particular city or province; many were originally pawnbrokers (*montes de piedad*). Today the savings banks still supply important amounts of credit for particular types of business, especially farmers. They also continue to provide much useful documentation on the economy of their area and to carry out non-lucrative tasks (*obra social*), e.g. cultural and recreational projects, even though they are no longer required by law to devote stipulated proportions of the loans they provide to such projects of public interest.

The effective elimination of this requirement, and of other measures giving the savings banks protected status, means that there is now little practical distinction between them and the remainder of the banking system. In order to compete in this new environment, most savings banks have come together in larger entities covering several provinces or even the whole country. The sector is now dominated by just two institutions: the Barcelona-based Caixa, originally a mutual pension fund, and Caja Madrid. While it has enabled the savings banks to survive in name, this concentration has prevented their conversion into semi-public regional banks on the German model, specifically charged with industrial promotion in their area.

Spain's large banks were already a powerful interest group prior to 1975, their importance during the Franco era deriving essentially from the regime's extensive intervention in the country's economy, which made control over the sources of credit vital. To a certain extent that was achieved by direct intervention. The country's central bank, the Bank of Spain, was nationalized in 1962 and the government was a major supplier of business credit. By and large, however, Franco left the large private banks (*banca privada*) untouched, confident in the unquestioning support of the deeply conservative families which controlled them, and which acquired considerable power as a result.

Their influence was, if anything, enhanced by the delicate process of transition after 1975, to which a functioning banking system was essential in order to avoid complete economic collapse. As a result all the leading political players were at pains not to alienate the sector, including those on the left who might normally have hoped to curtail bank influence. Consequently the banks continued to control large swathes of Spanish industry through their shareholdings and their role as credit-provider. When large-scale investment funds appeared in the country they did so largely under the banks' aegis. Moreover, the coming of democracy allowed them to extend their influence in several ways.

Thus with the opening up of the media to private capital, the banks inevitably acquired a considerable degree of control in that vital sector. At the same time, they acquired a new, formalized role in the formulation of government economic policy. Since government control over the Bank of Spain was loosened in 1980, the larger banks have been assured representation on its Supervisory Board (*Consejo General*). Similarly, they are represented on the National Banking Authority (*Consejo Superior Bancario*), which has a statutory right to be consulted on interest-rate policy decisions.

The banks' influence has also been reinforced by their important role in financing the political parties [2.1.3]. It was reflected in the strenuous efforts made by the Socialist PSOE to cultivate contacts with them, before and after the party came to power in 1982. The key intermediary was its first Finance Minister Miguel Boyer, who himself later returned to a senior post in the sector. Under Boyer's successor, Carlos Solchaga, even closer links were established between the banks and the Finance Ministry, which itself operated semi-independently from the cabinet as a whole [1.4.4]. Under a succession of governments since then, economic policy has tended to reflect closely the desires of bankers.

It is not democracy that has most affected the banks' political influence, however, but the altered business environment it has brought about. Under the Franco regime the private banking sector operated in a way that had very little to do with modern business practice. Internally, decisions were taken by a bank's chairman, often a virtually hereditary post, with little regard for the opinions of other shareholders. The biggest banks operated as a cartel, preferring cooperation to competition in business as well as in lobbying government.

Since 1975 this situation has been radically altered, as Spain's economy has been opened up to the forces of free-market capitalism and international competition. One result was a succession of mergers which have reduced the number of leading banks to two. A first round of mergers and takeovers was triggered off by the failure of a number of smaller banks during and immediately after the transition. It resulted in the emergence of a group of seven major banks, known as the 'big seven': the Bilbao, Vizcaya, Central, Hispanoamericano, Banesto, Santander, and Popular. In 1987 a second period of upheaval began. It started with the crisis experienced by Banca Catalana, closely linked to Catalan prime minister Jordi Pujol and his regionalist supporters [3.2.1.2]. Soon, however, it spread to the big banks themselves.

The causes lay in the outdated practices characteristic of Spanish banks and in the 1987 Single European Act [4.1.1], under which there would be open competition between banks across the EC from 1993. Faced with the prospect of competing with more efficient foreign banks, whose advantages derived partly from sheer size, the more dynamic of the 'big seven' opted to break the gentleman's agreement that had previously governed relations between them. The result was an outbreak of forced mergers and takeover bids (*Ofertas Públicas de Adquisición/OPA*), often tacitly encouraged by the government.

The first two bids, by the Bilbao and then the Central for Banesto, failed. In 1989, however, the two great Basque banks came together to form the Banco Bilbao Vizcaya (BBV). Two years later the ailing Hispanoamericano was absorbed by the Central to form the Banco Central Hispano (BCH). Then, in 1994, after a severe crisis which led the government to exercise its emergency powers to intervene, Banesto was effectively acquired by the Santander, although technically the two remained separate. Meantime, a further major player was added by the merger and privatization of the state's banking interests under the name of Argentaria [5.4.1]. It was then acquired by the Bilbao Vizcaya, now known as BBVA, and finally – at least to date – the Santander and BCH merged to form BSCH (often referred to now as the 'Santander Group').

The seven have thus been reduced to just two, the Popular having been relegated to the second rank. Having secured their domestic position, BBVA and the Santander Group have been at the forefront of Spanish penetration into Latin America [0.4.2] and have also begun to expand in other regions. In 2004, for example, Santander took over Abbey, the sixth-largest bank in the UK and, in 2005, it acquired a 19.8 per cent stake in Sovereign Bancorp, the 18th largest bank in the USA. This meant that by the time it celebrated its 150th anniversary in 2007, it had become the twelfth largest bank in the world and first in the Eurozone by market capitalization. It is currently attempting to take over the major Dutch bank, ABN Amro, in an alliance with Royal Bank of Scotland. Meanwhile, not only does BBVA

Table 5.1 Spain's largest banks and building societies in 2005, ranked by assets

The 10 biggest banks
1. Banco Bilbao Vizcaya Argentaria BBVA
2. Banco Santander Central Hispano BSCH
3. Banco Español de Crédito
4. Banco Popular Español
5. Banco Sabadell
6. Bankinter
7. Banco Pastor
8. Barclays Bank
9. Banco Santander Consumer Finance
10. Deutsche Bank, SAE

The 10 biggest building societies
1. La Caixa
2. Caja de Ahorros de Madrid
3. Bancaja
4. Caixa Catalunya
5. Caja de Ahorros Mediterránea
6. Caixa Galicia
7. Ibercaja
8. Unicaja
9. Bilbao Bizkaia Kutxa
10. Caja España

own Mexico's second largest bank (BBVA Bancomer), it has also taken over American Compass Bancshares in the United States, and has recently entered the gigantic Chinese market through an alliance with a bank called China Citic.

5.3.4 Services

The service or tertiary sector (*sector terciario*) has come to dominate Western economies in recent decades. The same is true of Spain, albeit to a slightly lesser degree, with services now providing around 66 per cent of employment. This situation represents a remarkable change for the country; in 1960 services accounted for little over a quarter of the economy. Regionally, the most significant contributions are made by Madrid, Catalonia, Andalusia and Valencia, which together make up two thirds of the sector. It is an especially important sector from the point of view of women's employment, with about 85 per cent of Spanish women who are in employment working in services.

As in other countries it is difficult to generalize about the service sector, composed as it is of a wide range of highly diverse activities. Of these, two are especially important in terms of the employment they provide.

The first is wholesale and retail trade (*comercio mayorista y minorista*), which accounts for around one fifth of all service jobs in Spain. In recent years this share has been declining steadily as small shops (*pequeños comercios*) are driven out of business by the less labour-intensive large-scale outlets (*grandes superficies*), such as super- and hypermarkets. Their supremacy was reinforced by the 1995 Trading Act (*Ley de Comercio*), which among other measures partially deregulated shops' permitted opening hours (*horario comercial*). Unlike the case in most EU countries, in Spain the larger outlets are mainly in foreign ownership; French chains are particularly important, although the second largest is the Basque chain Eroski.

The second major subsector in employment terms is that of public administration and other services provided by public authorities (principally education, health and social services). All these activities expanded rapidly in the 1980s, at both central and regional level. Combined, they now account for almost as many jobs as wholesaling and retailing.

The most rapidly growing subsector in recent years has been that of business services. As well as banking [5.3.3], this includes insurance and the remainder of the financial services industry. Like the banks, they remained heavily protected up to the coming into effect of the EU's single market in 1993. Largely as a result the financial sector as a whole remained underdeveloped and inefficient by international standards, and offered a tempting target to foreign investors. The most notable exception to this is the insurance group MAPFRE, which has 250 associated companies located all around the world and especially in Latin America and Europe.

In terms of overall economic significance, a fourth service subsector stands out. Now, as for many years, Spain's ability to pay for its imports depends crucially on the tourist industry (*sector turístico*) [5.2.1], which accounts for 11 per cent of the country's GDP. After tailing off from the late 1980s, the tourist trade rose sharply again in the mid-1990s, when Spain benefited from the troubles suffered by several of its Mediterranean competitors. The authorities have also invested heavily in campaigns designed to distribute tourism more evenly over the country and the calendar year.

One major problem with tourism is the low average amount injected into the Spanish economy by each tourist who visits the country. In part this is a reflection of the continuing emphasis on mass tourism (*turismo de masas*). But it also derives from the dominant role played by foreign tour operators (*tour operadores*) in managing the trade. As in the case of industry [5.3.2], here is evidence of inability on the part of Spanish business to exploit fully the country's natural resources. But those resources are also key to another crucial issue surrounding tourism, which is the adverse ecological effect that large-scale tourist developments have had on the country, especially on its coastal regions [8.2.3].

5.3.5 Regional differences

As well as the massive sectoral shifts it has undergone in recent decades the Spanish economy has also experienced another sort of structural change. The geographical distribution of economic activity and wealth is markedly different now from what it was in 1960, or even 1975. The causes of change lie in the decline of certain established economic activities – traditional agriculture, heavy industry – and the rise of new ones, whose location is determined not by the presence of raw materials but by other factors, especially proximity to markets.

Up to the 1960s the two wealthiest and most developed parts of Spain were Catalonia and the Basque Country or, more precisely, the metropolitan areas of Barcelona and Bilbao. Otherwise industrial development was limited to a few smaller outposts, mainly along the northern Atlantic coast (*Cornisa Cantábrica*). Madrid, almost entirely because of its role as the centre of administration, was the single enclave of prosperity in a vast area covering both Castiles, and the entire south.

In the 1990s, however, this pattern was replaced by another in which wealth and development are concentrated in two connected strips. The more important extends down the Mediterranean coast from Catalonia, through Valencia and Murcia and into the easternmost Andalusian province of Almería. The other runs up the valley of the Ebro from Tarragona in Catalonia, through Saragossa, into Navarre before petering out in the inland Basque province of Alava. Together with the y-shaped area formed by these two strips, Madrid and the two island regions (Balearics and Canaries) now make up 'rich Spain'.

The reasons why these areas have prospered vary. In the case of Madrid, success is mainly attributable to the expansion of government and the growing attractiveness of capital cities in general as business locations. In the islands tourism has obviously played the leading role. It has also been vital to the rise of the Mediterranean coastal strip (*eje mediterráneo*).

This last area, however, also displays a number of features common to economically successful regions in developed countries. Thus it has little heritage of industrial blight, in terms of outdated plant and environmental damage. Its workforce is young and unwedded to the skills and practices of traditional heavy industry. It has a number of medium-sized centres, which provide an attractive working and living environment for incoming executives, as well as a major financial and business centre in Barcelona. Since the 1980s it has enjoyed an excellent system of internal communications. And it is also directly linked with one of the EU's main growth areas, the Mediterranean coastal area of southern France and northern Italy.

In all these respects conditions are very different along the northern Atlantic coast, the part of Spain which has lost most ground in the last few decades. From being among the country's most prosperous regions the Basque Country, and above all Asturias, have fallen down the regional league table. In the former case, a strong business tradition and a series of initiatives by a determined regional government have helped to alleviate the problems of industrial decline.

Andalusia, Extremadura, Castile-La Mancha and Galicia are the country's poorest regions, although the western part of Castile-Leon also contains pockets of extreme relative poverty. As such, they have been major recipients of EU regional aid. Rather more hopefully, there are signs that, as in the Basque Country, devolution is producing positive effects. There is some evidence that regional governments are more sensitive to the needs of regional economies, and quicker and more innovative in responding to them than Madrid. In a reversal of previous experience, the poorer regions were less badly hit by the recession of the early 1990s than the country as a whole. And, albeit slowly, the gap between them and their richer neighbours is narrowing.

5.4 Spanish companies

The basic building blocks of a country's economy are its individual companies. These can and do vary enormously in size, management structure and ownership within countries as well as between them. In Spain's case the last of these three features has been and remains of particular importance. Compared with the Anglo-Saxon countries in particular, in Spain the state's role as entrepreneur has been, and to some extent still is, an important one.

5.4.1 Public sector

The public sector of the economy embraces a number of activities that relate to the country's people as a whole. In most of the developed world, as well as administration itself they include responsibility for education, health and social services. In Spain too the state is a major employer in this capacity [5.3.4]. There, however, its role in the economy goes much further. For it has also owned, in whole or in part, a considerable number of firms operating in industries that elsewhere in the West are usually in private hands.

The Spanish state's first major venture into business was CAMPSA (*Compañía Arrendataria del Monopolio de Petróleos SA*), the oil and petrol monopoly created in 1927 by the then dictator, Primo de Rivera. However, it was under Spain's second twentieth-century dictatorship that the government became a major economic player. Partly from the same desire as that of Primo to prevent the penetration of foreign companies, partly because the state was the only significant source of capital after the Civil War, the Franco regime became involved in many diverse industries.

In 1941 Franco set up a state holding company, the National Industry Agency (*Instituto Nacional de Industria/INI*), to oversee the government's rapidly burgeoning interests. Some of these, however, he assigned to an expanded Directorate-General of State Assets (*Dirección General del Patrimonio del Estado/DGPE*), which dated from the previous century. By the time of his death these two bodies had a considerable presence in many sectors of the economy.

Thereafter the public sector grew further as a result of industrial restructuring in the 1980s [5.1.2]. In a number of industries acquisition by the state was the only way of preserving either jobs or a Spanish presence, or both. By 1988 the INI had become Spain's largest industrial conglomerate. More than 150,000 workers were employed in the widely diverse companies – over 50 in total – in which it had holdings.

In fact, along with the illogical division between the INI and DGPE, excessive diversity was one of the public sector's main problems. Another was the unproductive, loss-making character of many of the companies it had acquired. These considerations led the government to implement major changes. In 1981 the National Hydrocarbons Agency (*Instituto Nacional de Hidrocarburos/INH*) was created, bringing together the INI's various petroleum and petrochemical interests in a separate unit. In a number of other cases, companies in the same or related fields were merged in order to create more viable entities.

The Socialist governments of the 1980s also took steps to rationalize the overall structure of the public sector by clarifying the roles of the INI and DGPE. The latter, subsequently renamed as the State Assets Group (*Grupo Patrimonio*), became the holding company for a diverse range of operations, mainly related to some sort of government or monopoly service. A new holding company, Teneo, was set up within the INI, to oversee companies capable of showing a profit, and hence with potential for privatization.

The INI was left with direct responsibility for those firms which, for various reasons, were incapable of surviving unsupported in the marketplace, mainly in declining traditional industries. The division was by no means clear, however. The national airline, Iberia, which at that time was notoriously inefficient, was assigned to Teneo – indeed, the firms within the new group generally failed to show the desired profitability. On the other hand, the highly profitable telecommunications monopoly, Telefónica, was assigned to the State Assets Group.

From the late 1980s onwards the Socialist government began to privatize various state-owned companies. Some were sold off directly to private sector firms while several of the largest were floated on the stock market, including Telefónica, the electricity company Endesa, and the oil firm Repsol set up within INH in 1981 [5.2.1]. In the last two, as in most of the larger companies affected, the government retained 50 per cent of the stock, and thus a decisive voice in company policy.

Also partially privatized was Argentaria, the state banking corporation. This was created in 1991 by bringing together in a single federated entity a number of public financial institutions, including the Post Office Savings Bank (*Caja Postal de Ahorros*) as well as the Overseas Trade Bank and the Official Credit Agency [5.3.3]. By 1996 three-quarters of Argentaria's shares had been sold through the stock market; shortly thereafter it was acquired by the Banco Bilbao Vizcaya, one of the leading private banks [5.3.3].

This whole process was subject to virtually no public scrutiny; it was never debated in Parliament, and the key decisions seem to have been taken by the powerful Finance and Economics Ministry [1.4.4] in consultation with the banks. In line with this approach, one of the Socialists' last acts before they left office in 1996 was to dissolve the INI. Its functions were assumed by two new entities more independent of public oversight: the State Industrial Holding Company (*Sociedad Estatal de Participaciones Industriales/SEPI*) and the State Industry Agency (*Agencia Industrial del Estado/AIE*).

Iberia, which had previously had such a poor financial history, compounded its problems through the additional losses incurred when it expanded its Latin American operations in the 1990s and suffered additional setbacks when the first Gulf War in 1991 had a negative impact on airlines generally around the world. By 1994 the company was technically bankrupt and the Spanish government was given special permission by the European Commission to inject capital to bail it out, on condition that it would be privatized in the future. The process of privatization was completed in 2001, and it is now among the 100 most profitable companies in the country.

The remaining state holdings in a number of companies, including Repsol, Argentaria and Telefónica, were sold off during the period of the PP governments (1996–2004). Many observers felt that in most cases the effect was merely to create private rather than public monopolies, or situations of extreme market dominance. Nevertheless, none of the cases was referred by the government to the Competition Commission (*Tribunal de Defensa de la Competencia/TDC*). There were also more serious allegations that businessmen close to the PP were given favourable treatment in the sales. Telefónica, Spain's second largest company, came under the control of Juan Villalonga, a close associate of the then Prime Minister José María Aznar [10.4].

One privatized company, Endesa, has been at the centre of one of the most controversial takeover bids in recent years. It became a private entity in 1998 and was the object of a hostile takeover bid in 2005 by Gas Natural, a company which is mostly owned by the Catalan bank La Caixa. The latter is perceived as having a very close relationship with the PSOE, the current government party, while Endesa is noted for its proximity to the PP. In 2006 the German energy giant E.ON launched a bid for Endesa which was opposed by the Spanish government on the grounds that it wanted an indigenous Spanish company to control Spanish energy. This opposition was deemed anti-competitive by the European Commission, who ruled against the government. Meanwhile, however, the Italian energy company Enel in conjunction with the Spanish construction firm Acciona joined in the bidding and managed to acquire 92 per cent of Endesa. Thus, although the government may have managed to keep E.ON at bay, their goal of ensuring the existence of an indigenous Spanish energy leader has not been achieved, since Enel's participation alone accounts for more than half the group's participation in Endesa.

5.4.2 Private sector

The most obvious characteristic of Spanish private sector firms is their small size. Numerically both industry and the service sector are dominated by SMEs, that is small and medium-sized enterprises (*pequeñas y medianas empresas/pymes*). Nearly 80 per cent of firms employ fewer than 100 people. In fact, the most common form of business operation in Spain continues to be the sole trader (*comerciante*).

Of course, larger firms provide a disproportionate share of both employment and output. Yet even Spain's largest companies are relatively small by international standards. In 2004, seven figured among the world's top 500 by earnings. Of these, three were former state-owned monopolies – Telefónica (which is the fourth-largest telecomms company in the world by share value); Repsol-YPF (in 97th place), and Endesa, in 256th [5.4.1]. Two more were banks – Santander Central Hispano/BSCH (155th) and BBVA (268th) [5.3.3], one was an energy company – CEPSA (386th) – and one a construction firm, ACS (435th). Moreover, many of the largest firms in Spain are owned by foreign interests (see Table 5.2).

The problems posed by small scale have led to the formation of cooperatives in certain areas and sectors (e.g. wine production). The best-known example is the group founded in Mondragón, in the Basque province of Guipúzcoa, in the 1950s. Mondragón Corporación Cooperativa-MCC is one of the largest worker cooperatives in the world. Over the last fifty years, its activities have expanded throughout Spain and internationally, and now encompass a wide range of areas, accounting for over 260 different companies, including a domestic appliance manufacturer (Fagor), a supermarket chain (Eroski) and a savings bank (Caja Laboral-Euskadiko Kutxa).

Other than cooperatives, firms are of four main types. The first corresponds roughly to the British concept of the partnership (*sociedad colectiva*); in such firms the partners (*socios*) are personally liable in the event of bankruptcy (*insolvencia*). By contrast, in a limited partnership (*sociedad en comandita*) some or all of the partners have liabilities limited to their initial capital participation. Companies of these types are identified by the suffixes y *Compañía* (y *Cía*) and *Sociedad en Comandita* (SC) respectively. Neither is common in Spain.

The remaining two types of business association are forms of limited company, corresponding broadly – but not exactly – to UK private and public companies. The Spanish equivalent of the private limited company is the *Sociedad de Responsabilidad Limitada/SL*. For this type of enterprise there is no longer any upper limit on the

Table 5.2 Spain's largest companies, 2004

The top thirty Spanish companies by earnings (excludes financial sector)	
Company	Business
Repsol YPF (S)	Energy (hydrocarbons, gas)
Telefónica (S)	Telecommunications
Endesa (S)	Energy (electricity)
El Corte Inglés	Retail distribution (department stores, hypermarkets)
Compañía Española de Petróleo CEPSA	Energy (hydrocarbons, gas)
Telefónica Móviles España	Telecommunications
ACS	Construction and property
Mondragón Corp. Cooperativa	Finances
Iberdrola	Energy (electricity)
Altadis (S)	Cigarettes and tobacco; distribution (formerly Tabacalera)
Centros Comerciales Carrefour (F)	Retail distribution (hypermarkets)
Renault España (F)	Cars and components
Mercadona	Retail distribution (hypermarkets)
Grupo Ferrovial	Construction and property
Telefónica Internacional España	Telecommunications
General Motors Holding España (F)	Cars and components
Fomento de Construcción y Contratas	Construction and property
Gas Natural SDG (S)	Energy (gas)
Ford España (F)	Cars and components
Seat (F)	Cars and components
Unión Fenosa	Energy (electricity)
Grupo Eroski	Retail distribution (hypermarkets)
Peugeot Citroën Automóviles Hispania (F)	Cars and components
Volkswagen Audi España (F)	Vehicle dealers
Vodafone España (F)	Telecommunications
Iberia Líneas Aéreas España (S)	Air travel
Industria de Diseño Textil INDITEX	Clothing manufacturing and retail
Comp. de Distrib. Integral Logista	Transport and Courier Services
Auna Op. de Telecomunicación	Telecommunications
Acciona	Construction and property
Acerinox	Steelmaking

Notes: F = Foreign (non-Spanish) controlling interest. S = Current or former state holding.

company's capital (*capital social*) as recorded in the Register of Companies (*Registro Mercantil*); the minimum required is €3005. The capital is held in the form of shares (*participaciones*); as and when they are offered for sale the existing owners and the company itself have the right of first refusal. These and other stipulations ensure that the typical Spanish private limited company is a family firm (*empresa familiar*).

The minimum capital required to form a public company (*Sociedad Anónima/SA*) is €60,101. Public companies are distinguished from private ones by the fact that their shares (called *acciones* in the case of SAs) can be freely traded. In some, but not all cases, trade occurs through the mechanism of a stock exchange listing (*cotización*). Changes of share ownership do not have to be recorded in the Register of Companies, as is the case for private limited companies – hence the Spanish name.

By law, a public company is required to hold an annual general meeting of shareholders (*Junta de Accionistas*), which must approve the annual report and set a dividend. Between such meetings the company's affairs are run by the board (*Consejo de Administración*), made up of directors (*consejeros*) elected by the AGM. The board has the power to appoint one of its members as managing director (*consejero delegado*), who then exercises in the board's name the powers bestowed on it by law, and by the AGM.

5.5 Economic lobby groups

In modern capitalist democracies the most prominent of the lobbies which attempt to sway government policy are typically economically based. Specifically, they relate to the interests of the main factors of production: on the one hand, labour or the workforce, and on the other, capital and its owners, the employers. For various reasons neither is particularly powerful in Spain, which is one reason for a continuing tendency to institutionalize their influence.

5.5.1 Trade unions

Despite the country's belated industrialization, the Spanish labour movement dates from the late nineteenth century. Nonetheless, like the parties of the left to which the labour movement was allied, the country's trade unions long suffered from a lack of potential recruits and, latterly, from Francoist repression. Under the particular circumstances of the transition the unions acquired an enhanced status, but subsequently their influence has once again been eroded by a variety of factors.

5.5.1.1 Organization and status

The main Spanish trade unions (*sindicatos*) are actually 'confederations' of individual unions covering a particular industry or industries. In that sense they are more akin to the TUC than to individual British trade unions. Rather than in the professions they represent, they differ in their political orientation – or, more precisely, in the political tendencies with which they were originally connected.

Of these the most important of all was anarchism. Indeed in the 1930s the anarchist-linked National Labour Confederation (*Confederación Nacional de Trabajo/CNT*) was the country's largest political association. However, the loosely-organized CNT was virtually destroyed by the Franco regime, although it retains some following in certain industries.

The CNT's long-standing rival, the General Workers' Union (*Unión General de Trabajadores/UGT*), fared rather better after 1975. Closely linked to the Socialist PSOE since its foundation in the 1880s, the UGT had deep roots not just in several industrial areas (the Basque Country, Asturias, Madrid) but also in the rural south. It also had a well-known and popular leader, Nicolás Redondo. Its strength was further increased by absorbing much of the Workers' Trade Union (*Unión Sindical Obrera/USO*), a smaller body which had been active in opposition to the Franco regime. The UGT, however, had been reticent in that respect, and had consequently been outstripped in membership by a much younger organization.

Resistance to the dictatorship was the original aim of the Workers' Commissions (*Comisiones Obreras/CCOO*), which from the late 1950s spread to become a country-wide underground movement. In addition, CCOO enjoyed significant success in infiltrating the government-controlled unions, which were the only legal ones at the time [0.2]. Before long it came to be effectively controlled by the Communist Party (PCE), under whose direction its activities became both better organized and more overtly political. Its prominence in opposition, and that of its leader Marcelino Camacho who was imprisoned by the regime, meant that it enjoyed a high standing when the transition began.

At that time, when parties remained illegal, the unions briefly assumed a leading political role and their membership soared. This new importance was soon legally recognized. Many of the social provisions of the 1978 Constitution reflected union concerns. Rather more significantly, unions' right to defend their members' legitimate interests was included among the text's fundamental principles [1.1.2]. This and other constitutional provisions were given concrete form in the 1980 Workers' Charter (*Estatuto de los Trabajadores*) and the 1984 Trade Union Freedom Act (*Ley Orgánica de Libertad Sindical/LOLS*).

In particular, the LOLS consolidated the system of workplace elections (*elecciones sindicales*) established by the Charter. They operate on a list system similar to that used for parliamentary contests [1.3.1], the lists being presented by unions or other groupings of workers. In companies with over 50 employees the elected representatives (*delegados*) make up a workforce committee (*comité de empresa*) with the statutory right to be informed and consulted by the employer. In EU parlance these committees are often described as works' councils, so it is important to stress that, unlike the latter, they are representatives of the workforce, not forums for debate with the employer.

Unions' status in the new Spain was underlined between 1979 and 1985 by their involvement in a series of pacts on aspects of economic policy with government and employers. Yet, in most cases these brought only minor or intangible gains for union members, at the cost of considerable concessions. Union participation in them indicated not strength but weakness, traceable in part to Spain's persistent unemployment problem but also to certain features of the trade union movement itself.

First, after the brief surge experienced during the transition, the density of union membership – that is, the proportion of the workforce which is affiliated to a union – has sunk steadily. By the mid-1990s it was among the lowest in Europe, standing at around 15 per cent according to most estimates. This, in turn, is attributable to a number of causes.

The first cause is Spain's industrial structure, which is dominated by small and medium-sized firms [5.4.2], which everywhere have a low level of union membership. Secondly, there is no requirement to be a union member in order to vote in workplace elections. Thirdly, unions' incentive to recruit is further reduced by the fact that non-members must pay a contribution towards union funds (*canon sindical*). Finally, like parties, unions receive public funding (*financiación estatal*) – and that is based on the results of workplace elections, not membership figures.

The second feature of the union movement is that it is fragmented, with a number of smaller unions enjoying significant support in particular regions and industries. Thus the largest union in the Basque Country is Basque Workers' Solidarity (*Eusko*

Langileak Alkartasuna/ELA-STV), which has links to the nationalist PNV [3.2.2.2]. Other important regional unions are the Galician Interunion Confederation (*Confederación Intersindical Gallega/CIG*) and the Basque Workers' Commissions (*Langile Abertzale Batzordeak/LAB*). The latter are ideologically linked to Batasuna but, unlike that party [2.1.1], they have not been declared illegal.

Sectoral unions include a number of highly disparate groups. They range from those representing the police such as the United Police Union (*Sindicato Unificado de Policía*) and the Spanish Police Confederation (*Confederación Española de Policía*) to unions that represent workers in the expanding white collar occupations, the best established of these being the Confederation of Independent Public Servants' Unions (*Confederación de Sindicatos Independientes de Funcionarios/CSIF*). At the opposite end of the occupational spectrum is the Landworkers' Union (*Sindicato de Obreros del Campo/SOC*). The SOC is the heir to Andalusia's tradition of rural anarchism, and during the 1980s it organized direct action in favour of land reform [5.3.1]. Its ideological opposite is to be found in the company-sponsored employee associations established by some large firms. Despised by the rest of the movement as 'bosses' unions' (*sindicatos amarillos*), these are of particular significance in the retail sector, notably in the Corte Inglés chain of department stores and hypermarkets.

The wide differences between these smaller employees' representatives have inevitably led to disagreement on aims and strategy. Yet even despite the existence of these other organizations, UGT and CCOO dominate the union movement, regularly filling between 70 and 80 per cent of places on workforce committees. For that very reason their failure to agree a common strategy during the critical period of the 1980s was especially damaging to the unions' cause.

5.5.1.2 In search of a strategy

The roots of disunity between the two largest unions were to be found in the transition. At that time the communist-dominated CCOO [5.5.1.1] saw itself as an instrument to win political concessions from government as much as economic ones from employers, which implied the use of militant methods. It was thus the prime mover behind the high level of industrial unrest (*conflictividad laboral*) during the early part of the transition, frequently backing strikes in individual firms or calling them to support wider political demands.

Meanwhile the UGT [5.5.1.1] tended to take a more cautious line. It concentrated on workplace issues, specifically pay and conditions, and was much more disposed to pursue demands through negotiation, either with individual employers or with the government. That moderate approach proved more successful in winning concrete concessions, and by 1982 the UGT had overtaken CCOO in support at workplace elections [5.5.1.1]. When its sister party (*partido hermano*), the Socialist PSOE, came to power that year, the UGT leadership confidently expected to consolidate its position through privileged links to government.

As regards the UGT's interests as an organization, these hopes were largely fulfilled. In particular, the 1984 Trade Union Freedom Act [5.5.1.1] contained two provisions for which UGT had lobbied. It increased the period between workplace elections from two years to four, and gave the main role in collective negotiations not to company committees [5.5.1.1], but to union sections representing a whole industry (*sección sindical*). In both cases these measures favoured UGT at the expense of CCOO, which tended to be better established at workplace level.

However, UGT's expectations on behalf of its members were disappointed; from an early stage the government pursued economic policies which hit them hard [5.1.2]. In 1985 reform of the pension system, to the actual or potential disbenefit of many union members, led UGT leader Nicolás Redondo [5.5.1.1] to threaten resignation as a Socialist MP; two years later he carried out his threat in response to proposals for further cuts in social spending. Thereafter relations between the industrial and political wings of the socialist movement (*familia socialista*) deteriorated progressively, with the UGT increasingly joining CCOO in demanding that the government pay less attention to purely economic considerations and more to social ones.

It also adopted the more militant methods to which CCOO had clung, three times joining it to organize general strikes against government policy. The biggest of these stoppages was the first, called on 14 December 1988 (*14-D*) against government plans for special low-wage contracts for the young. The enormous turnout brought virtually the whole country to a standstill and demonstrated the unions' ability to command support well beyond their membership on particular issues. Some four years later a government decree cutting unemployment benefit provoked a second general strike. This stoppage, held on 27 May 1992 (*27-M*), commanded less popular support. The downward trend continued when UGT and CCOO issued their third joint strike call, in January 1994, directed as in 1988 against proposed labour market reforms.

Declining public support for such militancy, despite considerable sympathy with its motives, both mirrored the unions' relative impotence and further aggravated it. Although the youth employment plan was withdrawn in 1988 and minor concessions were made in 1992, in neither case did the unions' show of strength force a change in the general direction of government policy. Admittedly, unions' lobbying bore some fruit in the relatively favourable provisions of the 1994 Strikes Act (*Ley de Huelga*). But in general their influence remained low in the later years of Socialist rule.

The Spanish unions' plight was not unique. Throughout the West such organizations have had little success in preventing deregulation of economies, which in turn has further weakened their position. However, in Spain their position was particularly difficult in the 1980s. Time and again unions were in the impossible position of opposing the attempts of a Socialist government to repeal measures originally introduced under Franco. Once most such measures were gone their situation was, in a sense, eased. And, at the same time, the unions themselves have shown greater awareness of the need to escape the legacy of their past.

In both cases this has involved a change of leader, UGT's Redondo being replaced by Cándido Méndez in 1994, and CCOO's Camacho by Antonio Gutiérrez in 1987 (to be followed by José María Fidalgo in 1998). In the latter case the removal of Camacho was accompanied by a lengthy struggle to free CCOO from communist control, a process that was ultimately eased by the Communist Party's virtual collapse [2.5.2]. There has also been a sharp move away from militancy by both unions, the level of strikes declining throughout the 1990s. Instead both main unions have concentrated increasingly on workplace issues, leaving political ones to the parties.

This approach brought dividends with the coming to power of a conservative party anxious to establish its centrist credentials, and to defuse accusations of being anti-worker. As a result, PP governments showed a somewhat unexpected willingness to broker and even join deals between employers and unions. It is ironic that the CCOO, which remains the principal employee representative in most of Spain's larger firms, has been the more enthusiastic participant in this process. In 2001 it was the UGT which finally ended 13 years of cooperation between the two main unions by refusing to join the government and CCOO in signing the latest in a series of agreements on the pension system.

Even deeper dissension between government and unions became evident in the wake of the PP government's notorious second *decretazo* which placed restrictions on the unemployed and led to yet another general strike, held on 20 June 2002 (*20-J*). With the arrival in power of a new Socialist administration under the more conciliatory PM Zapatero, much more cooperation has been achieved and new agreements reached in relation to employment regulation. The rapprochement between the PSOE and its old trade union ally even led to the inclusion of one UGT stalwart, Manuel de la Rocha, in the party's electoral list for the March 2008 elections. Although this move was not part of any formal pact between the two bodies, the union was happy to declare that it viewed the development as a positive one.

Also under Zapatero, the issue of the extensive confiscations of trade union property which took place during and after the Civil War has been re-examined. This is a particularly sore point for the now depleted CNT [5.5.1.1] which in 1936 had an extensive membership list, exceding that of the UGT. Nonetheless, when compensation was paid to the unions in 2005, the latter union (which has been historically linked to the Socialist party) received a much larger amount than the former, leading to accusations of government favouritism.

5.5.2 Employers' organizations

If the development of Spanish trade unions was held back by the country's peculiar history, the same was even more true of their natural opponents, employers' organizations (*organizaciones empresariales*). Prior to 1975 there was in fact no country-wide organization representing employers, only a few regional associations in the more advanced parts of the country. The most significant of these was the Catalan Development Association (*Fomento de Trabajo Nacional/FTN*), a body dating back to the late nineteenth century when it had provided much of the impetus for Catalan regionalism [3.2.1.1].

When industrialization eventually began on a significant scale, in the 1960s, it did so under very special circumstances. The Franco regime's authoritarian policies ensured that, with occasional exceptions, the labour force remained docile and wage demands muted. At the same time the country's economic isolation effectively protected its businesses from outside competition [0.2]. It is understandable that employers saw little need to organize, even if they had been permitted to do so.

On the other hand, Franco's belief in strict state control led him to impose on the country's developing industries an extraordinary mass of regulations. They covered virtually all aspects of business activity, including prices as well as the labour market, and were only partially dismantled after the change in economic policy in 1959/60 [0.2]. Their stifling effect on business initiative latterly caused more enterprising employers to press discreetly for moves to bring the country's business environment in line with the much less restricted conditions of its democratic neighbours.

Once Franco had died, such deregulation became the central demand of the body set up in 1977 to represent the interests of employers at national level, the Spanish Employers' Confederation (*Confederación Española de Organizaciones Empresariales/CEOE*). As its title suggests, the CEOE is in fact a relatively loose alliance of employers' groups which have retained considerable independence. In total, they amount to some 2,000 organizations of primary association and 200 affiliated regional and trade organizations, among which the Catalan FTN continues to be prominent.

Individual firms typically belong to several of these affiliated associations. They acquired renewed importance after the mid-1980s, due both to the growing importance of regional government, and to the abandonment of the country-wide union–employer agreements of the previous decade. In any case, the stress placed by the CEOE's national leadership on deregulation has not always been well received by the small and medium-sized enterprises which form such a large part of the Spanish corporate sector (*sector empresarial*). For the protected conditions of the Franco era left many SMEs (*pymes*) technically ill-equipped and psychologically ill-prepared for the increased competition implied by deregulation.

These particular interests were reflected during the transition in the creation of a distinct Spanish Confederation of SMEs (*Confederación Española de Pequeñas y Medianas Empresas/CEPYME*). In 1980 CEPYME affiliated to the CEOE, but it continues to operate with considerable independence. Moreover, the smaller General SME Confederation (*Confederación General de Pequeñas y Medianas Empresas/COPYME*) remains outside the CEOE, as did a third association representing SMEs set up in the 1990s, the Family Business Institute (*Instituto de la Empresa Familiar/IEF*). And, in any case, many SMEs look to a different type of organization as the most effective channel for their interests.

Spain's Chambers of Commerce, Industry and Navigation (*Cámaras de Comercio, Industria y Navegación*) date from 1911 and are organized on a provincial basis. Like those in most continental countries, the Chambers have considerably greater practical importance than their British counterparts. They exercise statutory responsibilities relating to the general economic well-being of their area and are funded by the dues all local employers are required to pay. This compulsory affiliation naturally provokes some employer resentment. But the tensions frequently evident between the Chambers and the CEOE also reflect the fact that the Chambers represent interests specific to the CEOE's smaller members which sometimes seem to be neglected by its national leaders.

At the same time, larger firms also sometimes feel the need for alternative means of lobbying. In some cases this is done through the appropriate industry-specific organization, of which the most powerful is that representing the banks [5.3.3]. To represent interests common to all bigger firms, a number have banded together in the Business Circle (*Círculo de Empresarios*), which in some ways resembles the UK Institute of Directors. The management education it provides is in Spain promoted by a separate organization, the Association for Progress in Business (*Asociación para el Progreso de la Dirección/APD*).

As well as in this variety of organizations, the differing interests of Spanish employers have been reflected in apparent uncertainty on the CEOE's part about how best to influence public policy. Its first chairman was Carlos Ferrer Salat, of the Catalan FNT. Under his leadership the CEOE entered a series of broad agreements on economic and social policy with unions and government, an approach maintained after the Socialists came to power in 1982. It was radically changed, however, once Ferrer was replaced as chairman by José María Cuevas. Before his election in 1984 Cuevas had been involved in attempts to bring together all the forces of the right and centre-right in a party capable of challenging the Socialist government [2.4.1]. After it, he took a more confrontational attitude both to the PSOE and to the unions, with whom the CEOE signed no new agreements after 1984.

Instead, the CEOE concentrated on building up influence over the conservative opposition party, People's Alliance (AP), to which it gave considerable financial backing. When in 1987 AP switched to a policy line less acceptable to employers Cuevas abruptly withdrew this support [2.4.2]. The move was instrumental in AP's transformation into the People's Party (PP), and a switch back to more employer-friendly policies. Thereafter CEOE's renewed support, public and financial, was an important factor in the PP's rise to power in 1996.

This close link with the party of government obviously gave the CEOE greatly increased influence post-1996, yet it remained limited by other pressures on the PP. During the 1996 general election campaign, Cuevas publicly listed the CEOE's expectations of a conservative administration. The PP's leader, José María Aznar, was quick to deny that these demands were his party's policy. Desperate to portray itself as 'centrist' [2.4.3], it simply could not afford the appearance of being in the employers' pocket. Recognizing this, the CEOE displayed renewed interest in agreement with unions after the PP won that election.

Unsurprisingly, relations between the CEOE and the Socialist government that came to power in 2004 have been less friendly. Nonetheless, agreements relating to pensions (in 2005) and labour reform (in 2006) have been hammered out between the government, the employers and the trade unions [5.5.1.1]. But an agreement on pegging the standard minimum wage to the inflation rate from 2008 onwards was arrived at exclusively by the unions in negotiation with the government, without the involvement of the employers. This move was harshly criticized by Cuevas, who claimed that it ran counter to the notion of social dialogue, that is, the tacit agreement that major issues of economic policy should be negotiated between government, unions *and* employers.

Cuevas was also very critical of the new government's commitment to holding talks with ETA [3.2.2.1], an indication perhaps of the degree to which the CEOE is politicized. The CEOE stance was criticized in its turn, however, by Confebask, an association of some 13,000 companies in the Basque Country whose businesses have often been the target of unwelcome attention from ETA. The latter has extorted payment from them of what it calls the 'revolutionary tax' (*impuesto revolucionario*). Given this pattern of extortion and the record of killings and kidnappings perpetrated on business people in the Basque Country by ETA over several decades, Basque employers have tended to be more supportive of the government's efforts to advance the peace process than their counterparts in the CEOE at national level. In 2007 Cuevas retired, to be replaced as Chairman by Gerardo Díaz Ferrán.

5.6 Glossary

absorción (f)	company takeover
acciones (fpl)	shares in a public company
acuicultura (f)	aquaculture
adquisición (f)	purchase; takeover
Agencia Industrial del Estado (f)	State Industry Agency
ajuste (m)	adjustment; reduction
ajuste de plantilla (m)	job losses, redundancies
ajuste presupuestario (m)	cut in (government) spending
apertura (f)	opening-up (of economy to outside world/competition)
arcas del estado (fpl)	government coffers, the Treasury
atomización (f)	fragmentation (of economy), existence of many small firms
autónomo (m)	self-employed person
banca privada (f)	the private banking sector
barreras aduaneras (fpl)	customs barriers
barreras no tarifarias (fpl)	non-tariff barriers
bienes de equipo (mpl)	capital goods
bolsa (f)	stock exchange
caja de ahorros (f)	savings bank
caladero (m)	fishing ground
calentamiento (m)	overheating (of the economy)
Cámaras de Comercio, Industria y Navegación (fpl)	Chambers of Commerce, Industry and Navigation
canon sindical (m)	contribution towards union funds
casa matriz (f)	parent company
círculo de empresarios (m)	business circle
comerciante (m)	(sole) trader
comercio (m)	trade; shop
comercio exterior (m)	foreign trade
comercio mayorista y minorista (m)	wholesale and retail trade
Comisiones Obreras (fpl)	Workers Commissions (trade union associated with the Communist Party)
Comité de Empresa (f)	workforce committee
concentración parcelaria (f)	rationalization of landholding structure
Confederación Española de Pequeñas y Medianas Empresas (f)	Confederation of Small and Medium-Sized Enterprises
conflictividad laboral (f)	industrial unrest
consejero (m)	company director
consejero delegado (m)	managing director
Consejo de Administración (m)	Board of Directors
contingente (m)	(import) quota
contratación (f)	hiring (of labour)
contrato a tiempo parcial (m)	part-time contract
contrato de aprendizaje (m)	contract of apprenticeship

contrato de duración indefinida (m)	permanent contract
contrato temporal (m)	temporary/fixed term contract
contribuyente (mf)	taxpayer
convenio colectivo (m)	collective agreement
cotización (f)	share price; exchange rate; social security contribution
crisis (f)	crisis; recession
cuentas de las administraciones públicas (fpl)	government accounts
cuota empresarial (f)	employer's social security contribution
déficit comercial (m)	trade gap
déficit exterior (m)	foreign deficit
déficit público (m)	public sector deficit
delegado (m)	elected representative
desarme arancelario (m)	removal of customs barriers
desequilibrios territoriales (mpl)	regional imbalances
despido (m)	dismissal, sacking
destrucción de empleo(s) (f)	job losses
deuda del estado (f)	government debt/bonds
economía sumergida (f)	informal/black economy
eje mediterráneo/atlántico (m)	Mediterranean/Atlantic coastal strip
elecciones sindicales (fpl)	workplace elections
empleo (m)	employment; job
empresa deficitaria (f)	loss-making firm
empresa familiar (f)	family firm
empresa nacional (f)	Spanish firm; domestic firm
empresa transnacional (f)	transnational company
Encuesta de Población Activa (f)	Official Labour-force Survey
endeudamiento público (m)	public/national debt
enfriamiento (m)	cooling-down
Estatuto de los Trabajadores (m)	Workers' Charter
estructura agraria (f)	structure of land-ownership
excedente (m)	surplus
éxodo rural (m)	rural depopulation, flight from the land
explotación (f)	farm, (land)holding
falta de movilidad laboral (f)	lack of mobility in the labour market
familia socialista (f)	socialist movement
financiación estatal (f)	public funding
fiscalidad (f)	taxation; tax rate
fiscalidad indirecta (f)	indirect taxes
fondo de cohesión (m)	cohesion fund
fusión (f)	merger
grandes superficies (fpl)	large-scale retail outlet
grupo (m)	group (of companies), conglomerate
hacienda (f)	tax authorities
holding (m)	holding company
horario comercial (m)	permitted shop opening hours
impuesto revolucionario (m)	extortionary 'tax' imposed by ETA on firms in the Basque Country
impuesto sobre el empleo (m)	'jobs tax'
impuesto de sociedades (m)	corporation tax
impuesto sobre el valor añadido (IVA) (m)	value added tax (VAT)
impuesto sobre la renta de las personas físicas (IRPF) (m)	income tax

indemnización (f)	compensation; severance pay
industria (f)	industry; firm
industria auxiliar (f)	component industry/firm
insolvencia (f)	bankruptcy
Instituto Nacional de Empleo (INEM) (m)	National Employment Agency
invernadero (m)	greenhouse
Inversión Extranjera Directa (f)	Foreign Direct Investment (FDI)
inversión extranjera (f)	foreign investment, inward investment
investigación, desarrollo e innovación (I+D+i)	research and development and innovation
jornalero (m)	day labourer
jubilación anticipada (f)	early retirement
Junta de Accionistas (f)	Annual General Meeting (AGM)
latifundio (m)	large estate
mentalidad empresarial (f)	entrepreneurial spirit
mercado laboral/de trabajo (m)	labour/jobs market
mercado nacional (m)	domestic market
minifundio (m)	very small farm/holding
minorista (m)	retailer
moderación salarial (f)	wage moderation
monte de piedad (m)	pawnbroker
obra social (f)	non-lucrative work (of savings banks)
oferta pública de adquisición (opa) (f)	takeover bid
organizaciones empresariales (fpl)	employers' organizations
Organización de los Países Exportadores de Petróleo (OPEP) (f)	OPEC
parcela (f)	plot (of land)
paro juvenil (m)	youth unemployment
participaciones (fpl)	shares in a private limited company
pesca costera (f)	inshore fishing
pequeños comercios (mpl)	small shops
población activa (f)	labour force
poder adquisitivo (m)	purchasing power
política cambiaria (f)	exchange rate policy
política monetaria (f)	monetary policy
presión fiscal (f)	tax burden
primicias (fpl)	early-season produce
productos (mpl)	products; (agricultural) produce
productos elaborados (mpl)	finished products
pyme (f)	SME (small/medium-sized firm)
reciclaje (m)	retraining; recycling
reconversión (industrial) (f)	industrial restructuring
reforma agraria (f)	land reform
reforma de la protección por desempleo (f)	reform of unemployment legislation
Registro Mercantil (m)	Register of Companies
riego (m)	irrigation
rigidez (f)	(source of) rigidity (in the labour market)
Salario Mínimo Interprofesional (SMI) (m)	standard minimum wage
saneamiento (m)	rationalization; streamlining; setting on sound financial footing

sector (m)	sector; industry
sector agropecuario (m)	agriculture
sector alimenticio (m)	food and drink industry
sector automovilístico (m)	vehicle/car industry
sector empresarial (m)	corporate sector
sector forestal (m)	forestry sector
sector lácteo (m)	dairy industry
sector minero (m)	mining industry
sector pesquero (m)	fishing industry
sector secundario (m)	industry
sector terciario (m)	tertiary (services) sector
sector turístico (m)	tourist industry
sindicato (m)	trade union
sobreexplotación (f)	over-exploitation; overfishing
sociedad anónima (f)	public limited company
sociedad colectiva (f)	partnership
sociedad de responsabilidad limitada (f)	private limited company
sociedad en comandita (f)	limited partnership
Sociedad Estatal de Participaciones Industriales (f)	State Industrial Holding Company
socio (m)	partner
subvención (f)	subsidy
tasa de actividad (f)	participation rate, economic activity rate
tasa de desempleo/paro (f)	unemployment rate
tasa de inflación (f)	inflation rate
tour operadores (mpl)	tour operators
trabajador cualificado/sin cualificar (m)	skilled/unskilled worker
trabajador por cuenta ajena (m)	employee
Tribunal de Defensa de la Competencia (m)	Competition Commission
turismo de masas (m)	mass tourism
Unión General de Trabajadores (f)	General Workers' Union

6

Social challenges

In spite of the economic prosperity it enjoys, Spain faces some major social challenges, most of them typical of advanced Western democracies. Many of these are issues of social cohesion that beset other countries, given the particular disadvantages that certain groups of people have to cope with. Some specific issues stand out in the Spanish case, given the phase of the country's development, its geographical location, and, in some respects, the enormous advances that have been made in recent years in the fields concerned.

This chapter examines some of the more important of these social challenges. It looks first at the situation with regard to immigration, which has proven to be particularly complicated in the Spanish case. It then considers the degree to which the situation of women has changed in the relatively short period since the transition to democracy, as well as a number of issues which relate generally to male-female relationships, including divorce, abortion and domestic violence. The major advances in the area of same-sex relationships are then outlined, and the chapter concludes with a discussion of the ways in which the country is coping with, respectively, the ageing of its population and the needs of its disabled people.

6.1 Immigration

6.1.1 From emigration to immigration

For centuries, Spain was a country of emigration, with the most intense periods of emigration lasting, firstly, from the late 1890s to the 1930s, and then from the mid-1950s to the mid-1970s. In this second stage, over a million Spaniards left the country in search of work in the more industrialized northern European economies, mainly France, Germany, Switzerland, Belgium and the UK but also, to a lesser extent, in North and South America. Remittances sent back to Spain by these workers proved invaluable to a home economy which was struggling to develop, and helped to redress the country's balance of payments during those years [5.2.1].

This trend was reversed in the 1970s, due to the oil crisis of 1973 and the subsequent recession experienced in the industrialized countries. In that context, new restrictions were imposed on immigration in those host countries, with the result that Spanish emigrants started to return home. Added to this, a growing number of nationals from third countries also began to choose Spain as their destination for emigration, and this trend became more pronounced in the 1980s, especially in the second half of the decade when the country's economy was expanding rapidly [5.1.2]. The number of foreigners residing in Spain doubled between 1970 and 1985 and then again from 1985 to 1990, by which time the figure stood at over half a million. These migrants, however, were still mostly affluent northern Europeans, many of them British or Scandinavian retirees, and only a minority were immigrant workers from poorer countries.

In more recent times, further improvements in Spain's prosperity, along with membership of the EU, have made the country more attractive for the latter. The result is that, by 2007, the country had a total foreign population of more than four million, or about 10 per cent of the total. This figure refers to those who have been registered (*empadronados*) in the census of population. It therefore includes both the three million or so immigrants who have entered the country with the required documentation, i.e., 'legal immigrants', as well as many who are 'illegal immigrants' (*ilegales/indocumentados/sin papeles*).

A large majority of the total number of immigrants now resident in Spain – both legal and illegal – are migrant workers, mostly from North Africa, Latin America and Eastern Europe. By nationality the largest groups come from Morocco (more than half a million), Ecuador and Romania (more than 400,000 in each case). Most of the immigrant population in Spain is concentrated in the larger cities (especially Madrid and Barcelona), along the Mediterranean coast (with high numbers in Valencia, Almería, Murcia, Girona, Málaga and Alicante) and on the islands (Canaries and Balearics). Across the entire country, however, the presence of foreign workers is becoming increasingly visible, even in small towns and rural areas, often due to the labour needs of the agriculture industry.

There are clusters of particular nationalities of immigrants in certain areas, including, for example, North Africans (*magrebíes*) in Almería, Pakistanis in Barcelona, Ecuadorians in Murcia and Latin Americans generally in Madrid. The latter have been coming to the country in large numbers for more than a decade, a form of migration which has been facilitated by the fact that Spain and her former colonies share a common language. In 2006 the number of Latin American residents in Spain – including those from Portuguese-speaking Brazil – was 1.7 million, with Ecuadorians forming by far the largest proportion, followed by Colombians and Argentinians. In the same year, it was estimated that there were more than 200,000 Bolivians living in Spain, of whom just 60,000 were believed to have the required documentation. Also in 2006, police reports suggested that about 500 illegal immigrants were entering Spain daily through Barajas airport in Madrid, of whom 90 per cent were said to be Bolivians.

The first systematic attempt to regulate the legal situation with regard to immigration came with the introduction in 1985 of the first Aliens Act (*Ley de Extranjería*). This was a restrictive piece of legislation, framed largely in response to the need, on the eve of Spain's joining the European Community [4.2.1], for the country to be seen to tighten up on the inward flow of migrants. The Act established a clear distinction between legal and illegal immigrants, but even legal immigrants were afforded only their basic human rights under the Constitution. Those without documentation were not accorded any substantial rights and were liable to face immediate deportation.

In the early 1990s, new visa requirements began to be imposed on North Africans and on nationals of certain Latin American countries. Measures were also taken, however, to put in place a genuine immigration policy rather than simply responding to the need to meet European requirements. A process was established whereby immigrants could achieve legal status, and plans were devised to assist with their integration into Spanish society. The government set up special bodies to coordinate policy in the area and established agencies to ensure more accurate recording of data relating to migration, including the Permanent Immigration Observatory

(*Observatorio Permanente de Inmigración*). The 1985 Act was amended by Royal Decree in 1996, to reflect this progress. The result of these changes was that administrative requirements for immigrants were made more flexible, and provisions were put in place for permanent work and residence permits to be granted.

A new all-embracing Aliens Act was introduced in 2000. This extended the rights of both documented and undocumented migrants and established a means by which the latter could achieve legal status after two years of residence and could access social, health and education services. This law passed through the Cortes without the support of the minority People's Party (PP) government itself, which viewed its more liberal provisions as constituting a magnet to attract further immigrants (*efecto llamada*).

After the PP achieved a majority in parliament at the general election held later the same year [2.4.4], however, the government modified the terms of the Act, introducing further restrictions on entry. The right of association was likewise removed from undocumented migrants, which meant they were forbidden from joining trade unions or striking. The government also tightened up on the conditions under which other family members could come to the country to join migrants already there (*reagrupación familiar*), while also introducing measures to speed up the process of expulsion. The period of residence required in order to achieve legal status was increased to five years, employers who took on illegal immigrants faced harsh penalties (including the possible closure of their businesses), and transport companies were obliged to report passengers who did not use return tickets. The harshness of the Act provoked street demonstrations and widespread protests by humanitarian groups, and these objections were borne out when, in 2003, several of the provisions in the Act were overturned in the Constitutional Court.

The Socialist government which came to power in 2004 adopted a much more liberal approach. It rapidly introduced measures to regularize the situation of immigrants who were already in the country. Under the terms of this 'extraordinary regularization' (*regularización extraordinaria*), those immigrants who had been in the country for at least six months were entitled to apply for papers to enable them to stay legally. As well as that, applications for work permits now had to be made by the employers of the migrant workers rather than by the workers themselves. More than 700,000 applications were submitted, and the result was a huge increase in the number of documented immigrants in the country. The degree to which things were changing and the impact these immigrants were having can be gauged by noting that, in the year 2006, total social security contributions increased by more than one billion euros over the previous year.

Illegal immigrants make up a large proportion of the total, existing largely on the margins of Spanish society, usually outside the range of both the social services and the country's taxation regime. It is notoriously difficult to establish exactly how many 'illegal immigrants' there are in Spain. If we subtract the number of documented immigrants from the total number of foreigners as reported in the census, we get a figure of just over one million. Since the census figure may not reflect the real situation, however, many observers believe that the correct number of illegal immigrants is much higher than that.

People enter the country illegally by road or through airports, of course, but the most dramatic – and most dangerous – means of entry in recent years has been by sea crossing. The shortest route is from the North African coast of Morocco. It is estimated that, since 1999, more than 100,000 North Africans have crossed the Straits of Gibraltar in flimsy boats (*pateras*) in an attempt to reach Spain by this means. Many have not succeeded and have drowned in the attempt.

An alternative route – longer, and more dangerous – is to go from the west African coast to the Canary Islands. Again, immigrants taking this route typically sail in another type of poorly-equipped boat – called *cayucos* – and often their journey ends tragically too. This means of entry into Spain reached a peak in 2006, when 31,000 people arrived on the Islands [4.2.3]. Many hundreds have died in the attempt, however, including no fewer than 150 people who drowned on one occasion in October 2007 when their boat broke up.

A third entry route from Africa is from Morocco via Ceuta and Melilla. Since the late 1990s, these have been the preferred means of entry for many Africans, who attempt to cross the fences that mark the borders between Spanish and Moroccan territory. The people who manage to enter Spain by these means usually arrive in a dreadful condition. Those who have crossed by sea have often travelled long distances before embarking, having left with insufficient quantities of food and water. They frequently pay exorbitant sums of money to be allowed to make the crossing, and are typically themselves the victims of human traffickers who put them on the boats and abandon them to their fate. Those who reach Spain alive and who are detained on arrival are housed in reception centres (*centros de acogida*), which are often overcrowded and poorly resourced, until they can be repatriated.

Using one or other of these routes, large numbers of sub-Saharan Africans have managed to enter the country without the required documentation. From Morocco alone the number who entered Spain illegally in 2003 stood at around 17,000, although this number has declined in subsequent years due to the cooperation that Spain has received from Morocco in implementing a range of security measures [0.4.3].

These measures have included strengthening the security in place along the frontier with Ceuta and Melilla. The borders between the latter and Morocco, the country which surrounds them, have been fortified significantly. The barbed-wire fences surrounding the enclaves have been increased in height, while sensors, video cameras and watch-towers have also been installed, in an effort to avoid a repetition of the incident in 2005 when the fences were stormed by a massive number of people attempting to gain entry simultaneously. Six of the immigrants died at that time, four of them shot by Moroccan police, while it was reported that many others who had not succeeded in entering found themselves stranded in the desert without food or water.

Surveillance at sea has also been made more effective with the creation of a new EU-level security agency called Frontex which has helped to reduce the numbers of immigrants entering the Union along its southern coasts [4.2.3].

The EU has also strengthened the legal measures designed to control the flow of migrants. In 2002, it introduced visa restrictions for Latin Americans wishing to enter Europe, and these are gradually being applied to all the countries in the Schengen area, that is, the group of 24 European countries – including Spain – that allow completely free movement across their borders, without any passport controls [4.1.2]. Hence, Ecuadorians have needed a visa to enter Spain since June 2003, and

Bolivians since April 2007. The Spanish government also now requires airlines to gather background information from passengers entering from non-Schengen countries.

An agreement between Spain and Morocco obliges the latter to re-admit not only their own nationals but also those from third countries who have entered Spain illegally through that country. Repatriation agreements also exist in regard to other African countries including Nigeria, Mali, Guinea-Bissau, Mauritania and Senegal.

6.1.2 Economic and social implications of immigration

The new immigrants have been an important factor in Spain's rapid economic growth over the last decade. They represent about ten per cent of those in employment, which makes Spain the country with the highest proportion of foreign workers in the EU. They are particularly prominent in sectors where Spaniards prefer not to work. In 2005, for example, they constituted 33 per cent of home-cleaners and carers, one fifth of all construction workers, 14 per cent of agricultural workers and one tenth of those working in catering. Their economic importance is reflected in the fact that responsibility for immigration-related matters was transferred from the Ministry of the Interior to the Ministry of Labour and Social Affairs in 2004 [1.4.4].

Remittances from immigrants to their home countries have increased in line with the increased immigrant population, amounting in 2006 to more than four billion Euro. These sums are larger than the total amount of Spain's official aid to less developed countries, and obviously benefit the economies of those countries. The trade in remittances itself clearly benefits Spanish banks, however, since they charge commission on them. Given the relatively high rate of such commissions, many immigrants prefer to use the services of remittance agencies (*remesadoras*) which charge lower rates.

Immigrants also have an important social impact. For instance, the birth rate in Spain has been extremely low for several decades, bottoming out at 1.2 births per woman of child-bearing age in 2000 (while the 'replacement rate' needed to ensure stable population is around 2.1). Since most immigrants are relatively young people and often start families in Spain, they have helped to push the rate back up, so that it stands now at 1.37, with 16 out of every 100 children in Spain being born to mothers who are non-nationals.

Naturally, this also has an impact on the educational system. Between the academic years 1999–2000 and 2004–2005, the number of non-national children in primary schools in Spain jumped from 44,000 to 198,000; in the basic secondary school cycle from 30,000 to 125,000, and at Baccalaureate level from 6,000 to 19,000. Along with the increased numbers of foreign children comes a greater demand for classes in Spanish language and culture, but also a demand for tuition in the languages, cultures and religions of the immigrant communities. Reflecting the fact that there are more than one million Muslims resident in Spain, courses which introduce Islamic religion and culture are now taught in many schools in Andalusia and Aragon, as well as in Ceuta and Melilla. In 2006, the government funded a Spanish-language textbook on Islam for schoolchildren. In Getafe, a town to the south of Madrid, where nearly 12 per cent of the population are immigrants, local council staff have access to classes on Arab language and culture.

On the other hand, problems of racism and rejection of the newcomers are also a fact of life in Spain. After terrorism, unemployment and housing, immigration is seen by Spaniards as the fourth most serious issue facing Spanish society, and a 2007 poll indicated that 62 per cent of Spaniards believed that there were too many immigrants in the country. Most would see racism as a relatively minor problem, although it is estimated that there are about 4,000 racist attacks every year and approximately 60 murders with a racist, xenophobic or neo-Nazi dimension to them.

Occasionally, serious incidents take place involving an entire community. One of the worst to date occurred at El Ejido, in Almería province, in February 2000. Following an incident in which a 20-year-old woman was stabbed to death, allegedly by a Moroccan agricultural labourer, a substantial proportion of the town's indigenous population embarked on an orgy of violence and destruction directed against his compatriots, most of whom lived in shanty accommodation outside the town. Twenty-two people were injured and 46 arrested. The conflict ended with an agreement to give compensation to the immigrants involved and to build improved accommodation for them.

There is a disproportionate number of immigrants involved in certain areas of criminal activity. For example, four fifths of female prostitutes in Spain are foreign women, typically from Latin America, many of these being victims of human trafficking. Meanwhile, gangs of youths of Latin American origin (*bandas latinas*) have begun to appear in deprived areas of some cities, notably Madrid. These are gangs of disaffected adolescents, many of them from Ecuador, Colombia and the Dominican Republic, who are posing new problems for the Spanish police with their turf wars and violent initiation rites.

There is a strong perception in Spain, partly justified, partly exaggerated, that there is a direct relationship between immigration and crime in general. A survey carried out by the European Commission against Racism and Intolerance found that 60 per cent of Spaniards linked the two. This view is reinforced by the fact that 30 per cent of inmates in Spanish prisons are non-nationals, about half of whom are Moroccans, Colombians or Algerians.

In a more positive vein, constructive steps have also been taken by the Spanish government to facilitate the entry of migrants – specifically, African migrants – who wish to work and contribute to Spanish society. These include the creation and funding of training centres (*escuelas taller*) for potential immigrants in several African countries. These centres aim to provide training opportunities for people who may either be offered work contracts in Spain or opt to stay in their home countries to train others. To date centres have been set up in Senegal, Mauritania, Mali, Gambia and Guinea-Bissau. Courses include training in areas such as fishing, agriculture, health care, construction and the hotel and catering trade.

6.2 The situation of women

Until fairly recently the situation of women in Spanish society was in important respects almost medieval. In Franco's time, a Spanish woman could not own her own passport, open a bank account or sign a contract. Until 1975 married women were legally required to obtain their husbands' permission before undertaking any activity outside the home. Married women who engaged in a sexual relationship outside their marriage were deemed to have committed the crime of adultery under the law, regardless of the circumstances; a married man who was an adulterer was considered to have committed a crime only if the adulterous act had taken place in the family home, or if it was public knowledge, or in the event that he was living with a mistress. Although it was possible – with considerable difficulty – to annul a marriage or obtain a legal separation, divorce was banned, as were contraception and abortion.

Opposition to contraception, divorce and abortion was in line with the teachings of the Catholic Church, which had a strong influence on the social policies adopted by the Franco regime [0.2]. The waning of this influence, especially in the late 1960s and 1970s, facilitated the emergence of more liberal attitudes on these questions, although working out political and legal solutions proved to be tricky enough. Although contraception was legalized without much fuss in 1978, divorce and abortion proved to be more of a challenge for governments during the transition period.

In 1981 the then government took steps to legalize divorce, but split apart in the process [2.2]. It is a sign of how times had changed, however, that many of the aspects of the measure that led to public dissatisfaction were clauses restricting the availability of divorce rather than the opposite. These included the fact that a spouse had to cite grounds in order to petition for a divorce and could only do so if he or she had been legally separated for at least a year.

Added to that, the attitudes of the overwhelmingly male Spanish judiciary in applying the law often made it seem ineffective, with the result that many couples initially preferred to avoid the complications involved in a divorce procedure by simply living apart, a practice often referred to as 'Spanish style divorce' (*divorcio a la española*). As a result, Spain has had one of the lowest rates of divorce in Europe until recently.

A revised law brought in by the Socialist government in 2005, however, has made it easier to obtain a divorce, and has led to an increase in the rate. Now, a spouse does not have to obtain a legal separation before getting a divorce, nor is it necessary to cite any grounds. It is possible to apply for a divorce as early as three months after getting married, or even earlier if a spouse is being abused by their partner. A further innovation introduced by the new law means that the judge can decide to grant shared custody, even against the parents' wishes, if this is deemed to be to the benefit of the child or children of the marriage. Recent surveys indicate that the new law is having a dramatic effect on the take-up of divorce. The number of divorces registered in 2006 was more than 74 per cent up on the previous year, with the rate increasing dramatically in the case of people who had been married for less than twelve months, while the number of separations had dropped by 71 per cent.

Again after much public debate, and in spite of the strong opposition of the Catholic Church, limited abortion was legalized in 1985. The conditions for abortion are the strictest in the EU outside Ireland, with the grounds on which a termination may be carried out being limited to three. These are when there is grave danger to the physical or mental health of the mother; in cases of rape; or when the foetus is damaged. The vast majority of abortions – in 2005, almost 97 per cent – are carried out on the basis of the first of these conditions. Although a 1991 decision by the Supreme Court seemed to establish the possibility of using social grounds as a further justification, this has not gained general acceptance. There are repeated calls for the law to be revised in order to allow for abortions to take place freely up to a certain time limit (possibly twelve weeks). This type of law based on time-limits (*ley de plazos*) is, of course, vehemently opposed by those groups – the Catholic Church among them – who denounce the practice of abortion in general.

As it stands, gynaecologists who have carried out abortions have been periodically prosecuted for ignoring the conditions laid down in law or for interpreting the notion of danger to the mother's health – especially her mental health – too widely. Even clinics that practise abortions which are totally in compliance with the legislation, however, are often targeted – sometimes violently – by the groups who oppose it.

On the other hand, many doctors who consider themselves to be conscientious objectors to abortion refuse to perform any terminations. As a result, only a small percentage of abortions are carried out in public hospitals: in 2005, just 3 per cent. In certain autonomous regions it is difficult for a woman to get a termination. In six Spanish regions – including, for example, Navarre – legal abortions have never been carried out at all. In these cases, women are obliged to travel to another region or to go abroad to have an abortion.

Illegal abortions are relatively commonplace. Some of the more notorious prosecutions in this area in recent years have involved abortion clinics in Barcelona which carried out illegal abortions on women from Spain as well as from other countries. Perhaps because of the clandestine or semi-clandestine nature of these practices, the country's official abortion rate is one of the lowest in the EU, although between 1987 and 2005 the number of abortions per annum increased from 16,000 to over 90,000.

More generally, the defence of women's rights and the enhancement of women's lives have been the stated aims of the National Women's Bureau (*Instituto de la Mujer*) since it was set up in 1983 by the Socialist government of the time. Acting as an independent agency under the aegis of the Ministry of Culture (though later transferred to the Ministry of Labour and Social Affairs), it aims to foster the involvement of women in all areas of political, cultural and socio-economic life in Spain. The Bureau has produced various Women's Equal Opportunities Plans (*Planes para la Igualdad de Oportunidades de las Mujeres*). Nonetheless, these have been characterized by a distinct lack of specific proposals, and it is hard to escape the conclusion that their main purpose may have been the improvement of the government's image among women. To its credit, however, the Bureau did pioneer the establishment of centres for battered wives (*mujeres maltratadas*).

The issue of domestic violence (*violencia doméstica*) has long been an acute problem in Spain, where about 60 women are murdered by their partners or ex-partners every year. Until recently, however, the extent of government action did not reflect the seriousness of the problem. Since the late 1990s, these cases and instances of domestic violence generally have been receiving greater attention in the media, as have the related court judgements, which have often entailed relatively lenient sentences for the offenders. The outrage felt by the public prompted the Socialist government, in 2004, to pass a 'Gender Violence Act' (*Ley Integral contra la Violencia de Género*), with the support of the opposition.

This law introduced a wide range of provisions to assist and protect victims of 'gender violence' (*violencia de género*), including stricter sentences for those convicted of such violence and more general use of barring orders, as well as measures aimed at increasing awareness of the issue. Offenders, 90 per cent of whom are men, can now find themselves having to relinquish their rights to the family home and their access to their children, or being obliged to undertake rehabilitation programmes.

Two new bodies were created to help deal with the problem, a Gender Violence Office (*Delegación de Gobierno contra la Violencia de Género*) within the Ministry of Labour and Social Affairs and the Monitoring Office for Violence against Women (*Observatorio Nacional de Violencia sobre la Mujer*), and there are now 46 Spanish courts that deal exclusively with crimes of violence against women. Additionally, the issue forms part of the syllabus of the new school subject called Education for Citizenship (*Educación para la Ciudadanía*) [7.3.2.1].

Within two years of the law being passed, nearly 50,000 men had been sentenced under its provisions, although the number of women murdered by their partners or ex-partners is as high as ever. One startling fact is that one in every three women murdered in 2007 was a foreigner, a statistic which is in line with a general trend towards an apparent increase in gender violence among immigrants. Those women who are in the country illegally are particularly vulnerable, given their reluctance to report their situation to the police for fear of being deported [6.1.1].

Similarly, the existence of the Bureau and changes in legislation have not brought about full equality of opportunity for men and women, although improvements have been made in this area too. The unemployment rate among women (11.6 per cent in 2006) is almost twice the figure for men, and women still tend to have lower paid jobs than similarly-qualified men, earning on average 20 per cent less than them. Women occupy just 5 per cent of management positions in private companies and 14 per cent in the public sector.

A recent report from the government-funded Social Research Centre (*Centro de Investigaciones Sociológicas*/CIS) [1.5.3] suggested that Spaniards perceived women as being at a disadvantage compared to men with regard to salary, opportunities for employment, promotion prospects and access to posts of responsibility in both public and private companies, as well as in terms of the possibility of achieving work-life balance. In fact, the only area where women were not seen as being disadvantaged was access to education.

Nonetheless, significant changes have been made. One domain which was, traditionally, exclusively male is the army, but since 1988 women have been permitted to join. Now, women constitute about 12 per cent of army staff and 5 per cent of officers [9.2.2]. In 2005, a woman was made captain of a warship for the first time. Although these figures are modest enough, they mean that the Spanish armed forces are the first in the EU and third in the world in terms of the proportion of female membership in their ranks. On top of this, the Spanish government made history by appointing the first ever female Minister of Defence in 2008.

Indeed, gender equality has been an important element of the Socialists' agenda since they came to power in 2004. Prime Minister Zapatero has followed through on his pledge to achieve gender balance in cabinet and appointed a majority female cabinet in April 2008, even though the more weighty portfolios still tend to be handled by men [1.4.3]. And, in 2005, the PSOE government carried out a reform of the Divorce Law which stipulated that failure to share domestic duties and the care of any children in the marriage could be held against the offending partner – in practice, in virtually all cases, the male – in any divorce settlement.

Furthermore, a major new law was added to the statute books in 2007, the Effective Equality Act (*Ley para la Igualdad Efectiva de Mujeres y Hombres*). The Act introduced new provisions aimed at combating sexual harassment (*acoso sexual*) and discrimination (*discriminación*) against employees who become pregnant. It also brought in new measures to encourage equal opportunity in the workplace, as well as obliging companies to achieve a ratio of 40 per cent female membership on their boards of directors within eight years. It extended maternity leave entitlements in certain cases, as well as extending parental leave for fathers to a period of 15 days. There are also new non-contributory benefits for mothers under 21 years of age. In the political sphere, quotas were set for the minimum numbers of women candidates to be included on parties' electoral lists.

6.3 Other social challenges

6.3.1 The situation of homosexuals

The very liberal view of homosexuality that is reflected in the legislation in force in Spain today offers a stark contrast to the intolerance that homosexuals endured during the Franco era. Then, any way of life that did not conform to strict Catholic dogma was considered anathema, and, under laws enacted by the regime between 1954 and 1970, anything up to 5,000 people were imprisoned for homosexuality. In fact, a law passed in 1970 allowed for the 'rehabilitation' of gays and lesbians by a variety of means, including the possible use of electric shock therapy. This law was revoked in 1979, although it was not until 2001 that legislation was passed requiring that police files on people arrested under the Act be destroyed.

Despite the repressive legislation, a clandestine gay cultural scene emerged in the 1960s, centred mainly in the trendy resorts of Sitges and Ibiza. The first gay organization was formed in 1975, the Catalan Gay Liberation Front (*Front d'Alliberament Gai de Catalunya*/FAGC), although it was not made legal until five years later, by which time similar organizations had begun to appear in other parts of Spain. In Barcelona in 1977, while homosexuality was still banned under the 1970 law, FAGC organized the first gay pride rally, which was harshly suppressed by the police.

Until as recently as 1986, soldiers in the Spanish army who were convicted of homosexuality could be discharged or imprisoned for anything between six months and six years. During the 1990s, the first openly gay districts appeared in the country, these being the Chueca district of Madrid and the Eixample in Barcelona. Chueca was the scene of a crowded street party lasting several days in June 2007 when Madrid hosted the Euro Pride festival.

The first law aimed at enshrining the specific rights of homosexuals in a range of areas of life was passed in Catalonia in 1998. Called the 'De facto Partners Act' (*Ley de Parejas de Hecho*), it stipulated that cohabiting gay couples would have many of the rights enjoyed by heterosexual couples with regard to inheritance, employment and pension entitlements, on presentation of a sworn statement (*certificado notarial*) setting out their situation. These rights did not, however, include the right to adopt children. In subsequent years, regional governments all over Spain followed the example set by Catalonia.

At the level of central government, the Socialists fulfilled their election promise to introduce legislation granting equal rights to gay and heterosexual couples in 2005, despite trenchant opposition from conservative political and social groups. The 'Homosexual Marriage Act' (*Ley de Matrimonio Homosexual*) achieved international media coverage and made Spain just the third country in the world to allow same-sex marriages, after the Netherlands (in 2001) and Belgium (in 2003). The conservative People's Party opposition has since filed an appeal – as yet unresolved – against the law in the Constitutional Court.

During the first year that the law was in force, some 4,500 gay couples got married, and up to July 2007 about 10,000 couples, out of an estimated gay population of 4 million, had tied the knot. The army saw its first gay wedding between two soldiers in 2006, although it is interesting that by 2002 the Civil Guard [9.3.1], formerly such a strongly conservative body, had already begun to allow gay couples to cohabit in its barracks.

Although a poll conducted in 2006 indicated that 66 per cent of the Spanish population favoured the new law, support for these liberalizing measures has been far from unanimous. Not only does the People's Party object to it, but the Catholic Church has also made clear its strong opposition. Both have joined forces with conservative pro-family values groups to organize demonstrations and issue public condemnations of the 2005 Act. Some of Spain's more reactionary mayors have even refused to marry gay couples, although the relatively liberal PP mayor of Madrid, Alberto Ruiz-Gallardón [2.4.5], defied his own party by personally conducting a gay marriage in 2006. Meanwhile, one conservative judge in Murcia was disciplined for decreeing that a mother in a lesbian relationship should have custody of her children taken away from her. The most consistent pattern of aggressive homophobia has been shown by neo-Nazi groups, a minor but vocal element in Spanish society that includes homosexuals among its range of targeted victims. Again, Catalonia has led the way in opposing this trend with its plans to introduce legislation banning homophobia in 2008.

Spain made history in this area again in 2007 when it became the first country to officially recognize the historical persecution of gays and lesbians. Homosexuals who were punished for their 'deviance' during the Franco dictatorship are now entitled to compensation of €12,000 each as well as a monthly pension of €800. Unfortunately, the measure came too late for most of the people concerned, as only about fifty of the victims were still alive to enjoy this benefit at the time the law was implemented.

Also in 2007, provision was made for married lesbian couples to attain the legal status of parents if one of the partners gave birth following fertility treatment. In the same year, another major advance was made in relation to gender equality with the passing of the 'Gender Identity Act' (*Ley de Identidad de Género*). This law grants transsexual people, diagnosed with gender dysphoria, the right to change their name and their gender as registered on their passports and identity cards (*Documento*

Nacional de Identidad/DNI) without having to undergo a sex-change operation or going to court. Finally, in that year also, the controversial new school subject of Education for Citizenship was introduced, which includes as part of its syllabus the fostering of tolerance of diversity, including an appreciation of homosexuality [7.3.2.1].

6.3.2 Providing for old age

Despite the mitigating effect of immigration [6.1.1], Spain is still a country with a very high proportion of old people. In 2006, 17 per cent of the population was aged over 65, that is, almost 7.5 million people, of whom nearly two million were over 80. Not only has life expectancy risen dramatically (80.2 years in 2005), the country's traditionally high birth rate is now among the world's lowest, standing at 9.98 births per thousand inhabitants in 2007, which puts Spain in 190th position out of 217 countries studied.

The ageing of the Spanish population is more noticeable in rural areas than in cities: among people who live in towns of less than 2,000 inhabitants, one in four is over 65. And non-nationals now form a significant proportion of the elderly population, the majority of these being pensioners from northern European countries – a quarter of them from the UK – living mainly on Spain's Mediterranean coast.

Not only are Spaniards living longer, but it is much less usual than in the past for younger relatives to be on hand to look after them. Up to a few decades ago, those younger family members – especially women – would normally have their parents living with them, with only a small number of older people living in institutional care in 'asylums' (*asilos*). Now, like their contemporaries elsewhere in Europe (although not quite to the same degree), the younger generation are increasingly unwilling to assume the task of caring for their parents by having them live in their homes. One result is that, according to the most recent housing census, almost 1.4 million people over the age of 65 live alone, of whom just over 1 million are women.

Naturally, this situation translates into a strong demand for geriatric hospital provision, as well as for non-medical provision in the form of old people's homes (*residencias de tercera edad*). But, because it used to be the norm for old people to be looked after by their families, the country had virtually no provision for the elderly until recently. One advantage of this, however, is that most publicly run old people's homes are relatively new and in good condition. The majority of these (70 per cent) are private, and these provide 75 per cent of the places required by the elderly population. Religious orders and institutions run 60 per cent of private homes, but, although the latter are generally of a higher standard than other private institutions, they are threatened by a sharp drop in the number of nuns in Spain.

More than half of the elderly people who reside in institutions pay for their care out of their own resources, with just one in every five being subsidized by the state (*régimen de concierto*). In the case of public homes, places are funded either entirely by the state or through a system of joint payment (*copago*), with the amount of the contribution from the resident depending on the person's resources. The extent to which public funding is available varies from region to region, but most regions' budgets are insufficient to cover the need that exists for subsidized places in private homes, and there are not enough places in public homes to meet current needs either. Elderly people are frequently obliged to resort to funding a place in a private institution by mortgaging the family home (*hipoteca inversa*), with the loan being repaid on the person's death, either through the house being sold or by the heirs providing the necessary finance.

Residential facilities have been supplemented by provision of various types of community-based care (*asistencia comunitaria*). They include sheltered housing (*viviendas tuteladas*), a home-help service (*servicio de ayuda a domicilio*) and helpline facilities (*tele-asistencia domiciliaria*). In addition the existing network of pensioners' day centres (*hogares del pensionista*) has been extended. More innovatively, the Socialist governments of 1982–96 introduced a substantial programme of subsidized holidays for the elderly (*vacaciones de tercera edad*) and health cures (*termalismo*). Given that their pensions have also been mainly unaffected by cutbacks since 1985, all in all the elderly have been among the major beneficiaries of the expansion of social provision.

Despite these advances, one major difficulty for Spain's elderly is the fact that pensions are still among the lowest in Europe, which reflects the generally low wage levels in the country. What also keeps pension levels low is the fact that Spaniards make social security contributions over just a 35-year period, whereas the norm in the EU is a period of 40 or even 45 years. We can get an idea of the dramatic increase in the cost of pensions to the Spanish taxpayer by considering that the bill stood at just €30 billion in 1998, but had risen to nearly €50 billion by 2006.

The significance of the role played by older people in contemporary Spain can be gauged by the recent change in name of IMSERSO, the government body responsible for overseeing social services. Run under the aegis of the Ministry of Labour and Social Affairs, this used to be the 'Migration and Social Services Bureau' (*Instituto de Migración y Servicios Sociales*), but the acronym now stands for the 'Elderly and Social Services Bureau' (*Instituto de Mayores y Servicios Sociales*). Given that it has been estimated by the OECD that as much as 35 per cent of the population will be aged 65 or over by 2050, we can expect that the Bureau will gain in significance in future decades as this sector of the population continues to play an important role in Spanish society.

6.3.3 Disabled people

The distance travelled by the country in terms of the care it provides for disadvantaged groups is reflected in the contrast between the wide range of benefits for both the elderly and the disabled set out in the 2006 Dependency Act (*Ley de Dependencia*) and the treatment which these groups received during the dictatorship. Under the Franco regime state provision for the disabled (*minusválidos/discapacitados*) – other than what was available in the 'asylums' which provided institutional care for them, as well as for the elderly [6.3.2] – was limited to social security payments for those most seriously affected.

The only major exception was the National Association of the Blind of Spain (*Organización Nacional de Ciegos Españoles/ONCE*), set up by Franco in 1938 to support those blinded fighting – on his side – in the Civil War. Until recently, the Association had never been a drain on the state, since it earned more than sufficient income from the various lotteries that it ran. It has traditionally provided thousands – currently, more than 20,000 – of its own members with employment selling tickets (*cupones*) for the lotteries.

Nowadays, its activities have expanded to include education and training courses, as well as programmes aimed at introducing its members to a range of types of employment, and its brief now also extends to groups suffering from other forms of physical disability (*discapacidad*). In effect, ONCE has come to be an alternative means of tax-raising to pay for disabled provision.

At one stage, the organization's financial situation became so strong that it was able to play an important role in the Spanish media sector, and it still maintains strong interests in that area, including 100 per cent ownership of the news agency Servimedia [10.3]. ONCE's financial situation changed in 2004, however, when lottery sales fell and the organization registered losses for the first time ever. Nonetheless, it had astutely signed an agreement with the Spanish government earlier that year which meant that the government would subvent any losses it incurred, which amounted to €75 million in 2005.

The country's disabled people currently represent around 9 per cent of the population, nearly 60 per cent of whom are over 65 years of age. The first step taken in the new democracy to cater for these was the passing of the 1982 Disabled Persons Integration Act (*Ley de Integración Social de los Minusválidos/LISMI*). As well as extending the system of payments to the disabled, and increasing their size, the LISMI introduced support for carers (*terceras personas*) and a mobility allowance (*subsidio de movilidad*). The Act also set guidelines for disabled access to public premises.

Over the next decade various types of smaller care units were opened with the aim of providing specialist and more personalized care for particular groups. Some serve the severely mentally handicapped and physically disabled (*centros de atención a minusválidos psíquicos/físicos gravemente afectados/CAMP/CAMF*). Others are rehabilitation centres for the physically disabled (*centros de recuperación de minusválidos físicos/CRMF*). Still others offer sheltered employment to those unable to deal with the world of work (*centros ocupacionales*).

More recently, the emphasis has been on the development of new forms of assistance for the disabled. IMSERSO [6.3.2] now runs the National Centre for Personal Independence and Technological Aids (*Centro Estatal de Autonomía Personal y Ayudas Técnicas/CEAPAT*). Spain has also participated in various EU programmes aimed at the disabled. Nevertheless, provision remains highly uneven in quantity and quality across the country.

The 2006 Dependency Act established a categorization of degrees of disability, setting out three different levels and providing for different types of support to be offered to people depending on their category. The assistance provided under the terms of the Act includes home help [6.3.2], day centres (*centros de día*), residential care (*atención residencial*) and help with the adaptation and improvement of accessibility of family homes (*ayudas para la adaptación y accesibilidad del hogar*). These services are funded partly by central government and partly by regional governments (with each of these providing 35 per cent of the overall cost). But a proportion of the cost, up to 30 per cent, is also paid by the people receiving the service themselves, although their contribution varies according to their income (*ingresos*) and assets (*patrimonio*). An agreement reached in 2007 between IMSERSO and ONCE will mean that a further €16 million will be invested in a range of projects aimed at helping elderly and disabled people to live more self-sufficient lives (*vida autónoma*) and to improve their mobility.

The one million Spaniards who are deaf (*sordos*), partially deaf (*discapacitados auditivos*), or deaf-blind (*sordociegos*), will benefit under the 2007 Sign Language and Oral Communication Act (*Ley de la Lengua de Signos y Medios de Apoyo a la Comunicación Oral*). This will improve the provision of sign language facilities in Castilian and Catalan, these being the only two languages in Spain with recognized signed versions. The Act also reinforces people's right to use signed languages, as well as providing greater access to interpreters and specialized teachers. Under the terms of the Act, two new bodies were created, the Office for the Normalization of Spanish Sign Language (*Centro de Normalización de la Lengua de Signos Española*) and the Spanish Subtitling and Audiodescription Centre (*Centro Español de Subtitulado y Audiodescripción*).

6.4 Glossary

acoso sexual (m)	sexual harassment
asilo (m)	asylum; old-style home (for children, the old, etc.)
asistencia comunitaria (f)	care in the community
atención residencial (f)	residential care
ayuda a domicilio (f)	home-help
ayudas para la adaptación y accesibilidad del hogar (fpl)	adaptation and improvement of accessibility of family homes (for disabled)
bandas latinas (fpl)	gangs of youths of Latin American origin
centro de acogida (m)	reception centre
centro de atención a minusválidos psíquicos/físicos gravemente afectados (m)	centre for the severely mentally and physically disabled
cayuco (m)	small boat (used by illegal immigrants from sub-Saharan Africa)
centro de día (m)	day centre
centro ocupacional (m)	sheltered employment unit
certificado notarial (m)	sworn statement
copago (m)	system of joint payment (by individual and state)
cupón (m)	lottery ticket
discapacidad (f)	disability
discapacitados auditivos (mpl)	partially deaf people
discriminación (f)	discrimination
divorcio a la española (m)	Spanish-style divorce
Documento Nacional de Identidad/DNI (m)	national identity card
Educación para la Ciudadanía (f)	Education for Citizenship (school subject)
empadronados (mpl)	people registered in census
escuelas-taller (fpl)	training centres
hipoteca inversa (f)	mortgage repaid on borrower's death
hogar del pensionista (m)	pensioners' day centre
ilegales/indocumentados/sin papeles (mpl)	illegal immigrants

ingresos (mpl)	income
Instituto de la Mujer (m)	National Women's Bureau
ley de plazos (f)	abortion legislation based on time limits
magrebí (mf)	North African (inhabitant of Maghreb)
minusválido/discapacitado (m)	disabled person
mujer maltratada (f)	female victim of physical abuse; battered wife
Organización Nacional de Ciegos Españoles/ONCE (f)	National Association of the Blind of Spain
patera (f)	small boat (used by illegal immigrants from North Africa)
patrimonio (m)	assets
planes para la igualdad de oportunidades de las mujeres (mpl)	women's equal opportunities plans
reagrupación familiar (f)	immigrants joining family members in new country
recuperación (f)	recovery (from illness); rehabilitation (of the disabled)
régimen de concierto (m)	system of state subsidies for old people's homes
regularización extraordinaria (f)	extraordinary regularization (of immigrants)
remesadora (f)	remittance agency
residencia de ancianos/tercera edad (f)	old people's home
servicio de ayuda a domicilio (m)	home-help service
sordo (m)	deaf person
sordociego (m)	deaf-blind person
subsidio de movilidad (m)	mobility allowance
tele-asistencia domiciliaria (f)	helpline facility
termalismo (m)	health cure
vacaciones de tercera edad (fpl)	subsidized holidays for pensioners
vida autónoma (f)	self-sufficient/independent life
violencia de género (f)	gender violence
violencia doméstica (f)	domestic violence
vivienda tutelada (f)	sheltered housing unit

Social welfare, health and education

Following on from the discussion of key social challenges in the previous chapter, here we first offer a general account of Spanish social welfare and health service provision, and then outline the situation with regard to education. Not only do these three areas account for a significant proportion of government expenditure, opinion polls repeatedly indicate that they are also areas to which Spanish people show a very strong commitment.

The country has had to make up a lot of ground in this field in recent decades. Social services were either neglected or inadequately resourced under the dictatorship and health provision has had to expand rapidly in recent years in order to cope with the needs of a population of more than 45 million people. To some extent both of these sectors have lagged behind the country's general economic development and certainly Spain spends less per head of population on these areas than other developed countries. Spending on education is also less than the average for developed countries, and the country is clearly still struggling to ensure adequate good-quality educational provision for its people. Despite the shortcomings, however, the country has made huge progress in all three areas over the last half-century, and, with regard to certain aspects of provision, the services available in Spain are of a very high quality and compare well with those in other European countries.

7.1 Social security

The origins of social security provision in Spain go back to the beginnings of the twentieth century. In 1900 compulsory insurance against accidents at work was introduced; in 1907 the National Social Insurance Agency (*Instituto Nacional de Previsión/INP*) was created. Later, under Primo de Rivera's dictatorship and the Second Republic, provision was extended in small ways. However, only under the Franco regime did a genuine social security system come into being. The unusual circumstances and nature of its development bequeathed substantial problems to the regime's democratic successors, which still plague the system to some extent today.

7.1.1 Francoism's legacy

Francoism's first attempt at establishing a unified system of social security came with the 1963 Social Security Framework Act (*Ley de Bases de la Seguridad Social*). This brought together a number of existing forms of benefit including old age, widows' and invalidity pensions (*pensiones de vejez, viudez e invalidez*). Most of these were far from generous; nor was there any mechanism for adjustment in line with inflation. In 1970, flushed with the economic success of the intervening years [0.2], the regime decided to make good these deficiencies.

The 1970 reforms improved a number of existing benefits (*prestaciones*) and extended coverage to new areas. In the medium term, their impact was disastrous. One reason was that they further accentuated the complexity and overlap which, despite supposed unification in 1963, characterized the Francoist system. It included numerous exceptional schemes (*regímenes especiales*) for particular groups of workers, as well as other anomalies. While significant sections of the population had no social security cover, some individuals were receiving multiple pensions from different parts of the system.

This bureaucratic complexity aggravated the second, and principal problem bequeathed by the 1970 reforms: their high cost. From 1973 on, economic boom turned to recession [5.1.1], causing a slump in the system's income, which was derived totally from the contributions (*cuotas*) paid by employers and employees. At the same time, the downturn also meant a rapid rise in the number of unemployed, for whom the 1970 reforms had increased the coverage and level of benefit.

The Franco regime's social security legacy thus turned out to be a considerable financial burden on its successors. In 1979 the system's outgoings exceeded its income for the first time. By 1986 its annual deficit had reached 24 per cent of budget. By European standards this figure was normal, or even low. In Spain, however, politicians and public alike were accustomed to the idea that the system should pay for itself.

The deficit accordingly gave rise to much talk of a 'crisis' in the social security system, and of a massive shortfall (*agujero*) in its finances. That there was, and is, a problem of how to finance the welfare state cannot be denied, but in essence it is one common to all developed countries. The distinctive issues facing the Spanish system in the early 1980s were, first, the alarming speed with which the financial situation was deteriorating and, second, the fact that welfare benefits remained relatively poor in a number of areas.

7.1.2 Reform and its limits

As in other areas, it was only when the Socialist Party (PSOE) reached power in 1982 that real steps were taken to tackle the social security 'crisis' [7.1.1]. Initially this was done by cutting some benefits, starting with the most costly of them: pensions. In 1985 some pension payments were reduced, and the number of years' contributions necessary to receive an old age pension increased. The government also sought to make savings on unemployment benefit by tightening up the requirements for entitlement and reducing the period of payment.

These changes focused attention on those jobless (over 60 per cent) who received no support. In 1989 a number of regional governments introduced a form of general income support, or social wage (*salario social*), to help them. The central government, however, refused to countenance a country-wide scheme because of concern about its potential cost. Instead, it addressed the problem as part of an attempt to restructure overall provision.

This was the intention of the 1990 Social Security Act (*Ley de Seguridad Social*). Like earlier legislation, the Act distinguishes between financial benefits (*prestaciones económicas*) and benefits in kind (*prestaciones técnicas*). However, it also introduced a distinction between contributory benefits (*prestaciones contributivas*) and non-contributory ones. The intention was for the latter to be financed, not from contributions, but from general government revenue. The separation was finally completed in 1999.

Non-contributory benefits include all benefits in kind, of which by far the most important is health care. They also include subsistence payments to those who, for certain specific reasons, need support, but have not paid into the system for long enough to qualify for the relevant form of contributory benefit. The most important such payments provide income support for the unemployed (*subsidio de desempleo*), as well as basic pensions (*pensiones asistenciales*) for the old and permanent invalids.

A range of new benefits were introduced during the tenure of the Socialist government elected in 2004. For instance, since July 2007, the parents of every newly-born or adopted child in Spain receive €2,500 (*cheque-bebé*) on the arrival of their child. Meanwhile, with effect from January 2008, people under 30 years of age renting a home for the first time receive a €600 loan, along with assistance with the payment of their rent for the first four years.

These latter payments, along with pension payments, are administered by the regional governments, except in the case of Ceuta and Melilla, where the payments are made by IMSERSO [5.2.4.1]. Non-contributory unemployment benefit, on the other hand, is administered by the National Employment Agency [5.2.4.1].

Contributory benefits are payable only to those who have made sufficient contributions to the system, on the basis of a number of defined circumstances (*contingencias*). The most important is pensionable status, which covers old age, permanent invalidity, and the condition of widow or orphan. Payments under this head account for over two-thirds of the total budget. The other main ones are unemployment and temporary incapacity for work (*incapacidad temporal*). Family support (*prestaciones familiares*), which is essentially child benefit, is also a contributory benefit.

These payments are administered by the National Social Security Agency (*Instituto Nacional de Seguridad Social/INSS*), which is attached to the Ministry of Labour and Social Affairs. Because of the amounts involved, the system's accounts are kept separate from the general government budget and require parliamentary approval in their own right. While their situation was eased by the removal of non-contributory benefits, it was far from solved. Indeed, insofar as the reforms increased welfare coverage, they actually aggravated the financial situation to some extent.

Again, pensions and unemployment benefit were obvious places for the conservative PP governments of 1996–2004 [2.4.4] to seek savings. With regard to the second, they relied essentially on other economic measures reducing the number of unemployed, a strategy that did bear fruit as the unemployment rate eventually declined [5.2.4.2]. On pensions, however, those governments took a very different line; they sought to build on the cross-party Toledo Pact of 1995, in which the main political parties had agreed not to use pensions for electioneering purposes.

Accordingly, between 1996 and 2001 the government signed a series of further agreements with the trade unions [5.5.1] on means of rationalizing the pension system. These certainly helped to stabilize the INSS budget, which showed a surplus in 1999, and has continued to do so since then. Two years earlier the improving situation had enabled a much-needed cut in employers' contributions to the system [5.2.4.2]. Moreover, despite the continued existence of several exceptional schemes [7.1.1], basically those for farmworkers, domestic workers and the self-employed, the system is also much simpler.

However, considerable problems remain. Overall spending on benefits is comparatively low by international standards and still devoted disproportionately to the jobless. A number of needy groups, especially those of recent appearance such as single-parent families and young people living independently, are neglected by the system. Above all, given the rapidity with which Spain's population is ageing [6.3.2], pension costs are bound to rise in the future. Hence the current government's concern to extend provision through personal 'pension plans', possibly as part of company schemes, beyond their present rather rudimentary coverage.

7.2 Health care

Spain spends somewhat less than other developed countries on health care (*asistencia sanitaria*) – around 8.1 per cent of GDP in 2004, compared with the OECD average of 8.9 per cent. Nevertheless, health spending represents a major burden on public finances, and one that is rising fast. Part of the cause, as in other countries, is the speed with which medical advances occur. However, the problem has been particularly acute in Spain, because until relatively recently the quality of health provision (*oferta sanitaria*) was poor.

7.2.1 The Spanish NHS

It is true that the Franco regime introduced compulsory health insurance (*seguro obligatorio de enfermedad/SOE*) for ever larger groups of workers; by 1975 nearly 80 per cent of the population was covered by it. Yet the resultant system was complicated, wasteful and prone to abuses, in particular the practice of doctors holding posts in both the public and private sectors simultaneously (*pluriempleo*). What is more, only around a fifth of hospital facilities (*instalaciones hospitalarias*) were in public hands, most being run more or less directly by the Church. In 1978 a National Health Agency (*Instituto Nacional de la Salud/INSALUD*) was set up to coordinate provision. However, the move did not change the system's essential features: high dependence on private care and inadequate services.

For reasons of both ideology and efficiency this situation was unacceptable to the Socialist government elected in 1982. It therefore introduced a series of reforms, the framework for which was set out in the 1986 General Health Act (*Ley General de Sanidad/LGS*). The LGS provided for the creation of a National Health Service (*Servicio Nacional de Salud/SNS*) modelled, as the name suggests, on the British NHS rather than the contributory systems common in continental Europe.

Accordingly, the basic principle of the SNS is availability of care free of charge at the point of delivery. By the 1990s universality of free provision had effectively been achieved. However, users are required to bear 40 per cent of the cost of prescriptions (*recetas*), unless they are entitled to exemption, which is the case, for example, of pensioners and their dependants [6.3.2]. Charges also apply to dental and psychiatric care (*asistencia odontológica y psiquiátrica*).

The 1986 Act placed administration of the SNS in the hands of INSALUD. It provided for the creation of regional health services (*servicios autonómicos de salud*) and district health authorities (*Áreas de Salud*), the latter serving a population of between 200,000 and 250,000. Each district is required to contain at least one district health complex (*Centro de Salud*), consisting of a general hospital and other facilities. In many cases these were based on the old health campuses (*ciudades hospitalarias*) in which various general and specialist hospitals were grouped together.

These arrangements applied to hospitals and other facilities run by INSALUD. For those run by private operators the Socialists adopted a similar solution to the one they had already applied in education [7.3.1.2.1]. Private hospitals may receive public funding, but only if they sign a maintenance agreement (*concierto*) with the health authorities covering the conditions under which they provide care. During the 1980s the government undertook a massive building programme which greatly reduced the importance of privately run facilities. Yet they still account for around one third of the overall number of hospital beds in Spain. Most have become maintained hospitals (*centros concertados*). However, although 40 per cent of patients treated in private hospitals are paid by the SNS (*asistencia concertada*), a significant minority continue to operate on a purely private basis.

Ironically, almost as soon as the SNS had been conceived its national character was undermined by the transfer of health care responsibilities to seven of the country's autonomous regions [3.1.3]. Those regional health services now not only exercised administrative functions but also had powers over policy and funding. At the end of 2001 agreement was reached on extending health devolution to the remaining regions, and this process has been rolled out across the country since.

In tandem with these changes, INSALUD was restructured into a much smaller body called the National Health Administration Institute (*Instituto Nacional de Gestión Sanitaria*) whose main function is simply to look after the administration of health services in Ceuta and Melilla. The SNS now comprises the state's health administration function plus those of the various autonomous regions. The former relates to overall coordination of the Spanish health system and strategic planning at a national level, along with the negotiation of international agreements in the area of health and the processing of legislation relating to pharmaceutical products. The regions, on the other hand, are responsible for planning and delivering health service provision in their respective geographical areas, including the provision of medical staff.

Each of the regions has its own health budget, of course, but they have experienced severe difficulties in attempting to work within those budgets. In 2005, for example, they accumulated a deficit of €4.5 billion, and had to be bailed out by the state, the only exceptions being Navarre and the Basque Country.

In an attempt to ensure coordination between the two levels of government, the Joint National Health Council (*Consejo Interterritorial del Sistema Nacional de Salud/CISNS*) brings together representatives of both. It has been unable to prevent disparity in health resources between regions, however, and this is often, though not always, to the detriment of the poorer ones. A report in 2007 pointed to the availability of what were termed 'better services' in Aragon, Navarre, Cantabria, Asturias and the Basque Country, while the Canary Islands, Valencia, Murcia and Madrid were said to have 'deficient services'. The CISNS had its coordinating role reinforced when the new Health Cohesion and Quality Act (*Ley de Cohesión y Calidad*) was passed in 2003.

In 1997 the PP government, in order to encourage the involvement of alternative providers, opened the way to the creation of health trusts (*fundaciones sanitarias*) which allow for private or sectoral interests to invest in health care facilities. Originally confined to new facilities, these were later extended so that they may now also run existing ones. The best-known trust facility is the hospital at Alcorcón, near Madrid, but others are active in a wide range of care types, including general practice and preventive medicine. Currently, this model of health care provision is more prevalent in regions where the People's Party is in control of government.

7.2.2 Resource problems

The country's health care spend may be below the average among rich countries, but Spaniards enjoy excellent health according to the most commonly used indicators. The country's infant mortality rate (*tasa de mortalidad infantil*), which as late as 1960 stood at 43 per thousand, is now just 4.3 per thousand – lower than that of the USA and of several EU countries. Life expectancy (*esperanza de vida*) is one of the highest in the EU, having reached 83.5 years for women and almost 77 years for men. Yet for all the positive statistics, and despite the real achievements of recent years, the Spanish health service is regularly perceived as being in crisis.

The best-known symptom is the persistence of lengthy waiting lists (*listas de espera*) for many types of treatment. These caused renewed controversy in late 2001. During the negotiations on completing the devolution of health powers [7.2.1], a number of regional governments asserted that the lists provided by the central authorities for their regions grossly understated the true situation. Whatever the truth of those accusations – and it seems clear that a degree of manipulation had been taking place – the lists are indicative of significant resource difficulties in the system as a whole.

Thus there is a shortage of qualified nurses (*enfermeros titulados*) and nursing auxiliaries (*auxiliares de clínica*). Spain also continues to have insufficient hospital beds (*camas hospitalarias*) for its needs. Provision of acute beds (*camas de agudos*), for instance, is below the EU average, and long-stay beds, especially for medical geriatric care, are also in fairly short supply. In addition, the available beds are unevenly distributed, being scarcer in rural areas and the south.

Spain has proportionately more doctors than any other developed country, a situation which reflects the massive increase in those studying medicine since 1980. But this same influx has aggravated the problem of poor training; many graduates feel the need to work abroad after qualifying to acquire the practical experience which is virtually non-existent in most medical faculties in Spain.

Across the country generally more specialists are needed, however, and those already in the system are poorly distributed. Paediatricians are particularly abundant at a time when Spain's birth rate continues to be low. In addition many doctors are unemployed, because the system cannot afford to employ them. As a result, junior doctors especially have tended to be dissatisfied. Some of their senior colleagues, too, were offended by the 1987 ban on their occupying several posts simultaneously [7.2.1]; since then they have had to devote themselves to a single job (*dedicación exclusiva*).

The main resource problem, however, continues to be a steady increase in health costs. As these rose in the late 1980s and early 1990s, the government introduced a National Health Service Consolidation Plan (*Plan de Consolidación del SNS*) in

1992/93. The basic principle behind this Plan was a clear division between policy-making and the provision of care, with the Health Ministry now defining exactly the types of health care which Spaniards are entitled to receive free of charge and setting performance targets. These criteria then serve as a means of measuring performance in each of the country's regions [7.2.1].

The Socialist government also moved to stem another source of rising costs, those for medicines. Unannounced, it raised prescription charges substantially in 1993, a move soon dubbed *medicamentazo*, but one which had the effect of reducing the annual increase in the cost of medicine over the following three years from 16 per cent to less than 5 per cent. The People's Party government elected in 1996, however, while advocating an extension of private health provision and greater management freedom for public hospitals, repeated this tactic of increasing prescription charges with a further notorious *medicamentazo* in 1998.

By then, the government had also negotiated an agreement with the drug companies on the use of generic drugs, thereby making medicines more affordable. At the time this measure was taken, generic drugs represented just 1 per cent of the Spanish medicines market, a paltry proportion in comparison with other Western countries, in some of which generic drugs make up over 50 per cent. More recently, the Socialist government has introduced a new law to further promote the use of generic drugs with the aim of reaching a level of 20 per cent.

7.2.3 Primary care

A further effect of the emphasis on specialist care [7.2.2] is that inadequate resources are directed to primary health care (*atención primaria de salud/APS*). Again, this is not a phenomenon unique to Spain, and the dangers associated with neglecting it were recognized in the 1986 General Health Act. Its aims explicitly included health awareness and the prevention of illness, and it stressed the importance of non-specialist care in achieving them. These good intentions have been honoured more in the breach than the observance, however, with the vast bulk of resources going on specialist care delivered in hospitals. In 2003, for example, primary health care accounted for just 16 per cent of the total spend on health, while in terms of staff deployment, only 20 per cent were working in primary care, with the remaining 80 per cent being specialist staff.

As a result, the local health centres (*centros de salud*) through which primary care is delivered are underfunded by comparison with hospitals. Even more than the latter, they suffer from a lack of nursing staff. Moreover, few doctors wish to become GPs (*médicos de cabecera*). Until recently organization of primary care was also poor; even now that an appointment system (*cita previa*) has been introduced waiting times are frequently long and consultations short. Small wonder that, like their counterparts in other countries who face a similar problem, many Spaniards go directly to relatively well-equipped hospital accident and emergency units, thus increasing the pressures on them.

As is the case in those other developed countries, the biggest health problems facing Spain derive from the scope and depth of the social and economic changes that have taken place over the last few decades. Alcohol consumption by the young has grown rapidly, and Spaniards still smoke more than most, with women in particular having a high level of tobacco consumption, despite the advent of anti-smoking legislation. There has been a massive shift from manual labour to desk-bound employment. The country's traditional diet, thought to be the principal cause of good health and long life, is changing dramatically; young Spaniards now ingest as much cholesterol as their contemporaries in northern Europe.

These changes have impacted on Spaniards' health in ways that are similar to their European counterparts, although the relevant indicators suggest that, in some respects, Spaniards are still coping better than others with these new lifestyles. The data for 2004, for instance, suggest that Spain was below the European average in terms of the number of deaths per 100,000 inhabitants with regard to nearly every cause of death apart from AIDS. In relation to death from heart disease, for example, Spain was third from the bottom of the European league.

On the other hand, the record on fatal accidents at work is poor, as it is in relation to road deaths, especially deaths attributable to drunken driving. In 2004, there were 113 deaths on the roads per million inhabitants, compared with the EU average of 95; about 40 per cent of those involved speeding and/or drink-driving. These indicators suggest that health awareness and illness prevention are even more vital in Spain than elsewhere as a factor in improving health levels, and, indeed, in maintaining existing ones. Yet, like other aspects of primary care, they continue to be the poor relations of the Spanish health system.

One area has proven to be an exception. Spaniards have traditionally been inveterate smokers, with only the Greeks consuming greater quantities of tobacco per head of population in Europe. In 2005, deaths attributable to smoking amounted to 16 per cent of the total. To address the problem, a controversial smoking ban (*Ley Antitabaco*) was introduced in 2006 which forbade smoking in workplaces and most public venues. Smaller bars and restaurants could opt to allow smoking or not, while larger establishments were required to provide a ventilated area for smoking which would be separated from the rest of the building. Although implementation of the new Act has been uneven across the country, with some bars in particular flouting the law, initial indicators suggest that it is having an effect, as the sales of cigarettes and cigars have declined by 6 per cent or more.

7.3 Education

As Spain returned to democracy after 1975, its educational system was beset by a number of fundamental difficulties. The Franco regime had fostered a traditional, elite-oriented approach to education, which meant that levels of educational attainment generally were very low, with less than 100 per cent participation even in primary school, and with higher education being reserved for a tiny proportion of the population. The Catholic Church had a preponderant influence in the system, owning and operating a large number of the schools and embedding its own principles so deeply that the content of the education received by children continued to reflect those principles even after the transition to democracy had been completed. Along with this, much of the curriculum at all levels of the educational system was of poor quality and not geared towards the needs of a modern economy, with insufficient vocational training, poorly-trained teachers and a university sector with a less than wholehearted commitment to research activity.

In the last phase of the dictatorship, the 1970 General Education Act (*Ley General de Educación/LGE*) constituted a belated attempt to rectify matters. It implicitly shifted the emphasis onto mass education, and lengthened the period of compulsory education, raising the leaving age to 16 in theory, as well as seeking to end selection at age 10. It also introduced new provisions for vocational training (*formación profesional/FP*).

Within a decade it was clear that the provisions in the new Act were inadequate and that the educational facilities available in the country did not even match the aims set out in it. In effect, little was done to ease the chronic shortage of school premises in urban areas, where they were most needed, and no adequate budget was made available to finance the LGE's ambitious plans for vocational education. In large part as a result, a significant number of children continued to leave education at 14.

In addition to this problem of drop-out (*abandono*), adherence to traditional methods and content led to an alarmingly high percentage of pupils failing to complete even their compulsory studies successfully (*fracaso escolar*). At university level, the content of courses remained essentially unchanged, with teaching methods largely based on learning by rote in conventional lectures. In particular, the curriculum of technical subjects was ill-suited to the economic needs of the late twentieth century. With the growth in population in the 1970s, resulting from the Francoist emphasis on encouraging large families, numbers began to increase at all levels in the system, and the generally poor quality of what was available became even more obvious.

It was not until the arrival of the Socialists in power in 1982 that any more fundamental reforms were implemented, although, since then, changes have been introduced and improvements made more or less continually. These changes have been instituted in many cases by central government but, as regional governments have gradually assumed responsibility for the administration of education in their geographical areas, they have also introduced changes. The remainder of this section looks first at the way governments have attempted to address the issues relating to education and then at how educational studies are structured as a result of these various reforms.

7.3.1 Organizational reform

Education was a major priority for the government elected in 1982. More than almost any other sector of the economy it benefited from the growth of public spending over the next decade. Between 1985 and 1991 alone the government education budget rose by some 70 per cent in real terms. During this time the organization of virtually the entire education system, at both university and school level, was overhauled. Deficiencies continued, however, and both the conservative People's Party governments of 1996–2004 and, again, the PSOE governments elected since 2004 have attempted, each in its way, to address them.

7.3.1.1 Higher education

The university system (*universidad*) was more affected than any other sector of education by the advent of mass access. From about 60,000 in 1962/63 the number of students enrolled rose to 650,000 in 1980 and more than 1.5 million in 2000, giving Spain a proportionately larger student population than any other Western country. Although numbers have declined slightly in recent years, this massive increase occurring over the space of a few decades resulted in unsatisfactory conditions for university students and teachers alike. It also held back the already urgent modernization of higher education in the areas of syllabus content, teaching methods and research activity. All of these – but particularly the last – were regarded by the PSOE as crucial to the country's economic performance, which explains the speed with which the party addressed the university issue on coming to power in 1982.

7.3.1.1.1 The LRU

The Universities Reform Act (*Ley de Reforma Universitaria*/LRU), the Socialist government's first major education law, was passed in 1983. One of its main aims was to do away with the post of temporary lecturer (*profesor no numerario*/PNN), which had originally been introduced as a stop-gap measure. Because their legal status was anomalous under existing legislation, the PNNs' pay and conditions were far from satisfactory. Yet in the meantime they had come to represent 60 per cent of teaching staff – and a constant source of discontent.

The LRU therefore abolished the category, which disappeared in 1987. Instead it established a clear distinction between tenured staff, made up of professors (*catedráticos*) and permanent lecturers (*profesores titulares*), and other lecturers. These latter were to make up no more than a fifth of total staff. They included junior lecturers (*ayudantes*) – mainly those completing a higher degree – and teaching associates (*asociados*), part-time teachers who were also practitioners in the relevant field. Unlike those of the PNNs, their teaching loads were supposed to be commensurate with their other duties.

In practice, however, these changes have not worked out as planned, in part due to the difficulty of reallocating resources. Some departments in established but less popular subjects, such as history, are over-staffed. Others cannot appoint sufficient tenured staff to meet student demand, so that the new non-tenured posts have become almost as widely abused as the PNNs. Moreover, large as the increase in resources has been, it has not kept pace with rising student numbers. In that regard the large increase in student grants (*becas*), admirable in that it has widened access to higher education, has only served to make the situation worse.

More generally, the LRU focused on a long-standing problem of Spanish higher education, the strict and bureaucratic control traditionally exercised by the central government over the universities. By the 1980s it was felt that this centralist approach had stifled individual institutions' initiative and flexibility, preventing them from finding solutions to the problems they faced. The LRU therefore granted universities a greater degree of freedom to manage their own affairs. Institutions were allowed to elect their own vice-chancellors (*rectores*), while the management boards (*juntas de gobierno*) these headed were given extensive control over internal policy.

Autonomy was strictly limited however, as universities were subject to considerable outside influence. One channel for it was the University Court (*Consejo Social*), of which sixty per cent of the membership are representatives of local trade unions and employers. The intention is to ensure that universities are responsive to the economic needs of their immediate catchment areas but there is little evidence that this has been achieved. A more effective, though less institutionalized, form of outside influence is the election of vice-chancellors. This is frequently politicized, in that different candidates are closely associated with particular political parties or factions within them. As a result, educational considerations can get entangled with political ones, especially those of the regional governments which now supply much of universities' funding.

At the same time, under the complex arrangements for devolution made in the 1980s [3.1], the central government retains powers to 'coordinate' education, and specifically the universities. Under the LRU these powers were exercised through the Universities' Council (*Consejo de Universidades*), attached to the Education Ministry. Despite supposed autonomy, many university decisions still had to be referred to the Council. As a result the delays traditionally typical of Spain's centralized system continued to occur, as for example with the introduction of new undergraduate course structures [7.3.2.2].

The autonomy that has been granted has not had entirely positive results. Appointments and promotions became a purely internal responsibility – previously they had been controlled by the Ministry in Madrid. The change led to a tendency towards academic in-breeding (*endogamia*), in other words, departments appointing their own ex-students and promoting members of existing staff. On the other hand, that could also be seen as a fair reflection of the lack of geographical mobility in Spanish society as a whole [5.2.4.1].

7.3.1.1.2 Competition

Overall, the results of the LRU were patchy, at best, and discontent among both students and staff remained high. Moreover, the Socialist government became increasingly worried about continuing low standards of teaching and research. Faced with such intractable problems, latterly it latched on to the currently fashionable notions of competition and choice as solutions to the universities' ills.

Probably the least significant step in that marketizing direction has been the establishment of new private universities. It was envisaged in the LRU and its details finally regulated in 1990, with the first new institutions coming into operation in 1993/94. Up to that time the only non-state institutions authorized to award higher degrees were the four given that privilege by the Franco regime. Of these, three were long-standing Church foundations (see Table 7.1); the fourth was the University of Navarre, set up in the 1960s by Opus Dei. All have small intakes and, in general, high academic reputations.

This is not true of the new private foundations, whose intake consists largely of students who have failed to pass the far from demanding entrance examination for the public universities. The sole exception is the San Pablo University Centre; based on a Church-run former university college, this resembles the four older Church universities. Yet like them its standards are high because its intake is small – and for that reason it does not represent a meaningful competitor to the public universities.

The number of public universities has grown dramatically since 1980. Institutions were founded in those regions which had previously lacked one; in others where population increase or dispersal restricted access to existing universities additional

Table 7.1 Spanish universities

Region	University	Notes	Students 1999/2000 (in thousands)	2005/06
Andalusia	U de Almería	N	15	12
	U de Cádiz	N	23	19
	U de Córdoba		21	18
	U de Granada		61	56
	U de Huelva	N	14	11
	U de Jaén	N	16	14
	U de Málaga		40	35
	U Pablo de Olavide (Sevilla)	N	5	10
	U de Sevilla		76	59
Aragon	U San Jorge (2005)	CN		*
	U de Zaragoza		43	36
Asturias	U de Oviedo		42	32
Balearic Islands	U de las Illes Balears		14	14
Basque Country	U de Deusto	C	15	11
	U de Mondragón	P	3	4
	U del País Vasco/Euskal Herriko Unibersitatea		60	47
Canary Islands	U de La Laguna		25	25
	U de Las Palmas de Gran Canaria		25	21
Cantabria	U de Cantabria		14	12
Castile-La Mancha	U de Castilla-La Mancha	N	33	28
Castile-Leon	U de Burgos	N	11	9
	U Católica de Ávila	CN	*	*
	U Europea Miguel de Cervantes (2002)	PN		1
	U de León	N	16	13
	U Pontificia de Salamanca	C	8	7
	U de Salamanca		34	29
	U SEK (Segovia)	N	1	1
	U de Valladolid		36	31
Catalonia	U Abat Oliba-CEU (2003)	CN		*
	U Autónoma de Barcelona		37	44
	U de Barcelona		62	64
	U de Girona		13	12
	U Internacional de Catalunya	P	2	4
	U de Lleida		11	7
	U Politècnica de Catalunya		33	32
	U Pompeu Fabra	N	7	8
	U Ramón Llull	P	13	13
	U Rovira y Virgili, Tarragona	N	11	12
	U de Vic		2	4
Extremadura	U de Extremadura		27	25
Galicia	U de A Coruña	N	26	22
	U de Santiago de Compostela		42	33

Table 7.1 (continued)

Region	University	Notes	Students 1999/2000 (in thousands)	2005/06
	U de Vigo	N	31	24
Madrid	U de Alcalá de Henares		20	24
	U Alfonso X el Sabio	P	8	10
	U Antonio Nebrija	P	2	3
	U Autónoma de Madrid		32	33
	U Camilo José Cela (1998)	PN	1	2
	U Carlos III de Madrid	N	13	18
	U Complutense de Madrid		104	85
	U Europea de Madrid	P	6	9
	U Francisco de Vitoria (2001)	PN		3
	U Politécnica de Madrid		44	37
	U Pontificia Comillas	C	9	7
	U Rey Juan Carlos (Móstoles)	N	6	19
	U San Pablo-CEU	CN	8	8
Murcia	U Católica San Antonio (1996)	CN	-	5
	U de Murcia		31	28
	U Politécnica de Cartagena	N	6	6
Navarre	U de Navarra	C	12	15
	U Pública de Navarra	N	10	8
Rioja	U de La Rioja	N	7	7
Valencia	U de Alicante	N	29	29
	U Cardenal Herrera-CEU (1999)	CN		7
	U Católica de Valencia San Vicente Mártir (2003)	CN		6
	U Jaume I de Castellón	N	13	12
	U Miguel Hernández (Elche)	N	7	10
	U Politécnica de Valencia		34	36
	U de Valencia Estudi General		58	48
Distance	UNED		141	165
learning	U Oberta de Catalunya	P	12	45

Notes: C = Church foundation; N = Post-1975 foundation; P = Private foundation; * = under 800 students.

ones were established (see Table 7.1). Within this expanded public sector, choice was encouraged by enabling universities to offer new degree courses of their own design [7.3.1.1]. The Socialists also began moves to relax the formerly tough rules on universities' catchment areas, and so allow students to attend any university throughout the country [7.3.1.1.3].

Other measures used by the government to promote competition recalled those taken in the UK. Thus universities were encouraged to seek funding from the private sector, a factor which has been apparent mainly at postgraduate level. In 1993 the government established a national quality assessment plan covering universities' teaching and research (*Plan Nacional de Evaluación de Calidad de las Universidades*). In the latter area a clear trend was established of concentrating university-based research in a small group of leading institutions. The rest, it seems, were to be left to face the problems of mass teaching, with neither a genuine research base nor adequate resources.

7.3.1.1.3 The LOU and its revision

The conservative governments that succeeded the Socialists from 1996 were conscious of the need for further changes, and, by 2001, had introduced a measure of their own called the Universities Act (*Ley Orgánica de Universidades/LOU*). Under this the universities' management boards [7.3.1.1.2] were renamed (*consejos de gobierno*), and student representatives were excluded from them. The university assembly (*claustro*), made up of the representatives of the university community (students, administrative and teaching staff), was reduced to a purely representative body, and lost the right to elect the vice-chancellor. Instead the VC was to be elected by the university community as a whole who would vote on the basis of a weighted franchise, which meant that teaching staff controlled 70 per cent of the votes. This change was intended to reduce the extent of political influence in the university, but, given the extent of the campaigning subsequently carried out by candidates for official positions, it is doubtful whether it had the desired effect.

The change which would have affected students most was the intention to abolish the old, country-wide university entrance examination (*selectividad*). In the event, however, this proposal was never implemented because government policy subsequently changed once the PSOE regained power in 2004 [7.3.2.1]. The PP's plan, however, was that universities would assume full responsibility for their own admission requirements, despite the fact that such a change would have undermined previous moves to encourage greater geographic mobility of students [7.3.1.1.2]: from 2000/01 universities have been required to open at least 20 per cent of places to applicants from outside their own region (*distrito único/abierto*).

It was accordingly decided to introduce a new standardized school-leaving examination, although again this was never actually brought into being, since the PSOE changed that policy also once they took charge of government in 2004 [7.3.2.1]. The university entrance examination is still in place, with universities being left free to conduct such additional tests as they consider necessary. In particular, these are needed for the more popular courses, which have an intake limit (*Numerus Clausus*). Special arrangements continue to exist for mature applicants.

Teaching staff were among the most affected by the LOU, and, at least for a number of years, some of these changes were actually introduced. All appointees to tenured posts [7.3.1.1.1] would now be required to pass a standard (i.e. Spain-wide) examination of their aptitude for university teaching (*habilitación nacional*), before being interviewed or tested by individual universities. In addition, two new types of non-tenured posts were created. Lecturers (*ayudantes doctores*) had to have completed a higher degree and must not have been attached to the university to which they were applying for two years prior to making their application for the position. Senior lecturers (*profesores contratados*) had to have at least two years' post-doctoral research experience. Among other goals, these changes were clearly aimed at ending the tendency for 'in-breeding' [7.3.1.1.1].

Finally, the LOU introduced various changes with regard to the university system as a whole. It set up a Higher Education Quality and Assessment Agency (*Agencia Nacional de Calidad y Evaluación/ANCE*) to oversee teaching and research assessment. The old Universities' Council [7.3.1.1.1] was replaced by a University Coordination Council (*Consejo de Coordinación Universitaria*), on which private universities [7.3.1.1.2] were represented with full voting rights. In a concession to the Catholic Church, the establishment of Church-run universities was made slightly easier than that of private universities in general.

Given the sensitivity about the Church's educational role, that was one reason for opposition to the LOU, but not the only one. Students were incensed at the lack of any firm provision for an extended system of grants, without which increased mobility seemed likely to remain the preserve of the rich. They were also concerned at the continuing possible need to sit separate tests in various universities.

On the other hand, staff felt they were having mobility forced on them, while the vice-chancellors were upset at being required to present themselves for re-election within six months. And, like opposition politicians and the regional governments who were charged with implementing the changes, they complained about the lack of identified resources to carry them through. These various strands came together in a series of vociferous demonstrations against the Act.

Although those protests could not prevent its approval, only some of its provisions ever came into force, since a considerable number of amendments were introduced in 2007 when further changes were made by the Socialist government. In the PSOE's version of the law, the University Coordination Council is replaced by the General Conference on University Policy (*Conferencia General de Política Universitaria/CGPU*). The CGPU will bring together representatives of the Ministry and representatives of the regions in a body which has responsibility for devising general policies for university education and for overseeing curricular and financial matters. In effect, this means that the autonomous regions will have enhanced powers in relation to the administration of the universities, including the power to stipulate how lecturers will be appointed within their region.

The main thrust of the changes that the new government introduced, however, was to increase the autonomy of the universities themselves. Universities now have the right to devise the details of their own course structures (*planes de estudios*) once they receive permission to proceed with the creation of a particular degree and once they follow general guidelines laid down by the Ministry and the region. Furthermore, each university assembly can now decide whether that university's vice-chancellor is to be elected by the university community as a whole, as heretofore, or appointed by the assembly itself.

The examination of aptitude for university teaching which had been introduced under the LOU was revoked in the 2007 amendments, and a new system based on certification (*acreditación*) was created. To achieve certification, a person wishing to apply for a university position is to be vetted by a committee of experts who will assess the applicant's experience and professional credentials, so that universities can then select their preferred candidate from among those who have been successful. The clause requiring applicants not to have been attached to the university to which they are applying for two years prior to their application was also revoked.

In an attempt to promote research activity in the universities, these revisions to the Act stipulate that research-active lecturers can be granted a period of leave of up to five years in order to work in spin-off companies (*empresas de base tecnológica*), that is, companies created to commercialize scientific advances. More generally, at least 50 per cent of teaching staff in the university must hold doctoral degrees, and academics with doctorates are also favoured in the sense that any who are in permanent posts have more voting rights in the weighted voting system in operation in university assemblies than those who are not doctors.

Finally, the mobility of researchers – both national and international – is to be fostered by the creation of a new funding programme called the Miguel de Unamuno Programme (*Programa Miguel de Unamuno*).

7.3.1.2 School provision

At school level, the main issue in the 1980s was the status of Spain's private schools, the great majority of them run by the Church. The reason was partly financial. Over the decade to 1982 maintenance grants to private schools had increased by a factor of over 70 despite the fact that such schools remained largely free of state control. Under measures passed in 1980 they were allowed to select their pupils according to their own criteria; they were even allowed to charge fees (*tasas*), and over half did so. When the Socialists came to power in 1982 they were understandably keen to change this situation.

7.3.1.2.1 The LODE

The Socialists' second major education reform, the Right to Education Act (*Ley Orgánica del Derecho a la Educación/LODE*), was passed by Parliament in 1984. The LODE addressed the questions of public subsidy and social division, as well as others related to the running of schools. It implicitly recognized that private schools would continue to have considerable importance. But it also redefined the balance of power between them and both the government and parents, in such a way as strictly to limit their educational and social influence.

In order to receive public funds under the LODE, schools had to sign an agreement (*concierto*) agreeing to fulfil a number of conditions. Most fundamentally, maintained schools (*centros concertados*) had to provide compulsory education free of charge. They are also required to keep proper accounts subject to government scrutiny and to refrain from any supplementary profit-making activities. The LODE also stipulated that government approval was required for maintained schools' statement of educational philosophy (*ideario*). The impact of all this on the approach adopted by such schools is limited, however; in particular, there are indications that some maintained schools may help their students' prospects of entering preferred university courses by enhancing the marks they are awarded at school-leaving level.

In addition the LODE barred Church and other private schools from practising selection if they received financial support. Access to maintained schools could be restricted only by the same resource considerations as in the public sector. In other words, where selection was unavoidable due to excessive demand for places it should follow only the criteria laid down by the state; these gave priority to children of poorer families and those living close to the school concerned.

Maintenance agreements under the LODE also required a School Council (*Consejo Escolar*) to be set up. Some 40 per cent of the Council's members are elected by the teaching staff, and the same proportion by parents and pupils. Only the remaining 20 per cent represent the school's operators. Individual School Councils in turn elect the National Schools' Council (*Consejo Escolar del Estado/CEE*). The CEE's 80 members are drawn in specified proportions from representatives of the same three basic interests – staff, pupils and parents, and private school operators – and of the government.

The CEE, first constituted in 1986/87, has only advisory powers and in practice has not proved an effective channel of public input into education policy. The individual Schools Councils, however, have had a major impact, since they considerably reduced the absolute power previously enjoyed by private school operators over internal management. They elect the school's headteacher (*director*) for a three-year term, and are responsible for appointing and dismissing staff. This latter provision in particular is intended to protect teachers' academic freedom (*libertad de cátedra*), restricting the ability of school operators, and specifically the Church, to influence the way subjects are taught.

The LODE provoked one of the most bitter political confrontations of the 1980s. At a time when the Right was finding it hard to make any real progress in attracting popular support [2.4.2], the Act provided a rallying point for opposition to the government. It brought articulate, better-off parents reluctant to give up the privileges of private education into alliance with the Church and those close to it. Together these interests staged a mass campaign against the proposals. Eventually the case went to the Constitutional Court [1.1.3], which in 1985 found against the objections.

7.3.1.2.2 Freedom and diversity

Central to the debate over the LODE was the notion of educational freedom. The government held that the Act promoted the freedom not just of teachers but also of children and parents. Subject only to resource constraints, it ensured free access to all state-funded schools, and allowed greater public participation in their operation. The conservative opposition, on the other hand, argued that the LODE restricted freedom by placing constraints on the providers of education. Yet, despite these fundamental differences the Act's provisions are now, by and large, an accepted part of the Spanish education system.

There are a number of reasons for this acceptance. First, selective private schools have continued to function outside the LODE's framework. They receive no public support and continue to cater for a small but significant social group with the resources to pay the fees they charge. They provide not only a high level of education but also entry to a network of contacts in the business and political worlds.

Second, it remains possible in practice for maintained schools to erect price barriers to access. For even within the public sector the notion of 'free' education relates only to teaching in the narrowest sense. Schools can and do charge for 'extras' such as sports and recreational facilities, meals and even supervised self-study. As a result, the ability to use income as a selection criterion – the real concern of many of the LODE's most vociferous opponents – has been retained.

Private establishments still account for a higher percentage of the Spanish school system than any other in Western Europe, that is, around one third of all provision at primary and secondary levels. On the other hand, with public control over the bulk of such schools assured by the system of maintenance agreements some of the old divisions have been reduced, if not eliminated. And the fact that autonomous regions are now increasingly providing funding for the purchase of textbooks has also helped to even out some of the differences.

If these factors have made schooling more uniform, a new element of diversity was introduced by the devolution of education powers to the regions. Begun in the 1980s, this process was finally completed in 2000. By then diversity had come to be seen as desirable in itself, and encouraging it was one of the principal aims of another major reform carried out by the Socialists: the 1995 Schools' Participation, Assessment and Management Act (*Ley Orgánica de la Participación, la Evaluación y el Gobierno de los Centros Docentes/LOPEG*). The LOPEG introduced an assessment scheme for state and maintained schools, but also encouraged them to develop distinctive educational plans (*proyectos educativos*) which would allow parents to exercise a degree of choice between them.

Like the LODE [7.3.1.2.1], the LOPEG caused considerable controversy. This time, however, the government received tacit support from maintained-school operators, pleased at the partial return of control over their schools' educational philosophies. On the other hand, the new Act was bitterly opposed by the teaching unions and the Left, who had backed the reforms of the 1980s, as well as by the conservative opposition, the People's Party (PP), which had resisted those. This realignment of forces indicated how the debate on school provision had moved on since the 1980s, but also the extent to which educational issues had become secondary to party political interests.

Once the PP came to power it put considerable emphasis on the notion of choice, in particular parents' supposed right to choose freely their children's school. However, the principal organizational changes included in the first major piece of education legislation that they proposed ignored this issue, while curtailing parental choice in another regard. Under the provisions of that government's 2001 Education Quality Act (*Ley de Calidad de la Educación/LOCE*) [7.3.2], headteachers were no longer to be designated by the elected School Council [7.3.1.2.1], but were to be named by the relevant regional ministry.

As it happened, this Act was never fully implemented, since the PSOE took over the reins of power in 2004 and introduced a new Education Act (*Ley Orgánica de Educación/LOE*) in 2005. Under the terms of this Act, headteachers are to be appointed by a committee made up of representatives from the regional administration, teachers and the School Council. The latter has some of its former powers restored to it, although it does not regain the power to approve or manage the school budget. A further controversial issue in the new law is the fact that maintained private schools will now be funded exclusively with public money, a measure which is designed to enhance parental choice in the selection of schools for children, but which its critics maintain diverts funds towards the private sector which ought to be employed for the creation of new public schools.

7.3.2 The structure of education

The reforms which have taken place over the last 25 years have affected not only the principles underlying the education system and its institutional structure but also the structure and nature of the studies themselves. Indeed, the situation has been one of almost constant change. For, on the one hand, implementation of structural reforms is inevitably gradual, spread over a period of years; and, on the other, even before one set of modifications is complete, the trend has been for another to be already under way.

7.3.2.1 School education

It is in schools that the most complex changes have occurred. For the most part they derive from the third major reform carried out under Socialist rule, the Education System Structure Act (*Ley de Ordenación General del Sistema Educativo*/LOGSE). Passed in 1990, the LOGSE was a massive and ambitious piece of legislation which affected all schooling at secondary level and below, as well as vocational education.

The LOGSE's provisions were introduced on a rolling timetable from 1991/92, replacing those of the 1970 General Education Act one school year at a time. The changes introduced by the LOGSE begin with the 0–6 age group, the whole of which is defined by the LOGSE as part of the educative process. Under the old system many kindergartens (*jardines de infancia*) and infants' schools (*escuelas de párvulos*) provided children of this age group with little more than supervision. Now, in theory at least, they are receiving education closely linked to that at primary level in nursery schools (*escuelas infantiles*) – hence the abandonment of the old denomination of 'pre-school education' (*educación preescolar*). The cycle is divided into two stages: education for the 0-3 age group, which is not compulsory, and that for the 3-6 age group, which is.

At primary level the LOGSE also brought in major changes. Formerly, this was referred to as 'basic' education (*Educación General Básica*/EGB), and covered an unusually long period by international standards, from age 6 to 14. Under the new system primary education (*educación primaria*) runs from age 6 to 12, in line with international norms, and is divided into three two-year stages (*ciclos*). These arrangements were accompanied by other changes intended to correct many of the faults of the old EGB. In theory, at least, the maximum class size is now 25, subject matter has been brought more into line with contemporary requirements and more project work introduced.

However, the most far-reaching and controversial changes were in secondary education, which under the old system had been both divided and divisive. Prior to the introduction of the LOGSE, only pupils who obtained the basic-level pass certificate (*graduado escolar*) had been allowed to proceed to academic secondary education, modelled on the French Baccalaureate (*Bachillerato Unificado Polivalente*/BUP). Those who failed received a leaving certificate (*certificado de escolaridad*) and were supposed to go on to vocational training [7.3.2.3]. Successful pupils wishing to go on to higher education took a one-year pre-university course

(*Curso de Orientación Universitaria*/COU). Together with BUP and the first level of vocational training, COU made up the secondary sector (*enseñanzas medias*/EEMM).

The LOGSE's arrangements were very different. They introduced a common programme of compulsory secondary education (*educación secundaria obligatoria*/ESO), covering the 12–16 age group. Since it was now attended by all pupils, the stigma of primary school 'failure' was removed. In addition, ESO was free so that the school-leaving age was now 16 in practice as well as theory. It consisted of two two-year stages, the second of which included a significant vocational element; the aim was to encourage more talented youngsters to follow the vocational path thereafter. On successful completion of ESO pupils received a secondary pass certificate (*graduado en educación secundaria*), giving an attainment profile. Standards of achievement were to be monitored by a new National Educational Quality and Assessment Agency (*Instituto Nacional de Evaluación y Calidad del Sistema Educativo*), which was renamed the Institute of Evaluation (*Instituto de Evaluación*) in 2006.

Only at age 16 does the new system involve a division into academic and non-academic streams. The first now comprises a shortened Baccalaureate (*Bachillerato*), of two years' duration, which has taken over the functions of the old COU. Along with that, the format was no longer to be standardized. Pupils could now choose between four options (*especialidades*): natural and health sciences, humanities and social sciences, technology, and the arts. One of the LOGSE's achievements, with a view to the country's economic needs, has been the popularity and prestige of the technology option.

More generally, though, the LOGSE reforms have not been seen as particularly positive. Criticism has focused on the new compulsory secondary phase. Levels of achievement are often low, with a considerable proportion of pupils failing to achieve a pass; as a result, the term 'failure' has re-emerged, this time at secondary level. Many secondary schools (*institutos*) are overcrowded, while in rural areas pupils often have to travel considerable distances to reach them. There have also been problems in ensuring that children from minority groups do indeed receive secondary schooling.

Furthermore, teachers' recruitment has proved problematic, as has their quality. That is largely because the move from primary now occurs earlier than before, so that the first two-year stage has been taught mainly by former primary teachers (*maestros*) up to now. Indeed the two stages are typically taught in different buildings, and in many cases have remained effectively separate.

In view of these problems, and given its own political standpoint, the conservative People's Party was highly critical of the LOGSE before it came to power in 1996. It nonetheless allowed implementation to be completed, while preparing its own set of reforms. These were included in the LOCE enacted in 2002 [7.3.1.2.2], although the latter, in its turn, was never fully implemented.

Among other measures it contained, the Act would have introduced a new subject – advocated by the Catholic Church, which runs about one sixth of the country's schools – entitled 'Society, Culture and Religion' (*Sociedad, Cultura y Religión*). It would also have brought in a country-wide secondary leaving examination (*reválida*) to replace the university entrance examination [7.3.1.1.3]. The latter provoked particular concern among critics since pupils' final mark was to be an average of the mark from that examination and their record of attainment at school (*expediente*) which, they claimed, could have given private school pupils an unfair advantage. Other measures proposed, but not implemented, included the reintroduction of streaming (*separación por rendimiento*) which had not been allowed under the LOGSE.

With the sudden suspension of the implementation of the LOCE and the introduction of new educational measures, the Spanish school system experienced an aggravated sense of confusion during the 2004/05 academic year. Pupils in some autonomous regions who had begun to study courses under the LOCE had to readjust to new approaches, and new textbooks had to be issued to cope with the changes.

The changes which the Socialists introduced, codified in their 2005 Education Act, the LOE, included various curricular changes which entailed paying greater attention to cultural and religious diversity. One of the more controversial innovations was the creation of a subject called Education for Citizenship (*Educación para la Ciudadanía y los Derechos Humanos*). The latter, offered in the last year of primary and the first year of secondary school, addresses questions related to democracy and democratic values, the environment and issues around gender and sexual orientation, as well as respect for religious and cultural diversity. It has been strongly criticized by the PP, the Catholic Church and conservative organizations. Also under the LOE, pupils are allowed to repeat a certain number of years' schooling, one in primary school and two in ESO. They can also, however, progress to the following year if they are carrying two failed subjects (or even three under certain circumstances).

One area of the curriculum which has traditionally been served very badly in Spain, but where progress is now beginning to be made, is the teaching of languages, both foreign and regional. Although OECD reports suggest that attainment levels in general literacy are below par, efforts have been made to improve the quality of the teaching of languages other than the mother tongue, and to make greater use of foreign language assistants in public schools. Along with this, bilingual teaching (in Spanish and the relevant co-official language) of subjects across the curriculum is now well established in regions where such languages exist. The most striking innovation, however, has been the increased provision in state schools of bilingual education in Spanish and another European language: most commonly, this is English, but there are also schools providing education through French and, to a small extent, German. To date, approximately one thousand schools of this sort have been established across the country, operating at kindergarten, primary or secondary level, including FP. In regions with co-official languages, these schools provide trilingual education.

7.3.2.2 Higher education

In the higher education system (*enseñanza superior*), change in the structure of studies was begun by the 1983 Universities Reform Act (LRU) [7.3.1.1.1]. It involved the introduction of new qualifications (*títulos*) and degree courses (*carreras*) as well as major changes to course structures. As in schools, change has been gradual, but most of the provisions of the LRU are now in place.

The greater part of the university system is made up of the academic faculties into which each university is divided. Faculties now offer undergraduate degrees (*licenciaturas*) based on a standard four-year programme (in place of five years, as had been the system previously). The only significant exception to this is the degree in Medicine which takes six years to complete.

The undergraduate programme consists of two parts (*ciclos*), each normally of two years' duration, the first being intended to provide a range of subjects (*asignaturas*) which constitute foundation knowledge, while the second introduces an element of specialization. This is achieved through a system of core subjects (*troncales*), other compulsory subjects (*obligatorias*) and options (*optativas*), some of the latter to be drawn from a specified list and others to be chosen at will by the student (*optativas de libre elección*). The faculties also offer studies at postgraduate level; a programme involving taught classes and a thesis leads to a doctorate (*doctorado*), normally within five years.

As well as revising the structure of programmes in order to offer four-year degrees, the range of subjects which can form the basis of a degree has been updated. In Spain official degree titles must, by law, be drawn from a listing established by the government. The age of the list valid in the 1980s was a major reason for the outdated nature of many degrees, and in 1986 the government gave the task of drawing up a new one to the Universities' Council [7.3.1.1.1]. Yet it was well into the 1990s before many degree titles finally received the Council's approval.

Moreover, despite regional and university autonomy [7.3.1.1.1], the course structures of new and revised degree courses had to be approved by the Council [7.3.1.1.3]. That process caused further delays. It also revealed the fact that the legal requirements on course content were far too demanding for the new four-year structure. Consequently in 1997 the government reduced the number of 'credits' required, thus triggering off a further round of changes to course structures. Despite these problems, however, the range of officially recognized degrees offered by universities has been increased from 65 to 190.

In addition, some shorter, practice-oriented postgraduate qualifications have been introduced with the approval of regional educational authorities. These are known in Spain as *másters* and, as in the UK, normally involve a taught element followed by a dissertation.

University schools (*escuelas universitarias*) are also of a hybrid nature. Most of their three-year diploma courses (*diplomaturas*) are vocational or semi-vocational in nature, in specified areas such as nursing and primary teaching. Others, notably those in business studies and engineering, differ little from the early stages of courses offered elsewhere in the system. In general, however, they have enjoyed lower prestige.

This is decidedly not the case with the Advanced Technical Schools (*Escuelas Técnicas Superiores/ETS*). The ETS are broadly comparable to UK engineering faculties, offering a variety of undergraduate courses leading to a qualification as engineer or architect. Entry is subject to strict limits, and demand for places is high. Like the university faculties, the ETS also offer postgraduate studies. In Madrid, Barcelona and Valencia they are grouped together in separate Technical Universities. These have now lost their specialist nature by the addition of faculties where non-technical disciplines are studied.

The Spanish university system continues to evolve rapidly, and further changes are currently being introduced in response to the convergence process mapped out at European level in the 1999 Bologna Declaration. A royal decree of October 2007 (*Real Decreto de Ordenación de Enseñanzas Universitarias*) provides for a set of changes related to the Bologna process, including the abolition of both *licenciaturas* and *diplomaturas*. These will be replaced by a system which will have three levels of qualification as follows:

– a Bachelors Degree (*grado*) of four years' duration;
– a Masters Degree (*máster*) lasting a further year;
– a Doctorate (*doctorado*), to be completed in a further three years.

Undergraduate degrees will be organized around five thematic areas: Arts & Humanities; Sciences; Health Sciences; Social & Legal Sciences, and Engineering & Architecture. The basic Engineering degree will be reduced to four years, but this qualification will be more or less equivalent to the current diploma in technical engineering, while a full qualification in the subject will require a Masters degree. Degrees in Architecture, Medicine and Veterinary Science will continue to be of five years' duration.

7.3.2.3 Vocational training

Vocational training (*formación profesional/FP*) has long been a problem area within the Spanish education system. Although its importance was formally recognized by the 1970 General Education Act, vocational provision remained inadequate in terms of both quantity and quality. Although the 1970 Act in theory established a three-level system, in practice only the basic level (FP1), for 14- to 16-year-olds, was developed to any significant extent; the third, advanced level (FP3) was never implemented at all.

The main problem, however, was not paucity of provision but public perception. Because of the selective nature of secondary education [7.3.2.1], FP1 came to be regarded as a sink for those who had failed to complete primary education successfully. As fewer and fewer able students opted for it voluntarily, FP acquired a poor reputation among employers as well as parents. A similar problem was apparent also at higher levels. Despite the poor quality of many university courses, further aggravated by overcrowding, young Spaniards continued to display the traditional obsession with academic qualifications (*titulitis*), irrespective of the job prospects they offered.

By the 1980s these inadequacies were generally accepted, and attempts were made to address them in several social contract agreements which were drawn up in the early years of that decade. Thus the 1984 Social and Economic Agreement (AES) set up a Solidarity Fund specifically to promote vocational training. A General Vocational Training Council (*Consejo General de Formación Profesional*) was established, with representatives of government, trade unions and employers. The AES also led to the setting up of training workshops (*escuelas-taller*) and craft training centres (*casas de oficios*).

As a result of these and other *ad hoc* measures, the system began to lose all semblance of an overall structure. Restoration of logic to the vocational sector was an important aim of the 1990 measure known as the LOGSE [7.3.2.1]. As part of this, basic vocational training (*FP de base*) was integrated into the new, unified secondary stage [7.3.2.1]. From there pupils may pass to an intermediate stage, designed to last two years and organized in the form of modules (*módulos*). Successful students become qualified technicians (*técnicos*).

The LOGSE also provided for pupils to pass from the revised Baccalaureate [7.3.2.1] to an advanced level of vocational training; subsequently it has become possible to do so directly from the intermediate level. Access involves an entry test (*prueba de acceso*); it in turn provides an alternative path into higher education.

Despite these changes problems have persisted in the vocational area. Above all, even the more advanced vocational courses still involve little – or no – practical experience (*experiencia laboral*). Increasing this was a major aim of the 2001 Vocational Education Act (*Ley de Formación Profesional*), which established a national system of vocational qualifications, some of which could be obtained purely by experience. Further provision for vocational education was contained in the LOE as well as in a decree issued in 2006 which related specifically to this sector.

New measures introduced by this legislation include the following:

– It is now possible for workers in certain professions to obtain a certificate testifying to their competence in that area; this can then be used to obtain exemption from modules within the FP cycle of studies;
– A distance education element has been introduced for students wishing to obtain a qualification in FP;
– To fully complete the FP cycle, students will have to carry out a project in their field;
– New subjects introduced into the FP cycle include Entrepreneurship; Risk Prevention; Innovation; and Quality Assurance, all of which relate to areas in which the Spanish labour market has traditionally been deficient;
– A new System of Vocational Education Qualifications is to be introduced, based on the national system of vocational qualifications.

At higher level, both the advanced technical schools and university schools [7.3.2.2] provide vocationally oriented courses. In particular, training for primary teaching takes place in special university schools (*escuelas universitarias/EU*), some of which have now been converted into Faculties of Education, although many are still generally known by their old title *EU de Magisterio*. Several of them are run privately. Under plans proposed by the PSOE government in 2007, training for primary education, including kindergarten level teaching, will entail students taking a full four-year degree programme in education. One year of the programme will be completely practical.

Up to now, students who wish to become secondary teachers have been required to take a five-year degree and then obtain the Certificate of Teaching Aptitude (*Certificado de Aptitud Pedagógica/CAP*). The CAP, a programme lasting approximately six months, has been consistently criticized as providing inadequate training. In 2007 the PSOE government approved a plan to phase it out and to introduce a system whereby those intending to teach at secondary level would be required to undertake a Masters degree after their new four-year primary degree. To enter the Masters programme, graduates will need to have attained an intermediate level in a foreign language.

Under the system established in 1970 the CAP was taught at a College of Education (*Instituto de Ciencias de la Educación/ICE*), attached to a university. For the past few years, these have gradually been disappearing. Their functions are being assumed by the regionally based Teachers' Centres (*Centros de (Encuentro de) Profesores*), which previously provided in-service training (*formación continua*) of various sorts.

7.3.2.4 Further, continuing and special education

Several forms of further and continuing education are available in Spain. Some, like the people's universities, are community-based; most, though, are provided by official bodies, at national, regional and municipal level. The central government has attempted to coordinate these in a national programme of adult continuing education (*educación permanente*), with limited success.

A major part of continuing education consists of distance-learning programmes designed to allow adults to achieve conventional qualifications. Organizations dealing with the primary and secondary levels were set up during the Franco era. They were later joined by Spain's equivalent of the Open University (*Universidad Nacional de Educación a Distancia/UNED*). The Open University of Catalonia (*Universitat Oberta de Catalunya*) is a recently established, privately-run institution. In addition, special arrangements, including a separate entrance examination, exist for those aged 25 and over who wish to enter the conventional higher education system.

A more recent innovation is the concept of 'compensatory education'. This comprises a wide range of programmes aimed at individuals who need to make up lost educational ground in order to enter the job market. Target groups include drug addicts and those who, for whatever reason, failed to complete normal school education.

Special education, on the other hand, is concerned with overcoming learning disabilities of various sorts. Traditionally provision for children affected by such disabilities, where it existed at all, tended to be strictly separated from mainstream education, and often had little genuinely educational content. More recently the accent has been on overcoming such divisions. The Schools Integration Programme (*Programa de Integración Escolar*) aims at the teaching of disadvantaged children in mainstream classes wherever possible; only in extreme cases is separate provision now envisaged.

7.4 Glossary

abandono (m)	dropping out
acreditación (f)	certification
asignatura (f)	subject
asistencia concertada (f)	public subsidization of private hospitals
asociado (m)	teaching associate
ayudante (m)	junior lecturer; assistant
ayudante doctor (m)	lecturer

Bachillerato (m)	Baccalaureate
Bachillerato Unificado Polivalente (BUP) (m)	old-style selective Baccalaureate
beca (f)	student grant
carrera (f)	degree course
casa de oficios (f)	craft training centre
catedrático (m)	professor
Centro de (Encuentro de) Profesores (m)	Teacher Centre
centro concertado (m)	grant-maintained school
centro no concertado (m)	non-maintained private school
Certificado de Aptitud Pedagógica/CAP (m)	Certificate of Teaching Aptitude
certificado de escolaridad (m)	old-style school-leaving certificate
ciclo (m)	stage (of school course); part (of degree course)
claustro (m)	university assembly
concierto (m)	maintenance agreement
consejo de gobierno (m)	university management board (since 2001)
Consejo de Universidades (m)	Universities' Council
Consejo Escolar (m)	School Council
Consejo Social (m)	(University) Court
Curso de Orientación Universitaria (COU) (m)	pre-university year
diplomatura (f)	diploma (course)
director (m)	headteacher
distrito único/abierto (m)	system under which students may apply to any university, not only those in their own region
Educación para la Ciudadanía y los Derechos Humanos (f)	Education for Citizenship
educación permanente (f)	continuing education
educación preescolar (f)	pre-school education
educación primaria (f)	new-style primary education
Educación Secundaria Obligatoria (ESO) (f)	new-style secondary education
empresa de base tecnológica (f)	spin-off company
endogamia (f)	(academic) 'in-breeding', tendency for universities to recruit staff internally
enseñanza básica (f)	old-style basic education
enseñanza obligatoria (f)	compulsory education
enseñanza superior/terciaria (f)	higher/tertiary education
enseñanzas medias (fpl)	old-style secondary education
escuela de párvulos (f)	infant school
escuela-taller (f)	training workshop
Escuela Técnica Superior (f)	Advanced Technical School
escuela universitaria (f)	university school
especialidad (f)	option
expediente (m)	record of attainment
experiencia laboral (f)	practical experience
formación continua (f)	in-service training
formación profesional (f)	vocational training
fracaso escolar (m)	failure to complete compulsory education successfully
grado (m)	Bachelors Degree
graduado en educación secundaria (m)	new-style secondary pass certificate

graduado escolar (m)	old-style basic-level pass certificate
habilitación nacional (f)	single, Spain-wide examination of aptitude for university teaching
ideario (m)	school's statement of educational philosophy
instituto (m)	secondary school
Instituto Nacional de la Salud/INSALUD (m)	National Health Agency
Instituto Nacional de Seguridad Social/INSS (m)	National Social Security Agency
jardín de infancia (m)	kindergarten
libertad de cátedra (f)	academic freedom
licenciatura (f)	undergraduate degree (course)
maestro (m)	primary teacher
Magisterio (m)	primary teacher training
máster (m)	Masters Degree
módulo (m)	module
obligatoria (asignatura) (f)	compulsory class
optativa (asignatura) (f)	optional class chosen from specified list
optativa de libre elección (f)	unrestricted optional class
pensiones asistenciales (fpl)	basic pensions
plan de estudios (m)	course structure
prestaciones (fpl)	benefits
prestaciones familiares (fpl)	family support
profesor contratado (m)	senior lecturer
profesor no numerario (PNN) (m)	temporary lecturer
profesor titular (m)	permanent lecturer
proyecto educativo (m)	educational plan
prueba de acceso (f)	entrance test/examination
rector (m)	vice-chancellor, principal
reválida (f)	national secondary school leaving examination
seguro obligatorio de enfermedad/SOE (m)	compulsory health insurance
selectividad (f)	university entrance examination
separación por rendimiento (f)	streaming
Servicio Nacional de Salud/SNS (m)	National Health Service
tasa (f)	fee
tasa de mortalidad infantil (f)	infant mortality rate
técnico (m)	qualified technician (new-style vocational qualification)
titulitis (f)	obsession with academic qualifications
título (m)	qualification, certificate, degree
troncal (asignatura) (f)	core subject
universidad (f)	university; the university system

8

The environment

Environmental issues have moved centre-stage throughout the world, as concern continues to grow over the effects of climate change (*cambio climático*) and the damage caused by pollution. All countries – no matter what stage of development they may be at – are implicated in this process. Despite the fact that there has been a notable lack of leadership among politicians in the country with the biggest economy in the world, the United States, most political leaders are now committed to instituting changes in order to avoid causing further harm to the environment and in order to deal with the potential damage – in particular, global warming (*calentamiento global*) – that may be caused in the long term. The Kyoto Protocol (*Protocolo de Kioto*) of 1997 constituted an attempt to deal with the situation at the international level, while the 2007 Bali Summit (*Cumbre de Bali*) took the matter a step further by, amongst other things, drawing the USA more fully into the process.

Spain has been involved in those efforts and has undertaken to reduce its emissions and control development in line with the targets set. We shall see below that only limited success has been achieved in meeting those targets to date. This is also the case in terms of the degree to which the country complies with norms agreed at the European level: Spain still has some of the highest levels of harmful emissions in Europe and is among the group of countries having the most difficulty in reaching their environmental targets. Given that Spain long missed out on the advantages of growth, it is perhaps not surprising that it has prioritized economic development and has been slow to face up to its environmental problems. This chapter begins by looking at the problems caused directly by pollution. It then goes on to examine underlying changes to the country's landscape and their effects in both ecological and economic terms. Finally it considers the response to these issues in terms of attempts to protect Spain's environment.

8.1 Pollution

Precisely because of its nature as a single system, it is hard to classify into distinct categories the impact of human activities on the environment. In Spain as elsewhere, the changes they produce in one aspect inevitably have knock-on effects in others, often apparently unrelated. Perhaps the best starting point is to examine the process known as pollution (*contaminación*), that is the changes produced in the chemical make-up of the elements essential for human and other life: air, water and the earth itself.

8.1.1 Air pollution

Despite its relatively favourable geographical location at the edge of Western Europe, exposed to the prevailing Atlantic winds, Spain has serious problems of air pollution (*contaminación atmosférica*), mostly related to the emission of various greenhouse gases (*gases de efecto invernadero*). While emissions per head of population are about average for Europe, the country is relatively underpopulated, and the damage caused by such pollution is severe, so that Spain is deemed unlikely to be able to meet the targets set by the Kyoto Protocol. It is estimated that, currently, about 16,000 deaths per year can be attributed to contamination of the atmosphere in the country.

This problem is mostly associated with the high volume of traffic in the major cities. The country's two main metropolitan areas, centred on Madrid and Barcelona, have extremely high densities of road traffic, to which successive governments have reacted only belatedly and without great success. They have also been slow to encourage the use of unleaded petrol (*gasolina sin plomo*), which only became cheaper than leaded varieties in 1990. They have failed to develop public transport and the use of rail for commuter traffic, opting instead to foster the growth of motorways and presiding over a huge increase in road traffic. Passenger transport grew by 84 per cent between 1990 and 2003, while the transport of goods grew in the same period by 99 per cent, and most of this involves lorries and cars. Levels of nitrogen dioxide (*dióxido de nitrógeno*/NO2), for instance – emitted mainly by road traffic – are generally high in urban areas. Already, in 13 Spanish cities, levels exceed the target limit which has been set for 2010. They are particularly high in the region of Madrid, with the capital itself and the towns of Getafe and Alcorcón being the most serious offenders, along with the cities of Valencia and Barcelona.

Emissions from industry and from other sources, including domestic heating systems, are also a major factor in atmospheric pollution. The activities principally to blame are the chemical industry, oil refining and petrochemical manufacture, and the generation of electricity in fossil-fuel-fired power stations (*centrales térmicas*). Again, the areas most seriously affected are the urban areas, including some of those that were developed as industrial zones during the Franco regime, such as Huelva on the southern Atlantic coast; the eastern Mediterranean ports of Cartagena and Tarragona; and Puertollano, in the province of Ciudad Real.

One noxious product of industrial activity is sulphur dioxide (*dióxido de azufre*/SO2), the levels of which are particularly high in the area around Oviedo in Asturias and in the Corunna/Arteixo region in Galicia. Similarly, levels of ozone (*ozono*/O3) exceed acceptable limits in several cities in Andalusia and the Madrid region, although emission rates for carbon dioxide (*dióxido de carbono*) across the country are still lower per inhabitant than in other EU member states.

The air-pollution problem is exacerbated in Spain's case by the predominating meteorological conditions: high levels of solar radiation favour the formation of gases such as ozone, and the lack of rainfall means that harmful particles generally remain suspended in the air. These conditions lead to increased levels of respiratory problems among the population at large and a higher incidence of cardiovascular diseases, allergies and asthma, while also adding to the infant mortality rate [7.2.2]. In the case of Madrid, its geographical position in a shallow, elevated basin, along with the climatic phenomenon of temperature inversion, gives rise in winter to the characteristic 'beret' of visibly polluted air hanging over the city.

Somewhat belatedly, and partly in response to pressure from Europe, legal measures have been taken to attempt to deal with this problem. The most notable piece of legislation is the 2007 Air Quality Act (*Ley de Calidad del Aire y Protección de la Atmósfera*). In line with the practice in other EU states, it provides for target-setting in relation to atmospheric pollution and periodic reviews of the situation, as well as obliging regional governments to classify the different territories in their regions in terms of their prevailing levels of pollution. It establishes a range of measures to control emissions, and provides for the introduction of a system of vehicle taxation based on emissions.

Another environmental problem affecting Spain's urban areas, although not strictly speaking pollution, is regarded as such in semi-technical language: noise pollution (*contaminación acústica*). It is a field where international comparisons are fraught with difficulties, due to differences in measurement techniques; so figures suggesting that Spain rivals Japan as the world's noisiest country must be treated with caution, particularly as they have been contested by Spanish official bodies.

Nevertheless – and despite the introduction of a new law banning excessive noise in 2003 – even these authorities' own data make clear that noise levels in central Madrid regularly exceed international guidelines. Moreover, those figures relate to background noise levels and do not take into consideration the situation of workers involved in particularly noisy activities. In such cases, the effects on individuals depend on the observance of prescribed safety precautions, often lax in Spain.

8.1.2 Water pollution and dumping of wastes

The problems the country faces in the area of water quality are some of the most severe of all. They derive from emissions of various sorts, as well as from the dumping of waste products, a practice which also has other damaging effects.

As elsewhere, a major cause of water pollution (*contaminación del agua*) is industrial emissions. Their severity in Spain can be traced largely to the very special conditions of industrial development during the Franco era. Many of the industries which grew up then used technically outdated processes whose viability depended partly on low labour costs, but partly on the absence of regulations requiring firms to bear the costs of reprocessing harmful wastes (*residuos*). Two especially important examples were the chemical industry and paper manufacture; in the Basque Country in particular emissions from paper mills (*papelerías*) produced very high levels of river pollution.

By the 1970s many towns and villages depended for employment on highly polluting activities, and the absence of controls was taken for granted. In this situation the further wave of industrialization in the 1980s had catastrophic effects. Between 1983 and 1988 production of toxic wastes increased by 300 per cent, and even the government ministry responsible admitted that less than a third of the total was being monitored. Inevitably a significant proportion found its way into water courses.

Mining activities of various sorts are another notorious source of pollution. In 1998 the collapse of a retaining dam at an operation near Aznalcóllar, in Seville province, released millions of cubic metres of toxic water and mud into the River Guadiamar. Much good agricultural land was severely damaged as a result, although mercifully it proved possible to minimize the impact on the Doñana wetland area [8.2.3].

Just over a decade earlier, in 1987, 20,000 water birds died in Doñana when their habitat suffered contamination (*intoxicación*), the cause on that occasion being pesticides used by rice farmers. In general, agriculture is another major source of pollutants of surface and ground water (*aguas superficiales y subterráneas*), since newer, more intensive practices employ considerable amounts of pesticides and artificial fertilizers (*abonos químicos*). These are widely used in greenhouse production of early fruit and vegetables along the Mediterranean coast, especially in Huelva and Almería provinces.

Spain's households also contribute significantly to water pollution because of low levels of sewage treatment. Despite the construction of new treatment plants (*depuradoras*), significant amounts of raw sewage continue to be pumped directly into water courses; less than half of all domestic sewage is adequately treated. The problems are particularly grave in areas of rapid population growth, and in some coastal areas. Along the Mediterranean coast, for example, as much as 30 per cent of sewage passes untreated into the sea.

Spain's coastal waters (*aguas litorales*) are also affected by dumping of solid wastes. Particularly important in this regard are the mining operations carried out at Portmán, east of Cartagena on the Murcia coast. Lead and zinc have been mined there for centuries, but it was under the Franco regime that a massive open-cast operation got under way. One of the largest of its kind in the world, this involved washing earth directly into the bay using a mixture of sea water and highly toxic chemicals, including cyanide and sulphur. Although the mines have now closed, the bay is still silted up and badly contaminated; a large area on the landward side is a veritable moonscape. Plans are in place, however, to clean up the area, and it is expected that the bay will recover over the next few years.

Another instance of irresponsible dumping of wastes is the case of the chemical company Ercros in Tarragona province, which in 2003 was convicted of dumping toxic waste into the river Ebro at the entrance to the Flix reservoir. It is estimated that the clean-up operation will cost in the order of €200 million; a 2006 order to the company that it pay a proportion of this cost has been appealed by it.

Inevitably a major contributor to pollution of the seas around Spain is the oil industry. Spillages from tankers – some of which may be deliberate – occur on a regular basis, many in the vicinity of Galicia. One major incident occurred in the winter of 1992/93, when the tanker *Aegean Sea* ran aground off Corunna with considerable damage to marine life, including economically important shellfish stocks.

The most notorious and damaging incident, however, was the case of the tanker *Prestige*, a Greek-operated ship flying a Bahaman flag of convenience, which sank off the Galician coast in 2002. It was carrying 77,000 tons of heavy fuel oil (*chapapote*), of which 64,000 tons spilled immediately from the wreck, with 125 tons per day leaking into the sea subsequently. Had the ship been towed into a port, the damage might have been contained more effectively; as it happened, both Madrid and the regional government were severely criticized for opting to tow the vessel out to sea. From that location, oil contaminated thousands of kilometres of coastline and a vast swathe of the sea off the Galician coast, causing fishing to be suspended in the area for six months. More than a thousand beaches along the Spanish and French coasts were polluted.

Although the reaction of the Spanish and Galician governments was clearly inadequate, and they appeared unwilling to acknowledge the seriousness of the situation, volunteer efforts were more effective, as people came from all over Spain and from other parts of Europe to assist in cleaning up the mess and to rescue wildlife caught up in the disaster. A new environmental movement called 'Never Again' (Galician: *Nunca Máis*) emerged, founded by activists in the area, and the incident served to dramatically increase general levels of awareness of environmental issues. Although there is still oil in the wrecked tanker, and although it continues to leak into the sea, the effects of the slow leak are not dramatic at the moment, but there is a danger that the rusting hull of the vessel will rupture, which would mean further serious problems of contamination.

At least until relatively recently, deliberate dumping at sea has also been practised in a number of cases with the active encouragement of the Spanish authorities. For 15 years from 1974 they allowed a chemical firm to dump titanium dioxide waste in the ocean 55 km off Cádiz, until protests from local people forced a reassessment of the situation. Up to 1983 foreign nuclear waste (*residuos nucleares*) was dumped at a site 700 km off the Galician coast, making it the world's largest off-shore deposit of such material.

More recently Spain's own mounting stocks of nuclear waste have begun to pose a major problem. By the 1990s over 500 tons of highly radioactive waste were stored at the country's power stations; by the year 2020 the figure is expected to rise to some 6,000 tons. As in other countries the search for permanent sites has met with understandable resistance from people in the areas potentially affected. At the end of 1992 the first permanent disposal site (*cementerio nuclear*) for low and medium-level waste was opened, at El Cabril in Córdoba province. Although the first of Spain's nuclear power stations, at Zorita in Guadalajara, was decommissioned in 2006, the search for alternatives to fossil fuel means that nuclear power stations, of which there are currently six in Spain, are likely to continue to provide energy for the country in the future, with the resultant ongoing problems associated with the disposal of nuclear waste.

Finally, the more mundane topic of general household and other non-toxic solid waste is also problematic. Apart from being extremely intrusive visually, the wholly or partially uncontrolled dumping evident around so many Spanish settlements can also be dangerous. In 1996 an official dump at Bens, outside Corunna, collapsed over a cliff, killing one person and causing extensive damage to the surrounding terrain. This particular case did have a positive impact, however. Subsequently Corunna has set in place a coordinated disposal system which includes household waste separation (*recogida selectiva*), and which has achieved international recognition as a model.

Although recycling and waste separation have become more common features of Spanish towns and cities in recent years, this is an area where Spain continues to lag behind its counterparts in the developed world, partly because increased affluence has led to increased amounts of waste being dumped. One estimate suggests that the production of urban waste increased by 40% in the period 1996–2003. Despite the examples of good practice around the country, such as the Galician one mentioned above, waste separation by householders is still often a voluntary matter. Local authorities have been slow to put in place recycling arrangements in their waste collection systems, although the 2007 Waste Plan (*Plan Nacional de Residuos Sólidos*) encourages such recycling and threatens tougher financial penalties for companies who dispose of waste irresponsibly. As usual, there are regional differences in behaviour; the indications are that regions such as the Balearic Islands, the Basque

Country, Navarre and Rioja make more of an effort to recycle their waste than others.

8.2 Landscape change

Environmental damage does not, of course, begin and end with the question of pollution. As well as the relatively direct effects of waste dumping and other emissions, change in the environment as the result of human actions also involves more complex and longer-term processes. Some operate at continental or world scale; thus Spain too is affected by the thinning of the ozone layer (*capa de ozono*) or the greenhouse effect (*efecto invernadero*). Other such processes, however, are more localized, in the sense that they operate exclusively or with particular intensity within individual countries. In Spain, two are especially important.

8.2.1 Deforestation and reforestation

The story that in ancient times a squirrel could travel from Gibraltar to the Pyrenees without touching the ground may be apocryphal. What is undeniable is that Spain's once vast woods have been severely depleted over the centuries. It is true that deforestation has been partially reversed in recent years, but that has brought new problems.

It was the Franco regime, from the 1940s on, that began to reverse the process of deforestation, but not for ecological considerations – nowhere had they reached the political agenda at that time. Instead its massive programme of reforestation was promoted by economic concerns. The species planted were chosen for their rapid growth, many of them imports to Spain such as the Australian eucalyptus. In addition to the implications in terms of habitat change [8.2.3], this policy has also had an unintended side effect which works against its original objective.

For, as well as growing quickly, eucalyptus and the various species of pine introduced also burn easily. And the biggest threat to Spain's woodland (*bosque*) today comes from the forest fires (*incendios forestales*) which became alarmingly frequent in the 1980s and have literally flared up again repeatedly since 1994. Such fires have hit the new species hard, but not exclusively.

Evidently other factors are at work too, some of which are inherent to the Mediterranean climate and vegetation prevalent in much of the country. Summers are long, hot and dry, lightning a frequent occurrence; indigenous woodland also burns relatively easily, and is intermixed with highly inflammable stretches of scrubland (*monte*). Yet these factors do not explain the upsurge of fires, especially as one of the worst hit regions has been Galicia, where the climate is Atlantic in nature.

One cause there and elsewhere in the country is the declining economic value of Spain's woodland, most of which is privately owned. With wood no longer used significantly for heating, there is no incentive to carry out the work of selectively lopping branches, collecting fallen ones and clearing undergrowth. The resultant dense mass of live and dead timber both burns easily and makes extinction difficult; it cannot, however, explain why fires start so frequently.

That can only be the result of human action, which is increasingly impacting on woodland. Population growth and changing leisure patterns are bringing more people into the Spanish countryside; many, unlike their forebears, are completely unacquainted with it. Carelessness of various types undoubtedly causes many fires. Nor are the countryside's own inhabitants blameless in this regard; one recent study in the Valencia region found careless burning of stubble (*rastrojo*) and pasture land (*pastizales*) to be the main cause of fires.

These are not always the result of mere carelessness, however. Rural resentment against re- and afforestation is based on a number of grounds including loss of farming land and damage to it allegedly caused by woodland wildlife. Nor is it restricted to farmers; in some areas it appears to have become part of local tradition, perhaps dating back to the loss of former common lands in the nineteenth century. Sometimes, too, burning of woodland seems to be used as a means of settling private disputes. For all these reasons, some fires – no one can be sure what proportion – are undoubtedly the result of deliberate action by local people.

Finally it is suspected that larger interests are also at work. In some cases logging firms (*industrias madereras*) have been accused of responsibility, their alleged object being to buy up large quantities of fire-damaged, but still usable wood at knock-down prices. However, the most serious allegations have been levelled at property developers (*empresas inmobiliarias*), especially in areas close to the Mediterranean coast where there is a lot of pressure for out-of-town housing developments (*urbanizaciones*).

There prime building land is often wooded, and subject to planning restrictions. Some of the worst fires have removed the woodland such restrictions were designed to protect – and hence also the arguments against development. Economically that can be very attractive not just for the developer but for the local economy as a whole. For that reason suspicion has occasionally been voiced against local councillors; the interests of their municipality, and also the prospect of party or personal rake-offs [2.1.3], provide possible motives for collusion with fire-raisers.

To the extent that such suspicions are justified, it is clear that more than environmental measures will be needed to remove the main contemporary threat to Spain's woodland. However, that is not to say that such measures cannot help, and indeed in a number of areas they are being taken. Both central and regional governments have undertaken campaigns designed to increase environmental awareness [8.3.2]. More directly, Galicia has had particular success with simple measures designed to stop fires spreading once started, for example through the systematic cutting of firebreaks (*cortafuegos*).

A 2003 Forestry Act (*Ley de Montes*) places responsibility for managing mountain lands on the regional governments. In an attempt to discourage the deliberate setting of fires for economic reasons, the law makes it illegal for local authorities to re-zone burned lands as building land for a period of 30 years after a fire has taken place.

8.2.2 Desertification

Deforestation is a particularly serious problem in Spain because it, in turn, is one of the main causes of a second process of long-term landscape change – desertification. Here a terminological point should be clarified. Internationally a distinction is drawn between desertification – the process by which arid land becomes effectively incapable of sustaining life, in other words a desert – and desertization, the abandonment of an area by its human population. The same distinction is also made in official Spanish usage. In Spain, however, the latter phenomenon was already well known as 'depopulation' (*despoblación*). As a result, the less clumsy *desertización* is frequently used, even by experts, when speaking of landscape change in areas of the country which were long since virtually uninhabited.

Such desertification, most commonly associated with Africa, is a threat facing a number of countries in southern Europe. Since the early 1980s Italy and Greece have participated, along with Spain, in a joint Campaign against Desertification in the Mediterranean Region (*Lucha contra la Desertificación en el Mediterráneo/LUCDEME*). However, the scale of the problem is considerably greater in Spain, and affects some 30 per cent of its territory. Already the country has Europe's only genuine desert, an area in Almería – a province with 70 per cent of its land affected by desertification – famous as a Western film-set. But desertification is also a real threat in other provinces of Andalusia, in parts of the Extremadura and Valencia regions, and above all in the interior of Murcia.

Deforestation [8.2.1] is clearly an important factor in the erosion which is the prelude to desertification. In Spain this is caused less by wind (*erosión eólica*) than by the action of water (*erosión hídrica*). Here, as with deforestation, the Mediterranean climate plays a key part, with its highly irregular rainfall pattern (*pluviometría*). Lengthy dry spells are typically broken by torrential rainstorms (*trombas de agua*), which in the absence of tree cover wash away large amounts of topsoil.

Agricultural practices (*técnicas agrícolas*) have also contributed to erosion. In Castile, in particular, extensive cereal farming put a premium on bringing as much land as possible under the plough. With the advent of mechanization more marginal land, especially on slopes, was cleared of its natural vegetation and worked with heavy tractors, becoming more vulnerable as a result. Elsewhere overgrazing (*sobrepastoreo*) or other inappropriate land-uses produced similar results. The inefficient methods and general neglect typical of the large estates of the south [5.3.1] may also have played a part.

In recent years such factors have probably become less important; in particular the EU's encouragement of land set-aside (*abandono de tierras*) has taken much marginal agricultural land back out of production. Yet the threat of desertification has not been diminished, and indeed was accentuated by the almost total absence of rainfall throughout much of southern and central Spain during the period 1990–95. The drought (*sequía*), however, may only have served to divert attention from the most serious cause of desertification, which, although water-related, is not climatic but synthetic in origin.

Its cause is excessive use of what is becoming a scarce resource world-wide, particularly in countries where supply is uncertain, such as Spain. There rising water demand comes from various sources. Both domestic and industrial consumption are partly to blame; in some localities, especially on the Andalusian coast, heavy watering of golf courses is also a factor. However, the main cause is the recent large increase in the amount of agricultural land under irrigation.

This technique is used both for intensive fruit and vegetable farming, concentrated along the south-eastern and southern Mediterranean coast, and for other crops, most notably rice, of which the Murcia region is now a major producer. The effect has been a significant reduction in the water table in a number of areas – it appears to be particularly marked on Gran Canaria, where water demand comes mainly from tourism. The consequence is to increase the danger of erosion and thus desertification.

In some coastal areas the drop in the water table has allowed sea water to enter the underground reserves known as aquifers, which in turn affects water used for irrigation. Thus in Almería the presence of salt in irrigation water is thought to be responsible for a reduction in crop yields. More importantly, it gives rise to excessive concentrations of salt in the earth (*salinización*), a further cause of desertification.

Even without sea water contamination it is known that irrigation can produce the same result. High salt concentrations in Extremadura are believed to have been caused in this way when local farmers were encouraged to abandon traditional crops on unirrigated land in favour of others, especially asparagus, which require irrigation. Extremadura has now joined the list of Spanish regions where desertification is a significant danger.

8.2.3 Ecological and economic impact

Both deforestation and desertification are extreme examples of a more general phenomenon. Climate and landscape change results in the loss of natural habitats and so leads to a decline in biodiversity. It is an important issue in Spain, which hosts a considerable number of rare, even endangered species. Western Europe's last brown bear colony is perhaps the best-known example, but there are many others, often surprising. The evergreen oakwoods of Extremadura, for instance, are the world's largest, and home to the black vulture and other bird species found nowhere else in Europe.

Alongside the oakwoods themselves, Extremadura also contains large expanses of a habitat effectively unique to Spain, the thinly oak-covered parkland known as *dehesa*. It is, in fact, an artificial landscape, produced by partial deforestation to allow various forms of extensive agriculture (wheat-farming, pig-rearing, cork collection, etc.). The uneconomic nature of such activities in conventional terms has led to pressures for more profitable uses, irrigation and so potential desertification. However, whether or not that drastic stage is reached, upsetting the delicate balance of uses which maintains the *dehesa* in its current condition will inevitably lead to serious losses in terms of biodiversity.

Wetlands (*zonas húmedas*) are by no means unique to Spain but are important there because of the country's location on the migration routes of various species of waterfowl. As well as by direct reclamation for agricultural use, their area is being steadily reduced by increasing irrigation and the consequent fall in the water table [8.2.2]. Three of the most important wetland areas have received some protection through designation as national or regional parks [8.3.1]. Such measures, however, do little to maintain the water table; in the largest wetland area of all, the Coto Doñana, it is estimated to be falling by around one metre every year.

Landscape change is detrimental not just in ecological terms but also in the economic ones that dominate official thinking. Especially as the country seeks to diversify its tourist industry away from the Mediterranean coast, it is coming to be recognized that the attractiveness of landscapes – and habitats – is a key asset in maintaining Spain's market leadership. This applies not only to the conservation of hitherto unspoilt areas but also to the improvement of conditions in existing tourist areas whose appearance has suffered particularly from development's visual impact (*impacto paisajístico*).

This comes from a number of sources. One is the massive transport projects undertaken in the 1980s. Another is the common problem of uncontrolled – and sometimes even controlled – dumping of rubbish on the fringe of settlements in full view of the public. Much the most important form of visual impact, however, is tourist accommodation itself, whether in the form of medium- to large-scale holiday villages or as individual second or holiday homes.

For many years such developments were subject to only minimal planning controls; in any case they were frequently constructed without the requisite permission. The 1988 Coastline Act (*Ley de Costas*) was intended as a means of controlling such building, and introduced a ban on all construction within 100 metres of the shoreline. But this regulation has frequently been breached by both developers and local authorities. In many instances, builders have paid large sums of money to councillors in order to ensure that the land they are interested in is classified as being suitable for building houses and apartments (*suelo urbanizable*).

The most notorious of the corruption cases of this type to date is one which has come to be known as the Malaya Operation (*Operación Malaya*), centred on the City Council of Marbella in Andalusia. In 2005, an investigation began into the activities of certain councillors – members of the People's Party (PP) that controlled the city at the time. This has since led to the arrest of more than 100 people, including the former Mayor of the Council. Alleged offences include bribery (*cohecho*), misappropriation of public funds (*malversación de caudales públicos*), perverting the course of justice (*prevaricación*) and influence-peddling (*tráfico de influencias*). By 2006, the scandal had grown to such proportions that the government took the unprecedented step of dissolving the Council. Legal inquiries are ongoing at the time of writing, and have themselves become the object of some controversy [9.1.4]; these inquiries have extended to the activities of several other local authorities.

Dwellings which have been built illegally in this manner have rarely been demolished in the past, although a new Coastline Act passed in 2006 is beginning to have an effect. During 2007 a total of 665 constructions which had been built illegally were demolished in various locations along the Mediterranean coast. The unfortunate people who bought the apartments and houses in question have been promised compensation, but this is likely to be minimal and late in coming. Meanwhile, in Cabo de Gata-Níjar National Park in Almería province, construction has been halted on what was to be an enormous hotel called El Algarrobico – being built without proper planning permission – and a demolition order has been placed on that building too.

The early years of the 21st century have seen prolific construction activity in Spain, with the result that this sector has been a major contributor to the country's economic growth [5.1.3], and its dominance is reflected in the lack of control exercised by local authorities. Some steps have been taken, however, to try to ensure that developers behave more responsibly in relation to the community at large. A Land Act (*Ley de Suelo*) passed in 2007 obliges developers to reserve 30 per cent of residential land for 'social housing' (*viviendas de protección oficial/VPO*) and to cede up to 15 per cent of land on which they intend to build to local authorities for the provision of green space (*zonas verdes*) or for community use (*edificaciones de interés público*). Time will tell whether these measures, along with the decline in construction activity since late 2007, will help reduce the negative impact of development on Spain's coasts.

8.3 Protection of the environment

When, in the early 1990s, Spain was a candidate to host the EU's future environmental authority the government was embarrassed by the revelation that none of its ministries included the term environment in its title. At the time, many of the comments passed were unfair since few governments paid more than lip-service to ecology. However, it is true that Spain was not well-placed to undertake the task of protecting the environment (*defensa del medio ambiente*), not least because it lacked coherent structures to do so. It is only in recent years that such structures are coming into being, and that the government is starting to take the issue seriously.

8.3.1 Environmental authorities

The oldest Spanish authorities with specifically environmental responsibilities are those which run the country's National Parks. They date back to 1918, when the first two were designated. The first park of all originally encompassed the Covadonga area of Asturias, but was expanded in 1995 to cover a much wider area of the Picos de Europa mountain range. The national network (*red estatal*) is currently composed of fourteen parks (see Table 8.1).

Table 8.1 National Parks

	Area in hectares	Year set up	Province
Ordesa y Monte Perdido[a]	15,608	1918	Huesca
Teide[c]	18,900	1954	Tenerife
La Caldera de Taburiente	4,690	1954	Tenerife (La Palma)
Aigüestortes i Estany de Sant Maurici[a]	14,119	1955	Lleida
Doñana[a]	50,720	1969	Huelva/Seville
Timanfaya	5,107	1974	Gran Canaria (Lanzarote)
Las Tablas de Daimiel	1,928	1980	Ciudad Real
Garajonay	3,984	1981	Tenerife (La Gomera)
Archipiélago de Cabrera[b]	10,021	1991	Balearics (Mallorca)
Picos de Europa	64,660	1995	Asturias/Cantabria/Leon
Cabañeros	39,000	1995	Ciudad Real/Toledo
Sierra Nevada[a]	86,208	1999	Granada/Almería
Islas Atlánticas[b]	8,480	2002	Galicia (Pontevedra/A Coruña)
Monfragüe[a]	17,852	2007	Cáceres (Extremadura)

Notes:
[a] Control transferred to Regional Government.
[b] Officially designated a 'land–sea park' (*parque marítimo-terrestre*).
[c] Declared World Heritage Site by UNESCO in 2006.

Five are located in the island regions of the Balearics and Canaries; two are in the Pyrenees; one is intended to protect the Sierra Nevada in Andalusia, where the highest peaks in the peninsula are located (Mulhacén and Veleta), while the one in Cabañeros protects a rare habitat in Spain's central plateau. Two others (Doñana and Daimiel) are in wetland areas in the south and south-central areas of the country respectively, while the latest addition to the list encompasses four small archipelagos off the coast of Galicia. In addition a further important wetland in the Ebro Delta has been designated a Regional Park by the Catalan regional government. The Monfragüe area of Extremadura, which includes some of the country's most valuable habitats [8.2.3], was initially declared not a National but a Nature Park (*Parque Natural*), adding it to a list of some 120 such parks in the country, although it was subsequently upgraded (in 2007) to the status of National Park.

Each of the National Parks has a Strategic Plan (*Plan Rector*), setting out aims and policies. Yet while they undoubtedly offer a degree of protection to sensitive areas, they also increase pressures on them by attracting visitors. Nor can the parks offer protection against practices carried on outside their boundaries which nevertheless impact strongly within them. The 2007 National Parks Act (*Ley de Parques Nacionales*) sets out the respective responsibilities of central government and the regional governments in relation to national parks. The idea behind this is to transfer the bulk of the responsibility for this area to the regional governments, leaving Madrid with responsibility for devising and operating an overall strategic plan for all parks. Certain regions, including Catalonia, Andalusia, Aragon and Extremadura, have already taken on this role (see Table 8.1). Final designation of a park as a National Park is the responsibility of the Madrid government, and this designation may be removed if a park is not being properly managed.

Spain also has various other categories of protected countryside areas (*espacios naturales protegidos/ENP*). Most owe their status essentially to being areas of natural beauty (*parajes pintorescos*), although some are nature reserves (*reservas naturales*) and others are intended to conserve stocks of game. Although the level of protection offered is often inadequate, the number of such designated areas in the various categories has increased enormously over the last fifteen years. Notable among these are the Bird Protection Areas (*Zonas Especiales de Protección para las Aves/ZEPA*) and the Areas of Community Interest (*Lugares de Interés Comunitario/LIC*). The ZEPA aim to protect those areas which are home to the large variety of birds in the country, many of which are characteristic of Spain, including birds such as eagles and storks, while the LIC define the boundaries of Special Conservation Areas (*Zonas Especiales de Conservación/ZEC*). In certain regions, as much as 20–30 per cent of the territory is – at least nominally – protected under such designations as these.

After the original National Parks, the next public authority with environmental responsibilities to be set up was the National Nature Conservancy Agency (*Instituto Nacional para la Conservación de la Naturaleza/ICONA*). Created in 1971 under the auspices of the Ministry of Agriculture, Fisheries and Food, ICONA had wide and rather ill-defined responsibilities covering a number of aspects of conservation, as well as for fighting forest fires [8.2.1]. It also had the task – a considerable one in Spain – of issuing shooting and angling permits.

A year after ICONA's establishment the importance of environmental considerations for government was recognized, at least formally, with the creation of an Interministerial Environment Committee (*Comisión Interministerial del Medio Ambiente*). This was dissolved in 1987, however, since when coordination has taken place through the Under-secretaries' Committee [1.5.2] and a special cabinet committee. Meanwhile, the 1978 Constitution had included something close to an injunction to set up a government agency specifically to protect the environment. The Environment Directorate-General (*Dirección General del Medio Ambiente/DGMA*) set up the same year inside the then Public Works Ministry fell well short of that. Not till 1990 was the DGMA given its own Secretary of State [1.5.2], and only in 1993 was the term 'environment' included in the Ministry's title.

In 1996, however, a separate Environment Ministry was finally created. Known as MIMAM, it assumed the responsibilities of the old DGMA. It also incorporated ICONA, which became the Nature Conservancy Directorate-General (*Dirección General de Conservación de la Naturaleza*). However, despite the disappearance of a separate Industry and Energy ministry, MIMAM was not given responsibility for energy conservation, which went initially to the Economics Ministry instead, and later, in 2004, to the Ministry of Industry, Tourism and Commerce. Urban and rural planning powers were retained by the renamed Development Ministry [1.4.5], and subsequently passed on to the Housing Ministry created in 2004. And the Nature Protection Service (*Servicio de Protección de la Naturaleza/SEPRONA*) set up by the Civil Guard [9.3.1] is responsible to the Interior Ministry.

8.3.2 Shifting priorities

As well as juggling with administrative structures, from 1982 successive governments have taken a number of legislative and other initiatives to protect the environment. In recent years in particular, a large number of new laws have been passed aimed at bringing together and rationalizing the legislation in the area of environmental protection.

The first major advance was the 1985 Water Act (*Ley de Aguas*), which established a National Water Board (*Consejo Nacional del Agua*) to supervise the usage and condition of the country's supplies. In the following year framework legislation [1.3.3] on toxic wastes was introduced, and a decree issued requiring that an environmental impact analysis (*declaración de impacto medioambiental*) be carried out for all infrastructure developments and other large-scale projects. Later in that decade came the Coastline Act [8.2.3] and the Countryside Conservation Act (*Ley de Conservación de Espacios Naturales*), both of which have been revised more recently (in 2006 and 2007 respectively).

The concept of environmental offence (*delito ecológico*) appeared in Spanish law for the first time in 1983, but the years since then have seen little enforcement of this notion. The first successful prosecution did not take place until 1988, when emissions from a Catalan power station were held responsible by the courts for damage to 30,000 hectares of woodland and pasture land. However, the station's manager was given only a month's prison sentence; a requirement to reduce future emissions by fitting filters was suspended on 'economic grounds'.

Subsequently the pattern of infrequent prosecutions has been maintained, as has the tendency to show leniency to corporate offenders. On the other hand, an individual fire-raiser found guilty in 1996 of damaging an area of ecological value was given a ten-year sentence. As with the creation of specialist agencies [8.3.1], some regions have led the way in this area too by appointing special environmental prosecution services (*fiscalías de medio ambiente*). Yet, given the slowness with which the Spanish legal system acts [9.1.4], it is questionable whether prosecution can ever provide even minimally effective protection to the environment.

The 1988 Catalan trial served to highlight the underlying problem which afflicts all attempts to protect Spain's environment. It was punctuated by demonstrations from workers at the plant concerned. Fearful of losing their jobs, they were protesting against the environmentalist groups whose pressure had forced the manifestly reluctant authorities to act. In general, and despite the widespread dissatisfaction with traditional parties [2.1.1], environmentalist parties have made little impact on the Spanish political scene.

Even more significantly, the court which delivered the 1988 judgment was not the only official body to explicitly reject their priorities. When the government announced plans for the building of 15 noxious-waste disposal plants by 1994, one of its declared aims was to avoid placing financial costs on the waste producers. Much more often, the order of priorities is implicit, as in official reluctance to prosecute environmental offenders. At the regional and municipal level it is evident in connivance at the manipulation of bathing water quality figures and evasion of planning restrictions.

More subtly, a belief in the absolute priority of economic growth (*desarrollismo*) is built into administrative structures and government thinking. Despite the creation of an Environment Ministry (MIMAM), several of central government's environment-related responsibilities remain in the hands of ministries principally concerned with promoting economic activity rather than supervising and controlling its unwanted effects [8.3.1]. Moreover, many of MIMAM's staff came originally from ICONA, an organization dominated by foresters (*ingenieros de montes*) whose values were essentially those of traditional engineers. A similar ethos prevails in its waterworks section, which has repeatedly been shown to have the greatest political clout.

The 2001 National Water Plan (*Plan Hidrológico Nacional/PHN*), for which MIMAM is responsible, illustrates the point well. It paid lip service to the objectives, set out in the 1985 Water Act, of preventing water pollution and overuse. Yet it failed to address them. Instead, it was mainly concerned with engineering projects, the largest of which was a plan to engineer a transfer of water (*trasvase*) on a massive scale from the Ebro to the Segura, for the benefit of farmers in Valencia and Murcia. As well as opposition from environmentalists, it therefore provoked a major outcry in Aragon and Catalonia, both of which stood to lose considerable amounts of water.

Although work on this project had already begun, in 2004 it was modified significantly by the new Socialist government, whose policy was to favour the construction of desalination plants (*desaladoras*) to convert sea water to drinking water, rather than just transferring river water from one region to another. These plans were formulated in a new Water Management Plan (*Actuaciones para la Gestión y Utilización del Agua/AGUA*) in 2005, whose stated aims were to improve both the quality of the water supply and irrigation methods as well as promoting desalination. AGUA is not without its detractors, however: the desalination process is criticized for having a high cost in terms of energy use and for leaving residues of brine which can damage fauna and flora.

The 1993 National Reforestation Plan (*Plan Nacional de Reforestación/PNR*), was an attempt to reverse previous errors by offering four times more financial support for planting indigenous species than non-indigenous ones [8.2.1]. Yet under the PNR, replanting depended on individual farmers' acceptance of grants, with the result that it is inevitably small-scale and uncoordinated. Nor does the PNR affect land outside agricultural use where erosion is already under way. Moreover, although the financial arrangements are clearly beneficial in a sense, they do nothing to ensure that the choice of species is made on the basis of appropriateness to the terrain concerned. In essence, the PNR was not an environmental measure but an agricultural one. In 2000, a new plan – the National Forest Strategy (*Estrategia Forestal Española*) – was developed, as the Spanish element of a European-level strategic plan, to highlight the environmental benefits of afforestation and to try to improve the country's standing in that area relative to other member states.

Indeed, the prodigious output of legislation during the period of the PSOE government (2004–) [2.3.4], combined with numerous laws introduced under the previous administration – many instigated by agreements at European level – along with environmental provisions contained in revised Statutes of Autonomy in the regions, have led to a plethora of plans and strategies covering all aspects of the environment in recent years. These include areas such as air pollution, where plans cover the management of the right to produce emissions and, in line with recent international developments, the purchase and sale of such rights, as well as the major water plans mentioned above.

An action plan for further development of alternative energy sources was drawn up in 2005. This at least is one area where significant progress has been made. The level of renewable energy use in the country is higher than the EU average, and Spain is the second largest producer of electricity from wind in the world. Other alternative sources with a recognized potential for development include the use of biomass, and, particularly perhaps, solar energy, although the latter currently accounts for less than 1 per cent of energy production. Given that Spain's economy has been growing faster than most in the last decade [5.1.3], it is not surprising that energy consumption has also grown, albeit only slightly. In line with global and European aspirations, however, the aim of the 2003 Spanish Energy Strategy (*Estrategia de Ahorro y Eficiencia Energética*) is to achieve a reduction of 7.2 per cent in the period 2004–2012. The energy strategy is overseen by the National Energy Commission (*Comisión Nacional de Energía*) which was set up in 1998.

New plans have also been put in place for the disposal of various types of waste. These cover topics such as urban waste, recovery of contaminated soils, disposal of vehicles and used tyres and batteries, as well as dealing with waste generated by building and demolition work. Other plans address the need to mitigate the negative effects of tourist development and to control transport and transport infrastructure.

Although implementation of plans and the enforcement of regulations continues to be patchy and inconsistent, the tendency in Spain is towards greater environmental awareness both at the institutional level and among individual citizens. The fact that most parts of the country now have at least some Green political groups is perhaps indicative of a shift in priorities, although, to date at least, politicians from those groups have not achieved much electoral success.

The decision taken by EU leaders in 2007 to aim for a 30 per cent reduction in greenhouse gas emissions by 2020 constitutes a serious challenge to a country like Spain. It is likely to lead to a more acute sense of the urgent need to control the environmental effects of economic activity. That same group also set targets of 20 per cent for renewable energy and a 20 per cent improvement in energy efficiency by 2020. The fact that, at least in the first of these, the Spanish performance is better than most gives some hope that improvements in this field will continue.

8.4 Glossary

abandono de tierras (m)	set-aside
abono químico (m)	chemical/artificial fertilizer
aguas litorales (fpl)	coastal waters
aguas residuales (fpl)	sewage
aguas subterráneas/superficiales (fpl)	underground/surface water
bosque (m)	woodland
cabecera de cuenca (f)	headwaters
calentamiento global (m)	global warming
capa de ozono (f)	ozone layer
cementerio nuclear (m)	nuclear-waste dumping facility
centrales térmicas (fpl)	fossil-fuel power station
cohecho (m)	bribery
conciencia (medioambiental) (f)	(environmental) awareness
Consejo Nacional de Aguas (m)	National Water Board
contaminación acústica (f)	noise pollution
contaminación atmosférica (f)	air pollution
cortafuegos (m)	firebreak
Cumbre de Bali (f)	the Bali Summit meeting (on climate change)
defensa del medio ambiente (f)	protection of the environment
deforestación (f)	deforestation
delito ecológico (m)	environmental offence
depuradora (f)	sewage treatment plant
desarrollismo (m)	belief in absolute priority of economic growth
desertificación (f)	desertification
desertización (f)	depopulation; desertification (see 8.2.2)
efecto invernadero (m)	greenhouse effect
empresa inmobiliaria (f)	property company/developer
empresa maderera (f)	logging company
erosión eólica/hídrica (f)	wind/water erosion
espacio natural (m)	countryside area
fiscalía de medio ambiente (f)	environmental prosecution service
gasolina sin plomo (f)	unleaded petrol
impacto paisajístico (m)	visual impact
incendio forestal (m)	forest fire
industria maderera (f)	logging company
ingeniero de montes (m)	forester
intoxicación (f)	contamination
inundación (f)	flood

malversación de caudales públicos (f)	misappropriation of public funds
medio ambiente (m)	environment
medio físico (m)	natural environment
monte (m)	scrubland
papelería (f)	paper mill
paraje pintoresco (m)	area of natural beauty
pastizales (mpl)	grazing land
pluviometría (f)	rainfall pattern
prevaricación (f)	perverting the course of justice
Protocolo de Kioto (m)	Kyoto Protocol
rastrojo (m)	stubble
recogida selectiva (f)	(household) waste separation
reforestación (f)	reforestation
regadío (m)	land under irrigation
repoblación forestal (f)	(see *reforestación*)
reserva natural (f)	nature reserve
residuos (mpl)	waste(s)
salinización (f)	salinization, excessive build-up of salt
sequía (f)	drought
sobrepastoreo (m)	overgrazing
técnica agrícola (f)	agricultural practice
tráfico de influencias (m)	influence-peddling
tromba de agua (f)	sudden, tropical downpour
urbanización (f)	development (i.e. group of houses)
viviendas de protección oficial/VPO (fpl)	social housing
zona húmeda (f)	wetland area

Justice, defence and public order

This chapter looks at issues of relevance to the rule of law and questions relating to justice and defence. It begins by examining the guarantor of Spanish justice, the country's legal system. The following sections consider first the armed forces and how their role has developed in recent decades, and then the institutions charged with combating threats to the rule of law: the various police forces and the prison service. The last section considers the delicate relationship between protecting Spanish society from the effects of crime and preserving civil liberties.

9.1 The legal system

One aspect of Spain's limited experience of democratic politics [0.1] is that its judiciary has historically tended to be more or less directly controlled by the government of the day. Executive influence was especially widespread under the Franco regime and took a number of forms. Offences that would in most countries be considered a matter for the civilian courts fell under military jurisdiction; judges' career chances were under direct government control. As a result, the executive's role in the administration of justice was a thorny issue facing democratic governments after 1975.

9.1.1 The General Council of the Judiciary

In order to ensure judicial independence the 1978 Constitution created a General Council of the Judiciary (*Consejo General del Poder Judicial/CGPJ*), modelled on similar bodies in France and Italy. Two years later detailed arrangements for the Council's appointment and operation were set out in the 1980 Judiciary Act (*Ley Orgánica del Poder Judicial/LOPJ*). In essence, the CGPJ's purpose was to remove from government control personnel decisions affecting the judiciary.

Thus under the 1980 Act it had sole responsibility for all such matters, including the selection of members of the judicial service (*carrera judicial*), appointment to particular posts, and promotion to higher courts. Its remit also includes conduct of any disciplinary proceedings relating to members of the judiciary, although – somewhat anomalously – its decisions in this regard can be challenged in the Supreme Court [9.1.3].

Furthermore, the CGPJ examines proposed legislation of all types, advising the government as to its compatibility with judicial procedures and the Constitution. It can itself propose changes in the organization of the judiciary and court system. It must be consulted by the government before the latter appoints a new Attorney-General [9.1.2], and it nominates two members of the Constitutional Court [1.1.3] as well as Supreme Court judges [9.1.3]. Finally, it is responsible for nominating from among its own members the Supreme Court's chair, who then automatically assumes that of the CGPJ itself.

In addition to its chairperson, the Council consists of 20 ordinary members (*vocales*) appointed for a five-year period. Eight must be lawyers with at least 15 years' professional experience; the remaining 12 are drawn from the judiciary itself. Under the 1980 Act the members were also elected in two different ways: 12 by the legal profession and eight by the two Houses of Parliament. As a result, control over the judiciary effectively remained in the hands of lawyers appointed by the Franco regime, most of whom were conservative, even reactionary in outlook.

After the Socialist Party (PSOE) reached power for the first time in 1982 it felt that the Council majority was blocking reforms which it had been democratically elected to carry out, both within the judicial system and more broadly, for instance over the limited legalization of abortion. In 1985 it therefore passed a second Judiciary Act. This law changed the arrangements for appointing the Council itself, all of whose 20 ordinary members were now to be elected by Parliament with a three-fifths majority. The effect of this change was to politicize all appointments to the Council; indeed, as long as the PSOE enjoyed a sufficient parliamentary majority it appointed its own nominees at will. However, once its majority was eroded in the later 1980s vacancies could only be filled if there was agreement between government and opposition. In the wake of the 1993 general election this was not forthcoming and vacancies remained unfilled.

After a minority conservative government came to power in 1996 however, the main parties finally agreed on candidates for the vacant seats. But the new administration nonetheless remained keen to reform the method of the Council's election – which, given the legislation's entrenched status [1.3.3], required agreement with the opposition. This was eventually achieved in May 2001, as part of a wider pact [9.1.4].

Under the new arrangements, eight Council members are elected by the two Houses of Parliament with a three-fifths majority. The remaining twelve are also elected by MPs, but from a slate of 36 candidates presented by the legal profession. These candidates, in turn, are presented by the various organizations representative of the legal profession, in proportion to their membership, or by non-affiliated lawyers and judges who can obtain sufficient signatures in support.

Rather than removing political influence, this delicate compromise is really an attempt to balance its different forms. For the various professional organizations are divided essentially along political lines, the larger ones being firmly conservative in outlook. As a result the Council too is made up of identifiably left- and right-wing factions, the latter clearly in the majority at present. In early 2002, when the Council was faced with the task of filling four vacancies in the Supreme Court, the conservative faction imposed its favoured candidates for all of them.

More recently, the Council's own membership has been a cause of major controversy. In early 2007, a new Council was due to be formed for a five-year term, but the two associations failed to agree on its composition, with the conservative faction arguing for a return to the pre-1985 arrangements, whereby the Council itself would have the right to elect twelve of its own members. At the time of writing, the issue of ensuring that a new Council is formed is an urgent priority for the Socialist government.

9.1.2 Public interest

While judicial independence is crucial to the rule of law, democratic principles also require that the public interest in a correctly functioning legal system may somehow be asserted. This, too, is the subject of various constitutional provisions. First and foremost, the elected government of the day has a number of responsibilities in this area which, as in most continental European countries, are discharged through the Ministry of Justice.

The Ministry has a number of different roles. It drafts government legislation in consultation with various bodies, in particular the Lawyers' Association (*Colegio de Abogados*) to which all lawyers belong. It administers the legal system's physical infrastructure, such as court houses (*palacios de justicia*). And it runs the government's own legal service (*Servicio Jurídico del Estado*).

The Justice Minister is in an inherently delicate position when taking many decisions. As a member of an elected government he or she may, indeed must, bear in mind political criteria, while adhering strictly to the law as head of the legal authorities. Because of this special position the Justice portfolio is normally kept separate from other ministerial responsibilities. There was therefore considerable concern when, in 1994, it was amalgamated with the Interior Ministry [1.4.4]. The conservative government elected two years later opted to return to the practice of appointing a separate Justice Minister, and this situation persists to the present day.

The second instrument of the public interest within the legal system is the government attorney service (*ministerio fiscal*). This body is responsible principally for acting as public prosecutor in criminal cases. As such, attorneys (*fiscales*) initiate the examination stage of cases [9.1.3], and thereafter cooperate with the police and the examining magistrate in assembling the evidence. At the subsequent trial they lead the prosecution case.

In addition, the attorney service has a general brief to monitor the functioning of the courts to ensure that verdicts are implemented and that procedures are properly carried out. Its members enjoy wide powers to intervene in cases where they have grounds to believe that the public interest is affected. The service is headed by the Attorney-General (*Fiscal General del Estado*), nominated by the government after consulting the General Council of the Judiciary.

Particularly after the 1985 reform of the Council [9.1.1], this arrangement inevitably placed a question mark over the Attorney-General's independence from government. Concern reached a peak in the early 1990s, when the then Socialist government appointed a known party supporter to the post, with the Council's approval – at a time when the succession of scandals involving government members [2.3.2] made his role as defender of the public interest particularly important. In the event his appointment was eventually overturned by the Constitutional Court on a technicality, and subsequently governments of both main parties have adopted a more sensitive attitude to the issue. On the other hand, they have also tended to shy away from their constitutional duty to call the Attorney-General, and the service as a whole, to account for its actions in general.

Finally, the Constitution also includes provisions for more direct public involvement in the judicial system, but these have been implemented only partially and with hesitation. Thus not until 1995 was a measure to regulate the operation of trial by jury (*jurado*) passed. Even then there was very little preparation in terms of public education, giving rise to considerable concern among both lawyers and the public about the practical effects. Similarly the constitutional right to instigate a private prosecution (*acción popular*) has had little practical effect because of the conditions surrounding its use. For only officially recognized legal representatives (*procuradores*) are permitted by law to present cases to a court. And the costs of litigation will be borne by the state only if sufficient public interest can be demonstrated, a very difficult task indeed.

9.1.3 Courts

Justice is dispensed in Spain, as in most countries, in the form of legally binding decisions made by courts. Prior to 1975 several types of institution enjoyed the power to impose these. They included Church courts (*tribunales eclesiásticos*), as well as the tribunals operated by certain professional organizations and by the military (*tribunales de honor*). The 1978 Constitution recognizes the jurisdiction of these latter within the specifically military sphere. With this single exception, however, it explicitly denies legal jurisdiction to all organs other than the courts of the state's own judicial system.

Along with civil and criminal courts, this comprises four other categories unknown in the United Kingdom or Ireland which deal with specific areas of the law (see Table 9.1). In addition, the court system is structured on the basis of a conceptual division of the judicial process into stages. The central, indeed the only one in many cases (*causas*) is that of trial (*enjuiciamiento*). The approach is investigative rather than adversarial: it is the presiding members of the judiciary, rather than the parties' representatives, who examine witnesses. The court may examine several witnesses together, as a means of resolving contradictions in their

Table 9.1 Court types

Name	Type
Tribunal Supremo	Supreme Court
Audiencia Nacional	(Spanish) High Court
Tribunal Superior de Justicia	regional high court
Audiencia Provincial	provincial court
juzgado de lo civil	civil court
juzgado de lo penal	criminal court
juzgado de lo social	employment court
juzgado de lo mercantil	commercial court
juzgado de violencia sobre la mujer	special court for dealing with gender violence
juzgado de lo contencioso-administrativo[a]	administrative court
juzgado de vigilancia penitenciaria[b]	prison supervision court
tribunal tutelar de menores	children's court
juzgado de distrito	old-style district court
juzgado de paz	municipal court
juzgado de primera instancia	court of the first instance
juzgado de primera instancia e instrucción	new-style district court
juzgado de última instancia	final court of appeal

Notes:
[a] Deals with disputes between private individuals and state authorities.
[b] Deals with matters relating to the application of prison sentences imposed by the courts.

evidence (*careo*). If one of the parties has legitimate grounds to question the court's verdict (*sentencia*) or sentence (*condena*) the case may pass to a further stage, that of appeal (*recurso*).

In criminal cases the trial is preceded by another stage, that of examination (*instrucción*). During it the court authorities are responsible for gathering the relevant evidence, in the form of exhibits and statements. The results are then presented to the court trying the case, in a report (*sumario*). It is a fundamental principle of the system that, in a given case, no two of these stages should be handled by the same court.

The conceptual hierarchy of courts overlaps with a second, geographical one, higher levels of which cover larger areas as well as subsequent stages of procedure. It was subject to considerable reform by the 1988 Court Structure and Functions Act (*Ley de Demarcación y Planta Judicial*). The only tier left unaffected by the Act was the lowest, made up of the municipal courts (*juzgados de paz*) with jurisdiction over minor civil and criminal offences (*faltas*). They are presided over by a single Justice of the Peace (*juez de paz*), who is not required to have any legal training.

The fundamental change introduced by the 1988 Act was the establishment of new courts at the level of court districts (*partidos judiciales*) to replace the former district courts (*juzgados de distrito*). These so-called 'courts of the first instance and examination' deal with the bulk of cases. They act as appeal courts for cases tried before justices of the peace, a role in contradiction with their title. In other civil cases they act as a genuine court of the first instance, i.e. as the court by which the case is first heard. In most criminal cases they act as the examining court (*juzgado de instrucción*). These reformed district courts are again presided over by a single member of the judiciary (*juez*). Roughly equivalent to a Scottish sheriff, unlike JPs he or she must be a trained lawyer.

Another change brought about by the 1988 Act was the creation of special provincial criminal courts. They try lesser offences, that is, those subject to a maximum prison term of three years (*arresto menor*). Previously such trials had been heard by the district courts which had examined them, in violation of the principle that different stages of a case should be the responsibility of different courts. Along with the special provincial children's, prison, employment and administrative courts, they complete the category of lower courts.

Courts at higher levels of the system are distinguished in several ways. They are collegiate, that is, they are presided over by a bench composed of several judges (*magistrados*). They consist of several divisions (*salas*), concerned with different types of cases. And they also generally deal with appeals from lower courts rather than with first hearings. An important exception to this last distinction is provided by the provincial courts (*audiencias provinciales*) which, in addition to hearing appeals from below, also try criminal offences too serious to be heard by a lower court.

The next level consists of the Regional High Courts (*tribunales superiores de justicia*) established as a result of devolution in the 1980s, which consist in each case of three divisions. These relate to civil and criminal cases (which are heard in the *Sala de lo Civil y Penal*); administrative cases (heard in the *Sala de lo Contencioso-Administrativo*), and employment cases (in the *Sala de lo Social*). For matters relating exclusively to the region concerned they provide the final court of appeal (*tribunal de última instancia*). In cases where country-wide issues are involved, further recourse may be had to the High Court (*Audiencia Nacional*), established in 1977. Its criminal division also tries cases in certain fields, including falsification of the coinage, contamination of foodstuffs and medicines, and drug trafficking. To allow it to do so it has four special examining courts, one each relating to appeals, criminal cases, administrative cases and employment cases (*Sala de Apelación; de lo Penal; de lo Contencioso-Administrativo; de lo Social*).

Finally, the Supreme Court (*Tribunal Supremo*) is concerned with resolving appeals relating to the interpretation of legislation. Its decisions in such cases constitute a body of case law (*jurisprudencia*). This is collected and published by the General Council of the Judiciary [9.1.1] for use by lower courts as a source of guidance, additional but subordinate to legislation. The Court consists of five divisions, four of which deal with civil, criminal, administrative and employment matters. The final one is a military division (*sala de lo militar*), to which appeal may be made from the separate military courts.

9.1.4 A system in crisis

The workings of both the Central Council of the Judiciary [9.1.1] and the provisions for democratic control over the legal system [9.1.2] have given rise to considerable concern among experts in Spain. But the widespread popular perception of a system in crisis has a different cause. It is the courts' inability to deal with the cases which come before them within a reasonable time period. Examples are numerous, but perhaps the most notorious is the case, uncovered in 1981, of several hundred people who suffered poisoning as a result of consuming contaminated cooking oil (*síndrome tóxico*). Government officials allegedly involved in the scandal were eventually brought to trial fifteen years later, in 1996.

Various reasons can be identified for such grave delays. Crime has become more common and changed significantly in nature [9.5.1]; the volume of legislation has risen massively. The judicial system has been starved of resources. In 1982 Spain's spending under this heading was only a tenth of the EC average and, despite considerable increases in the interim, it remains relatively low. Consequently, and again despite considerable increases, the judiciary is understaffed by Western standards.

Delays also result from the complex nature of judicial procedure, however, in particular the division of functions between the public attorney, the examining court and that responsible for the trial [9.1.3]. Even simple cases can generate a lengthy interchange of judicial opinions (*autos*) between them. Yet another factor is the very steep rise in cases taken out against public authorities and coming before the administrative courts (see Table 9.1).

The Spanish legal system has also displayed a worrying propensity to commit errors, ranging from the loss of personal items submitted in evidence to wrongful imprisonment as the result of mistaken identity as well as failure to have sentences carried out. The latter situation – in late 2007, half a million criminal court sentences were waiting to be put into effect – has given rise to numerous cases where individuals have committed crimes while waiting to have prison sentences implemented. Among the more serious instances have been cases involving violence and even murder, including the notorious case of the abduction and killing of a five-year old girl called Mari Luz Cortés in Huelva in 2008. The cost of injustices is, in financial terms, insignificant, but the effect of such problems on public attitudes has been such that, at times over the last number of decades, the courts, the judicial system and the law itself have been drawn into disrepute.

The 1992 Emergency Court Procedures Reform Act (*Ley de Medidas Urgentes de Reforma Procesal*) constituted one attempt to address these issues. Implementing the Act proved difficult, however. For example, little progress was made in reducing the bench in higher administrative courts to a single judge, in order to allow more cases to be tried. Subsequently, a cross-party agreement on legal reform was reached in Congress in May 2001. This Pact on the Reform of the Justice System (*Pacto por la Justicia*) contained an ambitious programme of reforms which were meant to be introduced gradually over the succeeding years. The targets enunciated in the Pact were not fully achieved, however, due to wrangling between the major parties (the PP and the PSOE), with the result that, at the end of 2003, the agreed procedures for implementing change were abandoned. Some of the reform elements have been instituted, however, and improvements have been made across a range of issues.

For example, Regional High Courts, which have taken on an increasingly prominent role, are now allowed to hear criminal appeals. The map of court districts (*mapa judicial*) has also been redrawn to bring it more into line with contemporary population patterns, and a system of regular reviews of the map is now in place. In conjunction with that redistribution new district civil courts have been established. Presided over by a single member of the judiciary, they were intended to relieve the overloaded general district courts [10.1.3].

Another outcome of the Pact was the formulation in 2002 of a Charter of Rights for Citizens in respect of the administration of justice (*Carta de Derechos de los Ciudadanos ante la Justicia*). This sets high standards for the legal system, and is aimed at ensuring that the various organs and agents of justice adhere to principles of openness and transparency, while delivering justice faster and more conscientiously to the citizen. Allied to this was the development of a much more extensive network of offices for dealing with complaints relating to the legal system (*unidades de atención al ciudadano*). The activities of these offices are reported on publicly on an annual basis, with the nature of the complaints received being itemised under the various principles set out in the Charter. While it is clear that there is still much room for improvement in the system, the degree of openness achieved and the level of acceptance of the rights of citizens in the area of justice augur well for future progress in the area.

While it was in office the conservative PP government also agreed on a range of legal reforms with those regional governments which had at that time already acquired control over legal matters in their territories. At the time, the autonomous regions concerned comprised Andalusia, the Canaries, Catalonia, Valencia, Galicia, Navarre and the Basque Country, and the agreement entered into was rolled out to other regions as they acquired such powers later. The main thrust of this agreement centred on the development of new offices (the so-called *Nuevas Oficinas Judiciales*) around the country which were intended to provide a faster and more efficient legal service, both in terms of administering the affairs of the courts and judiciary, and in terms of communicating more efficiently with the public. This meant, among other things, developing the physical infrastructure in terms of the construction of new buildings, lengthening the working day of public servants who dealt with legal matters, and making appropriate use of modern technologies.

Although the quality and transparency of legal administration have improved, there are still major concerns about the lack of separation between the justice system and politics. These concerns focus on the political nature of judicial appointments, in general, and on how close some members of the judiciary are to political parties, in particular.

One person who, for many Spaniards, exemplifies that connection is the examining magistrate (*juez de instrucción*) Baltasar Garzón, who even sat briefly as a Socialist MP after 1993 [2.3.2]. However, he subsequently fell out badly with his party over his desire to crack down on corruption, while his tenacious investigation of the GAL affair eventually led to the imprisonment of a Socialist ex-Minister [10.4.2]. Later, Garzón attempted to bring both the former Chilean dictator Augusto Pinochet and the then Italian Prime Minister Silvio Berlusconi to trial in Spain, the latter for alleged offences in relation to his media holdings [5.3.2].

In both cases the conservative government was clearly unhappy with his actions, as it was with his attempt to bring to justice the perpetrators of crimes against the tens of thousands of people – including many Spaniards – who disappeared or were killed during the Argentinian dictatorship in 1976–83. In 2003, dozens of former officials of the military regime, including two former dictators, Jorge Videla and Emilio Massera, were arrested in Argentina on the basis of an extradition request filed by Garzón. They were freed when the Spanish authorities announced that they accepted that the Argentinian authorities would try them.

In the same year, Garzón prepared a 700-page indictment outlining the case against Osama bin Laden, the head of the international terrorist organization al-Qaeda, as well as some 35 other men, alleging that they partially planned their terrorist activities in Spain, and that some of them had helped to organize the 9-11 attacks in the United States. Eighteen of the people concerned were eventually convicted in a Madrid court and were given long prison sentences. The actions taken against such individuals by Garzón are based on a provision in Spanish law which affords universal jurisdiction in prosecuting crimes such as genocide and terrorism committed outside the country, either by Spaniards or by nationals of other countries.

Garzón's most recent high-profile actions relate to the efforts he has made to limit the activities of hard-line Basque nationalists. First he ordered the arrest of leaders of the political party Batasuna in October 2007. Then, in February 2008, he made a ruling suspending the activities of the two main pro-independence Basque parties that had not already been made illegal, ANV and EHAK [3.2.2.4]. One direct consequence of this was that no radical Basque party could legally present itself at the March 2008 general election. Given the tenacity with which he adheres to his principles and his willingness to take an independent stance, it would be difficult to claim that Garzón is subservient to politicians, although his critics certainly feel justified in claiming that he is inclined towards self-promotion (*protagonismo*).

On the other hand, the direct or indirect influence of politicians, the government itself or of powerful businessmen associated with political parties has indeed been evident in other instances. One notorious case was that of Javier Gómez de Liaño, who in 1997 instigated proceedings against the PRISA group in a complex dispute involving pay-TV [10.4]. His action, which was in line with the PP government's known wishes, was later rejected by the Supreme Court, and he himself had to answer charges of perverting the course of justice (*prevaricación*).

Another case of alleged misbehaviour on the part of a judge arose in the context of the Malaya planning scandal [8.2.3]. The affair had already led to the dramatic imprisonment and/or removal from office of numerous officials associated with Marbella Town Council but in February 2008 it took an even stranger twist, this time involving the examining magistrate, Francisco Javier de Urquía Peña. Urquía had been given responsibility for the Hidalgo Operation (*Operación Hidalgo*), which meant that he was attempting to uncover the network of money-laundering manoeuvres associated with the millions of euro which had changed hands illegally between developers, politicians and local authority officials in Marbella. At the time of writing, Urquía himself stands accused of accepting bribes in the course of his duties and has been suspended by the CGPJ.

9.2 The military

Although the 1978 Constitution drew a clear distinction between the role of the armed forces, focused on national security, and the role of the police, focused on public order, that distinction was blurred during the Franco regime. The army was frequently employed by the regime to exercise control in civil situations, most notably to control striking workers and students during the most turbulent years of the later Francoist period in the 1960s and 1970s. Franco had been brought to power by the military [0.1], whose personnel were by and large fiercely loyal to him, and many vehemently opposed the moves to democracy after his death. Furthermore, the Spanish military had a long history of intervening in politics going back over 150 years. Little wonder, then, that well into the 1980s it continued to be seen as a significant threat to the country's stability.

9.2.1 Transition and the army

Throughout the transition to democracy [0.3] the question of how to keep the three armed forces (*fuerzas armadas*/FFAA) out of politics was perhaps the most important one facing Spain's new rulers. In fact, their concern was focused almost exclusively on the army (*Ejército de Tierra*). Not only was it by far the largest of the three services (*ejércitos*); it had also been particularly closely involved in the former regime and was most heavily impregnated with Francoist beliefs.

Not only that; the army had also been involved in running the country to an extraordinary degree. Serving officers habitually held ministerial posts unconnected with military affairs; they exercised administrative responsibilities of many types and at various levels; they helped run the economy's huge public sector; they were even involved in private business, being invited on to the boards of a number of important companies.

These activities were clearly different from those normally expected of the army in a democracy. The same was true of its operational role during the Franco era. Rather than defending Spain against external threats, the army acted essentially as an internal occupation force, defending the regime against its own people. It was accordingly deployed on a territorial basis, in military regions each under the command of a captain-general. In each province a military authority (*Gobierno Militar*) worked alongside the civilian one [1.5.2], and the army was frequently called in to maintain public order.

Finally, the army had an important ideological role, exercised through the system of compulsory military service. As well as providing the army with the necessary manpower, this was seen by many officers as a means of inculcating into the country's young men the fundamental principles of the regime: unquestioning respect for authority, represented above all in the person of Franco, fervent Spanish nationalism and contempt for any vaguely socialist, or even liberal ideas.

Against this background it is scarcely surprising that, after the death of its former leader, the army should have been the main centre of extreme reactionary thinking and activity (*involucionismo*). Between 1976 and 1980 a succession of coup plots was uncovered, the most serious being the Galaxia affair named after the Madrid café where it was planned. In 1981 a coup attempt was actually launched [0.3.3]. The wholly negative reaction it evoked, which ranged from the monarch to the mass of ordinary Spaniards, was a salutary lesson for the reactionaries. But as late as 1985 it would seem that a plot to assassinate King Juan Carlos, involving senior army officers, reached an advanced stage of planning before it was thwarted.

The centrist governments of 1976–82 were keenly aware of the dangers posed by the army's predisposition to plotting coups (*golpismo*). After the inaugural 1977 election a senior army figure convinced of the need for change, Lieutenant-General Manuel Gutiérrez Mellado, was brought into the cabinet as Deputy to Prime Minister Adolfo Suárez. Given special responsibility for defence matters, his task was to ensure that the army's opportunities to intervene in politics were removed.

The 1977 cabinet changes also ended the practice of according ministerial rank to the heads of the three armed forces. Instead, a Ministry of Defence was set up, to whose political authority the service chiefs were subordinate. Military direction was placed in the hands of a new Joint Chiefs-of-Staff Council (*Junta de Jefes de Estado Mayor*/JUJEM). The following year the Constitution distinguished the role of the armed forces in defending Spain against external threats from that of the civilian security forces [9.2.2].

The Constitution's characteristic ambiguity was evident in other key aspects of the military's role. On the one hand, its mission to defend Spain's sovereignty and territorial unity was given the status of a fundamental principle [1.1.2]. On the other, much less prominence was given to a specification that all the military's actions, including any related to national unity, are carried out under the supreme command of the monarch, itself subject to endorsement by democratically elected authorities [1.2]. It has sometimes been argued that this left the door dangerously open for the army to take unilateral action supposedly in the national interest. Yet in practice what mattered was not the Constitution's wording but the army's readiness and effective capacity to act unconstitutionally.

Sensibly, the government moved to limit both these factors. Before standing down as Defence Minister in 1979 to make way for a civilian, Gutiérrez Mellado took steps to reform pay scales and so reduce the risk of discontent. Under Suárez's successor, Leopoldo Calvo Sotelo, legislation was introduced to allow the dismissal of officers for alleged incompetence. This second measure was, in effect, a recognition that the government's real control over the army remained dangerously limited. Gutiérrez Mellado had been publicly insulted on several occasions by officers opposed to his reforms. And a number of the instigators of the 1981 coup attempt had previously been convicted of involvement in the Galaxia plot but had received only laughable sentences.

9.2.2 Modernization and reform

This situation changed in 1982, with the arrival in office of a Socialist administration with a massive popular mandate and a clear parliamentary majority [2.3.1]. From this much stronger position the new government effectively called the army's bluff, invariably taking quick and decisive action against recalcitrant officers in marked contrast to its predecessor. Crucially, however, it also recognized that the army's tendency to intervene in politics was due not only to political conviction but also to officers' grievances over pay, conditions of service and professional satisfaction. Accordingly Narcís Serra, Defence Minister from 1982 to 1991, set out to address these concerns, which in some respects had been aggravated under the former regime.

That was largely because Franco's maintenance of a large officer corps constantly replenished from the military academies had left the country with a top-heavy army – of the 1975 strength of 220,000, over 24,000 were officers (*oficiales*). As a result, even though individual officers' pay was poor, the overall wages bill was high and represented a major constraint on purchase of modern equipment. At the same time, promotion remained strictly based on length of service (*ascenso por antigüedad*). This ensured that mediocre officers reached senior positions while more able colleagues languished lower down the scale, with ample time to channel their frustration into political plotting.

The promotion issue was traditionally a sensitive one, and Serra shrewdly chose to finesse it. Merit criteria for promotion, introduced by the previous government at the levels of major and brigadier, became general. However, they applied only to active commands, the number of which was greatly reduced. Those who failed to meet the new standards continued to receive pay and even promotion, just as they would have done under the old system, but were transferred to a bizarrely named 'active reserve'. These measures improved officer quality and provided a means of sidelining potential troublemakers. In the longer term they also cut the real wages bill: more immediately they allowed financial juggling to free up funds for spending on hardware.

That in turn was essential for the second front of Serra's strategy, which was to involve the army in new, strictly defence tasks. It was a route on which Calvo Sotelo had already embarked by taking Spain into NATO. The PSOE had opposed that move when in opposition, but reversed its position once in office [2.3.2]. Well before 1996, when the country became fully integrated into NATO [0.4.1], its forces were regularly involved in joint exercises with those of its democratically run neighbours. Once a joint European Union corps was established, Spain was quick to join it.

Participation by the Spanish armed forces in UN peace-keeping missions has been another means to the same end. In 1989, in Angola, seven Spanish officers (*cascos azules*) became the first to take part in such a mission. Within three years Spain had become the largest single contributor to UN forces, and to date the Spanish army has been deployed on humanitarian or peace missions in more than a dozen countries and regions, including, in recent years, Rwanda, Chechnya, Kosovo and Afghanistan. While there is widespread public support for the role played by the army in these instances, there was very little for the controversial decision by the conservative People's Party government in 2003 to send Spanish troops to support the US-led occupation of Iraq, and most Spaniards welcomed the Socialist government's decision to recall the troops in 2004 [2.3.4].

The PSOE governments of the 1980s and 1990s redeployed the army along lines more in accord with an external defence role, a process begun by the plan known as META (*Modernización del Ejército de Tierra*). The posts of captain-general and, later, provincial military governor were abolished. In 1984 the JUJEM [9.2.1] was reorganized and its head renamed Chief of the Defence Staff (*Jefe del Estado Mayor de la Defensa*). A second major plan approved in 1994, and known as Norte (*Nueva Organización del Ejército de Tierra*), provided for closure of many installations no longer needed and a slimmer, restructured army.

These moves, together with the effects of time, have brought a gradual change in military attitudes. In 1989, when Serra again addressed the promotions issue by introducing fast and slow tracks for promotion as low down the scale as major, his move provoked some immediate controversy but no lasting problems.

Admittedly, the army today still contains some extreme reactionaries with the will to intervene in politics. But happily they no longer have the capacity to do so, their links to powerful political and economic interests now being as limited as their public support. When, in 2006, the head of the army, General José Mena Aguado, appeared to publicly threaten intervention to protect the unity of Spain in response to the draft new Statute of Autonomy for Catalonia [3.2.1.3], he was promptly dismissed by the government. Far-right parties have enjoyed negligible success since 1975 [2.6], while the newspaper *El Alcázar*, which openly backed a return to authoritarianism and was closely linked to various military plots, was forced to close in 1988 due to its pitiful sales.

Within the forces themselves debate has switched away from political issues to the technical question of their ability to carry out their new external defence role. In part it focused on Spain's level of defence spending. Although this has been rising consistently over the last ten years, in the 1990s the country had the lowest level of spending on defence in NATO outside Luxembourg, a situation that gave rise to severe logistic problems. But during most of that decade the main topic of discussion was possible professionalization of the military.

One reason for this was the increasing rejection of military service among the young. But in the new, less political climate some army opinion too began to favour scrapping it, on efficiency grounds. The Socialist governments in power up to 1996 showed great caution in responding to such suggestions, despite the potential electoral benefits. One reason was their awareness that abandoning conscription altogether would be costly. However, the PSOE also remained wary of the traditionalist feelings of army officers, many of whom remained suspicious of democracy into the 1990s.

The decision to professionalize was thus not taken until after the election of a conservative government, which could afford to take such feelings more lightly. In 1999 the Armed Forces Personnel Act (*Ley de Régimen del Personal de las Fuerzas Armadas*) was passed, introducing the principle of full professionalization. The last intake of conscripts enlisted the following year and, in 2001, obligatory military service was suspended by the government. Although it is not quite officially abolished, the effect of the suspension is that young people are no longer obliged to join up, but are free to so do if they wish to opt for such a career path.

One problem with this solution appears to be that young Spaniards are little more attracted by a professional military career than they were by compulsory service. But if there is some reluctance among Spaniards to become involved themselves in the armed forces, there are large numbers of young immigrants who see the armed forces as offering opportunities for them to earn a good wage and to become more integrated into Spanish society. Nationals of 19 different countries – including most Latin American countries, plus Equatorial Guinea – have the right to join the army, navy or air force, and Ecuadorians, Colombians and Bolivians have been particularly keen to do so. They are permitted to stay in the army for a period of up to three years; to remain longer, they must take out Spanish nationality.

Overall, the number of immigrants enlisting has grown, just as the numbers of immigrants into Spain generally have increased in the early part of this century [6.1.1]. Initially, in 2002, the percentage of foreigners allowed to join the forces was capped at 2 per cent of the total. But this quota has since been increased twice, so that it now stands at 9 per cent. Currently, among the 78,000 personnel who make up the armed forces, there are 4,300 immigrants, or 5 per cent of the total. Plans are in place to increase the number of personnel to 85,000, however, with the result that the potential exists for the forces to recruit up to 7,650 foreign members.

The 1999 Act also sealed another important change. Since 1988 women had been allowed to serve in the Spanish forces, but with certain restrictions as to the activities they might undertake. These restrictions were removed by the Act, which accords both sexes equal status within the services, and recruitment of female members got under way in earnest, so that, currently, more than 12 per cent of army personnel are women. Perhaps even more than the end of conscription this step shows how much the military has changed since Franco's death.

9.3 The forces of public order

In Spain policing powers are exercised by a number of bodies. Under the Franco regime these included the country's military [9.2], and the overlap in functions was reflected by the prevalence of militarist and authoritarian attitudes throughout the various forces concerned, with the result that, in some ways, vestiges of that Francoist past remain even to this day.

9.3.1 Civil Guard

Spain's oldest public order force is the incongruously named Civil Guard (*Guardia Civil*). Set up in the nineteenth century to counter the problem of banditry on country roads, it retains a number of military characteristics. Not only do Civil Guard officers (*guardias*), like policemen in many countries, carry arms. They are deployed, often far from their home region, in barracks (*cuarteles*), and thus separated from the local population they serve.

Traditionally the Civil Guard's services to travellers in distress caused it to be known affectionately as *La Benemérita* (The Admirables). However, during and after the Franco era it became the subject of considerable public suspicion, because of doubts about its commitment to democracy. Mainly drawn from Spain's Military Academy, its officers have tended to share the reactionary views typical of their Army colleagues [9.2.1].

These problems burst into the open with the participation of some Civil Guards in the 1981 attempted coup [0.3.3]. The Socialist government elected the following year placed the force under the command of Lieutenant-General Sáenz de Santa María, previously head of the National Police [9.3.2]. He was given the task of quelling unrest; once he was judged to have done so he was replaced by the Civil Guard's first ever civilian commander, Luis Roldán.

Only in time of war is the Civil Guard now responsible to the Defence Ministry, otherwise its political head is the Interior Minister. As a sop to officers' feelings – and in defiance of the EU's declared policy of phasing out all paramilitary police units – the Civil Guard's standing orders continue to reaffirm its military character. However, their detailed provisions are clearly closer to those of a police force.

These various moves have largely put a stop to overt insubordination, but not to all the Civil Guard's problems. They were aggravated by the activities of Roldán [9.5.1], which left the Civil Guard with an unnecessarily large and unwieldy central staff, infected with corruption. However, the force's problems go far beyond the influence of a single person.

Its officers have over the years been involved in human rights abuse of detainees, especially but not exclusively ETA suspects. The Intxaurrondo barracks in San Sebastián has been at the centre of a number of such allegations. In 1996 its former head, Lieutenant-General Rodríguez Galindo, was convicted in connection with the disappearance, torture and murder of two young Basques in the 1980s [9.5.2]. Some of his subordinates, and officers elsewhere, have been found guilty of involvement in criminal activities, including drug trafficking. There is evidence, too, of politically motivated violence by Civil Guard officers, one of whom was charged with Spain's first race killing, of a young woman from the Dominican Republic.

In part the Civil Guard's problems can be traced to underemployment, now that relatively few Spaniards live in the rural areas that are its prime responsibility. In the early years of this century, the government attempted to combat this problem by extending the force's activities. Specialist units were created to deal with coastal patrolling and with environmental problems such as forest fires, dumping of toxic wastes and protection of endangered species [8.3.1].

Given their tradition of political conservatism and the severity of the methods they have often employed in dealing with suspected offenders, it is perhaps not surprising that the force has come under attack over the years from the radical Basque separatist group ETA [3.2.2.1]. To date, more than 200 members of the force have been killed by them. Indeed, in the early 1980s, Civil Guard members were the principal targets of the organization. Most recently, ETA's resumption of violence in December 2006 soon led to the deaths of two young Civil Guards who were murdered by ETA members in 2008 in a village in the south of France.

With the increased concern over terrorism since the 9-11 attacks in the United States, and particularly after the terrorist atrocities committed in Madrid in 2004 [9.5.4], the aspect of the Civil Guard's activities relating to Spain's international frontiers has taken on a new importance and has led to its taking an active part in counter-terrorist activities. Partly as a response to this, and in an attempt to ensure that the Civil Guard continues to become a more modern and more accountable force, in September 2006 the Socialist government brought the Civil Guard and the National Police Force (CNP) together under a Joint Command (*Mando Único*). The person placed in charge of the two forces was, in fact, the then Director of the Civil Guard, Joan Mesquida.

9.3.2 Police

The CNP (*Cuerpo Nacional de Policía*) is the country's largest purely civilian policing agency. It was formed in 1986 by amalgamating two existing forces, the General Force (*Cuerpo General*) and the National Police (*Policía Nacional*), until 1978 known as the Armed Police (*Policía Armada*). Both of these were established by the Franco regime, and the second in particular was closely associated with its repression of civil liberties.

Yet, unlike the Civil Guard [9.3.1], the CNP managed to throw off that aspect of its past fairly quickly. To a large extent that was thanks to the work of Lieutenant-General José Antonio Sáenz de Santa María, the force's commander from 1979 to 1982, under whose leadership it took an active part in suppressing the 1981 coup attempt [0.3.3]. Sáenz de Santa María also set up the Special Operations Group (*Grupo Especial de Operaciones*/GEO). The latter has had a creditable record in ending terrorist sieges and similar operations, and was involved in the siege of an apartment in Madrid in the wake of the 11-M bombings, on which occasion a member of the force was killed when the bombers blew up the flat [9.5.4].

Of course, the past had a certain weight. Inevitably, many senior positions continued to be held by officers promoted under the old regime. Indeed, for many years those known to hold more progressive ideas were persistently marginalized by the Interior Ministry, which has overall responsibility for the police. In 1994 Juan Alberto Belloch took over as Interior Minister. As a lawyer, former judiciary member and also Minister of Justice, he was well aware of the problems caused by the lack of change in senior police personnel. Accordingly, he took action to put younger officers in charge.

The decision in 2006 to unify the command of the Civil Guard and the CNP [9.3.1] was taken in the context of an overall restructuring of the Interior Ministry undertaken following an election pledge by the Socialist government. The most obvious benefits of the move related to the need for the pooling of resources – and intelligence – between the two, especially in the areas of organized crime and international terrorism. The change meant that the newly created Joint Command would report directly to the Minister of the Interior, liaising with the Antiterrorism Coordination Agency (*Centro Nacional de Coordinación Antiterrorista*). This Agency, created in the wake of the 11-M massacre [9.5.4], is also located within the structure of that ministry, and brings together the CNP, the Civil Guard and the National Intelligence Service (*Centro Nacional de Inteligencia*).

As part of those 2006 reforms of the Interior Ministry, two new high-level departments were created within it, both of which reflected the changing nature of Spanish society. The first of these was the International and Foreign Affairs Office (*Dirección General de Relaciones Internacionales y Extranjería*) which would coordinate police activity relating to immigration [6.1]. The second was the Office of Support for Victims of Terrorism (*Dirección General de Apoyo a las Víctimas del Terrorismo*). Both of these new departments would pool the resources of the Civil Guard and the CNP in relation to the matters which were their responsibility.

These measures were aimed at ensuring that all the state's security forces (*fuerzas de seguridad del Estado/FSE*) could carry out their task more effectively, and went some way to compensating for what had for years been chronic undermanning and lack of resources, especially in the case of the CNP. This issue was particularly apparent in the CNP's efforts to deal with major crime, which it was increasingly concerned with, to the detriment of the pettier varieties which tend to preoccupy people on a day-to-day basis. The streamlining of the FSE was also an attempt to reduce the level of antagonism between the two main forces, which, given their overlapping functions, had on occasion even led to CNP officers and civil guards coming to blows over successful drug hauls.

There have also been problems of overlapping functions between the CNP and some of the country's various other civilian forces, the most numerous of which are the local police (*policía municipal*). In larger towns these are responsible for local by-laws, including parking regulations. Considerably wider responsibilities are wielded by the forces under the control of the Basque and Catalan governments (*Ertzaintza* and *Mossos d'Esquadre*), which have taken over much of the CNP's remit in their respective regions, while the Policía Foral have played an important role in policing Navarre. Plans to set up other police forces at the level of the autonomous regions are contained in several of the revised Statutes of Autonomy which have come into effect in recent years. Given this trend, it is likely that the enforcement of law and order at the local level will be increasingly devolved to the regions while issues relating to major criminal activity and to national and international threats to the country's security remain the concern of the CNP and the Civil Guard.

9.4 The prison service

Prisons in Spain are the responsibility of the Directorate-General of Prisons (*Dirección General de Instituciones Penitenciarias*), which forms part of the Interior Ministry. Down the years the country has produced a number of notable penal reformers, and in general prison conditions have been fairly good. In recent years, however, there has been growing concern, for a number of reasons.

Like the courts and the police, prisons (*centros penitenciarios*) have been placed under an increasing burden by the changing nature of crime [9.5.1]. One result of that has been a steep rise in the number of prison inmates (*reclusos*); between 1983 and 2005 alone this rose from under 15,000 to over 60,000. In a number of establishments the result has been severe overcrowding (*masificación*). Furthermore, there is a lack of adequate prison staff (*funcionarios de prisiones*). That in turn compounds the security problems posed by outdated facilities, which have led to a number of spectacular escapes from custody, most notably by businessman-turned-politician José María Ruiz Mateos [2.6] and former Civil Guard commander Luis Roldán [9.5.1].

The problems are aggravated by chronic delays in the court system [9.1.4], which means that prisons have to deal with many remand prisoners (*presos preventivos*). Their numbers first rose sharply during the transition period after 1975, due partly to a rise in offences. But the increase was also the result of a 1980 measure which greatly tightened up the conditions governing release on bail (*libertad bajo fianza*). Specialist remand facilities proved quite inadequate to cope with these twin pressures.

As a result, remand prisoners – substantial numbers of whom would later be acquitted – were held in unsatisfactory conditions, and alongside convicted prisoners (*condenados*). The same problem applied to juvenile offenders, and to first offenders (*primeros*), who, in theory, should be kept separate from repeat offenders (*reincidentes*). In 1983 the new Socialist government revoked the 1980 amendment to the bail regulations and placed a limit on the time which prisoners might spend on remand (three years for those accused of serious crimes, 18 months in the case of minor offences).

The change led to a massive exodus from the prisons, thought to have contributed to a further rise in offences. Subsequently the government introduced a third change, increasing the limits on remand time (to four and two years, respectively). It has succeeded in stabilizing the situation to a considerable degree, although remand prisoners still account for a considerable proportion of the total.

The other main issues facing the prison system relate to inmates at the other end of the scale, that is, those convicted of serious crimes of violence. Spain has one high-security prison (*centro de alta seguridad*), located at Herrera de la Mancha. However, few of the most controversial prisoners convicted of violent crimes are held there. These are ETA members convicted of terrorist offences [3.2.2.1]. ETA and its supporters claim to regard these as political prisoners (*presos políticos*), and persistently demand special treatment for them. The government's policy towards them has varied, tending sometimes towards concentrating them in a small number of prisons, sometimes towards dispersal among many.

This latter policy was designed to make it easier for individual ETA members to renounce violence and opt for reintegration into society (*reinserción social*). That approach has been criticized from the political right, since it involves early release of convicted terrorists. In the 1990s many conservatives demanded that the courts should be able to require sentences to be served in full (*cumplimiento íntegro de penas*). The resultant debate took on some of the symbolic significance of that in the UK over reintroduction of the death penalty (*pena de muerte*), which in Spain is forbidden by the 1978 Constitution.

The Socialist government of the time argued that the Constitution also outlaws full-term sentencing. Its argument was based on the constitutional principle that one of the aims of imprisonment should be rehabilitation of offenders (*resocialización*). For one thing, locking up prisoners for longer periods in itself works against rehabilitation. Moreover, early release is one of the most important of privileges (*beneficios penitenciarios*) which act as an incentive for prisoners to join actively in rehabilitation programmes.

On these grounds, the new Criminal Code passed in 1995 [9.5.3] left the question of privileges, including early release and parole (*libertad condicional*), in the hands of the prison supervision courts (see Table 9.1). The maximum prison term to be served in normal circumstances is set at 20 years. However, exceptions are allowed where consecutive sentences (*penas múltiples*) are involved, above all if any of the offences concerned is particularly serious. The 1995 Code also includes a number of steps designed to address the problems of overcrowding and reoffending, although their implementation has been dogged by resource problems.

9.5 Crime and civil liberties

Declining respect for the law is a common complaint among some older Spaniards, and it is true that the number of offences rose sharply after Franco's death. On that basis it was sometimes argued that democracy had made Spain less safe and law-abiding. Yet, in so far as international comparisons are possible in a field where statistics are notoriously hard to interpret, the country's crime rate remains relatively low. Rather than the incidence, it is the nature of crime that has changed most radically, in ways that make it much more of a problem. On the other hand, abuses of human rights and the law by public authorities, which were such a feature of the former regime, have not entirely gone away.

9.5.1 Changing nature of crime

Certainly the number of offences (*delitos*) recorded in Spain rose substantially in the fifteen years after Franco's death. However, since then it has tended to level off. Today the official level of crime (*delincuencia*) is around one-third of that in the UK or Ireland. Even allowing for under-reporting it seems clear that crime is not a major problem, although the fact that it was previously so little known inevitably conditions public perceptions of the present level.

To that general sense of insecurity (*inseguridad ciudadana*) has been added in recent years a fear of the threat of terrorist attacks, and especially, in the wake of the 11-M atrocities [9.5.4], the threat from international terrorism. But there is a generalized fear of offences affecting both individuals' property (e.g. house-breaking, car theft, bag-snatching) and their physical safety (muggings and other, more serious forms of assault). The latter offences are concentrated in specific areas, particularly the depressed outlying parts of larger cities (*barrios periféricos*) and, to a lesser extent, tourist areas. The vast majority of offenders come from deprived backgrounds, turn to crime when young and then re-offend, in most cases repeatedly; many, especially the younger ones, are drug users. The problem is thus essentially one for the appropriate social services, which lack the resources necessary to deal with it.

Central government's response to public concern has tended to concentrate more on policing. In 1992 it introduced the Public Safety Act (*Ley de Seguridad Ciudadana*), better known as the 'Corcuera Act' after the then Interior Minister, the main aim of which was to clamp down on drug-related offences. However, the methods it proposed provoked considerable controversy, and it was eventually declared unconstitutional [9.5.2].

Two years later Corcuera's successor, Juan Alberto Belloch, announced a Civil Liberty and Public Safety Plan (*Plan de Libertad y Seguridad Ciudadanas*). The Plan's title betrayed the need to improve public perceptions of the police, and its central idea was to get more police on the streets in a preventive role. But neither such neighbourhood policing (*policía de barrio*), or a later scheme based on community policing (*policía de proximidad*), have enjoyed great success. Not surprisingly, given the lack of police manpower [9.3.2].

What is more, over the last decade the police have had to devote an increasing proportion of their scarce resources to various types of less frequent but much more serious offences. Thus there have been a number of extremely unpleasant attacks on women and children of the sort with which the UK has become depressingly familiar, but which were previously all but unknown in Spain. Even more worrying is the rise in organized crime, especially in Madrid and along the Mediterranean coast, a development thought to be associated with Mafia-type gangs. As elsewhere, their activities are often related to the drug trade, in which indigenous gangs such as the Galician clans have long been involved. In recent years, organized crime has been increasingly associated with certain immigrant groups, including Eastern Europeans, especially in the larger cities [6.1.1].

Organized crime is closely related to money-laundering (*blanqueo de dinero*), which the Spanish authorities claim to be especially rife in Gibraltar. But Spain, like other developed countries, is not immune from the problem, which in another sense is simply one aspect of the wider phenomenon of white-collar crime (*criminalidad de cuello blanco*). The last two decades have seen various cases of large-scale financial fraud in the private sector. Perhaps the most notorious names are those of Mario Conde, one-time chairman of the Banesto bank, and Javier de la Rosa, who headed the Spanish operation of the Kuwait Investment Office (KIO).

Other cases have involved more or less senior figures in the public sector. One even involved the former Governor of the Bank of Spain, Mariano Rubio, who was found to have engaged in various forms of insider dealing. Another was that of the first civilian head of the Civil Guard, Luis Roldán [9.3.1], who was discovered to have made a fortune from rake-offs on tenders for building new barracks and other projects. The political parties, too, have been involved in such influence-peddling [2.1.3].

Politics is also linked, of course, to terrorism. On the one hand, the terrorist activities carried out by ETA would be defended by its supporters as being a purely political phenomenon. While that might have been sustainable before 1975, the evolution of its activities since then marks them out as essentially criminal in nature [3.2.2.1]. As well as numerous members of the public, its victims have included public officials, local, regional and national politicians (one of them a former cabinet minister) of various persuasions, and Francisco Tomás y Valiente, a former chairman of the Constitutional Court.

Several times it has seemed that the police have been on the point of destroying ETA. In 1998/99, it maintained a ceasefire (*tregua*) for over a year, and, more recently, it appeared that a major breakthrough had been achieved by the PSOE government under José Luis Rodríguez Zapatero, when a 'permanent ceasefire' was declared in March 2006. Unfortunately, the peace process which was under way at that time broke down [3.2.2.4] and the ceasefire was eventually terminated also.

Sadly, ETA continues to exist – and continues to kill, albeit rarely, and with markedly depleted forces at its command. The bombings and other attacks are only occasionally lethal but the intimidation associated with them is a phenomenon that ETA's opponents have long been familiar with, especially in small rural communities. An important agent of this is the young camp-followers who are also responsible for regular outbursts of street violence (*kale borroka*) that involve burning buses, attacking police officers and similar activities.

The other dimension of terrorism – brought home to Spaniards in the most brutal way possible in March 2004 – is that of international terrorist attacks inspired by Islamist fundamentalists and the deadly activities of groups such as al-Qaeda. The 11-M massacre [9.5.4] was one of the most lethal terrorist attacks to take place anywhere in Europe in modern times. On the one hand, it left Spaniards more determined than ever before to distance themselves from the foreign and international policies of the United States. On the other hand, they were more inclined to accept the need for vigilance and the imposition of high levels of security in their cities and towns, even if those security measures impinged to some extent on individual liberties.

9.5.2 Civil liberties

Undoubtedly the most severe breach of civil liberties to have been carried out by the forces of the state in Spain since its return to democracy was the 'dirty war' against ETA. It was carried on by a shadowy organization known as the Anti-terrorist Liberation Groups (*Grupos Antiterroristas de Liberación*/GAL), which killed 27 people and injured over 30 others, almost all in the French Basque Country, between 1983 and 1987. Few of their victims were important or even proven ETA activists; several were French citizens with no ETA connections whatsoever.

The first GAL members captured were mercenaries and common criminals, but in 1991 two Spanish police officers were convicted of recruiting and organizing these, the superior being José Amedo. Their subsequent confessions, above all Amedo's, incriminated not only their immediate superiors but politically appointed administrators in the Basque Country and the Ministry of the Interior. Other evidence established links to the secret service (CESID) and to the Civil Guard, especially the notorious Intxaurrondo barracks in San Sebastián [9.3.1].

In 1998 twelve senior government servants were convicted of involvement in one GAL operation, the botched kidnapping of Segundo Marey, a French citizen. Among them was José Barrionuevo, Interior Minister at the time, who was subsequently given a 10-year jail sentence. Two years later five more officials, including Intxaurrondo's commander Lieutenant-General Rodríguez Galindo, were convicted in a second case [9.3.1]. Galindo was sentenced to 75 years in prison, but was allowed out of jail on a conditional release after five years. Meanwhile, Barrionuevo, despite being given a ten-year sentence, spent only three months in prison, the rest of the time being suspended in one way or another, which included a pardon by the then

Prime Minister, the conservative, José María Aznar. Accusations that 'Mister X', the GAL's supreme commander, was actually Felipe González, Socialist Prime Minister from 1982 to 1996, were never substantiated.

The most recent trial related to the GAL affair took place in 2007, when Rafael Vera, who had been Secretary of State for Security in the 1980s, was convicted of using secret state funds to finance the operations of Amedo and his colleague. Vera had been one of the people convicted in the 1998 Marey affair, and had spent eight years in jail; on this occasion he was sentenced to just 18 months.

The GAL affair's significance is hard to exaggerate. For one thing, it undoubtedly made ending ETA's violence significantly more difficult [3.2.2.3]. Its negative impact in the Basque Country was greatly increased by an aspect almost as disturbing as the GAL's actions themselves: the persistent attempts by central government to obstruct investigations by journalists and individual judges, notably Baltasar Garzón [9.1.4].

Such obstruction did not even cease when the Socialists fell from power in 1996. Against the advice of the Central Council of the Judiciary [9.1.1], the new conservative administration refused to release government documents essential to the case without even submitting them for judicial review (*control judicial*) to establish their degree of sensitivity. This belated solidarity – the GAL affair had been a major plank of the conservatives' campaign to unseat González – was a timely reminder that the 'dirty war' almost certainly started under the centre-right governments of 1976–82, through the agency of the 'Basque-Spanish Battalion'.

At the same time, civil rights abuses in the fight against terrorism have stretched well beyond the GAL affair. Sadly, there have been repeated instances of maltreatment, torture and even death in detention. A number of senior officials have been implicated; in 1997 revelations about the treatment of an ETA suspect by the name of Elejalde led to the dismissal of the chief of police in San Sebastián, and the Civil Governor of Guipúzcoa province [1.5.2].

Many such cases have been concerned with the application of the Anti-terrorist Act (*Ley Antiterrorista*). Originally introduced in 1977 by the then centrist administration as an emergency measure, in 1985 it was normalized by the Socialist government. The Act allows for the suspension of normal safeguards for the rights of detainees, such as access to a lawyer, where they are suspected of terrorist offences. In 1988, however, police officers were convicted of having used it in the case of a common criminal known as El Nani, who died in custody after suffering severe maltreatment.

Worries about police malpractice of this sort were at the root of opposition to the 1992 Corcuera Act [9.5.1]. It proposed to give the police greatly increased powers to enter private premises in search of drugs; the phrase universally associated with it was 'kicking the door in' (*patada en la puerta*). Its opponents referred the measure to the Constitutional Court [1.1.3], which eventually found that it did indeed infringe constitutional safeguards for individual liberties and declared it invalid.

More generally, the governments of the post-Franco era have shown little desire to rein in or even investigate abuses by the security forces. Several scandals have occurred due to illegal telephone tapping (*escuchas telefónicas*) by national and regional police forces, and by the Defence Intelligence Service (*Centro Superior de Información de la Defensa/CESID*), the main Spanish secret service. In 1993 one such case forced the resignation of the Deputy Prime Minister, Narcís Serra, and six years later the Service's former head, Emilio Manglano, was jailed for his part in the affair.

The treatment of suspected illegal immigrants is another area of concern. The Aliens Act (*Ley de Extranjería*) in force up to 1999 [6.1.1] gave the Spanish authorities wide powers of deportation without recourse to the courts. Its replacement, passed in 2000 by the conservative government against the opposition of all other significant political forces, denied those suspected of entering the country illegally certain basic civil freedoms, such as the right of association or to join a trade union. And, over the course of the last six years, reports have emerged of the appalling conditions in two centres on the Canary Islands used to house Africans who had crossed clandestinely to the islands.

9.5.3 The 1995 Criminal Code

In the new democracy, it had been recognized for a long time that Spain's criminal code (*código penal*) required updating, but it was not until 1995 that a full revision of the code was carried out. Since then, two further major amendments have been made to it, but the basis of criminal proceedings in the country is still the 1995 Act.

The new code introduced changes which reflected the changing nature of crime [9.5.1] as well as the importance of democratic values which had become increasingly consolidated since Franco's time. Thus a new category of corporate offences (*delitos societarios*) was introduced, in an attempt to counter white-collar crime. They relate to company directors and carry a maximum penalty of three years' imprisonment, as well as heavy fines. Specifically covered are the falsification of company accounts, and the use of a majority holding to decide on actions contrary to the interest of other shareholders.

In the area of political corruption [2.1.3], the new code mainly increased the penalties for existing offences. Those involved in bribery of public employees (*cohecho*) may receive a fine and six-year prison term, as well as disqualification from public office (*inhabilitación*) for up to 12 years. One new provision related to conflict of interest; public employees who act as advisers to private persons or companies may now be heavily fined and barred from office for three years.

Other changes introduced by the code relate particularly to young offenders [9.5.1], and place the emphasis on preventing reoffending rather than punishment. Incapacity due to drug or alcohol addiction can now, under certain circumstances, exempt individuals from criminal responsibility, thus opening the way to rehabilitation outside prison. Those who refused to perform compulsory military or community service in the last years before they were suspended [9.2.2] were more likely to be fined than imprisoned.

The new code also includes a number of measures designed to reduce prison overcrowding and aid rehabilitation by keeping offenders out of prison as far as possible [9.4]. They extend the opportunities for courts to impose a suspended sentence (*suspensión de pena*), a possibility first introduced in 1983. A completely new concept is that of weekend imprisonment (*arrestos de fin de semana*), which may replace terms of up to two years at the rate of two weekends per week of sentence. With the agreement of the offender, fines or community service (*trabajos en beneficio de la comunidad*) may also be substituted.

Finally, the new code widened significantly the civil responsibility of the state for the actions of its employees. Compensation to members of the public for the errors and omissions of public bodies is now payable under much less stringent conditions. No longer must a claimant prove the direct responsibility of a particular employee, but need merely show that he or she was prejudiced by the 'operation of public services'. Moreover, responsibility is no longer limited to intentional acts (*delitos dolosos*) but extends to unintended ones (*delitos culposos*).

9.5.4 The 11-M and its aftermath

Many Spaniards felt that democracy itself was being threatened, not just in Spain but worldwide, after the terrorist attacks in Madrid on 11 March 2004, especially in light of what had happened in the United States in September 2001. The attack in Madrid, usually referred to as 'the 11-M' (*11-M*), began just before 8 o'clock on that Thursday, when bombs started to explode on a commuter train entering Atocha station. Around the same time, bombs also exploded in two other stations on the same Guadalajara-Madrid railway line, and two minutes after the first bombs went off, four bombs exploded in a train on an underground railway line just 500 metres from Atocha.

In all, ten bombs – which had been placed in rucksacks and left on the floors of carriages – exploded in four trains which were part of the commuter network taking people to work in Madrid. The final death toll turned out to be 191 people, with more than 2,000 injured, many seriously, which made it the most serious attack in Europe in peacetime since the 1988 Lockerbie disaster in Scotland. The reaction within Spain and around the world was one of shock and horror, and already on the afternoon of that same day demonstrations of solidarity began to take place around the country. On the following day those demonstrations reached record levels, with more than two million people demonstrating in Madrid, approximately 1.3 million in Barcelona and hundreds of thousands in other locations, including Brussels.

The Spanish general election was due to take place on 14 March, and, almost immediately, the question of who was responsible for the attack became a political issue. The indications from the PP government were that ETA was responsible, and at first this seemed a credible explanation given that members of that group had been arrested just two and a half months earlier, in December 2003, when they were attempting to plant two suitcase-bombs in another train station in Madrid. By the afternoon of the day of the attack, however, the police had already gathered some evidence – including a tape with Arabic verses from the Qur'an – that suggested that the perpetrators were not ETA but Islamist terrorists of Middle Eastern or North African origin. Although the government did not publicize this evidence until later, speculation continued to increase that an international terrorist organization, possibly al-Qaeda, was behind the attack. Indeed, the attack was claimed by al-Qaeda on the night of Saturday 13 March.

The government continued to suggest that ETA was probably to blame, however, and ordered Spanish embassies around the world to attribute responsibility to that organization. Meanwhile, opposition political groups in Spain, as well as most international commentators, were increasingly convinced that this was an attack organized by an Islamist group, possibly in retaliation for Spain's involvement in the war in Iraq [9.2.2]. Many media outlets in Spain were coming to the same conclusion, although those which were closest to the government, including the state broadcasters TVE and Radio Nacional de España, as well as the radio network Cadena COPE and the newspaper *El Mundo*, continued to support the view that ETA had been responsible [10.1].

In the event, on 14 March 2004, the elections went ahead, although, on the previous day – officially a 'day of reflection' (*día de reflexión*) when no political canvassing was allowed – there were vociferous protests outside the headquarters of the PP in Madrid. Despite being told that their behaviour was illegal, thousands of people turned out to demonstrate and to demand that the government 'tell the truth' about what had happened. By the day of the election, public opinion had swung firmly against the government, with the result that the PP fell from power, and the Socialists won [2.3.4], although it is also possible that the public reaction to the government's handling of the attacks simply led to a bigger majority for the PSOE than might have been the case otherwise.

By 13 March, five people had been arrested, based on evidence found on an unexploded bomb placed in one of the stations on the day. On 3 April, police located another group of suspects in a flat in Leganés in Madrid, all of them Muslims from the Middle East or North Africa. Rather than submit to the authorities, however, that group blew up the flat, killing themselves and a member of the elite police squad GEO [9.3.2].

Many others were arrested in the months and years that followed, several of them people who were already being held in Spanish jails for other crimes, and a major trial of suspected perpetrators took place, ending in October 2007. The outcome was that two Moroccan nationals who were adjudged to have placed the rucksacks on the trains were sentenced to a total of more than 42,000 years of imprisonment, while numerous others were found guilty of complicity with them or of involvement in terrorist organizations. A Spanish miner from Asturias was sentenced to 35,000 years for stealing the explosives used by the bombers, while other Spaniards were given lighter sentences for assisting with the transport or supply of the explosives.

Months after that trial, another Moroccan man accused of planting the bombs was arrested by the Moroccan authorities in February 2008. He was identified by the Spanish police on the basis of DNA evidence linking him to a comb found in the Leganés flat, and was taken in by the Moroccan police despite the fact that no extradition agreement (*convenio de extradición*) existed between Spain and Morocco [0.4.3]. Around the same time that the arrest took place, however, an agreement was reached between police forces in the two countries that allowed for a greater degree of cooperation between them than had been the case previously, including the sharing of intelligence and an arrangement whereby trials could take place in either country of people charged with offences committed in the other.

Controversy has continued to surround the events of the 11-M. Firstly, in terms of the competing hypotheses about the true perpetrators of the attack, with the PP consistently claiming that ETA was, or could have been, involved; meanwhile, that party continues to express resentment at what it sees as the PSOE's manipulation of the incident for electoral purposes. On the other hand, the Socialists – and majority opinion in the country – attribute blame to the Islamist group who were tried and convicted in court, and criticize what they see as the PP's ploy of attempting to gain electoral advantage at the time of the attack by attributing it to ETA, their avowed enemy [2.4.5]. The explanation offered by the prosecution at the trial, and eventually accepted in the court's judgement, suggested that the people who carried it out were a group of local Muslims who were acting more in emulation of al-Qaeda rather than as an al-Qaeda cell.

Secondly, the reactions of the victims and their families to the sentences varied, with some expressing satisfaction with the outcome and others demanding more exposure of what they claimed were hidden aspects of the investigations. The differences among the victims in this regard are reflected in the fact that two different associations of victims were created in the aftermath of the attack, each with a different political alignment.

The outcome in terms of material damage and, most especially, loss of life was tremendous. The scars of the attack have not gone away, in terms of the effect that it has had either on survivors and family members, or on society as a whole. Spain, like the USA after 9-11 and like Britain after the London bombings of July 2005, is a country resigned to facing the perennial threat of unexpected terrorist violence. The result is that Spaniards, like many people around the world, are now more willing to accept the restrictions placed by the authorities on their freedom of movement and the increased level of police surveillance associated with the aim of protecting the democratic society in which they live.

9.6 Glossary

acción popular (f)	private prosecution
antigüedad (f)	seniority
arresto menor (m)	custodial/prison sentence of up to three years
ascenso (m)	promotion
ascenso por antigüedad (m)	promotion based on length of service
Audiencia Nacional (f)	high court
audiencia provincial (f)	provincial court
auto (m)	judicial opinion
barrio periférico (m)	(deprived) outlying area of city
beneficios penitenciarios (mpl)	privileges granted to prisoners
Benemérita (f)	Civil Guard
blanqueo de dinero (m)	money-laundering
careo (m)	simultaneous examination by a court of several witnesses
carrera judicial (f)	judicial service
cascos azules (mpl)	blue helmets/berets, UN peace-keeping forces
causa (f)	case
centro de alta seguridad (m)	high-security prison
Centro Nacional de Coordinación Antiterrorista (m)	Antiterrorism Coordination Agency
Centro Nacional de Inteligencia (m)	National Intelligence Service
centro penitenciario (m)	prison

Centro Superior de Información de la Defensa/ CESID (m)	Defence Intelligence Service
código civil/penal (m)	civil/criminal code
cohecho (m)	bribery (esp. of public employee)
Colegio de Abogados (m)	Lawyers' Association
condena (f)	sentence
condenado (m)	convicted prisoner
Consejo General del Poder Judicial (CGPJ) (m)	General Council of the Judiciary
control judicial (m)	judicial review
convenio de extradición (m)	extradition agreement
criminalidad de cuello blanco (f)	white-collar crime
cuarteles (mpl)	barracks
Cuerpo Nacional de Policía (CNP) (m)	National Police Force
cumplimiento íntegro de penas (m)	serving full term of sentence
delincuencia (f)	crime
delito (m)	offence
delito culposo (m)	unintentionally prejudicial act
delito doloso (m)	intentionally prejudicial act
delito societario (m)	corporate offence
día de reflexión (m)	day before election (no polling allowed)
Ejército del Aire (m)	Air Force
Ejército de Tierra (m)	Army
enjuiciamiento (m)	(process of) trial
Ertzaintza (f)	Basque police force
escuchas telefónicas (fpl)	phone-tapping
falta (f)	minor offence
fiscal (m)	state attorney
Fiscal General del Estado (m)	Attorney-General
fuerzas armadas (fpl)	armed forces
fuerzas de seguridad del Estado (fpl)	state's security forces
funcionario de prisiones (m)	member of prison staff; prison warder
Gobierno Militar (m)	provincial military authority
golpe (m)	(military) coup
golpismo (m)	predisposition of military to stage coups
Grupo Especial de Operaciones (GEO) (m)	Special Operations Group (of National Police)
Guardia Civil (f)	Civil Guard
inhabilitación (f)	disqualification (from office)
inseguridad ciudadana (f)	sense of insecurity among the public
instrucción (f)	examination (stage of legal process)
involucionismo (m)	extreme reactionary beliefs and activity
Jefe del Estado Mayor de la Defensa (m)	Chief of the Defence Staff
juez (m)	member of judiciary
juez de instrucción (m)	examining magistrate
juez de paz (m)	justice of the peace
juicio (m)	trial (of a particular case)
Junta de Jefes de Estado Mayor (JUJEM) (f)	Joint Chiefs-of-Staff Council
jurado (m)	jury
jurisdicción universal (f)	universal jurisdiction

jurisprudencia (f)	jurisprudence, case law
juzgado (m)	court
kale borroka (f)	campaign of street violence by young ETA supporters
lavado de dinero (m)	(see blanqueo de dinero)
libertad bajo fianza (f)	release on bail
libertad ciudadana (f)	civil liberty
libertad condicional (f)	parole
magistrado (m)	judge
Mando Único (m)	Joint Command (for the Civil Guard and the National Police Force)
mapa judicial (m)	division of country into court districts
Marina (f)	Navy
masificación de presos (f)	prison overcrowding
ministerio fiscal (m)	government attorney service
Mossos d'Esquadre (mpl)	Catalan police force
oficial (m)	(military) officer
palacio de justicia (m)	court house
partido judicial (m)	court district
pena (f)	sentence
pena de muerte (f)	death sentence
penas múltiples (fpl)	consecutive sentences
poder judicial (m)	judiciary
policía de barrio (f)	neighbourhood policing
policía de proximidad (f)	community policing
Policía Foral de Navarra (f)	Navarre's police force
policía municipal (f)	local police
preso (m)	prison inmate, prisoner
preso preventivo (m)	remand prisoner
prevaricación (f)	perverting the course of justice
primero (m)	first offender
procurador (m)	officially recognized legal representative
recluso (m)	(see preso)
recurso (m)	appeal
reincidente (mf)	reoffender
reinserción social (f)	reintegration into society; rehabilitation of offenders
reserva activa (f)	'active reserve', status of promoted officers denied an active command
resocialización (f)	rehabilitation of offenders
sala (f)	division (of court)
sala de lo militar (f)	division of Supreme Court dealing with appeals from military courts
sentencia (f)	verdict
Servicio Jurídico del Estado (m)	government legal service
servicio militar (obligatorio) (m)	(compulsory) military service
síndrome tóxico (m)	poisoning as a result of consuming contaminated cooking oil (1981)
sumario (m)	report from examining court/magistrate
suspensión de pena (f)	suspended sentence
trabajos en beneficio de la comunidad (mpl)	community work
tregua (f)	(ETA) ceasefire
tribunal (m)	(see juzgado)

tribunal de honor (m)	military court; tribunal of professional association
tribunal eclesiástico (m)	Church court
Tribunal Superior de Justicia (m)	regional high court
Tribunal Supremo (m)	Supreme Court
tribunal tutelar de menores (m)	children's court
unidad de atención al ciudadano (f)	complaints office (in the legal system)
vocal (mf)	ordinary member (of committee, council, etc.)

The media

The media play an important role in Spanish society and, in one way or another, affect the daily lives of every Spanish citizen. Not only do they influence the way in which political decision-making takes place, but, increasingly, they relate to the way people live their lives in terms of raising social awareness, educating people about the world around them and providing both entertainment and opportunities for enhanced communication, locally, nationally and globally. Now more than ever, the media, in the extended sense of the term, are ubiquitous, and encompass a vast range of modes of communication, from print to digital media, from podcasts to high definition television. The main emphasis in this chapter is on the 'traditional' media of newspapers, radio and television, which are still the most dominant media in Spain today. The chapter opens with an examination of the close relationship that has existed and continues to exist between the media and the state.

10.1 Media and the state

In virtually every country around the world, there is a close link between the mass media (*medios de comunicación de masas*) and political activity generally. In the Spanish case, however, the relationship between the media and the state itself is particularly strong and often problematic. Spanish press, radio and, especially, television are intimately linked to the political process. The political allegiance of many of the major media outlets is readily identifiable, and political parties, while in government, generally exercise an inordinate degree of power and control over the organization and content of major newspapers and radio and television stations.

The Spanish media, like so many of the country's institutions, are heavily influenced by the experience of the Franco regime. Like many dictatorships, it censored media output. The principal media outlets were either directly under the control of the Ministry of Information and Tourism or in the hands of organizations, such as the Church, closely allied to the regime. Thus, vast swathes of the media were controlled – either directly or indirectly – by the government.

Under Franco's censorship (*censura*) legislation, both national and regional newspapers were kept under strict control. Radio was dominated by the state company Radio Nacional de España (*RNE*) [10.3] which broadcast alongside private stations sympathetic to the regime, while television, which started to broadcast in 1956, was in the hands of the government-owned Televisión Española (*TVE*) [10.4]. All of the state's media interests had as their prime task the dissemination of propaganda.

The first significant step in the direction of change was taken when the Minister in charge of the area, Manuel Fraga, introduced a new Press Law (*Ley de Prensa e Imprenta*, also known as the *Ley Fraga*) in 1966. This law allowed the media (at that time, mainly the printed media) to take a chance on publishing material which was critical of the regime or which the government might disapprove of. Daring newspapers such as *Madrid* or current affairs magazines (*revistas de actualidad*) such as

Triunfo or *Destino* offered alternative points of view to those endorsed at official level. But they operated in constant peril of being punished for what they published, for, while *prior* censorship of material was no longer required under this new Act, censorship still existed. Thus, they could be punished for the publication of views that were seen as being contrary to officially accepted political and religious values. Fines and closures were not unusual, the most spectacular of these being the closure of *Madrid* in 1971, followed by the physical destruction of that paper's premises.

After the death of Franco in 1975, the media played an important role in facilitating – and indeed leading – discussion of the changes that were taking place in the structure of the state and the political scenario that was unfolding. The transition period witnessed a veritable explosion of media activity in Spain, as the old Francoist press, the 'press of the National Movement' (*prensa del Movimiento*) withered away, and the old established print media, in particular, made way for new and more modern papers.

Chief among these was the stunningly successful daily *El País* [8.2], which first appeared in May 1976, and which served as a forum for advocating change, for debating the nuances of the process of transition and for explaining the intricacies of democracy to a Spanish public which was hungry for such information. When censorship was abolished by royal decree in 1977, the pace of change accelerated even further as the media developed and expanded, exploring the limits of freedom of expression (*libertad de expresión*) not only in the critique of political standpoints but in their treatment of social and sexual issues. That freedom of expression was underpinned by guarantees written into Article 20 of the 1978 Constitution [1.1].

Thus the media, and in particular the press, served as a 'parliament' (*Parlamento de la Prensa*) for the discussion of political ideas and a forum for debate and for testing opinions on social issues and other questions of national significance during this time. Later, on the night of 23 February 1981, when an attempted coup took place in the Spanish parliament, Spaniards sat by their radios to follow the events in Madrid [10.3].

On the other hand, the Spanish media's close links to and involvement with the political class has meant that political parties of all hues have consistently exercised a lot of influence over the management and editorial content of newspapers, magazines, radio stations and TV channels. Furthermore, as was the case during Franco's time, the government controls Efe, which is by far the largest Spanish-language news agency (*agencia de información/de noticias*) in the world. This position is unique among Western democracies and of particular significance in Spain, given the dependence of the country's many regional newspapers [10.2] on agency reports for national and international news.

There were obvious links between politics and the media too during the transition period. One of its protagonists, Adolfo Suárez [0.3.2], became prime minister in 1976 after having served as Director General of TVE [10.4] from 1969 to 1973. Suárez was a photogenic politician, with consummate communication skills, who used television to help push his agenda of change and reform. Television was also a key element during both the first general election in the new democracy in June 1977 and in the campaign for the 1979 election when Suárez's own party, UCD, was given massively wider – and more positive – coverage than all its opponents [2.2].

The use of the state television network for purposes of electoral advantage has been a consistent feature of the relationship between the state and television since then, regardless of which party happens to hold the reins of power. It was exemplified during the March 2004 general election when TVE not only supported the government's view of the 11-M massacre [9.5.4], but went so far as to change its programming to include a film about ETA, thereby further reinforcing the government's accusations against that organization. And this situation is mirrored at regional level by the involvement of politicians in regional television services [10.4].

In short, the Spanish media have consistently shown themselves to be susceptible to party political influence. *El País* has strongly supported successive Socialist (PSOE) governments while the conservative PP has received friendly coverage in its turn from various sections of the media, including especially the daily newspaper *El Mundo* [10.2] and the Antena 3 television station while RTVE's approach to its news coverage has frequently been aligned with the policies of the government of the day [10.4]. An example of the latter was the dubious role played by the state broadcaster in reporting the general strike of June 2002, the 20-J, when the company was sued in the High Court by the unions for its alleged under-estimation of the numbers of participants. The Court ruled in favour of the unions, and as a result RTVE were obliged to read out the Court's ruling on all their news programmes for a whole day [5.2.4.2].

Notable also is the support which the PP has continued to receive from *El Mundo* and Antena 3 for its theory that ETA, and possibly others, were implicated in the 11-M atrocity [9.5.4]. Indeed, in the immediate aftermath of the bombings, the media generally were willing to relay to the world the then government's version of events, although most people soon came to the conclusion that the attacks were the work of terrorists linked to al-Qaeda, a conclusion borne out by the outcome of the legal process that ensued.

The emergence of private TV and the granting of licences for mobile phones [10.4] are other areas where politicians have behaved in an apparently partisan manner towards the media. This was the case also during the development of regional television, to the extent that many observers would suggest that one of the key features of media coverage of politics in Spain is its general lack of objectivity.

10.2 The press

Although Spanish news dailies (*diarios informativos*) have a low readership (*audiencia/público*) by international standards, they nonetheless have a considerable significance. For, as elsewhere, and in spite of the advances that have taken place in telecommunications, in terms of news coverage the broadcast media to some extent live off the press, which consequently has an important agenda-setting role. At the Spanish level this is played by a relatively small number of actors, but the apparent concentration conceals a rich variety of local and regional papers.

Bald statements about Spanish newspaper readership require first to be put in context. Certainly sales (*difusión*) are not high by international standards, and are markedly lower in the south than in the north of the country. A recent study reported that there are 105 papers sold daily per 1,000 inhabitants, compared with, for instance, the UK's 318, Ireland's 191 or the EU average of 217. Nonetheless, given that there are no tabloid papers in Spain and that journalistic standards tend to be high, such comparisons need to be nuanced. For instance, it is worth noting that the consumption of quality press in the UK is some 90 per 1,000 inhabitants, not that different from the figure of 80 which we would get if we subtracted from the Spanish statistics the consumption of sports papers (*periódicos deportivos*) – the huge sales of which would presumably be much less if there were massive tabloid coverage of sport in Spain, as there is in Britain and Ireland.

At the time of Franco's death in 1975, the newspaper market was dominated by a limited number and range of titles. One of the more prominent was the traditional monarchist daily *ABC*, which dated back to 1903 and was published by Editorial Española, a company mainly owned by the big banks. Acquired in 2001 by the Correo group, which is itself now part of the media conglomerate Vocento, it continues to be successful. In the early 1970s it had the highest level of circulation (*tirada*) of any newspaper in Spain, and even today it occupies third place in the rankings for general newspapers (behind *El País* and *El Mundo*).

At that time it consistently espoused deeply conservative political views, as it continues to do to this day. The main point of difference between it and the regime was the newspaper's strong commitment to the Spanish monarchy, since it would have preferred to have seen it restored before Franco's death. Apart from that, the political views of its editors as well as their stance on social and moral issues tended to be in harmony with the thinking of the Franco authorities and the Catholic Church, with the result that left-wing parties and their policies were anathema to it.

This conservative stance has continued to be reflected in its editorial line, with the result that its criticism of the left in general, and of the PSOE in particular, has been trenchant over the years since then. Indeed, as its then editor Luis María Ansón later revealed, in the early 1990s it was involved in a concerted media campaign (*campaña mediática*) to oust the Socialist government of the time by just about any means, fair or foul. The decidedly old-fashioned look of the paper has been updated somewhat over the last few years, but, in terms of content, *ABC* still continues to reflect a generally conservative view of Spanish society. Despite its conservatism and PP sympathies, however, it is interesting to note that it does not support that party's version of the events of the 11-M [9.5.4].

Conservatism was also the hallmark of the other main daily newspaper of the time, *Ya*, which was controlled by the Catholic Church through a press group called Editorial Católica (Edica), and which went out of circulation in 1996. Edica also controlled a range of other titles, including the illustrated magazine *Blanco y Negro* which later became a supplement (*suplemento*) within *ABC*. Along with these, there were dozens of newspapers and magazines which were owned directly by the National Movement itself [10.1]. For the most part, these were publications that had been confiscated from Republican interests after the Civil War. Among them was the sports newspaper *Marca*, one of the few specialist publications of that period to have survived and thrived in democracy.

Also in existence at that time was the set of gossip and celebrity magazines (*prensa del corazón*) which are still such a prevalent sector of the print media in Spain. Notable among them were *Diez Minutos* and its more expensive equivalent *Hola*, weekly magazines (*semanales*) devoted to reporting on the lives of both Spanish and international celebrities (*famosos*). The latter went on to spawn the English-language offshoot *Hello*, as well as eventually publishing versions of the magazine in other countries, including Russia, Canada and Mexico.

The state itself also owned two press agencies at the time, Pyresa and Efe [10.1], which worked hand in glove with filmed news documentaries (*Noticiarios y Documentales Cinematográficos/NODOs*) in relaying news stories from Spain to the wider world, always in line with the regime's official policies.

The first major development in the modernization of the Spanish print media came with the creation of *El País*, in May 1976. The paper had been five years in the planning, and was the brainchild of a group of intellectuals who had jointly founded a concern known as PRISA (*Promotor de Informaciones SA*) in 1972. PRISA, founded and owned by Jesús de Polanco until his death in 2007, went on to become a major player in the Spanish media as well as outside Spain, with interests in a variety of papers, magazines, publishing companies and other media outlets [10.3; 10.4]. In 2006 it acquired a controlling interest in the media conglomerate Sogecable.

El País understood its mission as being to provide a modern, independent voice in the new democracy. It offered critical comment on the crucial issues facing the country at the time of the transition. The composition of the founding board of *El País* was an indication in itself of this independence and liberal ethos, ranging as it did from Polanco to Manuel Fraga, the former government minister from the Franco era [2.4.2], to the renowned economist Ramón Tamames, a member of the Spanish Communist Party.

Within eight months, *El País* had a circulation of 140,000. This has continued to rise, so that by the early years of this century it had exceeded half a million, with the result that the paper had an estimated readership of 2.2 million people. After a struggle for control of the shareholding and for editorial control in 1978–79, it has consistently been seen as being supportive – though not uncritically – of the PSOE.

It is now established as the leading national newspaper in Spain, and is read all over the Peninsula as well as in Latin America and Europe. It publishes 11 different editions, eight of which are regional Spanish versions of the paper (in Barcelona, Andalusia, Valencia, Madrid, Balearic Islands, Castile, Galicia and the Basque Country). There are also two European editions (published in Holland and Germany respectively) and one published in Mexico. As with other daily newspapers, circulation figures double in the case of the weekend edition (*dominical*) of the paper.

A few months after *El País* appeared on the streets, a second attempt was made at publishing an independent newspaper, in the form of *Diario16* (*D16*). This came on the back of the success achieved by the weekly current affairs magazine *Cambio16*, which had begun publication in September 1971, and was owned by the same family. The tone of the new paper was slightly more aggressive than that of *El País*, somewhere between the quality tone of the latter and that of a tabloid. In the late 1980s, however, a conflict between its founder, Juan Tomás de Sala, and its editor, Pedro J. Ramírez, over the reporting of the GAL scandal [9.5.2] led to the latter leaving the paper to found a new daily called *El Mundo*. Since many of the editorial team of *D16* had left with Ramírez, that paper then hit a serious crisis and subsequently foundered.

El Mundo, which began publication in 1989 and occupies a similar space to that which *D16* had carved out, was an instant success. Its meteoric rise was achieved by virulent editorial attacks on the Socialist government, backed up by aggressive investigative journalism that uncovered a number of scandals of the period. Some of the revelations, most notoriously a story about alleged nepotism by Prime Minister Felipe González, proved to be false. Ramírez's financial backing seemed to come mainly from anti-Socialist businessmen.

Later Ramírez was himself the victim of what appears to have been a revenge plot, when a video showing him engaging in unusual sexual practices acquired widespread notoriety. Nonetheless he continues to edit the paper, whose position in the conservative camp was underlined when partial control over it was acquired by the Teléfonica group, headed by a friend of the then PP leader, José María Aznar [10.4]. The paper continues to thrive, currently circulating more than 400,000 copies per day and publishing ten regional Spanish editions.

A more recent successful arrival is *La Razón*. Launched in 2000 by Ansón after he was removed from *ABC* and close in tone to a tabloid, it has reached a circulation level of approximately 200,000. *El País*, *El Mundo*, *ABC* and *La Razón* together account for just over a quarter of the total readership, and these effectively constitute Spain's national press. Apart from *ABC*, all those that survived the Franco era disappeared soon after 1975, while a number of new papers have come – and most of those have subsequently disappeared. These have included some attempts at producing sensationalist papers (*prensa sensacionalista/amarilla*), including *Claro*, which resembled a British-style tabloid. Brought out in 1989 by Editorial Española and the German Springer group, publisher of Europe's best-selling sensationalist daily, *Bild*, it survived for only three months.

The remaining 75 per cent of daily general news readership is made up by regional and local papers. The two largest are both based in Catalonia. Much the older is *La Vanguardia*, the flagship of the Godó group. The traditional paper of the Catalan middle classes, it was sufficiently conservative to remain independent under Franco, after whose death it was briefly the top-selling daily in the whole of Spain. However, its sympathy for Catalan regionalism has subsequently limited its appeal to its home region. Running in close second place to it in Catalonia is *El Periódico de Cataluña*, which forms part of the Zeta group. *El Periódico* is now the country's sixth-selling news daily (*diario informativo*), but its wider ambitions have also been thwarted; outside Catalonia it sells significantly only in Aragon.

Regional newspapers published in regional languages also made a comeback in the mid-1970s. The first one to be published since the time of the Second Republic was the Catalan-language *Avui*, which began publication in April 1976, backed by a wide range of shareholders from the region. It quickly gained a readership of over 100,000, although its circulation dropped to one third of that after a few years and now stands at 40,000.

In the Basque Country, two new papers began publication in 1977, *Deia* in May and *Egin* in September. The former espouses a moderate political position and publishes material mainly in Castilian. *Egin*, on the other hand, published in both Basque and Spanish, and was identified from its inception with extreme Basque nationalism, linked to the radical Basque party People's Unity. This paper was closed down in July 1998, its owners being charged with inciting terrorism, and its management team were jailed (although they were released in 1999). A new daily with a similar approach, *Gara*, appeared just six months after the closure of *Egin* [3.2.2.3]. This is now the paper most closely associated with radical Basque nationalism and the one used by ETA to give advance warning of its attacks. The same fate befell another newspaper of that ilk, called *Euskaldunon Egunkaria*, which had been founded in 1990 and had published exclusively in Basque. It was closed down in 2003. The arrest of the paper's editor and board of directors led to widespread protests in the Basque Country and allegations of torture and mistreatment. It too was replaced by a similar substitute called *Berria*.

Along with such papers as these, there is an abundance of regional papers published in Castilian, and the press market as a whole is, in fact, highly regionalized. Outside Madrid, which is obviously a special case, there is only one region – Castile-La Mancha – with no paper of its own apart from purely local dailies. Elsewhere, regional dailies in total comfortably outsell national ones. And, apart from in Andalusia where *ABC* is the most widely read individual paper, the best-selling daily is invariably a regional title. Indeed, in Asturias, the Canaries, Galicia and Valencia such papers fill the top three places, and in the Basque Country the top four.

Many regional papers form part of groups, some of which also own national dailies. One of the most notable of these is the Correo group, with a large stable of titles published mainly in the north of the country, including the Bilbao-based daily *Correo* itself (formerly titled *El Correo Español/El Pueblo Vasco*), *El Diario Vasco* and *El Norte de Castilla*, as well as the Andalusian titles *Ideal* and *Sur*. Controlled by conservative Basque business interests, the Correo group now sells more dailies than any other proprietor in Spain. It also became involved in the private television market, acquiring a 25 per cent share in Telecinco [10.4] in 1996, and has since gone on to become part of a large media conglomerate called Vocento. The latter was formed from the merger (in 2001) of Correo with another publishing house (*casa/empresa editorial*) called Prensa Española, which owns *ABC* as well as five regional papers. Other important newspaper groups owning several regional titles each are Prensa Ibérica, which includes the various regional editions of *La Opinión* as part of its stable, and the Zeta group, publishers of *El Periódico de Cataluña*.

Several of these groups also control sports newspapers. Zeta, for example, publishes *Sport*; PRISA, owners of El País, also own *As*, while Godó, the group that publishes *La Vanguardia*, also owns *El Mundo Deportivo*. The biggest-selling sports newspaper, however, is *Marca*, which has an estimated readership of some 2.3 million. This makes it the daily paper with the highest readership in Spain, if we discount the freesheet (*diario gratuito*) *20 Minutos* (with 2.5 million readers).

Marca in its turn is owned by a publishing house called Unidad Editorial, who also publish *Expansión*, one of the five business newspapers published daily in Spain. The latter has the highest circulation of all the business papers (approaching 80,000), and is consequently the one with the largest readership, currently estimated to be around 175,000. The other business dailies, in order of readership level, are *Negocio y Estilo de Vida*, *Cinco Días*, *La Gaceta de los Negocios* and *El Economista*.

Finally, it is worth pointing out that, in line with developments in other countries, many Spanish newspapers and magazines now make copious amounts of material available online. The widespread availability of broadband (*banda ancha*) makes it easy for consumers to download a digital version (*edición digital*) of their favourite publication. Indeed, the access that is available globally means that it is more difficult to be accurate about true readership figures, even if the digital editions of newspapers differ somewhat from the paper versions. Some are available free; others on subscription.

The internet (*Red*) clearly represents a threat to hardcopy versions of newspapers, and the response of the papers to it, in Spain as elsewhere, has been to offer more extensive coverage and a greater range of specialized supplements to encourage customers to keep buying the paper edition.

10.3 Radio

Spaniards are avid radio listeners (*oyentes*). On average, they tune in to radio stations for more than 100 minutes per day, and, of all the Spanish communications media, radio is the one which has experienced the most spectacular growth since the death of Franco. The first peak in that growth occurred during the period of the transition to democracy. In 1975, an average of 7.5 million Spaniards listened to the radio on a daily basis. By 1982, that figure had risen to 16 million. Since the late 1970s, successive issues of new licences have given rise to 'battles of the airwaves' (*guerra de las ondas*), with not only the broadcasters but also the government showing scant regard for national and international regulations limiting the number of radio stations (*emisoras*), most of which are local.

Politically, while the press constituted the key forum for discussion of issues relating to political change in the late 1970s, the importance of radio was firmly underlined on the night of 23 February 1981, the so-called 'night of the transistors', (*noche de los transistores*) when the Spanish people anxiously followed the events unfolding in the Cortes in Madrid on their radios, as an attempt was made by Colonel Tejero and his civil guard officers to carry out a coup and remove the democratically-elected government of the country [0.3.3].

By then, the state broadcasting station Radio Nacional de España (*RNE*) had been on the air for more than forty years, but new radio formats had already emerged, with new types of news magazine programmes being broadcast, such as 'Matinal', 'Hora 25' and 'Protagonistas'. In the late 1970s, the UCD government distributed some 300 or so new FM radio licences, mainly to sympathetic business and media interests. Some of these were survivors from the Franco era such as COPE, SER and Cadena Rato, while others were new groups formed around that time, notably Radio 80 and Antena 3. When the Socialist government distributed a further set of licences a decade later, the same pattern was repeated, although in this case the recipients of licences were often local authorities controlled by the governing party.

RNE had functioned as an arm of the government's propaganda machine during the Franco era, along with the other groups of stations owned and run by the National Movement at the time. The latter came together in 1972 as Radio Cadena Española, then merged with RNE in 1977, and in 1980 both merged with the state TV broadcaster, TVE [10.4], to become a new state company called Corporación Radiotelevisión Española, or RTVE.

Despite the emergence of a myriad of private and regional stations, RNE has maintained its strong position as one of the market leaders and its news coverage has a high level of credibility at national and international level. In line with trends among state-owned broadcasters in other countries, it has undergone several restructuring processes, converting it into a number of different channels, including channels dedicated exclusively to news, classical music and general pop music. Currently, it is structured as follows:

> *Radio 1*: general station
> *Radio Clásica*: classical music
> *Ràdio 4*: Catalan language programming
> *Radio 5 Todo Noticias*: 24-hour news coverage
> *Radio Exterior de España*: Short-wave service, broadcast around the world

By far the most dominant group of stations at national level, however, is Cadena SER (*Sociedad Española de Radiodifusión*). With its origins in the early decades of the twentieth century, it was the most successful of the privately-run radio stations during the Franco era. During the transition period, it acquired some of the new FM licences distributed by the government. But it was when the Socialist government allowed it to acquire Antena 3 Radio in 1992 that it expanded to a position of real dominance in the market. The latter was a station created by newcomers to the radio scene Antena 3, which began to broadcast in May 1982 and which, by the end of 1984, had bought out the other major newcomer, Radio 80, thereby managing to occupy fourth place in listenership ratings. The leader in listenership at the time was SER itself, followed by RNE and COPE.

Meanwhile, the media group PRISA, owners of *El País* [10.2], had begun buying into SER and, by 1985, were its biggest shareholders. Consequently, an action was brought against PRISA on the grounds of unfair competition, given that they now controlled the leading Spanish newspaper and a major radio station. The fact that the PSOE government of the time were willing to allow such a takeover provoked accusations from their rivals that the Socialists were giving favourable treatment to PRISA. By contrast, at Antena 3 Radio, the chat shows (*tertulias*) of their big-name broadcasters such as Antonio Herrero and José María García were consistently critical of the Socialists and supportive of the political line adopted by the conservative daily *El Mundo* [10.2]. PRISA, however, continued to expand and grow in strength during the 1980s and, by 1992, had also gained a controlling interest in Antena 3 Radio. After being taken over by PRISA, Antena 3 Radio went out of existence, with Herrero and García moving on to COPE.

At this point, SER had over 50 per cent of the entire listenership of general Spanish radio, a situation which led to further severe criticism of the PSOE government, and to a case being brought against it in the Supreme Court, where they were instructed to undo the purchase as it was deemed to breach anti-monopoly legislation. Although this judgement was later upheld in the Constitutional Court, the station has not yet acted on it, and currently claims that new laws governing the development of digital television and the promotion of pluralism [10.4] imply that there is in fact no legal limit to the number of broadcasting licences which can be held by any one group.

The gap left by the disappearance of Antena 3 Radio was partly filled by a new group of stations created by the powerful National Association of the Blind of Spain (*Organización Nacional de Ciegos Españoles*/ONCE) [6.3.3]. The group was formed by bringing together Radio Amanecer, acquired by ONCE in 1989, and the stations belonging to the old Cadena Rato and bought by ONCE in 1990. Onda Cero's star presenter for many years (until he moved to Punto Radio in 2004) was the veteran Luis del Olmo, who had been broadcasting on a succession of radio stations since the early 1950s. His programme 'Protagonistas', noted for its engagement with political issues and the social commitment of its presenter, was brought by him to Onda Cero and helped contribute to that station's early initial success, with the result that it quickly rose to third-ranking position in terms of listenership. Onda Cero was sold on to Telefónica in 1999, and was subsequently amalgamated with Antena 3 to form the Antena 3 Group. The main shareholder in that group is currently the publishing house Planeta, the biggest publishers of Spanish-language books in the world and owners of the newspapers *La Razón* and *Avui* [10.2].

Cadena COPE (*Cadena de Ondas Populares de España*) is a privately-owned network which has survived since Franco times, and is currently ranked second in listenership figures, although it remains some distance behind the dominant leader in general radio (SER). The group is controlled by a number of organizations associated with the Catholic Church. Its editorial content and political stance are generally seen as being sympathetic to the People's Party and as supporting a more conservative social agenda, in contrast particularly to that of SER. One of its flagship programmes is again a morning magazine programme with a star presenter. This one is called 'La Mañana' and is hosted by Federico Jiménez Losantos, a controversial figure who has gained notoriety, among other things, for calling on the King to abdicate and for vehemently supporting the version of the 11-M massacre espoused by the PP [9.5.4].

The number of public radio stations increased enormously with the advent of regional radio in the 1980s (to be followed, even more significantly, by regional television). These are funded partly by the autonomous governments and partly through revenue raised from advertising (*publicidad*). The first to appear were those based in the old 'historical communities' of Catalonia, the Basque Country and Galicia (Catalunya Ràdio, Radio Euskadi and Radio Galicia), and these were followed by radio stations for the Community of Madrid, Valencia and Andalusia. By the end of the decade, regional radio had become general throughout Spain.

Since then, radio in Spain has gone from strength to strength, both in terms of general radio (*radio generalista*) and specialist stations (*radio temática*). The discussion programmes on the former, in particular, provide and respond to many of the talking points of millions of Spaniards. In line with developments in print media and television, radio has been able to exploit the possibilities offered by more widespread internet availability in Spain and around the world. This has meant that listeners have enhanced access to radio stations via the Web and that they can download podcasts (*descargar podcasts*) of radio programmes or parts of them.

10.4 Television

Probably more than elsewhere, television is today the most important of the mass media in Spain. Almost all households have a set, and the average Spaniard watches television for nearly four hours a day. Two million people watch for more than ten hours, while 85 per cent of the population over the age of four years watch at least some television every day. The country is not unique in its addiction to television: in the UK, for instance, the average viewing time is more than four hours per day, while the figure for the average American household is over eight hours per day.

Even if news programmes (*telediarios*) play a relatively minor role in contemporary schedules (*programación*), TV's potential influence is enormous. One of the key features of Spanish television is its strong links to politics, and the role played by politicians in the running of the state television service in particular. A striking early example of this was the use made of television during the transition to democracy by PM Adolfo Suárez, who had been Director of RTVE during 1969–73 [10.1].

In fact, since its inception as TVE in 1956, Spain's national broadcaster has been closely linked to the political establishment. The legal framework put in place when the state company RTVE was established in 1980 was the Spanish Radio and Television Statute (*Estatuto de la Radio y Televisión Española*). Explicitly aimed at achieving objectivity and effective financial control of RTVE, it was meant to ensure minimal political involvement in the TV and radio stations that fell within its ambit, but its rules are not always strictly adhered to.

That legislation stipulated that the twelve members of the Board of Governors (*Consejo de Administración*) would be appointed by Parliament and that the government would appoint a Director General on the advice of the Board. These appointments were meant to last for the duration of the government's tenure, and, in theory, the DG could only be dismissed on professional grounds.

In reality, their terms have generally been considerably shorter than that, and governments have taken the opportunity to either dismiss Directors General or to put pressure on them to resign, whenever the politicians were unhappy with the treatment that government policies were receiving. The result has been that the positions of both the DG and the Board have been very unstable over the history of the station, and it has been difficult for successive DGs to establish strategies and to implement them. Rather, there has been constant flux and shifting in the management and administration of RTVE, with the resultant poor planning and inefficiency that that entails. Revised terms for the station, drawn up in 2006, mean that its legal status now more resembles that of a private company (although it is obviously still in state hands). In a bid to make the station more impartial, this revision also introduced a longer period of office for the Board – six years, two longer than that of government – as well as a new method of appointing a DG, who must now have the support of two thirds of the deputies in Parliament.

Partly due to its chronic inability to make long-term financial plans, partly from the refusal of government during the period 1983 to 1993 to subsidize the public broadcaster, and partly due to the competition which the arrival of private TV stations brought about from 1990 onwards, the station's finances have been in a notoriously sorry state for many years. Added to this, there have been frequent reports of mismanagement of funds and spending splurges. Some of the latter have led to well-publicized scandals, such as the case of Pilar Miró who was accused of spending up to eight million pesetas on clothes and gifts during her time as Director-General between 1986 and 1989. At the time that its governance was changed in

2006, a re-structuring plan was also introduced, aimed at getting the station's finances under control. Under this plan, a number of cost-cutting measures have been put into effect, the most notable being a massive reduction in staffing.

A similar scenario exists with public television at regional level (*televisiones autonómicas*). In the 1980s, even before private television was allowed to operate, permission was given for regional stations to begin broadcasting. As with regional radio, this occurred first in the historical communities, the justification being the need that those regional governments felt to promote the languages of their regions.

The first of these was a Basque station, now called Basque Radio and Television (*Euskal Irrati Telebista/EiTB*), which began broadcasting at the end of 1983. The following year TV-3, run by the Catalan Broadcasting Corporation (now called the *Corporació Catalana de Ràdio i Televisió/CCRTV*), came on the air. Despite the justification relating to promotion of the language, before long the Basque station had opened a purely Spanish-language channel. Regional channels soon followed in the other most populous regions (Telemadrid, Canal 9 in Valencia and Canal Sur in Andalusia), and, later, stations were set up in the Canary Islands, Extremadura, Asturias, Castile-La Mancha and other autonomous communities. Several of these regional channels claim high audience shares (*audiencias*), especially in Catalonia and Madrid.

In these stations also, the Director General and the Board are elected by the regional parliaments (with the latter requiring either a two-thirds or three-fifths majority of votes). They are therefore subject to a considerable degree of control from the respective regional governments. The result of this is that each of the stations tends to have an identifiable political bias, generally related to the party that happens to hold the reins of power.

In the case of state television and the public regional stations, funding sources comprise not just advertising, which provides the bulk of their income, and the sale of programmes, but also considerable government funding in the form of direct grants. There is no TV licence fee in Spain. As a result, not only is there a tendency towards political bias among these stations but there is a drain on public finances at both national and regional level. In total, between state television and the stations in the autonomous communities, the Spanish taxpayer currently contributes more than €2 billion per annum to fund public television. The funding being provided by the Catalan government to CCRTV for the period 2006–2009, for instance, is of the order of €1,100 million. This is a major source of grievance for the private television sector, which must rely solely on commercial activity for its income and considers that these grants constitute unfair competition. As a consequence, the latter has been calling for strict limits to be placed on the capacity of public television to generate funds from advertising.

Private television was introduced into Spain with the Private Television Act (*Ley de Regulación de la Televisión Privada*), passed in 1988 after a long period of gestation and much controversy. While in opposition (before 1982), the Socialist party expressed their dissatisfaction with the proposals. Extolling the virtues of public broadcasting, they alleged that private TV would be manipulated by business interests. Once they were in power, they took a different view, and eventually passed the Act in May 1988. The legislation abolished RTVE's monopoly on the right to broadcast, and set up a company, known as *Retevisión*, to manage the network. In addition it provided for the creation of three private TV stations (*televisiones privadas*), and set conditions for the concession of licences and their subsequent operation.

Of the six bidders who submitted proposals, those that eventually received licences were Antena 3, Tele 5 (since re-branded as Telecinco) and Canal Plus. The business interests behind these stations have been varied from the start, and, in the case of the first two, have been very unstable as shareholdings have changed hands frequently since they started broadcasting. Initially, no one individual or company could own more than 25 per cent of the total shares, and foreign involvement was also limited to a maximum of 25 per cent.

Many of the first shareholders in these stations were newspaper groups or publishing houses. Godó, publishers of *La Vanguardia* [10.2], were the original owners of Antena 3 as part of a consortium. In 1992 they were ousted by Zeta, publishers of the weekly magazines *Interviú* and *Tiempo* as well as *El Periódico* and *Sport* [10.2]. The publishing house Anaya originally owned Telecinco in conjunction with ONCE and three other investors, the most important of which was Fininvest (owned by the Italian business magnate and politician Silvio Berlusconi). PRISA, publishers of *El País* [10.2] owned Canal Plus, in partnership with the French station of the same name and a number of banks. Only the latter has proven to be a stable financial entity.

The private TV stations brought about a revolution in the habits of Spain's viewers (*televidentes*). Antena 3 was the first of the three to start broadcasting (in 1990) and it is currently the leading television station in terms of audience share, with about 23 per cent of viewers tuning in on a daily basis. It has had considerable success from the start, especially with home-grown sitcoms (*telecomedias*) such as 'Farmacia de guardia', although its attempts at producing 'reality TV' have been less fruitful. Other successes for the channel have included the Spanish edition of 'The Simpsons' and UEFA football matches. Its popular talkshow, 'El diario de Patricia', hosted by Patricia Gaztañaga, achieved notoriety in 2007 when a guest on the programme, who had unsuccessfully proposed on air to his ex-girlfriend, attacked and killed her five days after the show was aired.

Politically, Antena 3 is perceived as being broadly sympathetic to the PP, and has been so especially since, in 1998, Zeta's holding in the company passed into the hands of the former state telecommunications monopoly Telefónica [5.4.1], which at the time was controlled by a close associate of former PM José María Aznar. Telefónica went on to build up a major media empire through its media arm Admira, which acquired the radio station Onda Cero [10.3] as well as a stake in the publisher Unidad Editorial, whose stable includes Spain's top business and sports newspapers as well as the daily *El Mundo* [10.2].

Telecinco quickly followed Antena 3 on to air, and has since then been generally placed just behind that station in terms of audience share. It was created by Berlusconi, whose company, now called Mediaset Investimenti, currently owns just over 50 per cent of the station, in partnership with Vocento, owners of the Correo group of newspapers and of the daily *ABC* [10.2], and other smaller shareholders. The extent of Berlusconi's involvement has not always been clear, and indeed has given rise on occasion to judicial investigations [9.1.4].

Telecinco is essentially a commercial operation, and gives correspondingly little weight to news. Along with some homegrown drama, it has had a lot of success with American shows such as the various 'CSI' series, 'Beverly Hills', 'The X-Files', 'Twin Peaks', etc. It airs a highly successful daytime show, 'El programa de Ana Rosa', as well as offering the Spanish version of 'Big Brother' (*Gran Hermano*) and some other reality TV shows. The station has begun to move in the direction of digital TV, converting its production facilities and broadcasting two new digital channels, one devoted to cinema and the other to sport.

The third of the original licensees was Canal Plus, owned by a consortium headed by Canal Plus France and the PRISA group (through Sogecable) [10.2]. It was a subscription channel (*canal de abono*), transmitted on a scrambled signal, which meant that the viewer needed to buy a decoder (*descodificador*) in order to watch it, apart from the six hours per day during which it broadcast free to air. Its audience share was therefore considerably lower than that of the other two private channels or that of TVE1. Its strategy, however, was to occupy the high end of the market, prioritizing technical innovation and programming which included big football matches and new movies. This ensured that it operated on a sound financial basis, and it was in fact highly profitable. As with PRISA's flagship newspaper *El País* [10.2], it was broadly sympathetic to the Socialists, and flourished especially in the heyday of the PSOE during the early 1990s.

When the conservative PP government came to power in 1996, however, it seemed bent on cutting PRISA down to size. Thus the PP openly backed PRISA's rival Zeta [10.2] over the rights to screen top Spanish League football games, and attempted to prevent Sogecable from operating. The latter move gave rise to a protracted legal dispute, which the Supreme Court eventually decided against PRISA in 2001, but which the latter failed to implement, claiming that the decision was unconstitutional.

Good fortune came the way of Canal Plus and Sogecable/PRISA in 2005, however, when the new Socialist government agreed to their request to increase the amount of time that Canal Plus was allowed to air unscrambled broadcasts from six to 24 hours per day. By that time, Canal Plus had become Europe's third-largest pay TV station, and this move meant that it could finally become another 24-hour free-to-air channel. It also meant that the analogue frequencies which had carried Canal Plus could be used for other purposes.

These developments allowed Sogecable to create a new private channel called Cuatro which began broadcasting in November 2005, opting for a formula based mainly on American TV series and football matches. The new channel scored a major coup when it secured the right to broadcast many of the 2006 World Cup matches. Its audience share has gradually increased to the point where it now commands a respectable 8 per cent.

In 2005 also, the government removed the ban that had existed on companies holding more than a 50 per cent share in the radio market. This was also good news for PRISA as it meant that the 2001 Supreme Court verdict would not have to be acted on and that PRISA could continue as the legal owners of Antena 3 Radio [10.3].

From November 2005 the PSOE government's National Plan for Digital Television obliged all national TV stations to broadcast in digital format, and digital terrestrial television (*televisión digital terrestre/TDT*) began to be rolled out, to include both regional and local stations as well. By 2010, analogue TV will have disappeared from the Spanish television scene altogether, and, under the terms of the deal which allowed Canal Plus to go free-to-air, other media groups have been allowed to broadcast up to four channels each.

The change-over to digital TV not only brings with it an improvement in the technical quality of the signal received by suitably equipped television sets, but also allows for a huge increase in the number of channels offered. Already the list of national Spanish channels being broadcast amounts to more than twenty. A similar number of public regional channels are being aired in the various Autonomous Communities. Of those national and regional channels, at least a dozen are also broadcast internationally. Meanwhile, there are dozens of local TV stations, many of which operate as parts of networks, such as Popular TV which is owned by COPE, Localia TV, owned by PRISA and Une TV which belongs to Telecinco.

Further complexity is added to this situation by the fact that hundreds of channels now broadcast on cable and satellite platforms. These offer the wide range of options (*oferta televisiva*) that are now available in most developed countries, including Spanish-operated channels specializing in areas such as sport or movies as well as the international channels that offer news, sport, music, documentaries, etc., around the world. Spanish viewers have responded accordingly, welcoming both the increased provision and the opportunity to purchase the new high-specification television sets that have tended to go with it.

Also in line with international developments, one important recent trend is in the direction of integrating voice and/or video concurrently with pure data, or 'packetizing' (*paquetización*). This means that operators of cable and satellite broadcasting systems collaborate with telephone companies to offer the consumer a combination of television, telephone and internet. Such a three-part deal (called *triple play* in Spanish) is currently being developed by Sogecable in collaboration with Telefónica. With the increasing availability of broadband, and the massive expansion of the Spanish mobile phone industry (*telefonía móvil*), such options are likely to become more commonplace.

Already, the overlap between these various technologies is well advanced. In January 2008, when Antena 3 was launching a new series of the programme 'Los hombres de Paco', it offered consumers a preview of the first episode of the series over the internet, 36 hours before it was broadcast on TV. Over four million people still watched the television programme – nearly a quarter of all viewers on the day. A few days later, TVE1 followed suit with one of their programmes. Consumers can access programmes, and copious amounts of information about programmes, on the TV stations' websites (*páginas Web*), as well as facilities for various types of interaction.

In itself, of course, no amount of technological change will do much to improve the overall quality of the programmes. Most Spaniards would acknowledge that their various channels are dominated now as in the past by poor-quality entertainment (*telebasura*), with quizzes (*concursos*), variety and gossip shows, reality TV, sports and American series being the staple of most of them. Taking its cue from what has happened elsewhere in Europe, however, the Spanish government has at least compensated somewhat for the obsession with American-produced programmes by bringing in regulations that require TV stations to direct a proportion of their earnings towards domestic film production.

10.5 Glossary

agencia de información (f)	news agency
agencia de noticias (f)	(see *agencia de información*)
audiencia (f)	audience share (radio, TV)/readership (press)
banda ancha (f)	broadband
campaña mediática (f)	media campaign
canal de abono (m)	(TV) subscription channel
casa editorial (f)	publishing house
censura (f)	censorship
concurso (m)	(TV) quiz
Consejo de Administración (m)	Board of Governors (of Spanish Television Authority)
descargar podcasts	to download podcasts
descodificador (m)	decoder (to view subscription TV channels)
diario gratuito (m)	freesheet (free newspaper)
diario informativo (m)	news daily
difusión (f)	sales (of newspapers/magazines)
dominical (m)	weekend supplement/edition of newspaper
edición digital (f)	digital version of a publication
emisora (f)	(radio) broadcasting station
empresa editorial (f)	publishing company
famosos (mpl)	celebrities
guerra de las ondas (f)	'battle of the airwaves' (proliferation of competing radio stations)
libertad de expresión (f)	freedom of expression
medios (de comunicación de masas) (mpl)	(mass) media
noche de los transistores (f)	'night of the transistors' (night of failed coup on 23 February 1981)
oferta televisiva (f)	range of TV stations
oyentes (mpl)	(radio) listeners
página Web (f)	web page
paquetización (f)	packetizing (integration of TV, telephone and Internet)
periódico deportivo (m)	sports newspaper
prensa amarilla (f)	(see *prensa sensacionalista*)
prensa del corazón (f)	gossip magazines
prensa del Movimiento (f)	Francoist press
prensa sensacionalista (f)	sensationalist press (e.g., UK tabloids)
programación (f)	TV/radio schedule
publicidad (f)	advertising
público (m)	audience; readership
radio generalista (f)	general radio
radio temática (f)	specialist radio
Red (f)	the internet, the Web
revista de actualidad (f)	current affairs magazine
semanal (m)	weekly (magazine, etc.)
suplemento (m)	supplement
telebasura (f)	poor-quality TV programmes
telecomedia (f)	sitcom

telediario (m)	TV news programme
telefonía móvil (f)	mobile phone industry
televidentes (mfpl)	(television) viewers
televisión digital terrestre/TDT (f)	digital terrestrial television
televisiones autonómicas (fpl)	TV stations run by regional governments
televisiones privadas (fpl)	private TV stations
tertulia (radiofónica) (f)	radio chat show
tirada (f)	circulation (of paper)

The regions

This chapter gives pen-portraits of Spain's seventeen autonomous regions (*Comunidades Autónomas*/CCAA) and two 'autonomous cities'. They include the principal geographic and demographic features of each region, its politics, economy and media landscape, as well as any distinctive cultural characteristics. In addition, a number of basic statistics are summarized at the end of the chapter, in Table 11.1. It should be noted that the focus here is on regions' internal affairs. The impact on Spanish politics as a whole of regionalists – regionally-based parties which aim to protect regional interests – is dealt with in Chapter 3 [3.2].

11.1 Andalusia

Regional capital: Seville (*Sevilla*)
Main population centres: Seville (704,000), Málaga (560,000), Córdoba (322,000), Granada (238,000), Jerez de la Frontera (196,000), Almería (185,000), Huelva (145,000), Cádiz (130,000), Jaén (116,000), Marbella (124,000), Algeciras (111,000), Dos Hermanas (112,000)
Official name of regional government: *Junta de Andalucía*
Regional First Minister: Manuel Chaves (PSOE)
Composition of parliament following most recent regional election (2008): Andalusian Socialist Party (PSOE-A) 56; People's Party (PP) 47; Andalusian United Left-Greens (IULV-CA) 6

With almost 8 million inhabitants, Andalusia (*Andalucía*) is Spain's most populous region as well as being its second-largest by area. Andalusia's people live overwhelmingly in relatively large settlements – it has more cities with over 100,000 inhabitants than any other region – between which lie vast tracts of virtually uninhabited land. While the broad, low-lying valley of the Guadalquivir river forms the region's heart, it also includes such major mountain ranges as the Sierra Morena and the Sierra Nevada, the latter of which includes mainland Spain's highest peak, the Mulhacén. And, whereas Andalusia is blessed by a generally Mediterranean climate and magnificent scenery, both coastal and inland, it also suffers severe environmental problems, in the form of desertification [8.2.2] and the pollution caused by mining activities [8.1.2].

Many of the traditions and customs popularly associated with Spain, such as bullfighting and flamenco dancing, are in fact essentially Andalusian. This distinctive character has various roots, notably the region's lengthy occupation by the Moors – its name comes from the Arabic *al-Andalus* – and the strong gypsy presence there. With the prospect of devolution in the late 1970s feelings of regional identity acquired a new strength and coherence, ensuring that Andalusia joined the group of regions endowed with a higher level of autonomy [3.1.2].

One aspect of this awakening was the establishment of the Andalusian Regionalist Party (*Partido Andalucista*/PA) [3.2.3.1], which has remained a feature of the region's political landscape ever since. Indeed, from 1996 to 2004 the PA was a junior partner in the region's coalition government. Its success was strictly limited, though, not least by constant friction between supporters in different cities and provinces. In 2000, a breakaway group called the Socialist Party of Andalusia (*Partido Socialista de Andalucía/PSA*) formed – not to be confused with the PSOE in Andalusia, often referred to as the Andalusian Socialist Party (*PSOE-A*). To date the PSA has not had any significant success at the polls. Indeed, in the most recent regional election in 2008, the PA, the PSA and a range of other regionalist groupings ran together in an alliance called Andalusian Coalition (*Coalición Andalucista/CA*), and yet failed to secure even one seat.

As a result the regional government continues to be (effectively) controlled by the PSOE-A, as it has been since its foundation. Regional premier Manuel Chaves, a former central government minister, has been in office since 1991, and is one of the PSOE's most powerful 'barons' [2.3.4]. The communist-led United Left (IU) has seen its backing reduced over the years, although in the 2008 regional election, in coalition with Greens (IULV-CA), it managed to hold on to its six seats, a performance which was out of line with the general pattern of poor results that it obtained across the country in the general election held on the same date.

The conservative People's Party (PP) gained ground during the 1990s, in line with its improved performance in Spain generally. It even outpolled the Socialists in four of the region's eight provinces at the 2000 general election. However, it then slipped back in the 2004 election, only to increase its share of the vote again in 2008. It also improved its position in the regional election held on the same date, securing 47 seats, an increase of ten on 2004.

The Andalusian Statute of Autonomy was revised in 2007 [3.2.3.1], and the new text was approved by referendum in the region with a huge majority in favour (88 per cent). The term 'national reality' was introduced into the new text to describe Andalusia. This designation means that it approaches the status of 'historic nationality' accorded to the Basque Country, Catalonia and Galicia, but without quite having that status. The Statute also had the effect of extending the powers of the regional government in the areas of taxation and the administration of justice.

The two main public television channels are Canal Sur and Canal 2 Andalucía, to which was added (in 1996) a third, Andalucía Televisión, which broadcasts internationally. Newspaper readership is low, especially when one considers that the region is one of only two where the top-selling daily is the specialist sports title *Marca*. It is also atypically distributed in Spanish terms. Thus Andalusia is the only region where the most-read news daily is the conservative *ABC* [10.2], which was originally based in Seville. At the same time, though, papers produced in the region account for almost three-quarters of total readership. Yet none is a truly regional daily; each essentially serves its own city and province. The most important are *Diario Sur* and *Ideal* [10.2], printed in Málaga and Granada respectively, while *Diario de Cádiz*, *Córdoba* and *Diario de Sevilla*, the last a newcomer, all have significant readerships.

Farming remains central to Andalusia's economy, and indeed the region is the country's leading agricultural producer, with an emphasis on the traditional products of the region, wheat, olives and vines. More recently, efforts have been made to reduce the over-dependence on these, with an increase in the cultivation of other crops, including rice, beet and sunflowers. But with isolated exceptions, such as the market gardeners of Almería and Huelva [5.3.1], the sector is far from efficient, partly due to the legacy of large, unproductive estates (*latifundios*).

The Franco regime attempted to foster industry through the creation of growth poles (*polos de desarrollo*), which led to the development of chemical production in Huelva, shipbuilding around Cádiz bay and vehicle production at Linares, near Jaén. Yet precisely these industries were then disproportionate victims of industrial restructuring in the 1980s [5.1.2].

Consequently, Andalusia has been hard hit over the years by unemployment [5.2.4.1]. At its worst, in the early 1990s, joblessness in the region stood at around 30 per cent, with as many as three-quarters of young people out of work. The figures have improved somewhat of late, but remain among the worst in Spain after Ceuta, Melilla and Extremadura, and only the last of these regions has lower living standards than Andalusia. Massive investment in infrastructure, much of it co-financed by the European Union [4.2.2], and in the 1992 Seville Expo, appears to have had little impact, although the region has benefited from the development of a high-speed train (*Alta Velocidad Española/AVE*) which now connects both Seville and Málaga to Madrid.

Perhaps the key economic driver in Andalusia, however, is tourism. This is one of the warmest regions in Europe, and it has for many years attracted huge numbers of tourists, especially from northern European countries, most of whom come in search of beach holidays (*vacaciones de sol y playa*) at knock-down prices. Its famous coasts – the *Costa del Sol*, *Costa Tropical*, *Costa de Almería* and *Costa de la Luz* – are still the playgrounds of Europe. However, these same coastlines have suffered in varying degrees from the blight of uncontrolled building of apartments and hotels [8.2], even though its beaches manage to maintain relatively high standards of quality, a fact attested to by the total of 84 blue flags awarded to them in 2004.

11.2 Aragon

Regional capital: Saragossa (*Zaragoza*)
Main population centre: Saragossa (649,000)
Official name of regional government: *Diputación General*
Regional First Minister: Marcelino Iglesias (PSOE)
Composition of parliament following most recent regional election (2007): Socialist Party (PSOE) 30; People's Party (PP) 23; Aragonese Regionalist Party (PAR) 9; Aragonese Regionalist Committee (CHA) 4; United Left 1

Much of Aragon (*Aragón*) is mountainous and inhospitable – although often scenically beautiful, especially in the Pyrenean north – and has suffered severe depopulation over the last half century, a fact reflected in its very low population density – the second lowest of all Spain's regions after Extremadura. Moreover, given that almost 50 per cent of Aragonese live in Saragossa, the only settlement with a population of over 50,000, the average figure disguises the emptiness that characterizes much of Aragon.

The present-day region of Aragon formed only one, relatively unimportant part of the medieval 'Crown of Aragon', Castile's rival for the position of leading power in the Iberian peninsula. But it did form a distinct unit with considerable self-government within what was, in modern terms, a sort of federation. The experience has left a deeply-rooted feeling of identity among its inhabitants (known colloquially as *maños* and renowned for their constancy – or obstinacy, depending on one's viewpoint). It is reflected today in the pattern of newspaper readership, in which the *Heraldo de Aragón* far outranks all the Madrid-based titles.

Nonetheless, Aragon was granted only the standard level of autonomy in the first devolution round of the early 1980s [3.1.2]. This slight led to an upsurge of popular resentment later in the decade, effectively triggering a second round as part of which Aragon's powers were greatly extended. As part of these developments, the Aragonese Regionalist Party (*Partido Aragonés Regionalista/PAR*) [3.2.3.2] rose to become the second force in regional politics behind the Socialist PSOE. It was even able to claim the post of regional First Minister for a time as the price of helping the conservative People's Party (PP) to unseat the PSOE. Thereafter, however, the PAR lost some support and influence, while the regionalist vote was split by the emergence of a second, more left-wing grouping, the Aragonese Regionalist Committee (*Chunta Aragonesista/CHA*). As a result, the PP was able to consolidate itself as Aragon's largest party and the dominant force in its government. However, following the 1999 regional election the PAR joined forces with the Socialists to unseat the PP and form a PSOE-led coalition, which persists to the present.

Aragon's Statute of Autonomy was revised in 2007, and in it Aragon was accorded the status of 'historic nationality', previously reserved for the Basque Country, Catalonia and Galicia [3.2]. The Statute also extended the powers of the region in a number of areas including tax collection, the administration of justice and the creation of a regional police force. Other provisions include protection of the resources of the River Ebro, which is the source of diverted water for other regions. The Statute stipulates that specific quantities of water should be reserved for the use of the Aragonese.

Blessed by few natural advantages, Aragon was for centuries a rather poor region. In recent years its economy has been in transition from an agricultural base – with an important cereals sector – to one based on commerce and services, including tourism. The Ebro valley has emerged as an important development axis [5.3.5], with Saragossa as a key transport nexus within it. The PlAZA Logistics Complex (*Plataforma Logística de Zaragoza/PlAZA*), currently being completed near Saragossa airport, is set to become the biggest logistics and transport hub in southern Europe.

As a result of these developments, the region now has one of the country's lowest jobless rates and has seen a considerable increase in living standards, at least for the great majority of Aragonese living in the relatively small area affected. Their prosperity is nonetheless heavily dependent on a few major employers, notably the General Motors vehicles plant outside Saragossa.

The region is one of a small number that have been favoured with a high-speed train, the AVE [11.1], which in this instance links Saragossa – site of the Universal Exposition, *Expo 2008* – and Huesca to Madrid. It was only in 2006, however, that it acquired its own regional television station, Aragón Televisión.

11.3 Asturias

Regional capital: Oviedo
Main population centres: Gijón (274,000), Oviedo (215,000), Avilés (85,000)
Official name of regional government: *Gobierno del Principado de Asturias*
Regional First Minister: Vicente Álvarez Areces (PSOE)
Composition of parliament following most recent regional election (2007):
   Socialist Party (PSOE) 21; People's Party (PP) 20; United Left (IU) 4

Asturias is the cradle of the Spanish nation, since it was here that the long process of reconquest from the Moors began [0.1], specifically at Covadonga in the Picos de Europa mountains. Yet the same range divides Asturias geographically from the old Kingdom of Castile, of which it formed part, while the local dialect of Castilian (*bable*) is claimed by some to be a separate language – reasons enough for Asturias's status as one of Spain's traditional regions.

In modern times, the region's most distinctive feature was its industrial nature, the coal mines of its central valleys and the associated steel industry making it one of Spain's best-off areas. Since the 1970s, though, both sectors have been in crisis, leaving the region with grave economic problems and, in the former steel centre of Avilés, severe air pollution [8.1.1]. Since Spain's accession to the EU the situation has been aggravated by the difficulties of the previously important dairy industry [5.3.1]. The region's problems are compounded by lack of good communications and remoteness from major European markets. With above average unemployment rates, Asturias has slid down the league table of regional living standards to a position above only the poorest regions of the south.

The Asturian miners and steelworkers were traditionally staunch socialists, and their votes helped the PSOE to dominate regional politics in the 1980s. Conversely the decline of their industries severely hit the party which lost control of the regional government to the conservative People's Party (PP) in 1991. However, the PP's Asturian leaders soon fell out with their Madrid leadership. They eventually formed a breakaway grouping known as the Asturian Modernizing Union (*Unión Renovadora Asturiana/URAS*), whose modest success at the 1999 regional election helped return the Socialists to power. For the most recent regional election in 2007, URAS formed an alliance with the older Asturian Regionalist Party (Bable: *Partíu Asturianista/PAS*) but neither won any seats.

The regional institutions are located in Oviedo, one of the major population centres along with Gijón and the – now largely former – mining areas. The two main cities are very different in character, one an administrative centre, the other an industrial port, and have long been rivals. Each has its own daily: *La Nueva España*, the more widely read, being printed in Oviedo and *El Comercio* in Gijón. Both of them, and also *La Voz de Asturias*, outsell all the Madrid titles and between them dominate the market.

11.4 Balearic Islands

Regional capital: Palma (*Palma de Mallorca*)
Main population centre: Palma (375,000)

Official name of regional government: *Govern de les Illes Balears* (Catalan)
Regional First Minister: Francesc Antich (PSOE)
Composition of parliament following most recent regional election (2007): People's Party (PP) 28; Socialist Party (PSOE) 16; Majorcan Socialist Party-Nationalist Front-United Left-The Greens-Republican Left of the Balearic Islands (PSM-EN, EU-EV, ERIB) 4; Majorcan Union (UM) 3; Other local parties 8

In area terms the smallest of Spain's autonomous regions is that made up of the Balearic Islands (Catalan: *Illes Balears*). It consists of four islands, Majorca (*Mallorca*), Minorca (*Menorca*), Ibiza (*Eivissa*) and Formentera, of which Majorca is by far the most significant, containing some 80 per cent of the population. The islands, with their attractive climate, are fairly densely but evenly populated, with Palma as the only large city. Some 16 per cent of the population is non-Spanish – mainly affluent northern Europeans – which makes this the region with the highest proportion of foreign nationals in the country.

Historically the archipelago formed part of the 'Crown of Aragon' [11.2] and has a consequent tradition of self-rule, both as a unit and at the level of the individual islands, each of which has its own elected assembly (*consell*).

Most people on the Islands speak a form of Catalan, which has official status in the region. The regional government cooperates with the Catalan government in broadcasting material in Catalan in both directions, with Catalan television and radio stations being received on the Islands and, from the time it came into existence in 2005, the Balearic TV station (IB3) being received in Catalonia. The two main regional dailies, which comfortably outsell their rivals from the mainland, both appear in Castilian, however.

The Islands boast several political parties of their own, the most important being the Majorcan Socialist Party–Nationalist Front (*Partido Socialista Mallorquín-Entesa Nacionalista/PSM-EN*) and the more right-wing Majorcan Union (*Unió Mallorquín/ UM*). In fact they have a strong conservative tradition, and this made it possible for the regional government to be controlled by the People's Party from 1983 until 1999, when UM and PSM-EN, as well as smaller groupings from Ibiza and Formentera, joined with the PSOE to oust the PP and form a coalition government. The latter regained power with an absolute majority in 2003. At the most recent regional election in 2007, the PP again won most seats, but not enough to stop the PSOE getting back into government by forming a coalition with a range of regionalist parties.

Economically the Balearics have enjoyed considerable success over recent decades, and are now among Spain's most prosperous regions. Although there are some small-scale industries such as textiles and shoe manufacture, the Islands' advance has been based almost entirely on tourism, which makes up some 80 per cent of the economy by value, and the associated construction sector. There is awareness of the need to diversify both within and away from tourism, but efforts to do so have been hampered by the shortage of water on the Islands, which at times has to be supplied by tanker from the mainland.

The Islands' Statute of Autonomy was revised in 2007, augmenting the powers of the region in relation to taxation, justice and financial matters, making provision for the creation of a regional police force and strengthening the position of the Catalan language.

11.5 Basque Country

Regional capital: Vitoria (Basque: *Gasteiz*)

Main population centres: Bilbao (353,000), Vitoria (225,000), San Sebastián (Basque: *Donostia*) (183,000), Barakaldo (96,000), Getxo (85,000), Irún (60,000), Portugalete (48,000)

Official name of regional government: *Eusko Jaurlaritza* (Basque)/*Gobierno Vasco*

Regional First Miinister: Juan José Ibarretxe (PNV)

Composition of parliament following most recent regional election (2005):
Euzko Alderdi Jeltzalea-Basque Nationalist Party (EAJ-PNV)/Basque Solidarity (EA) 29; People's Party (PP) 15; Basque Socialist Party (PSE-EE) 18; Communist Party of the Basque Lands (EHAK) 9; Basque United Left (EB-IU) 3; Aralar 1

The Basque Country (Basque: *Euskadi*) lies at the meeting point of three very different parts of Spain: the Pyrenees, the Cantabrian coastal strip, and the Ebro valley on the edge of Spain's central tableland. Between them lies a region with a dramatic coastline of cliffs and coves, and consisting mainly of hill country rent by steep valleys. Today, though, few Basques live on the traditional upland farmsteads (*caseríos*). Instead the great majority are urban dwellers, in the Bilbao metropolitan area (*Gran Bilbao*), in the other cities and in numerous smaller centres.

The region may make up less than 1.5 per cent of Spain's territory – its three provinces are the country's smallest by area – yet it generates a very high proportion of foreign media coverage. The focus of attention is, of course, the area's strong nationalist movement. The impression often created is that the Basques are not really Spaniards at all – ironically, the nationalist argument in its most extreme form. As so often, the true picture is much more complex than that.

On the one hand there can be no doubt, not just that the region is different from the rest of Spain in many respects, but that most of its people feel a strong sense of common and distinct identity. But equally, when asked, the majority say that they feel both Basque and Spanish. And, at the same time, there are important differences within the region itself and among its inhabitants, so that it is often impossible to talk about what 'Basques' think or want.

Thus the Basque language (*euskera*) is nothing if not distinctive, being unrelated not just to Castilian Spanish but to any known tongue. But until recently the related culture was largely oral, its best-known expression a range of highly distinctive sports. By the 1950s the language's use was confined almost entirely to the countryside, while it was also divided into several very different dialects. From the 1960s on, attempts have been made to revive it on the basis of a specially constructed common form (*batua*), first through the creation of independent Basque-language schools (*ikastolak*) and later by the autonomous regional authorities. They have enjoyed considerable success. But even today most people in the Basque Country habitually use Spanish, especially in the region's southernmost province, Alava, where Basque cultural influence in general is very weak.

To a large extent it is the provinces that form the basis of Basque distinctiveness. Into the nineteenth century they enjoyed certain traditional rights (*fueros*), the best known being those of Vizcaya, associated with the town of Guernica (Basque: *Gernika*) and its Assembly Hall (*Casa de Juntas*). These included exemption from Spanish customs duties, and meant in effect that the Basque provinces (*Vascongadas*) were economically separate from the rest of Spain. What is more, even after the rights were suppressed in 1876 the provinces continued to collect their own taxes before remitting part of them as a reverse block grant (*cupo*) to the central government, as stipulated in regular financial agreements (*conciertos económicos*). In the case of Alava, which largely supported Franco's 1936 uprising [0.2], this privilege was retained even under his rule. And all three provinces continue to play an important part in Basques' perceptions and loyalties today.

In the arrangements for devolution made after Franco's death, the Basque Country's special situation was recognized by giving it privileged access to autonomy, the details of which were set out in its Statute of Autonomy [3.1.1]. Known as the Statute of Guernica, it was overwhelmingly approved by referendum in 1979, a result that underlined the strength of common Basque sentiment. Yet in a number of respects the Statute's provisions clearly reflected the special situation of the three provinces.

Thus devolution revived the system of financial agreements with Madrid, made not by the region, but with the individual provinces. Moreover, and uniquely in Spain, each of these has its own directly elected assembly (*Juntas Generales*) to oversee the provincial government (*Diputación Foral*). In the Basque Parliament, each of the three has equal representation, even though their populations differ widely. And, along with the other main institutions, the parliament is located in Vitoria, the capital of Alava, even though Bilbao is both the region's chief city and the cradle of its nationalist movement. The purpose was to give the Alavese a stake in a project for which many had no great enthusiasm.

Their feelings were exploited by a new political party, Alavese Unity (*Unidad Alavesa/UA*), which for a time in the 1990s attracted considerable support (see Table 3.2). However, by 2000 UA had effectively rejoined the mainstream conservative People's Party (PP) from which it had originally broken away. By that time the PP had moderated its initial sharp opposition to Basque self-rule and had accepted the region's autonomous status [2.4.3], all of which helped it to become the second strongest political force in the region in the elections held in 1998 and 2001. However, as soon as the PP won an absolute majority in parliament in Madrid in 2000, its attitude towards Basque nationalism began to harden. As a result of that shift, and possibly also because of the party's insistent attempt to blame the 11-M atrocity on ETA [9.5.4], its support dropped at the regional election of 2005, and it received fewer votes than the Basque Socialists (PSE-EE). The latter had traditionally enjoyed strong support in the region, but had seen that support eroded during the 1990s. It recovered to some extent in 2005, and consolidated its gains at the 2008 general election when it won nine of the 18 seats. The PSE-EE is the local organization of the PSOE in the Basque Country, although it also incorporates the regionalist grouping Basque Left (*Euskadiko Ezkerra/EE*).

Neither of the large Madrid-based parties has had much control over the political agenda in the Basque Country, however, since that agenda has generally been set by the nationalist movement, chiefly the Basque Nationalist Party (*Euzko Alderdi Jeltzalea-Partido Nacionalista Vasco/EAJ-PNV*, usually known as the PNV) [3.2.2.2]. Up to the 2008 election, the PNV had topped the poll at virtually every election, Spanish, regional or local, since 1977. Until 1986 it ran the region alone, and subsequently it has been the senior partner in a series of coalitions, until 1998 almost always including the PSE-EE. Since then, however, the PNV has governed together with Basque Solidarity (*Eusko Alkartasuna/EA*), and currently also with Basque United Left (*Ezker Batua/EB-IU*) [2.5.2]. EA split from the PNV in 1986 but at the 2001 and 2005 regional elections the two campaigned together [3.2.2.4].

Support for ETA's political wing has been in serious decline for over a decade. Originally that grouping was called People's Unity (*Herri Batasuna/HB*), but it was re-named Unity (*Batasuna*) in 2001. It was banned in 2003, however, for its alleged support of terrorism, although parties with similar ideologies and the same personnel have emerged at the various elections under a variety of names [3.2.2.4]. The two which are currently the most prominent are Basque Nationalist Action (*Acción Nacionalista Vasca/ANV*) – a party that achieved notable successes at the local elections in 2007 – and the Communist Party of the Basque Lands (*Partido Comunista de las Tierras Vascas/PCTV*; Basque: *Euskal Herrialdeetako Alderdi Komunista/EHAK*). Both of these parties are currently under threat of being banned also.

Relations between Madrid and the Basque government have been overshadowed in recent years by the announcement made by the Basque First Minister, Juan José Ibarretxe, that he intends to hold a referendum in the Basque Country in October 2008 on the issue of 'self-determination' (*autodeterminación*). By this is meant the question as to whether the Basque Country itself should be entitled to decide on the degree of autonomy or independence it has, without reference to the Spanish government.

Economically the Basque Country was distinguished by a rapid process of industrialization that began in the late nineteenth century. Industrialization acted as the trigger for nationalism [3.2.2.2], one of its offshoots being a separate Basque trade union organization [5.5.1.1]. Based originally on local iron ore reserves, it outlasted the exhaustion of the mines and saw the development of important steel and shipbuilding sectors in Bilbao and along the left bank (*margen izquierda*) of the Nervión estuary. In the 1960s industry spread out beyond this heartland to the valleys of Guipúzcoa and to Vitoria, which benefited from Alava's favourable location and financial privileges.

By the 1980s the farming and fishing so important to regionalists' view of the Basque Country were of only marginal importance. They were also hit badly by Spanish accession to the EU, while the traditional heavy industries were decimated by industrial restructuring [5.1.2]. Subsequently the region suffered from high levels of unemployment, especially among the young, and from a small but steady outflow of population. However, in recent years the efforts of successive regional governments have helped generate a gradual recovery, based partly on established industries, particularly machine tools, but also on the development of services. The modernized port of Bilbao has also played a significant part, with the striking new Guggenheim Museum, opened in 1997, attracting millions of visitors from Spain and abroad.

Finally, the Basque media landscape reflects many of the factors already mentioned. The two main regional television channels are ETB-1, which broadcasts exclusively in Basque, and ETB-2, which broadcasts in Spanish. The latter has an audience share of about one third – well ahead of any Spanish channel – while ETB-1's share stands at about 10 per cent. They are owned by the Basque Radio and Television Service (*Euskal Irrati Telebista/EiTB*) which also operates two international channels as well as five radio stations. Chief among the latter is Radio Euskadi, with 13 per cent of Basque listenership, just ahead of the Madrid-based SER. Two Basque-language daily newspapers, *Egin*, founded in 1977, and *Euskaldunon Egunkaria*, founded in 1990, were closed down in 1998 and 2003 respectively on the grounds of their alleged support for ETA [10.1], only to be replaced by similar papers called *Gara* and *Berria*. The market leaders in the region, however, both publish almost exclusively in Spanish; they are the Bilbao-based *Correo* and its San Sebastián stablemate *El Diario Vasco*.

11.6 Canary Islands

Regional capital: Las Palmas (*Las Palmas de Gran Canaria*)/Santa Cruz (*Santa Cruz de Tenerife*)

Main population centres: Las Palmas (377,000), Santa Cruz (223,000), La Laguna (144,000), Telde (98,000)

Official name of regional government: *Gobierno Canario*

Regional First Minister: Paulino Rivero Baute (CC)

Composition of parliament following most recent regional election (2005): Socialist Party (PSOE) 26; Canary Islands Alliance-Canary Islands Nationalist Party (CC-PNC) 17; People's Party (PP) 15; Canary Islands Alliance-El Hierro Independents (CC-AHI) 2

Located some 1000 kilometres from mainland Spain but a mere 100 from the coast of Africa, the Canary Islands (*Islas Canarias*) are unique among Spain's regions by dint of pure geography. As well as various uninhabited islets, the archipelago consists of Gran Canaria, Tenerife, Lanzarote, Fuerteventura, La Gomera, La Palma and El Hierro. Its considerable ecological value is attested by the fact that it contains no less than four of Spain's fourteen National Parks [8.3.1]. They contain a wealth of spectacular scenery, in particular various live volcanoes on Lanzarote and the extinct cone of Teide on Tenerife, Spain's highest point and a location which in 2006 was declared a World Heritage Site (*Patrimonio de la Humanidad*) by UNESCO.

The Islands' favourable climate supports a high density of population, most of which is concentrated on Gran Canaria and Tenerife. The two are traditional rivals, a situation reflected in the complex arrangements made for the regional institutions. Thus the regional parliament is located in Santa Cruz and the office of the Government Representative [1.5.2] in Las Palmas, while the regional First Minister's residence shuttles between the two cities every two years. In practice the regional ministries have offices in both cities, as does the Islands' television station, TV

Canaria. Their two best-selling dailies, *La Provincia* and *Canarias-7*, are printed in Las Palmas, the third, *El Día*, in Santa Cruz. All three have considerably larger readerships than the Madrid-based press.

Inter-island differences are also a feature of the Canaries' strong but hybrid regionalist movement. Some of its roots lie in left-wing activism during the 1970s, which was centred on Gran Canaria and at one point spawned an armed group, the 'Movement for the Self-Determination and Independence of the Canaries Archipelago' (MPAIAC). On Tenerife, by contrast, demands for autonomy came principally from centrist politicians.

Since 1986 these and factions from other islands have been united in the Canary Islands Alliance (*Coalición Canarias*/CC) [3.2.3.1]. Although there are ongoing tensions among its partners, CC has been the dominant political force in the regional parliament, governing in recent years as the senior partner in a coalition with the People's Party. This is despite the fact that the PSOE won more seats than CC in that parliament at the most recent regional election in 2007.

Long poor compared with mainland Spain, and still with a high unemployment rate of about 12 per cent, since the 1970s the Islands have experienced a considerable increase in their relative prosperity. This is based heavily on the tourist industry, which now accounts for 70 per cent of GDP and is made possible by a benign climate where temperatures are consistently pleasant almost all year round. A further factor in the Islands' advance has been recognition of the archipelago's unique situation in the form of special economic and fiscal arrangements. These involve exemption from certain taxes, as well as liberty of import and export.

Only one tenth of the territory is under cultivation, with most of that being devoted to growing cereals and potatoes, aimed at the peninsular Spanish market and the EU. Santa Cruz is the location of the country's oldest oil refinery, which, since it is situated within the city itself, is a cause of complaint from citizens unhappy with the pollution and security issues associated with it.

11.7 Cantabria

Regional capital: Santander
Main population centres: Santander (182,000), Torrelavega (55,000)
Official name of regional government: *Diputación Regional*
Regional First Minister: Miguel Ángel Revilla (PRC)
Composition of parliament following most recent regional election (2007):
People's Party (PP) 17; Cantabrian Regionalist Party (PRC) 12; Socialist Party (PSOE) 10

Historically an integral part of Old Castile, Cantabria is nevertheless geographically separate from Spain's central, Castilian plateau, perched on the northern slopes of the Picos de Europa and oriented towards the sea. The distinctive nature of its terrain is reflected in the popular term for the area – the Highlands (*La Montaña*). The name has been adopted by Cantabria's main daily, *Diario Montañés*, which utterly dominates the regional market, a further indication of the distinctiveness that led to the creation of the second-smallest of Spain's regions by population.

In line with its conservative traditions, Cantabria was one of only two regions governed throughout the 1980s by the Right, led latterly by the controversial figure of Juan Hormaechea. Having been ejected from the People's Party (PP), Hormaechea formed his own Cantabrian Progress Union (*Unión para el Progreso de Cantabria/UPCA*), which for a time proved strong enough to significantly destabilize regional politics. However, at the 1999 election the UPCA lost its last parliamentary seats, and the region was governed exclusively by the PP until they lost power after the 2003 regional election. Although on that occasion the PP won the highest number of seats of any party (18), it was ousted by a combination of the PSOE (13 seats) and the Cantabrian Regionalist Party (*Partido Regionalista de Cantabria/PRC*) which secured eight seats. The latter increased its strength at the 2007 election, again entering a coalition government with the PSOE, this time as the dominant partner.

Up until the 1970s dairying and a substantial steel industry brought the region a degree of prosperity. However, during the 1980s both these sectors suffered severe problems and the region slipped down the league of regional rankings. GDP per capita is now just slightly below the Spanish average, however, reflecting the fact that the region has experienced something of a recovery in recent years. As with the other regions along the north coast, it had been held back by poor communications and relative remoteness from major European markets. The newly-constructed Meseta motorway, connecting Santander with Castile, has mitigated these disadvantages somewhat, although this has been at considerable cost, since the difficult nature of the terrain has made this the most expensive motorway yet built in Spain. The status of Cantabria as a disadvantaged region changed from Objective 1 to Objective 2 in 2007, entailing a significant reduction in the amount of funding allocated to it by the EU.

The region was the birthplace, in 1857, of the Banco Santander, which is now Grupo Santander Central Hispano, the biggest banking group in the Eurozone and one of the biggest in the world.

11.8 Castile-la Mancha

Regional capital: Toledo
Main population centres: Albacete (162,000), Talavera de la Reina (84,000), Toledo (78,000), Guadalajara (75,000), Ciudad Real (70,000), Puertollano (50,000)
Official name of regional government: *Junta de Comunidades de Castilla-La Mancha*
Regional First Minister: José María Barreda (PSOE)
Composition of parliament following most recent regional election (2007):
Socialist Party (PSOE) 26; People's Party (PP) 21

Consisting of the arid southern half of Spain's central plateau, Castile-La Mancha (*Castilla-La Mancha*) is the most sparsely populated region of what is, by European standards, a rather empty country. A natural geographical unit, it has little historical basis – it is made up of New Castile but without its heart, Madrid, together with Albacete province, whose traditional links were with Murcia. As a result, it lacks a true centre. It is the only Spanish region without a significant daily newspaper of its own. Indeed, as in Andalusia, the sports daily *Marca* tops the readership rankings, with much of the remaining audience shared among the three main Madrid titles [10.2].

Castile-La Mancha is one of only two regions where no regionalist party has ever been represented in parliament. Indeed currently only the two largest Spanish parties have such representation. From 1983, when it was first established, up to 2004, the regional government was headed by the Socialist José Bono, who won an overall majority in parliamentary elections in the region on six occasions, and as a result became one of the PSOE's leading 'barons' [2.3.4]. In 2004 he resigned to take up the Defence portfolio in the Spanish government and was succeeded by José María Barreda who in turn went on to win an overall majority in the 2007 regional elections.

Although its inhabitants have a longer life expectancy than the average Spaniard, Castile-La Mancha has long been poor, and has suffered severe depopulation as a result. Its economy remains based on a rather inefficient agricultural sector, with the petrochemical complex at Puertollano representing its only major industry. However, parts of Toledo and Guadalajara provinces have obtained some spillover benefits from economic development around Madrid and, in the last decade or so, the region as a whole has experienced significant economic growth. The rate of industrial growth has been higher than the national average, as has growth in the construction sector. In line with the country as a whole, there has also been expansion in the services sector, especially tourism, as visitors discover the 'route of Don Quijote' and the other tourist attractions of the region. Together with better marketing of local food products these have brought an improvement in performance and moved the region away from the very foot of the regional prosperity league.

11.9 Castile-Leon

Regional capital: Valladolid

Main population centres: Valladolid (320,000), Burgos (174,000), Salamanca (160,000), Leon (137,000), Palencia (82,000), Ponferrada (67,000), Zamora (66,000)

Official name of regional government: *Junta de Castilla y León*

Regional First Minister: Juan Vicente Herrera Campo (PP)

Composition of parliament following most recent regional election (2007):

People's Party (PP) 48; Socialist Party (PSOE) 33; Leonese People's Union (UPL) 2

The region of Castile-Leon (*Castilla y León*) is not only Spain's largest by area but the most extensive such unit in the entire European Union; indeed, it is bigger than Portugal and several other EU member states. It consists of the northern half of Spain's central plateau, essentially the upper basin of the River Duero. Drained by emigration between 1950 and 1975, its population today is spread thinly and unevenly, concentrated mainly in the capitals of its various provinces.

A number of these, notably Burgos and, above all, Salamanca, are fine historic centres. They provide the main attraction of a growing tourist industry which has become a major factor in the regional economy. Traditionally that was based on cereals and these remain important today, although the main crop is now barley rather than wheat. The main industrial centre is Valladolid, which has managed to build on its designation by the Franco regime as a growth pole (*polo de desarrollo*) and to benefit from the establishment by the French car maker Renault of a major plant.

The establishment of Castile-Leon, which combines most of New Castile with the historically distinct – and older – region of Leon, was the cause of some controversy. Even once the merger was agreed the question of its headquarters remained, the new unit having no obvious natural or traditional capital. Eventually Valladolid's sheer size carried the day and all the region's political institutions were sited there, with its High Court located in Burgos as a concession to feeling there.

The lack of an undisputed regional centre continues to be reflected today in the pattern of newspaper readership. This is headed by the Valladolid-based *El Norte de Castilla*, the oldest newspaper in Spain, but with a considerably lower share than the leading titles in most other regions. The second most popular daily is the Madrid-based *El Mundo* – other nationwide papers also sell fairly well – while the third is the *Diario de León*. A number of other titles printed in the various provincial capitals also command significant market shares.

After a brief period of Socialist rule up to 1987 the region has been governed continuously by the Right, of which it is a traditional stronghold. An early regional First Minister was the future People's Party leader and Spanish Prime Minister, José María Aznar. Ever since the region's establishment the Leonese People's Union (*Unión del Pueblo Leonés/UPL*) has articulated resentment at Leon's incorporation into Castile, and regularly wins about a fifth of the votes in regional elections in Leon.

The region's original Statute of Autonomy came into force in 1983. It has been revised four times, most recently in 2007, with an entire section of the new document being devoted to setting out the role that the government of the region will have in managing and exploiting the water supplies associated with the river Duero. Other articles address issues such as the possibility of creating a regional police force and the transfer of responsibility for the administration of justice from Madrid to the region.

11.10 Catalonia

Regional capital: Barcelona
Main population centres: Barcelona (1,606,000), L'Hospitalet de Llobregat (248,000), Badalona (222,000), Sabadell (201,000), Terrassa (200,000), Tarragona (131,000), Lleida (126,000), Santa Coloma de Gramenet (119,000), Mataró (119,000), Reus (102,000), Girona (90,000), Cornella de Llobregat (84,000)
Official name of regional government: *Generalitat de Catalunya* (Catalan)
Regional First Minister: José Montilla (PSC)
Composition of parliament following most recent regional election (2006):
Convergence and Union (CiU) 48; Catalan Socialist Party (PSC) 37; Catalan Republican Left (ERC) 21; People's Party (PP) 14; Initiative for Catalonia–Greens–Alternative and United Left (ICV-EUiA) 12; Catalan Citizens' Party (CPC) 3

Catalonia (*Cataluña*/Catalan: *Catalunya*) is Spain's largest regional economy, with a GDP superior to that of several EU member states. Its population, second only to Andalusia, is unevenly distributed, being concentrated along the coast, above all in Barcelona and its surrounding satellite towns, and in a number of smaller inland centres such as Girona (Spanish: *Gerona*) and Lleida (Spanish: *Lérida*), both of which are now officially known by their Catalan names. The region lies across the most direct route into Spain from the EU's economic core area. In geographic terms, it resembles a microcosm of the country itself, the range of its landscapes passing from the high Pyrenees, through lower mountain ranges and a section of inland plateau, to the Mediterranean coast and the wetlands of the Ebro delta [8.3.1].

At the same time, however, Catalonia is also a highly distinctive region where support for autonomy has long extended across most of the political spectrum [3.2.1.1]. As a result it was given privileged access to devolution, its original Statute of Autonomy – known as the Statute of Sau – receiving overwhelming popular support in 1979 [3.1.1]. A revised Statute, granting greater autonomy to the region, came into effect in 2007.

The first regional election, in 1980, was won by the regionalist grouping Convergence and Union (*Convergència i Unió/CiU*), headed by its founder and leader Jordi Pujol [3.2.1.2]. Since 2003, however, the region has been governed by a three-party coalition led by the Catalan Socialist Party (*Partit dels Socialistes Catalans/PSC*). The PSC is an enthusiastic advocate of Catalan self-government and itself enjoys considerable autonomy within its parent party, the PSOE [3.2.1.1]. It shares power with two other left-wing parties, Catalan Republican Left (*Esquerra Republicana de Catalunya/ERC*), an old-established regionalist party, and an alliance of Greens and Communists called ICV-EUiA.

Tensions have occasionally been high between the members of the 'Tripartite' (*Tripartito*/Catalan: *Tripartit*) government, especially during its first term of office (2003–06) when it was led by the veteran Socialist Pasqual Maragall. The parties have cooperated more successfully since they regained power after the 2006 elections, with José Montilla as regional First Minister [3.2.1.3]. Meanwhile, the Catalan section of the People's Party (*Partit Popular/PP*), which for long viewed regionalism and autonomy with grave suspicion, has come to accept Catalan distinctiveness.

Its essential basis, and that of Catalan regionalism, is the existence of a distinct culture with its own language (*català*). Unlike Basque, Catalan has a long literary tradition and has always enjoyed high status, being used by large sections of the region's economic elites. It is also relatively easily learnt by incomers to the region – again in contrast to Basque – and is widely used today, despite attempts to stamp it out by the Franco regime. Understandably, following his death the new regional authorities felt the need to consolidate Catalan's situation, and introduced legislation to 'normalize' the language. It provided for increased use of Catalan by public authorities and within the education system, and enjoyed broad support.

Towards the end of the century, however, the CiU regional government introduced a further set of 'normalization' measures which further downgraded the use of Castilian Spanish in schools. Along with alleged discrimination in access to public sector jobs, this was seized upon by the PP's then leader in the region, Aleix Vidal-Quadras, as a means of rallying support from the region's non-Catalan speakers. But the other opposition parties backed the proposals, and Vidal-Quadras was eventually obliged to resign by the PP's own Madrid leadership. Nonetheless, dissatisfaction with the perceived 'imposition' of Catalan and criticism of the alleged obsession with issues of identity in the region continued. As a result, in 2005, a number of Catalan writers and academics created a new cultural grouping to give expression to these views. Out of that cultural movement emerged a new political party, the Catalan Citizens' Party (*Ciudadanos: Partido de la Ciudadanía*/Catalan: *Ciutadans-Partit de la Ciutadania/CPC*) which went on to win three seats in the 2006 regional election.

The other main dimension of Catalan distinctiveness is economic. Long the powerhouse of the Spanish economy, it has been further favoured by Spain's involvement in the process of European integration and parades its self-confidence through membership of the so-called Four Motors, a loose association with similarly dynamic regions in France, Germany and Italy. Catalonia's economic importance dates back to Barcelona's emergence as a major port and commercial centre in the Middle Ages. The contrast with Spain as a whole was accentuated from the mid-nineteenth century on by industrialization in and around the capital, a process centred on the textile and, later, metal industries.

More recently both of these industries have experienced some decline but, overall, Catalonia was relatively unscathed by the economic difficulties of the 1980s. New industries have emerged as leaders of the regional economy, notably petrochemicals, while the strength of the region's energy sector, with abundant supplies of both hydroelectric and nuclear power, has been another advantage. Above all, Catalonia has built on its traditional strength in trade and commerce to develop a thriving services sector within which both a massive tourist industry and business and financial services play significant parts.

Finally, Catalonia has its own flourishing media sector concentrated in Barcelona. The publicly-run Catalan Television Service (TVC) broadcasts on two conventional channels, TV-3 and Canal 33, of which the former is much the more popular with an audience share of around 25 per cent. Both broadcast in Catalan, but have been criticized for ignoring indigenous productions in favour of dubbed English-language material. The same is true of the cable channel K3. Two daily newspapers produced in Catalan, *Avui* and *El Punt*, printed in Girona, have respectable readerships, although they are outsold by *El País*. It, in turn, lags far behind the two market leaders, *El Periódico* and *La Vanguardia*, the flagships of the Catalan-based Zeta and Godó groups, two of Spain's largest [10.2].

11.11 Extremadura

Regional capital: Mérida
Main population centres: Badajoz (144,000), Cáceres (90,000), Mérida (54,000)
Official name of regional government: *Junta de Extremadura*
Regional First Minister: Guillermo Fernández Vara (PSOE)
Composition of parliament following most recent regional election (2007):
   Socialist Party (PSOE) & Regionalists 38; People's Party (PP) & Extremadura United (EU) 27

Separated by mountains from the main Castilian plateau and pressed against the Portuguese border, Extremadura is something of a backwater. That, and its mostly inhospitable climate, have condemned it to centuries of emigration and poverty. Indeed by most measures it still enjoys the dubious distinction of being the poorest of Spain's regions, as well as being one of the most thinly populated. On the other hand, and partly as a result, it possesses a richness of landscape and fauna unrivalled in Western Europe [8.2.3].

As in Andalusia, large unproductive estates (*latifundios*) are a feature of Extremadura's countryside. Agriculture continues to employ around 12 per cent of the workforce – almost twice the national average – although it contributes just 8 per cent of the region's wealth, measured in terms of its GDP. Industrial development is mainly linked to the exploitation of tobacco and local food products such as tomatoes, peppers and pork, which are processed in technologically advanced factories. Although the services sector, including public services, is crucial to economic survival, accounting for more than half the region's wealth, the one industrial sector where the region plays a significant role in terms of the country's economy is the production of both hydroelectric and nuclear power.

Rivalry between the capitals of Extremadura's two constituent provinces, the two most extensive in Spain, led its devolved institutions to be located in the smaller centre of Mérida. It has been run without a break by the Socialist PSOE, initially under First Minister Juan Carlos Rodríguez Ibarra, well-known for criticizing the ongoing devolution process as being unfair to Spain's poor regions in general, and Extremadura in particular. Currently the PSOE govern under First Minister Guillermo Fernández Vara with the support of regionalists, including Alliance for Extremadura (*Coalición Extremeña/CE*). The first regionalist grouping to be created in Extremadura was the centre-right party Extremadura United (*Extremadura Unida/EU*), formed in 1980; it currently has one deputy in the regional Assembly, having run in the 2007 regional election in an alliance with the PP.

11.12 Galicia

Regional capital: Santiago de Compostela
Main population centres: Vigo (294,000), Corunna (Galician: A *Coruña*) (243,000), Ourense (108,000), Santiago de Compostela (93,000), Lugo (92,000), Pontevedra (79,000), Ferrol (77,000)
Official name of regional government: *Xunta de Galiza* (Galician)
Regional First Minister: Emilio Pérez Touriño (PSdeG-PSOE)
Composition of parliament following most recent regional election (2005):
People's Party (37) 41; Galician Socialist Party (PSdeG-PSOE) 25; Galician National Alliance (BNG) 13

In many ways Galicia (Galician: *Galiza*) is Spain's most distinctive region. It is a land of rolling hills and steep river valleys fed by high rainfall. Its coastline is punctuated by the long, shallow inlets known as *rías* and makes up one third of the entire Spanish total. Separated from the rest of the country by mountains, the region's natural geographical links are with northern Portugal rather than Spain. The same is true of the Galician language (Galician: *galego*), while the lively indigenous culture is not Iberian in nature at all, but Celtic.

For these reasons Galicia had already been granted limited self-government under the Second Republic [0.1], and as a result was accorded the status of a 'historic nationality' in the 1978 Constitution. That gave it rapid access to relatively extensive autonomy [3.1.2], although Galicians themselves showed no marked enthusiasm; in the devolution referendum the turnout was a mere 30 per cent. The region has no undisputed centre, while its two largest cities, Vigo and Corunna, are old rivals. As a result, and given its historical significance, the new regional institutions were located in the much smaller Santiago de Compostela.

The lack of any great regionalist pressure in Galicia was, in fact, just one aspect of its general political and social backwardness. More than those of any other region its politics had been controlled by corrupt party bosses (*caciques*) and, in sharp contrast to the Basque Country and Catalonia, it had experienced no significant industrialization before 1975. Not surprisingly, it has been a stronghold for the Right over much of the last three decades, with Manuel Fraga, a native of the region and the doyen of contemporary Spanish conservatism [2.4.1], serving as its First Minister from 1989 until 2005.

The first break in the domination of the conservative People's Party (PP) – or, as it was then called, the People's Alliance (AP) – came in the late 1980s, when a local group broke away from that party and formed what they called the Galician Alliance (*Coalición Galega*/CG). With CG's support the local Socialists were briefly able to form a government, but at the next regional election in 1989 the PP swept back to power and CG melted away.

More recently, however, this situation has changed substantially with the rise of the Galician National Alliance (*Bloque Nacional Galego*/BNG) [3.2.3.2]. The BNG is an amalgamation of diverse left-wing groups, some in a moderate tradition stretching back to the 1930s, others born out of 1970s revolutionary ideas. These were skilfully welded together by Xosé Manoel Beiras, a leader whose personal charisma has itself contributed much to the BNG's success. At the 1997 regional election BNG overtook the Socialist PSOE to become the main opposition in the region's parliament. Four years later it once again outpolled the Socialists, albeit narrowly. In 2005, however, PSdeG-PSOE won 25 seats, 12 more than the BNG. Between the two, they formed a coalition government, finally ousting Fraga and the PP.

The Galician language is securely implanted at popular level – it is more extensively spoken even than its counterpart in Catalonia – and is widely used by authors of literature. The region's public television station, TVG, broadcasting in Galician, commands almost 15 per cent of the regional audience, although the only two newspapers published in Galician have small circulations. Yet Galicia has its own press, the penetration of the Madrid-based press being very low indeed. Instead Galicians opt for dailies produced in the region, and even in their own province. While *La Voz de Galicia*, printed in Corunna and Spain's sixth most popular title, heads the readership ranking by some way, the *Faro de Vigo* and *La Región*, produced in Ourense, both account for substantial shares.

Galicia's agricultural potential is limited by the fact that it has a high proportion of uncultivated land and by a land-ownership structure dominated by unviably small holdings (*minifundios*). The result, historically, was poverty and massive emigration, above all to Latin America [0.4.2]. Although agriculture was traditionally the backbone of the region's economy, it is now dominated, as elsewhere in Spain, by the services sector. The other activity with which Galicia has always been associated is fishing, and, while it contributes a relatively small proportion of the region's overall wealth, it is still the case that the Galician fleet accounts for half the Spanish total and exceeds that of any other EU country. Changes in recent decades, not least Spanish accession to the EU, have hit both agriculture and fishing hard, as well as what was the region's main industry – shipbuilding, based primarily in Ferrol.

Given the added difficulties of an extremely isolated situation in European terms, and poor communications, the region has continued to experience rather slow growth. However, some newer industries have prospered, such as the Citroën vehicles plant at Vigo and aluminium production in Lugo. Another notable Galician success story has been the development of Inditex, the company that owns Zara and a range of other clothes labels, from a small local concern based in Arteixo into the biggest fashion retailing group in Europe. The owner of Inditex, Amancio Ortega, has in passing become the richest person in Spain.

The trend away from pure beach holidays has also helped the substantial tourist sector. Moreover, there has been a considerable – although obviously unmeasured – flow of money into the region as the result of smuggling, both of tobacco and of other harder drugs. These factors have enabled Galicia to catch up somewhat with the rest of Spain, but it remains a relatively poor region. Moreover, rankings of overall well-being tend to place the Galician provinces very low indeed, with Lugo and Ourense right at the foot, due to their continuing low level of infrastructure and services.

11.13 Madrid

Regional capital: Madrid

Main population centres: Madrid (3,129,000), Móstoles (206,000), Alcalá de Henares (201,000), Fuenlabrada (194,000), Leganés (172,000), Getafe (156,000), Alcorcón (165,000), Torrejón de Ardoz (112,000), Alcobendas (104,000), Parla (95,000), Coslada (83,000), Pozuelo de Alarcón (80,000)

Official name of regional government: *Gobierno de la Comunidad*

Regional First Minister: Esperanza Aguirre (PP)

Composition of parliament following most recent regional election (2007):

People's Party (PP) 67; Socialist Party (PSOE) 42; United Left (IUCM) 11

Traditionally part of New Castile, when Spain's new regional map was drawn in the early 1980s the province of Madrid was established as a separate region (*Comunidad Autónoma de Madrid*/CAM) due to its radically different demographic and economic structure. Although its western and northern fringes take in the high peaks of the Gredos and Guadarrama mountains, the new region is by far the most densely populated in the country. The population is concentrated above all in the capital itself, Spain's largest city, but also in the satellite towns to its south-west and north-east that have grown with astonishing rapidity since the 1960s, when most were little more than villages.

Unlike other European capitals, Madrid long remained in essence a purely administrative centre, relatively unimportant in economic terms. Today, however, it is Spain's leading business centre. Its region lies second only to Catalonia in its national economic contribution, and its people are on average the best off in the country.

This growth has been based on a number of factors, in particular the advantage of a central location at the focus of the country's transport system and the growing importance of service industries, for which capital cities are favoured locations. These, particularly financial services as well as public administration, now form the mainstay of the regional economy, although there has also been substantial light industrial development, especially in the satellite towns (*cinturón industrial*). In recent years, construction has played a very important part in the economy of the region, partly based on a house-building boom and partly due to some major public infrastructure projects such as the development of the 'Calle 30' motorway. Other factors of significance are its importance as a tourist destination and the boost it received from Spain's entry into the EU. All of this has helped to ensure that CAM's economic growth rate has been the highest of any Spanish region in recent years.

Politically the region was initially governed by the Socialists. Subsequently, however, it followed the countrywide pattern of a swing to the Right but to a particularly marked degree, with the result that the People's Party has held power there since 1999, first with Alberto Ruiz-Gallardón as First Minister and, since 2003, Esperanza Aguirre [2.4.5]. There has been strong rivalry between Gallardón and Aguirre during all of this period, rivalry which came to a head in 2004 when the former – by then Mayor of the city – made an unsuccessful bid for leadership of the PP in Madrid, only to be defeated by Aguirre. The latter received the support of Mariano Rajoy, the PP's leader at national level, support which was again in evidence in 2008 when Rajoy refused to include Gallardón's name on the party's list of candidates for the general election, insisting that he remain in his position as Mayor instead.

The PSOE in Madrid has suffered its own internal difficulties too, leading to the resignation of prominent figures in the party, so that it continues to be in a weak position to challenge the PP for power. Predictably the regional parliament contains no regionalist representatives, although it did briefly include one in the 1980s.

The CAM is at the heart of the media industry in Spain, with the headquarters of most of the major newspapers, radio stations, TV channels and telecommunications companies being located in the capital. The main regional TV station is Telemadrid, which held a sizeable audience share in the 1990s but has since slipped to just over 10 per cent, about half that of Telecinco, the most popular channel in the region. Other regional TV channels in Madrid include La Otra, which broadcasts in digital format, a satellite station called Telemadrid SAT, and a private channel, Onda 6. The three public television channels are owned by Radio Televisión Madrid, which also controls the radio station Onda Madrid. The region's press is dominated by the three main country-wide titles, of which *El País* is by some distance the most widely read, although in recent years a number of freesheets (*diarios gratuitos*), including *Metro* and *20 Minutos*, have become very popular, especially in the capital.

11.14 Murcia

Regional capital: Murcia
Main population centres: Murcia (417,000), Cartagena (209,000), Lorca (90,000)
Official name of regional government: *Consejo de Gobierno*
Regional First Minister: Ramón Valcárcel (PP)
Composition of parliament following most recent regional election (2007):

People's Party (PP) 29; Socialist Party (PSOE) 15; United Left of Murcia (IURM) 1

On the map Murcia looks somewhat of an anomaly, a small wedge between the much larger regions of Andalusia, Castile-La Mancha and Valencia. Nor does it have any obvious distinguishing geographic or cultural characteristics. In fact, though, it is one of Spain's traditional regions, admittedly in conjunction with the neighbouring province of Albacete. But the latter's allocation to Castile-La Mancha when the new regions were created in the early 1980s responded fully to geographic logic, and if anything served to increase Murcia's own internal cohesion.

Traditionally, too, the region was plagued by the rivalry between its capital and the second city, Cartagena. The latter, a fine natural harbour and Spain's chief Mediterranean naval base, long sought the creation of its own, separate province. The issue now seems buried, however, at least to judge by the very high readership penetration enjoyed by the Murcia-based daily *La Verdad*. It dwarfs not just the region's other, more local titles, but also the country-wide ones.

The region's population is heavily concentrated along a coastal strip, the remainder of the terrain being mountainous and fairly inhospitable. In the past Murcia was notoriously one of the poorest parts of Spain, and lost heavily through emigration, above all to Catalonia where 'Murcian' became a general term for all poor incomers. In the last few years its population has been increasing at rates that are typically twice the national average, however, as the region's prosperity has improved and it has attracted large numbers of immigrants, especially from Morocco and Ecuador. Its economy used to depend heavily on mining, and this has left the landscape around Cartagena and La Unión badly scarred [8.1.2]. The mainstay of the economy is agriculture, which has shown consistent improvement in its performance over the last two decades, and in which many of its recent immigrants work. The most important products are soft fruits and vegetables, the production of which is made viable by the transfer of water resources to the region's main river, the Segura, from the Tagus. The National Hydrological Plan of 2001 projected further transfers to the Segura from the Ebro, but this project is now very much in doubt since it was radically revised by the Socialist government in 2005 [8.3.2].

Ensuring that Murcia has adequate supplies of water is, understandably, a vital priority for the region's political leaders. As in a number of other regions, these underwent a change of colour in the 1990s, when the People's Party (PP) replaced the Socialist PSOE in the regional government. Politically, Murcia is doubly similar to Madrid since, on the one hand, regional government continues to be dominated by the PP and, on the other, these are the only two regions where no regionalist party has ever sat in parliament.

11.15 Navarre

Regional capital: Pamplona (Basque: *Iruña*)
Main population centre: Pamplona (196,000)
Official name of regional government: *Gobierno de Navarra*
Regional First Minister: Miguel Sanz (UPN)
Composition of parliament following most recent regional election (2007):
    Navarrese People's Union (UPN) 22; Navarrese Socialist Party (PSN-PSOE) 12; Coalition for Navarre (NaBai) 12; United Left (IUN/NEB) 2; Navarrese Democratic Convergence (CDN) 2

The region of Navarre (*Comunidad Foral de Navarra*) may be relatively small, but it ranks second to none in the complexity of its nature and affairs. While the rivers of its wet, mountainous north drain to the Atlantic, the south forms part of the dry Ebro valley which runs down to the Mediterranean. In the former the Basque language (*euskera*) and its associated culture have a strong presence that is completely lacking in the more heavily populated south. In the centre lies a zone of transition which includes the Navarrese capital, Pamplona, the region's largest settlement by far. Yet, at the same time, few regions have a stronger and more cohesive sense of identity than Navarre.

The reasons are essentially historical. Navarre was once an independent kingdom extending north of the Pyrenees. Even after its incorporation into Spain, like the neighbouring Basque Country it enjoyed traditional rights (*fueros*) that effectively separated it from the rest of the country [11.5]. Even after the rights were suppressed in 1876 Navarre retained certain financial privileges, including the right to collect its own taxes. Moreover, these were maintained even under Franco, in recognition of enthusiastic Navarrese support for his 1936 uprising [0.1].

Thus when devolution got under way after his death, Navarre was unique among the new regions in already having a degree of self-rule. Its representatives insisted that the autonomy now to be granted be seen, not as a new departure, but as a direct continuation of existing arrangements. Consequently, it is the only region not to have a Statute of Autonomy as such. Instead its constitutional status is defined by the 1982 Act reaffirming its historic rights (*Ley Orgánica de Reintegración y Amejoramiento del Régimen Foral de Navarra*), known usually as the *Amejoramiento Foral*. In particular, this confirms the system of regular financial agreements (*convenios económicos*) under which Navarre collects almost all taxes before remitting a certain sum, or reverse block grant (*aportación*), to the central government.

A further complication was introduced by the fact that Basque regionalists claim Navarre as an integral part of the Basque Country; the 1978 Constitution even included special provision for the two regions to amalgamate [1.1.2]. While that is now recognized by all but extremists as a remote aspiration at best, Basque parties operate in Navarre and currently make up over a fifth of its parliament. They function within the Coalition for Navarre (*Nafarroa Bai/NaBai*) which was formed in 2003 and brought together former members of the banned Basque nationalist party, Unity (*Batasuna*), along with the more moderate Basque Nationalist Party (*Partido Nacionalista Vasco/PNV*). In the wake of the regional election in 2007, NaBai came close to forming a coalition government with the Navarrese Socialist Party (*Partido Socialista de Navarra/PSN*) and United Left (*Izquierda Unida/IU*), as the three had won enough seats between them to oust the conservative Navarrese People's Union (*Unión del Pueblo Navarro/UPN*) [3.2.3.1], but this option was disallowed by the PSOE leadership in Madrid, to the consternation of the local leadership.

Navarre's main political tradition is of militant conservatism, embodied by the Carlist movement [0.1]. However, in the 1980s Carlism's collapse enabled the PSN-PSOE to emerge as the region's first governing party. It was helped also by a split between mainstream Spanish conservatives and the UPN, whose chief concern was to protect the region's separate identity. In 1991, though, the UPN took over the regional government with support from the People's Party (PP), before itself suffering a breakaway by the less conservative Navarrese Democratic Convergence (*Convergencia de Demócratas de Navarra/CDN*). For a time in the mid-1990s this joined a Socialist-led coalition also involving Basque Solidarity (*Eusko Alkartasuna/EA*) [11.5]. Nonetheless, in 1999 the UPN, which had persuaded the PP to allow it a free run in regional elections, reasserted its leading role, and it is the party that has continued to dominate the region since then, either on its own or, since 2003, in coalition with the CDN.

Perhaps surprisingly given the complexities and even turbulence of its politics, economically Navarre has been one of Spain's major success stories in recent decades. Previously somewhat poor, from the 1960s on the region has undergone a massive but relatively painless process of industrialization, achieving some of the country's highest growth rates on the way. It also currently has the lowest level of joblessness in the country. Expansion was based partly on the region's advantageous location *vis-à-vis* European markets, but also on its privileged financial status which has enabled it to develop high quality communications and other infrastructure. Indeed, such facilities mean that in terms of overall well-being rather than just material prosperity, Navarre ranks first among all the Spanish regions, which includes having the longest life expectancy of all the regions – and that, despite the security problems posed by ETA's activities.

Before 1960 the regional economy was overwhelmingly agricultural. Today farming accounts for only a small share, although specialization in high-value crops such as asparagus means that it continues to make a significant contribution. Industry, most but by no means all of which is centred on Pamplona, is very diverse in nature. Metal industries of various sorts, including a major car plant near the capital, are most strongly represented, with vegetable canning and bottling also important.

In cultural terms, Navarre's diversity is acknowledged by official recognition for the Basque language. The two television channels controlled by the Basque government [11.5] have a 10 per cent share of the region's television audience. This region has the highest rate of newspaper readership in Spain, with by far the largest readership being enjoyed by the local *Diario de Navarra*, to the virtual exclusion of Madrid-based papers. The second paper in terms of readership is *Gara*, which is controlled by ETA's supporters.

11.16 The Rioja

Regional capital: Logroño
Main population centre: Logroño (147,000)
Official name of regional government: *Consejo de Gobierno*
Regional First Minister: Pedro Sanz Alonso (PP)
Composition of parliament following most recent regional election (2007):
    People's Party (PP) 17; Socialist Party (PSOE) 14; Party of the Rioja (PR) 2

The Rioja is the least extensive of Spain's mainland regions, and the smallest of all in demographic terms. Yet it is surprisingly diverse; much of the south is mountainous and empty, while the population is concentrated in small towns along the Ebro valley and, above all, in the capital, Logroño. Historically the area formed part of Old Castile, and includes the monastery at San Millán de la Cogolla, usually regarded as the cradle of the Castilian language.

However, it is geographically separate from the Castilian plateau and the main local daily utterly dominates the local press – in a region with more readers than the average. The region has even given birth to its own political formation, the Party of the Rioja (*Partido Riojano/PR*), which on occasion has held the balance of power in its parliament and been a junior partner in governments. The leading role in these, however, has been played by the major Spanish parties: in the 1980s mainly the Socialists, since 1991 the conservative PP.

Economically the Rioja is stable and prosperous. Its well-balanced economy includes an efficient and profitable agricultural sector, centred on cereals and the intensive production of fruit and vegetables, and a diversity of mainly light industries. Several of these use as their inputs local agricultural produce, the most famous being, of course, wine production.

11.17 Valencia

Regional capital: Valencia (Valencian: *València*)

Main population centres: Valencia (805,000), Alicante (Valencian: *Alacant*) (322,000), Elche (Valencian: *Elx*) (219,000), Castellón de la Plana (Valencian: *Castelló de la Plana*) (172,000), Torrent (75,000), Alcoy (Valencian: *Alcoi*) (61,000), Gandia (75,000), Sagunto (Valencian: *Sagunt*) (63,000), Benidorm (68,000), Orihuela (78,000), Elda (55,000)

Official name of regional government: *Generalitat Valenciana* (Valencian)

Regional First Minister: Francisco Camps (PP)

Composition of parliament following most recent regional election (2007):
People's Party (PP) 55; Socialist Party (PSOE) 37; Commitment for Valencia (CPV) 7

Long before the Rioja was a name known in the English-speaking world, Valencia was indelibly linked in the popular mind with oranges. They are still important for the present-day region of that name (*Comunidad Valenciana*), which produces 70 per cent of Spain's citrus fruit. Within the country it is associated above all with the irrigated market gardens known as *huertas*, whose products include rice as well as fruit and vegetables. And, in fact, almost 45 per cent of Spanish farm exports come from Valencia.

Today the region's economy is by no means exclusively agricultural. As part of the favoured Mediterranean coastal strip [5.3.5] it has developed and diversified, and now has substantial services and manufacturing sectors. Some industrial employers are large, such as the Ford car plant near the capital. Most businesses are small or medium-sized, however, and are spread over a range of light industries, such as tiles, concentrated around Castellón, and footwear. Fine beaches have also made for a substantial tourist industry, with Benidorm the best-known resort. As in other coastal zones, however, this has also had a significant downside in terms of the degree to which speculative building of apartment blocks and houses has spoiled the landscape [8.2.3]. The mix of economic activities includes several particularly affected by the underground economy [5.2.3], so that living standards in the region may well be higher than suggested by the relatively modest official figures.

Both economic activity and population are concentrated in and around the city of Valencia – the fourth largest in Spain – and in the medium-sized towns which dot the coastal strip. By Spanish standards this is a lush area, which benefits from the sometimes controversial transfer of water from the Ebro to its main river, the Segura [8.3.2]. Behind it lie ranges of hills, not particularly high but often forbidding; the Maestrazgo in the north of the region is a byword for difficult terrain.

The Valencian Community comprises the provinces of Alicante, Valencia and Castellón – the last of these being one of the wealthiest areas in the EU. It has a long history as a distinct unit, initially within the medieval 'Crown of Aragon' [11.2], while its capital is a long-established port and trading centre, the traditional rival of

Barcelona. Linguistically, too, it lies outside the Castilian orbit, with most of its people speaking what for most scholars is a dialect of Catalan. However, officially Valencian is now regarded as a distinct tongue. The regional government has gone so far as to withdraw from joint language-promotion programmes with its Catalan (and Balearic) counterparts in such areas as teacher training.

These political decisions were taken as a result of pressure from sectors of the lower middle class suspicious of all things Catalan. In the 1980s they were the driving force behind the rise of a new political party, Valencian Union (*Unió Valenciana/UV*) [3.2.3.1], which for a time attracted sufficient support to become a major player in regional politics and formed part of coalition governments. Initially its main impact, though, was to split the right-wing vote; the result was that the Socialist PSOE ran the region throughout the 1980s. Subsequently, UV's sharp decline had the opposite effect of ensuring a solid majority for the People's Party (PP).

In the early years of this century, left-wing regionalist parties such as the Valencian Nationalist Union (Valencian: *Bloc Nacionalista Valencià/Bloc*) and the Valencian section of United Left (Valencian: *Esquerra Unida del País Valencià/EUPV*) emerged as contenders for seats in the regional parliament. Encouraged by the fact that they had achieved a respectable share of the vote when they ran as individual parties in 2003, they had hoped to win enough seats to be in a position to support the PSOE in forming a coalition government at the subsequent election. They therefore entered into an alliance which also involved some other minor parties, including Greens, but in 2007 that alliance, called Commitment for Valencia (Valencian: *Compromis pel País Valencià/CPV*), secured only a very disappointing 7 seats, far fewer than the 19 that would have been needed to unseat the PP.

In April 2006, a new Statute of Autonomy came into effect, having been approved both by the government in Madrid and subsequently by the Valencian parliament (*Cortes Valencianas*; Valencian: *Corts Valencianes*). Salient features of this Statute include provision for the creation of a new police force at regional level and the stipulation that the Valencian Supreme Court will be the highest tier in the judicial system in the *Comunidad*. It also reaffirmed the status of Valencian as a separate language, not a dialect of Catalan.

Valencia has its own public broadcasting service which runs three channels. The oldest of these, Canal 9, commands an audience share of over 20 per cent and broadcasts mainly in Spanish, with the exception of its news programmes. The second channel, Punt 2, was created with a view to providing programming mainly in Valencian, and broadcasts a lot of home-produced material in that language and in Catalan. The third is an international channel, broadcast via satellite and internet, called TVVi; its content consists of selections of programmes from the other two channels, especially Punt 2. The Valencian language's presence is rather lower in the daily press, which is characterized by its diversity. On the one hand, the Madrid-based titles are relatively widely read. On the other, the three leading dailies are all regional, the two largest being printed in the capital and the third in Alicante.

11.18 Ceuta and Melilla

Ceuta and Melilla are two small enclaves on the Moroccan coast, both of which have formed part of Spain since the sixteenth century. Ceuta (population 77,000) lies just inside the Straits of Gibraltar, Melilla (population 69,000) rather further east, roughly opposite Almería. For administrative purposes Melilla's territory includes Spain's minuscule Mediterranean possessions, the Chafarinas Islands and the rocky islets of Alhucemas and Vélez de la Gomera.

Both cities are relatively poor, their per capita income amounting to some three-quarters of the Spanish average, although in recent years they have improved their position somewhat. Both are ports, Ceuta one of the most important in the Mediterranean thanks to its free port status, whereas Melilla's economy depends mainly on its large military garrison.

The two, which were made 'autonomous cities' in 1995, have been a constant source of low-level friction with Morocco. This came to a head in 2007 when the Spanish king and queen made an official visit to the cities, much to the chagrin of the Moroccan government [0.4.3]. Immigration has been a dominant political topic, often exploited by cynical political groups from the south of the Peninsula. The issue came to international attention in 2005 when six Africans died when attempting to gain entry by crossing the fence marking the border between the cities and the surrounding territory, four of them shot by Moroccan police [6.1.1].

11.19 Glossary

Alta Velocidad Española/AVE (m)	high-speed train
aportación (f)	grant
autodeterminación (f)	self-determination (of an autonomous region)
bable (m)	Austrian dialect
batua (m)	common form of Basque language
cacique (m)	corrupt party boss
Casa de Juntas (f)	Assembly Hall
caserío (m)	farmstead, typical of Basque Country
catalá (m)	Catalan language
cinturón industrial (m)	area of industrial development
conciertos económicos (mpl)/	financial agreements between region and
convenios económicos (mpl)	Madrid government
consell (m)	elected assembly for each of the Balearic Islands
Cortes Valencianas (fpl)	Valencian parliament
cupo (m)	reverse block grant (in Basque Country)
diario gratuito (m)	freesheet, free newspaper
ecotasa (f)	ecotax
euskera (m)	Basque language
fueros (mpl)	traditional rights in Navarre and the Basque Country
galego (m)	Galician language
ikastola (Basque)	Basque-language school
La Montaña (f)	local name for Cantabria
latifundio (m)	large estate in central or southern Spain
margen izquierda (f)	left bank of river (e.g., Nervión in Bilbao)
minifundio (m)	small land holding (e.g., in Galicia)
Patrimonio de la Humanidad (m)	World Heritage Site (UNESCO)
polo de desarrollo (m)	growth pole (for industry, in Franco times)
vacaciones de sol y playa (fpl)	beach holidays
valenciano (m)	Valencian language
Vascongadas (fpl)	Basque provinces

Table 11.1 Regional indicators

	Area (sq km)	Population[a]	Pop. density (per sq km)	Gross Added Value[b] (EUR bn)	Per capita GAV[c] (EUR)	Unemployment[d] (%)
Andalusia	87,560	8,059,461	92	112.0	14,500	14.0
Aragon	47,720	1,296,655	27	24.9	19,900	5.1
Asturias	10,604	1,074,862	101	17.4	16,500	8.1
Balearic Is	4,992	1,030,650	206	20.2	20,800	9.0
Basque Co	7,235	2,141,860	296	49.8	23,600	5.7
Canary Is	7,447	2,025,951	272	32.7	17,000	11.0
Cantabria	5,231	572,824	110	10.1	18,300	4.6
Cast-La Man	79,462	1,977,304	25	27.4	14,600	8.0
Cast-Leon	94,224	2,528,417	27	43.6	17,700	7.0
Catalonia	32,114	7,210,508	225	152.1	22,200	6.6
Extremadura	41,635	1,089,990	26	13.5	12,600	14.7
Galicia	29,575	2,772,533	94	41.2	15,200	7.5
Madrid	8,028	6,081,689	758	143.7	24,400	6.4
Murcia	11,314	1,392,117	123	20.5	15,600	8.3
Navarre	10,391	605,876	58	13.7	23,500	4.3
Rioja	5,045	308,968	61	5.9	20,000	5.6
Valencia	23,255	4,885,029	210	78.5	17,100	9.0
Ceuta	19	76,603	4,031	1.2	17,000	19.2
Melilla	13	69,440	5,342	1.9	16,800	17.5
Spain	505,864	45,200,737	89	810.8	18,700	8.6

Notes:

[a] 2007.; Source: National Statistical Office (*Instituto Nacional de Estadística*).[http://www.ine.es]

[b] 2005 (nearest thousand); Source: National Statistical Office (*Instituto Nacional de Estadística*).

[c] Annual figure for 2005. Source: National Statistical Office (*Instituto Nacional de Estadística*).

[d] Fourth quarter 2007 (unadjusted). Source: National Statistical Office (*Instituto Nacional de Estadística*).

Further reading

Introduction

Brennan, G. 1990 *The Spanish labyrinth*. Cambridge, Cambridge University Press.
Esdaile, C. 2000 *Spain in the Liberal Age*. Oxford, Oxford University Press.
Gillespie, R. and Youngs, R. (eds) 2001 *Spain: the European and international challenges*. London, Frank Cass.
Preston, P. 1986 *The triumph of democracy in Spain*. London, Methuen.
Ross, C. 2000 *Spain 1812–1996*. London, Arnold.
Tusell, J. 2004 *Dictadura franquista y democracia 1939–2004*. Barcelona, Crítica.

Chapter 1

Alcántara, M. and Martínez, A. (eds.) 2001 *Política y gobierno en España*, 2nd ed. Valencia, Tirant lo Blanch.
Heywood, P. 1991 Governing a new democracy: the power of the Prime Minister in Spain. *West European Politics* 14 (2).
Heywood, P. 1995 *The government and politics of Spain*. London, Macmillan (Chaps 2, 4, 8).
Newton, M. T. 1997 *Institutions of modern Spain: a political and economic guide*. Cambridge, Cambridge University Press (Chaps 1–6, 8).
Román, P. (ed.) 2002 *Sistema político español*. Madrid, McGraw Hill (Chaps 1, 2, 3, 9, 10, 13).
Sánchez Goyanes, E. 1989 *Constitución española comentada*. Madrid, Paraninfo.

Chapter 2

Balfour, S. (ed.) 2005 *The politics of contemporary Spain*. Oxford, Routledge.
Bell, D. (ed.) 1993 *Western European Communists and the collapse of Communism*. London, Berg (Chap. 6).
Fysh, P. and Hughes, N. 2001 Explaining the Populares' majority: the Spanish general election of 12 March 2000. *International Journal of Iberian Studies* 14 (1).
Heywood, P. 1995 *The government and politics of Spain*. London, Macmillan (Chaps 8, 9).
Hopkin, J. 1993 Reflections on the disintegration of UCD. *Journal of Association for Contemporary Iberian Studies* 6 (2).
Magone, J. 2004 *Contemporary Spanish politics*. Oxford, Routledge.

Pettit, P. 2008 *Examen a Zapatero.* Madrid, Temas de Hoy.
Román, P. (ed.) 2002 *Sistema político español.* Madrid, McGraw Hill (Chaps 5, 6).
Tusell, J. and Sinova, J. 1992 *La década socialista: el ocaso de Felipe González.* Madrid, Espasa.
Tusell, J. (ed.) 2000 *El gobierno de Aznar: balance de una gestión, 1996–2000.* Barcelona, Crítica.
Vázquez Montalbán, M. 2003 *La aznaridad: Por el imperio hacia Dios o por Dios hacia el imperio.* Barcelona, Mondadori.

Chapter 3

Amodia, J. (ed.) 1994 *The resurgence of nationalist movements in Europe.* Bradford, Bradford University Press (Chaps 10, 11).
Atkinson, D. 2000 Language legislation in Catalonia: the politics of normalization. *International Journal of Iberian Studies* 13 (2).
Balcells, A. 1996 *Catalan nationalism: past and present.* London, Macmillan.
Heiberg, M. 1989 *The making of the Basque nation.* Cambridge, Cambridge University Press.
Hollyman, J. 1995 The tortuous road to regional autonomy in Spain. *Journal of Association for Contemporary Iberian Studies* 8 (1).
Mansvelt-Beck, J. 2005 *Territory and terror: conflicting nationalisms in the Basque Country.* London, Routledge.
Morán, G. 2003 *Los españoles que dejaron de serlo: cómo y por qué Euskadi se ha convertido en la gran herida histórica de España.* Barcelona, Planeta.
Moreno, L. 2001 *The federalization of Spain.* London, Frank Cass.
Payne, J. 2004 *Catalonia: history and culture.* Nottingham, Five Leaves.
Roller, E. 2000 The October 1999 elections in Catalonia: the end of nationalist dominance in Catalan politics? *International Journal of Iberian Studies* 13 (2).
Ross, C. 1996 Nationalism and party competition in the Basque Country and Catalonia. *West European Politics* 16 (3).
Sullivan, J. 1999 Forty years of ETA. *History Today* 49 (4).
Zallo, R. 2001 *El país de los vascos: desde los sucesos de Ermua al segundo gobierno de Ibarretxe.* Madrid, Fundamentos.

Chapter 4

Bulmer, S. 2005 *The member states of the European Union.* New York, Oxford University Press.
Cooper, T. 2001 '¡Aleluya por Europa!' Press treatment of the European Union in Spain and the United Kingdom. *International Journal of Iberian Studies* 14 (2).
Gillespie, R. and Youngs, R. (eds) 2001 *Spain: the European and international challenges.* London, Frank Cass.
Martínez Chacón, E. (ed.) 2002 *Economía española.* Barcelona, Ariel (Chaps 5, 6).
Moreno Juste, A. 1998 *España y el proceso de construcción europea.* Barcelona, Ariel.

Piedrahita, S., Steinberg, F. and Torreblanca, J. I. 2006 *20 años de España en la Unión Europea (1986–2006)*. Madrid, Elcano Royal Institute.
Royo, S. 2006 *The European Union and economic reforms: the case of Spain*. Madrid, Elcano Royal Institute.
Squires, J. 1999 Catalonia, Spain and the European Union: a tale of a region's 'empowerment'. *International Journal of Iberian Studies* 12 (1).

Chapter 5

Berger, S. and Broughton, D. (eds) 1995 *The force of labour: the Western European labour movement and the working class in the twentieth century*. London, Berg.
Chislett, W. 2008 *Spain: going places. Economic, political and social progress 1975–2008*. Madrid, Telefónica.
Estefanía, J. 2007 *La larga marcha: Medio siglo de política (económica) entre la historia y la memoria*. Barcelona, Península.
Guillén, M. 2005 *The rise of Spanish multinationals*. Cambridge, Cambridge University Press.
Harrison, J. 1995 *The Spanish economy: from the Civil War to the European Community*. Cambridge, Cambridge University Press.
Longhurst, C. A. 1995 The Spanish labour market. In Cooper, T. (ed.) *Spain in Europe*. Leeds, All Saints College.
Longhurst, C. A. 1997 Poverty amidst affluence in contemporary Spain: a case of 'the poor you shall always have with you'? *International Journal of Iberian Studies* 10 (3).
Martínez Chacón, E. (ed.) 2002 *Economía española*. Barcelona, Ariel.
Murphy, B. 1998 Real and nominal convergence: Spain on the threshold of EMU. *International Journal of Iberian Studies* 11 (3).
OECD 2007 *Spain economic survey*. Paris.
Salmon, K. 1995 *The modern Spanish economy*. London, Pinter.
Salmon, K. 2001 Spanish foreign direct investment, transnationals and the redefinition of the Spanish business realm. *International Journal of Iberian Studies* 14 (2).
Tamames, R. 1996 *La economía española de la transición a la unión monetaria*. Madrid, Temas de hoy.
Tamames, R. 2000 *Estructura económica española*. Barcelona, Bosch.
Tamames, R. and Rueda, A. 2005 *Introducción a la economía española*. Madrid, Alianza.

Chapter 6

Brooksbank-Jones, A. 1997 *Women in contemporary Spain*. Manchester, Manchester University Press.
Comisión Europea Contra El Racismo Y La Intolerancia 1999 *Informe sobre España*. Equipo Nizkor.

Gold, P. 2000 *Europe or Africa? A contemporary study of the Spanish North African enclaves of Ceuta and Melilla.* Oxford, Alden Press.

INE 2004 *Extranjeros en España.* Boletín informativo del Instituto Nacional de Estadística.

INE 2005 *La salud de los españoles.* Boletín informativo del Instituto Nacional de Estadística.

INE 2006 *1 de octubre. Día internacional de las personas mayores.* Boletín informativo del Instituto Nacional de Estadística.

Mira, Alberto 2004 *De Sodoma a Chueca: historia cultural de la homosexualidad en España 1914–1990.* Madrid, Egales.

Oliver Alonso, J. 2006 *España 2020: un mestizaje ineludible.* Barcelona, Generalitat de Catalunya, Institut d'Estudis Autonòmics.

Ministerio de Trabajo y Asuntos Sociales 2007 *Tercer boletín estadístico del Observatorio Estatal de Violencia sobre la Mujer.*

Chapter 7

Boyd-Barrett, O. and O'Malley, P. (eds) 1995 *Education reform in democratic Spain.* London, Routledge.

European Observatory on Health Care Systems 2000 *Health care systems in transition: Spain.*

Gal Vallejo, C. 2007 *La asistencia sanitaria en el marco de la seguridad social.* Madrid, Ministerio de Trabajo y Asuntos Sociales, Centro de Publicaciones.

INE 2005 *Educación universitaria. Nuevas carreras, más universidades.* Boletín informativo del Instituto Nacional de Estadística.

Ministerio de Trabajo y Asuntos Sociales 2007 *Presupuestos de la Seguridad Social. Cifras y datos. Ejercicio 2007.* Madrid, Ministerio de Trabajo y Asuntos Sociales, Centro de Publicaciones.

OECD 2007 *Education at a glance 2007: Spain.*

Román, P. (ed.) 2002 *Sistema político español.* Madrid, McGraw Hill (Chap. 14).

Chapter 8

Bangs, P. 1995 The European Union and the Spanish environment. In Cooper, T. (ed.) *Spain in Europe.* Leeds, All Saints College.

Brooksbank-Jones, A. 1998 (Un)covering the environment: some Spanish perspectives. *International Journal of Iberian Studies* 11 (1).

Environment Ministry 2003 *Water in Spain.* Madrid.

Greenpeace España 2007 *Destrucción a toda costa 2007.*

Greenpeace España 2008 *Contaminación en España.*

INE 2007 *Medio ambiente y desarrollo sostenible.* Boletín informativo del Instituto Nacional de Estadística.

Chapter 9

Díaz Fernández, A. M. 2006 *Los Servicios de Inteligencia españoles: Desde la Guerra Civil hasta el 11-M. Historia de una transición.* Madrid, Alianza.
Merino-Blanco, E. 1996 *The Spanish legal system.* London, Sweet & Maxwell.
Ministerio de Defensa 2007 *La mujer en las Fuerzas Armadas en España.*
Ministerio de Defensa 2007 *Las Fuerzas Armadas españolas hoy.*
Román, P. (ed.) 2002 *Sistema político español.* Madrid, McGraw Hill (Chap. 11).
Woodworth, P. 2001 *Dirty war, clean hands: ETA, the GAL and Spanish democracy.* Cork, Cork University Press.

Chapter 10

Bustamante, E. 2000 Spain's interventionist and authoritarian communication policy: Telefónica as political battering ram of the Spanish Right. *Media, Culture and Society* 22 (4).
Deacon, P. 1994 *The press as the mirror of the new Spain.* Bristol, Bristol University Press.
Martínez Reverte, J. 2002 *Perro come perro: Guía para leer los periódicos.* Madrid, Crítica.
Román, P. (ed.) 2002 *Sistema político español.* Madrid, McGraw Hill (Chap. 8).
Smith, P. J. 2006 *Spanish visual culture: cinema, television, Internet.* Manchester, Manchester University Press.
Smith, P. J. 2006 *Television in Spain: from Franco to Almodóvar.* London, Tamesis.
Trenzado, M. and Núñez, J. 2001 Los medios de comunicación, in Alcántara, M. and Martínez, A. (eds.), *Política y gobierno en España*, 2ⁿᵈ ed. Valencia, Tirant lo Blanch.
Vara, A. et al (eds) 2006 *Cobertura informativa del 11-M.* Pamplona, Ediciones Universidad de Navarra, S.A.

Culture and society

Comellas, J. L. 2003 *Historia de los españoles.* Barcelona, Ariel.
Eaude, M. 2007 *Catalonia: A cultural history.* Oxford, Signal Books.
Graham, H. and Labanyi, J. (eds) 1995 *Spanish cultural studies: an introduction.* Oxford, Oxford University Press (Chaps 18, 20).
Hooper, J. 2006 *The new Spaniards.* Harmondsworth, Penguin.
Jordan, B. and Morgan-Tamosunas, R. 2000 *Contemporary Spanish cultural studies.* London, Arnold.
Richardson, B. 2001 *Spanish studies: an introduction.* London, Arnold.
Smith, P. J. 2003 *Contemporary Spanish Culture.* Cambridge, Polity.
Tremlett, G. 2006 *Ghosts of Spain.* London, Faber and Faber.
Woodworth, P. 2007 *The Basque Country: A cultural history.* Oxford, Signal Books.

Current development and statistics

Anuario El País (annual produced by newspaper of same name).
Anuario Estadístico de España (annual produced by the Spanish National Statistics Office INE).
International Journal of Iberian Studies.

Useful websites

www.la-moncloa.es – official Spanish government site, giving access to those of individual ministries and regional governments.
www.congreso.es; www.senado.es – official sites of the two Houses of Parliament.
www.admiweb.org – compendium of information on the Spanish public sector as a whole, with search facility.
www.areaplural.com – portal to wide range of political information (parties, regionalism, etc.).
www.ine.es – Spanish National Statistics Office.
www.cis.es – Spanish Sociological Research Centre.
www.elpais.es; www.el-mundo.es; www.abc.es – leading Spain-wide daily newspapers.
www.elperiodico.es; www.lavanguardia.es – leading newspapers in Catalonia.
www.diario-elcorreo.es – leading newspaper in the Basque Country.
www.oecd.org/eco/surv/esu-spa.htm – contains latest edition of OECD's annual economic survey.
http://europa.eu – European Union website
www.aimc.es/aimc.php – Asociación para la Investigación de los Medios de Comunicación (statistics on media in Spain).
www.eionet.europa.eu/seris/view_on_coverage?country=es – environmental information on Spain.
http://www.mtas.es/mujer/ – official website of the Women's Bureau.
http://www.poderjudicial.es/ – official website of the General Council of the Judiciary.

Index

Page numbers in bold type indicate main discussion of term.